FORGOTTEN PATRIOT
DOUGLAS HYDE

& THE FOUNDATION OF THE IRISH PRESIDENCY

Brian Murphy lectures in Communications at the Dublin Institute of Technology. A graduate of University College Dublin, he completed a PhD in Modern Irish History on the Irish Presidency. He has worked as a parliamentary researcher in Dáil Éireann and at the Department of the Taoiseach, as a speechwriter to two Taoisigh. A regular contributor to Irish media, he co-edited the bestselling book *Brian Lenihan: In Calm and Crisis* (2014).

Keep up to date with the author on Twitter @DouglasHyde1

This book is dedicated to the memory of my grandparents

Annie Moran 1901–94

James Moran 1903–80

&

John Murphy 1888–1970

Josie Murphy 1908–76

FORGOTTEN PATRIOT
DOUGLAS HYDE
& THE FOUNDATION OF THE IRISH PRESIDENCY

BRIAN MURPHY

The Collins Press

First published in 2016 by
The Collins Press
West Link Park
Doughcloyne
Wilton
Cork
T12 N5EF
Ireland

A CIP record for this book is available from the British Library.

Paperback ISBN: 978-1-84889-290-3
PDF eBook ISBN: 978-1-84889-590-4
EPUB eBook ISBN: 978-1-84889-591-1
Kindle ISBN: 978-1-84889-592-8

Design and typesetting by Patricia Hope, Dublin
Typeset in AGaramond
Printed in Poland by Drukarnia Skleniarz

CONTENTS

Abbreviations

DDA	Dublin Diocesan Archives
GAA	Gaelic Athletic Association
IRA	Irish Republican Army
NAI	National Archives of Ireland
NLI	National Library of Ireland
TD	Teachta Dála
UCDA	University College Dublin Archives
US	United States

Introduction

In 1737, the French Enlightenment philosopher Voltaire, in a letter to the future Prussian King Frederick the Great, stated that 'history can be well written only in a free country'.[1] In 2016, the events that gave rise to our own free country were brought into strong focus, as Irish society commemorated the centenary of the Easter Rising.

In the run-up to this significant anniversary, historians were prolific in assessing the momentous actions and the major personalities at the forefront of Ireland's struggle for nationhood. One figure, however, was largely conspicuous by his absence – Douglas Hyde.

Though Hyde was one of the most consequential of Irishmen, he is today very much a forgotten patriot. His public career has been given scant attention by historians, even though Hyde had arguably done more than any other individual to shape a distinct Irish identity and to encourage Irish people to regard themselves, in his own words, as a 'separate nationality'.[2] Hyde also railed against any notion that Irish people 'ought to be content as an integral part of the United Kingdom because we have lost the notes of nationality, our language and customs' and he sought to 'create a strong feeling against West-Britonism'.[3] His cultural proselytising precipitated the political revolution from which Irish sovereignty flowed.

Exactly 200 years on from Voltaire's musings about the drafting of history in a sovereign nation, the 1937 Constitution became the embodiment of the fullest form of Irish independence. The most important innovation in this new Constitution was the establishment of the office of President of Ireland as the effective head of state. Douglas Hyde would hold the distinction of being the first such office holder.

In the first year of Hyde's term, Harry Kernoff, a leading Irish modernist painter, created a stamp design linking George Washington and Douglas Hyde as the respective first presidents of their nations. This graphite sketch is still available to view in the National Gallery of Ireland.[4] Washington's endeavours, on behalf of the nascent United States, earned him the sobriquet of 'Father of Our Country'. In truth, such an accolade could also be applied to Douglas Hyde, given his work in preserving and promoting a distinct Irish national identity and subsequently as Ireland's first first citizen.

In America, Washington's work as Commander-in-Chief of the Continental Army and later as first President has secured him a rich historical legacy. Apart from the American capital being named in his honour and Presidents' Day, the official observance of his birthday, still being a national holiday, George Washington has more places in the United States named after him than any other individual. A 2013 survey of the Census Bureau's geographic database found that America's first President has ninety-four population centres called after him and 127 population centres where his name is found within a longer name.[5] Washington has also had seven mountain ranges, eight rivers, ten lakes and thousands of American public institutions and amenities named in his honour. Even outside the United States, Washington has been memorialised in far-flung destinations, with the naming in his honour of a Pacific Island owned by the Republic of Kiribati, a municipality in the Philippines and, in 1918, a main thoroughfare in Cork city after local residents decided they no longer wanted the street called after a British sovereign. Since 1869, Washington's image has adorned the dollar bill, the most common currency note in the United States.[6]

In comparison to George Washington, Ireland's first President fares much more modestly. Hyde's image briefly decorated the Irish £50 note from 1995 until 2002, when the punt was replaced by the euro. Of the very few public locations named after the first Irish President, arguably the best-known is the Douglas Hyde Gallery, a publicly funded contemporary art gallery, which opened in 1978, in the grounds of Hyde's alma mater of Trinity College Dublin. Ireland's reluctance to remember the service of past presidents is, perhaps, somehow encapsulated in an unfair and ungenerous 'joke', partly aimed at Hyde, told by a Fine Gael TD. In 1973, Oliver J. Flanagan suggested to his party's Ard Fheis that the reason why there were no streets named after any former Irish President was because there was 'no road long enough and no road crooked enough in Ireland to suit that purpose'.[7]

If apathy is, to paraphrase the Nobel laureate Elie Wiesel, a vice worse than anger, then Douglas Hyde's legacy has been particularly ill-served by Irish historians. In the sixty-seven years since Hyde's death, only two full-scale biographies of Ireland's first President have been written. The first, written by two American professors of English and Comparative Literature, was published in 1991.[8] Two years later, a two-volume biography by Risteárd Ó Glaisne, an Irish-language activist, teacher and journalist, was launched.[9] In more recent times, Cormac Moore, a leading Irish sports historian, produced a commendable book focusing on the GAA's scandalous decision to expel Hyde from its ranks.[10] However, the general indifference that Irish historians as a class have shown to Hyde's career belies the significance of his contribution.

Patrick Pearse, the titular head of the Easter Rising, seemed to understand intuitively the seismic impact that Hyde and the establishment of the Gaelic League would have on the course of Irish separatism. In 1914, Pearse wrote: 'the Gaelic League will be recognised in history as the most revolutionary influence that has ever come into Ireland. The Irish Revolution really began when the seven proto-Gaelic Leaguers met in O'Connell St . . . The germ of all future Irish history was in that back room.'[11]

Pearse was also quick to praise Hyde's influence on him personally, the loyalty he inspired and also the leadership he had provided in safeguarding Ireland's culture. A year previously, Pearse had written: 'I love and honour Douglas Hyde. I have served under him since I was a boy. I am willing to serve under him until he can lead and I can serve no longer. I have never failed him. He has never failed me . . . I can speak to him at once as friend to friend and as loyal soldier to loyal captain.'[12]

Ultimately, however, Pearse and Hyde would bitterly fall out, as the former embraced militant separatism at the expense, in Hyde's view, of cultural inclusiveness. After resigning from the presidency of the Gaelic League in 1915, in a scathing reference to Pearse and his supporters, Hyde said that 'these people queered the pitch and put an end to my dreams of using the language as a unifying bond to bring all Irishmen together'.[13]

In post-independence Ireland or, to borrow Voltaire's phrase, in our own 'free country', the writing of Irish history has tended to focus predominantly on those who opted for the militant path in the formative years of 1914 to 1923. Our process of commemoration also seems to have developed almost a hierarchy in the national pantheon with more attention being given to those who took up arms in the cause of Irish freedom than to those who provided the intellectual basis for a separate state. This is not a new phenomenon born out of the understandable emotion generated by the centenary of the Easter Rising. Official Ireland's non-recognition of Douglas Hyde's legacy was an issue that long rankled with his family. As far back as 1972, Hyde's daughter Una Sealy remarked in an interview, 'I have often thought if he had killed people he would have been considered great, but because he was such a gentle, refined person, no one bothered about him. He has been ignored for a long time. They left his grave twenty-three years without attending to it.'[14]

I first heard Douglas Hyde's name as a child in the place where he is still remembered best – his home county of Roscommon. My maternal grandparents lived almost across the road from the Dr Hyde Park, the county's premier GAA ground, which officially opened in 1971. As a child, I often kicked a ball in 'the Hyde' and if, at first, I imagined that the stadium was named in honour of a great Roscommon footballer of yesteryear, this misunderstanding was quickly corrected. My grandfather was one of the brave generation who fought for our free country and he was an active member of the South Roscommon Brigade of the IRA. He was also someone who had a deep affection for the Irish language and an enduring respect for the Irish-Ireland ideals of the Gaelic League. My grandfather spoke reverentially about Douglas Hyde.

My initial interest in the presidency also had a Roscommon connection. The first presidential election in my lifetime took place in 1990. I was a teenager and I found it an enthralling contest. Brian P.

Lenihan, the Fianna Fáil candidate, was our local TD in Dublin West and he had formerly represented Roscommon. Instinctively, he had our support. As my interest in the presidency deepened, I became aware that the office was a hugely under-researched area in Irish historiography. It is also one of the most misunderstood.

As far back as 1997, Professor Dermot Keogh bemoaned the fact that there is no published history of the presidency.[15] In the intervening years, there have been two biographical studies of former presidents, but both of these studies are largely weighted towards the portion of their respective lives preceding their tenures in Áras an Uachtaráin .[16]

The lack of historical research into the presidency, especially in regard to the office's early years, has allowed a number of misconceptions to take root. The most significant of these is that the formative presidencies were politically irrelevant. This train of thinking dismisses the presidency prior to 1990 as 'a retirement home', a largely ceremonial office, and a role far removed from the cut and thrust of political life.

I received my doctorate from University College Dublin in 2014 for a thesis that critically examined and highlighted the sizeable impact and engagement of the presidency in Irish politics and public life during the terms of office of the first three Presidents of Ireland (1938–1973). This book has its roots in my PhD thesis, which would not have come to fruition without the counsel of Professor Mary E. Daly. I was very fortunate to have her as my supervisor. She has been a source of great encouragement and wise advice to me since my days as an undergraduate student.

My research into the presidency was greatly facilitated by the professionalism and kindness of a number of archivists. Much of my research was carried out at the National Archives of Ireland and I wish to thank Tom Quinlan and all of the staff in Bishop Street, who were of real assistance to me. I am grateful also to Seamus Helferty, Kate Manning and Orna Somerville at UCD Archives Department; Maria O'Shea at the National Library of Ireland; Noelle Dowling at the Dublin Diocesan Archive and Ed Penrose at the Irish Labour History Society.

I am also obliged to Martin Fraser, the Secretary General at the Department of the Taoiseach, and Jerry Kelleher of the same department for granting me access to official records. Jerry's knowledge of the administrative history of the Irish Civil Service is outstanding and he consistently answered queries and steered me in the right direction.

I spent a hugely enjoyable day with Des and Anne McDunphy in their home in Malahide. Des kindly shared with me his recollections of his father and gave me access to his father's papers.

I want to thank Stephen Collins, Liam T. Cosgrave and Mary Cosgrave for facilitating my contact with former Taoiseach Liam Cosgrave. I want to acknowledge Eoghan Ó Neachtain and Pádraig Slyne, both of whom frequently came to my assistance when I struggled with documents written in the Irish language.

I owe a profound debt of gratitude to Bobby O'Sullivan, formerly of Coláiste Phádraig Christian Brothers Secondary School, Lucan. He was an inspirational teacher and he instilled in me a lifelong interest in history.

I want to thank all at The Collins Press for their courtesy, support and professionalism during the period this book was under production.

I am very grateful to everyone who assisted me in sourcing the photographs included in this book and for permission to reprint them. In this regard, I especially wish to thank Stephen Rae, Group Editor-in-Chief at Independent News and Media. My thanks are also due to Carcanet Press Ltd, Manchester, for allowing me to quote from the *Collected Poems of Austin Clarke* (copyright: the estate of Austin Clarke, 2008).

Loughlin Deegan and Joe Lennon undertook the time-consuming task of reading the manuscript at different stages. I am obliged to each of them for their generosity, their meticulous attention to detail and for many years of friendship. Any errors or omissions that exist are entirely my own responsibility.

I wish to acknowledge the scholarship of Jim Duffy, Robert Elgie, Gerard Hogan, Michael Gallagher and the late John Kelly, which was of huge assistance to me in explaining the powers and functions of the President of Ireland. I had many illuminating conversations on the subject matter of this book with Rory Brady and Brian J. Lenihan, both of whom had an in-depth knowledge of Irish political and constitutional history. It is a source of deep regret to me that both of them passed away before this book was published.

Other friends and colleagues were also helpful and offered valuable advice and insights throughout what I began to describe as 'my search for Hyde'. I want to thank, in particular, Bertie Ahern, Richard Aldous, Nevan Bermingham, Colm Brady, Maurice Bric, Marie Campbell, Niamh Cooper, Fergal Corcoran, Brian Cowen, Loughlin Deegan, Dominic Dillane, John Dolan, David Doyle, Fiona Faulkner, Tony Feeney, Philip Hannon, David Harmon, Eoghan Harris, Gerry Hickey (RIP), Gerard Howlin, Anne Hurley, Mandy Johnston, Susan Kiernan, Michael Laffan, Jennifer Langan, Ralf Lissek, John McCafferty, David McCullagh, Peter MacDonagh, Paul McGuill, Bobby Maher, Richard Maher, Robert Mauro, Ciara Meehan, Cormac Moore, Joe Moran, Gary Murphy, Donnacha Ó Beacháin, Margaret O'Callaghan, Ciaran Ó Cuinn, Seán Tadhg Ó Gairbhí, Patrick O'Herlihy, John O'Mahony, Mary O'Rourke, Des Peelo, Will Peters, John Pollock, Paul Rouse, Peter Ryan, Brendan Walsh, Noel Whelan and Zhen Yao.

Finally, my deepest appreciation goes to my parents, Kathryn and Eddie Murphy, and to my brother, John. I am truly grateful for all they have done for me. Their unstinting support in life has made this book and so much more possible.

1

25 June 1938

It had been a busy few days for Adolf Hitler, but Douglas Hyde had not slipped his mind.

It was Saturday, 25 June 1938 and, as Ireland's President-Elect prepared to leave the newly named Áras an Uachtaráin in Dublin's Phoenix Park for his inauguration ceremony, the Führer was beginning a weekend of relaxation in the Berghof, his Alpine retreat, near Berchtesgaden.

The previous week had seen Hitler juggle a number of competing demands on his time. His Nazi regime were currently in the process of finalising a decree forbidding Jewish doctors from treating Aryan patients and, days earlier, Hitler had personally ordered the destruction of Munich's Great Synagogue because it was situated next to the German Art Museum.[1]

Hitler was still nursing a sense of disappointment at a major German sporting setback. On the previous day, Friday 24 June, he had sent a message of sympathy to Anny Ondra, the glamorous actress wife of Max Schmeling.[2] The German boxer had been knocked out by Joe Louis in the first round of an eagerly anticipated world heavyweight title bout in Yankee Stadium, in a contest that had real political overtones. Hitler had lifted the night-time curfew across Germany so patrons could listen to the fight in bars. Schmeling's defeat by an African-American inflicted a significant blow to the Nazis' theory of racial superiority. During the build-up to the boxing match, a Nazi

Party publicist had told the world's press that 'a black man could never defeat Schmeling' and that the German's prize money would be used to build more tanks.[3]

In the early summer of 1938, three months on from the Anschluss, Austria was causing Hitler some frustration. Prior to departing for the Berghof, the Führer had refused to meet a delegation of Austrian Nazis, who had come to Berlin to complain at their lack of influence since Austria had been submerged into the Reich.[4]

Tensions were also mounting with the Soviet Union. German economic and diplomatic penetration into Iran was making Stalin increasingly nervous and was the subject of criticism in the Moscow state-controlled press.[5] Josef Stalin, the Soviet leader, had rightly concluded that Hitler's strategy was to use Iran as a source of raw materials for the German munitions industry and as a potential base for an attack on the Soviet Union. At the same time, Hitler was gradually progressing plans to 'smash Czechoslovakia at the first available opportunity'.[6] One of his final acts before escaping to the Bavarian Alps for the weekend was to conclude an exchange of formal letters in which Hitler and his Italian ally, Benito Mussolini, pledged to respect traditional Swiss neutrality.[7]

Though Ireland was at this stage somewhat peripheral to Hitler's dual quest for Aryan supremacy and German global domination, the fact that Douglas Hyde would be installed President of Ireland later that day had not escaped the Führer's all-encompassing gaze. The news of Hyde's emergence in April 1938 as the agreed candidate of the two largest political parties in Ireland for the new post had, according to Reuters' Berlin correspondent, 'evoked lively interest here'.[8]

Hitler, in particular, seems to have been intrigued by the prospect of a septuagenarian folklorist, retired university lecturer, linguist and Gaelic cultural icon becoming Ireland's first citizen. In the run-up to Hyde's inauguration in Dublin Castle on that Saturday, 25 June, Hitler 'ordered' the Berlin newspapers 'to splash' the Irish presidential installation ceremony.[9] Hitler's instructions created an unexpected financial boon for Irish photographers, many of whom received commissions from German newspapers to provide pictures of Hyde and the events in Dublin. Hitler's interest in the new Irish President was the subject of some speculation. *The News Review*, a British current affairs magazine, suggested that the intense German coverage was because 'Dr Hyde is married to a German woman' and also because 'the presidential scholar himself has acknowledged the help he had received from the research work of Gaelic experts on the academic staffs of Berlin and Bonn universities'.[10] Further speculation about the in-depth coverage centred on the rather tenuous connection that the senior civil servant in Hyde's new office 'will spend a holiday in Germany this summer'.[11] However, undoubtedly, the primary reason for Hitler's fleeting fixation with Douglas Hyde was that the coming into being of the new Irish presidency diluted Ireland's bonds with the British Empire almost to the point of disappearance. In the pre-Munich Agreement summer of 1938, Hitler may genuinely have hoped to avoid war with the United Kingdom, but he was also quite happy to highlight any geopolitical shifts that diminished the prestige of Germany's most formidable rival in Europe.

In the United States, Douglas Hyde was also getting plenty of publicity, but for very different reasons from in Germany. In fact, much of the favourable coverage that Hyde's inauguration generated in the US was rooted in the fact that the new Irish President's values stood in stark contrast to the totalitarian style of leadership that had become prevalent across Europe. Prior to Hyde's inauguration, a reporter from the mass-circulation *New York Times Magazine* spent a day with the President-Elect and noted that 'no man seemed more the antithesis of a continental dictator than this Irish poet as he sat there in his study surrounded by his treasures of Gaelic scholarship and folklore'.[12] Hyde's Protestantism was a strong feature of American newspaper coverage and there was praise for what was viewed as the broad-minded ecumenicalism of the Irish people in not insisting on a Catholic President. *The New York Times Magazine* opined that 'as a Protestant President in an overwhelmingly Catholic state', Hyde would be 'an earnest of the country's love of religious tolerance and peace among all sects in the community'.[13] Frank P. Walsh, a well-known New York attorney who had been a member of the American Commission on Irish Independence in 1919, told the Taoiseach, Éamon de Valera, that Hyde's unopposed election 'had made a deep impression in America. Every newspaper had front-paged the story, and when they followed it up with the reasons why the Irish people had conferred the highest honour at their command on this member of the [religious] minority the story made a deep impression.'[14]

The US Government was gratified by the selection of Hyde. At de Valera's request, President Franklin D. Roosevelt had recently indirectly intervened in the deadlocked Anglo-Irish negotiations. Roosevelt asked his newly appointed Ambassador to the Court of St James, Joseph Kennedy, 'to convey a personal message from me to the [British] Prime Minister, and to tell the Prime Minister how happy I should be if reconciliation could be brought about'.[15] De Valera believed that the intercession of the United States was significant and had caused the British to soften their position, leading to the conclusion of agreements that ended the Economic War and brought about the return of the Treaty Ports.

The US administration saw the choice of a Protestant President as evidence of Ireland's good faith in pursuing reconciliation and building a new dispensation of forbearance. This was a point that was elegantly made by Kennedy when he arrived in Dublin to collect an honorary degree just a fortnight after Hyde's inauguration. Kennedy told reporters 'America is very happy about the selection of your new President. It showed moderation. After all, Ireland is quite Catholic and the people of America feel that the country will get along well when it is handled like that. A spirit of tolerance is welcome to everybody.'[16] All four of Kennedy's grandparents had emigrated from Ireland to Massachusetts in the era of the Great Famine and, at a state reception in Dublin Castle, an emotional Kennedy spoke of the honour he felt in being welcomed by 'the warm handclasps of the great men of my own blood'.[17] He described 'the choice of Doctor Douglas Hyde to be the President of the state, [as] an act that is eloquent of that brotherhood and tolerance which remain the hope of mankind in an angry world'.[18] Developing the theme of a 'broad Atlantic' brotherhood of tolerance from which the US Ambassador to Britain saw Hyde's presidency as stemming, Kennedy said that when he considered 'the policies of your great leader, Éamon de Valera, of the British Crown and Prime Minister, and of the eminent statesman, President Roosevelt, who is my chief, I see a joined determination that blood shall not flow in this ocean again, the blood of brothers.'[19]

James Farley, the Postmaster General in President Franklin D. Roosevelt's cabinet and another grandson of Irish immigrants, had been so enthused by the choice of Hyde that he had brought a proposal to the US President 'to get Congress to send a special delegation to attend the inauguration of Dr Hyde'.[20] Farley ultimately had to resile from this initiative 'as it would violate the law of precedent' and presumably would have led to US Congressional delegations being compelled to attend similar ceremonies in other nations.

Hyde's election was very popular with Irish-Americans, but it also swayed opinion in communities traditionally hostile to Ireland. Judge Owen W. Bohan of the New York Court of General Sessions, who had been a prominent figure in the American Association for the Recognition of the Irish Republic in 1920, told the Irish Press that

> the election of a Protestant to the highest office in the [Irish] head of state here had created a profound impression in the United States. Indeed it has quite bewildered the Ku Klux Klan or the more bigoted Protestant elements in America. As far as Ireland is concerned they have been silent ever since, and newspapers which in the past were definitely against Ireland have changed their attitude.[21]

In Britain, the reaction to Ireland's new President was more muted. To the dismay of the British Government, even before the adoption of Bunreacht na hÉireann, the 1937 Irish Constitution, de Valera had managed to eliminate the Crown from the constitutional law of the Irish Free State.[22] Bunreacht na hÉireann further advanced this position and placed the President of Ireland – rather than the British monarch – at the apex of a constitution that was republican in character, but did not formally declare a republic. Although many Conservative MPs were unhappy that de Valera's new constitutional arrangement did not provide for the 'traditional role of the Crown in Ireland', Malcolm MacDonald, the Dominions Secretary, urged calm.[23] Neville Chamberlain's Government ultimately accepted this advice, in a step that some critics subsequently dubbed an early exhibition of appeasement. On 29 December 1937, the day Bunreacht na hÉireann came into operation, a British Government statement declared that they were 'prepared to treat the new Constitution as not effecting a fundamental alteration in the position of the Irish Free State . . . as a member of the British Commonwealth of Nations'.[24]

Article 57.1 of Bunreacht na hÉireann stipulated that the first President of Ireland should 'enter upon his office not later than one hundred and eighty days after the date of the coming into operation of this Constitution'.[25] When Hyde was unanimously elected President of Ireland on 4 May 1938, the British Government continued with their diplomatic equivalent of the stiff upper lip, despite the ire of the Tory backbenches. On 5 May 1938, as Westminster debated the recently concluded Anglo-Irish Trade Agreement, Colonel John Gretton, the Conservative MP for Burton, complained that in Ireland 'the Governor-General has gone and has been replaced by a President, who supersedes the representative of the King. The Crown is no longer recognised as having in any shape or form any weight, authority or influence whatsoever' and Brigadier-General Sir Henry Croft, Conservative MP for Bournemouth, expressed his dissatisfaction that 'the President was announced' in Ireland, which meant that the country had 'become, if not in name, in fact, something very near a republic'.[26] Though Chamberlain was present in the Commons for this entire debate, he studiously avoided commenting on the new Irish presidency. The Prime Minister also remained silent when, in the same debate, Sir William Davison, the Conservative MP for Kensington South, sought 'an assurance' that ex-unionists 'in Southern Ireland . . . will receive better treatment in the future than they have been receiving in the past'. However, David Logan, the Labour MP for Liverpool Scotland and an ardent sympathiser with Irish nationalist causes, rejected this criticism and gleefully reminded the British Parliament to 'not forget the Protestant President'.[27]

Hyde's inauguration was wilfully ignored by the British Government, with not one cabinet minister commenting on the events in Dublin. However, diplomatic courtesies were maintained in the form of the low-key presence of Geoffrey Braddock, the UK Trade Commissioner and the highest-ranking British diplomatic representative in Ireland, at the installation ceremony in Dublin Castle.[28] The *Daily Telegraph* and *The Times*, the two newspapers most closely associated with the British political establishment, paid scant attention to Hyde's inauguration. However, *British Pathé*, as part of their news digest for cinema-goers, filmed the scenes in Dublin and their commentator told British audiences that Hyde's installation was 'the greatest day in the history of the Irish Free State [*sic*]', 'the celebration of another victory for Mr de Valera' and an 'example of tolerance which is a model to many another nation'.[29] *The Observer* praised 'the wisdom' of Hyde's selection and the *News Chronicle* and the *Daily Express* accorded Ireland's new President extensive coverage.[30] The two latter papers even sent reporters to Ireland to interview Hyde. Robert W. Reid, a young reporter with the *News Chronicle*, spent some time with the President-Elect in his native Roscommon. His affectionate account of their meeting appeared in the British newspaper on the day prior to Hyde's inauguration. Reid described Hyde as 'tall, grey-eyed and looks ten years younger than he is . . . He favours moustaches after the style of Clemenceau to whom he bears a close physical resemblance. He wears tweeds, a cap and country-man's boots.'[31] Hyde explained to the English journalist his vision of an Irish-Ireland, which he emphasised as integral to his presidency, and said:

> I hope we shall now develop along the lines of a Gaelic nation . . . Gaelic not only in language but in music, games, literature and dancing. It may not come in my lifetime. It may not come in yours either. There are not as many people as I would like speaking Irish today, but I have insisted on having an Irish-speaking staff at the President's house. We are making progress, however, the children learn Irish in the schools, but the problem is to persuade them to continue its use as their mother tongue after they leave school. One good sign is the revival of Gaelic plays. The question of games is also important. The Irish have never been Anglicised in this respect. We have our own games, and I should like to see them played more widely. There is hurling for instance, and Gaelic football.[32]

On the morning of the inauguration, the *Daily Express* also published an interview with the President-Elect under the headline 'Dr Hyde is just a little homesick'.[33] Hyde had travelled to Dublin a few days prior to his installation ceremony and he had confessed to the *Daily Express* reporter that he was already missing home and that 'Frenchpark takes a lot of beating.'[34] English provincial papers, especially in areas of significant Irish immigrant population, such as the *Manchester Evening News*, the *Nottingham Journal*, the *Yorkshire Observer* and the *Birkenhead News,* which described Hyde as 'perhaps, the most universally loved individual in [Ireland]', treated the inauguration of Ireland's new President as a big news story.[35] In the Scottish capital, the *Edinburgh Evening News* lauded Hyde 'as one of the greatest scholars Ireland has ever produced' and welcomed his elevation as 'Dr Hyde will be no Hitler or Mussolini, nor is he expected to copy their example'.[36] The same paper also predicted that Hyde would quickly 'prove that the example of Czechoslovakia in appointing such a famous scholar as Dr Masaryk to be her first President was the wisest model which Ireland could follow'.[37]

In Northern Ireland, almost inevitably, the reaction to Hyde's inauguration broke down into tribal responses. The inauguration was uproariously celebrated in West Belfast and in other nationalist enclaves. Many Northern nationalists also travelled to Dublin 'to witness the pageantry of parades' associated with the inauguration ceremony and this was viewed as hardly surprising by Belfast's nationalist newspaper, the *Irish News*, 'since nothing so lavish, so significant in its meaning, or so nationwide in its appeal has taken place in Ireland since Tara was occupied by the ancient Kings'.[38]

In the unionist community, politicians competed with each other to express their indignation. The Northern Ireland Finance Minister, John Miller Andrews, described Hyde's inauguration as a 'slight on the King' and 'a deplorable tragedy'.[39] Dehra Parker, the Parliamentary Secretary to the Northern Ireland Minister for Education, complained that 'a man had been substituted as head of the southern state' and that 'the King had been insulted and rejected'.[40] She said that this was 'the final repudiation by the South of everything for which they in the North stood'.[41] Sir William Allen, the Stormont MP for Armagh, claimed that 'Mr de Valera had made a Protestant President of Southern Ireland simply to blindfold the people of England.'[42] Similarly, Hyde's Protestantism cut little ice with the *Belfast Telegraph,* which editorialised:

> The election of Dr Douglas Hyde as 'President' of Éire was obviously a mere tactical manoeuvre which has been exploited to the full as an example of 'religious tolerance' owing to the fact that he is a Protestant in religion. This artifice should deceive no one . . . We in Northern Ireland are firmly determined to remain under the King and the Union Jack, having no desire to exchange them for a President and the Republican Tricolour.[43]

The *Belfast Telegraph* also made it clear that it was not enamoured with the efforts to restore the Irish language, which had been Hyde's life work. It criticised the Dublin political establishment for a 'campaign waged with an intolerant fanaticism equal to that of any Communist or Nazi for forcing the study of the Gaelic language into the schools'.[44] The more liberal unionist Northern Whig, while sceptical of the new Irish presidency, was magnanimous towards Hyde and said that he would 'have the good wishes and the sympathy of all Northerners who esteem a genial and inoffensive and hitherto retiring scholar who suddenly has had quasi-political greatness of a dubious kind thrust upon him'.[45] Although the unionist community was far from impressed with the new Irish presidency, there was a distinct lack of personal animus towards Douglas Hyde. Despite her anger at 'the insult' to the King, Dehra Parker went out of her way to acknowledge that Douglas Hyde was 'a worthy estimable scholar'.[46] The Rev. Dr James Little, the Deputy Grand Chaplain of the Orange Order in Ireland, said that he would gladly welcome Hyde to Northern Ireland, although he did add with tongue in cheek that Hyde would be 'received with Orange musical honours, and the programme will conclude with "God Save the King", which I have no doubt, as a Protestant, would be sweet music to Dr Hyde's ears'.[47]

Hyde's selection as President of Ireland was a story with a truly global reach. Newspapers in Australia, New Zealand, South Africa and Argentina, countries in which Gaelic League branches had sprung up in or around the turn of the twentieth century, prominently covered the story. However, even in countries where there was a negligible Irish diaspora, Hyde was big news. Joseph Walshe, the Secretary to the Department of External Affairs, who was on a private holiday in the run-up to Hyde's inauguration, wrote to de Valera from Cairo to express his 'surprise' at the interest in Hyde and the fact that 'all the hundreds of papers in Egypt in various languages gave this appointment great publicity'.[48]

Douglas Hyde's inauguration day began with a journey to a bastion of Irish Protestantism, St Patrick's Cathedral, which had been an Anglican place of worship since 1537, following the English reformation. It was already bright and warm in Dublin on Saturday 25 June 1938, as Ireland's President-Elect prepared to depart the newly renamed Áras an Uachtaráin shortly before 9.30 a.m. For generations, the eighteenth-century house had been the residence of the viceroys who oversaw British rule in Ireland, but later that day it would officially become the residence of the first President of Ireland. Michael McDunphy, the fastidious Secretary to the office of the President, subsequently noted that 'although strictly speaking the President was not entitled to enter into occupation of his official residence until he had entered upon office', with Government approval, Hyde 'took up residence in Áras an Uachtaráin, formerly the Viceregal Lodge, on 20 June 1938'.[49] For the previous five days, Hyde had been tutored by McDunphy in the responsibilities of his new office and had been given a crash course in the protocols and ceremonial aspects of the installation proceedings, at which he would be centre stage.

Hyde was understandably nervous. His anxieties were rooted not just in concerns that the inauguration ceremony would pass off smoothly, but also in his own persistent doubts that he was too old for the presidential office.[50] The President-Elect was also uncomfortable in the formal attire he had been prevailed upon to wear for the day's ceremonies. In the run-up to the inauguration, newspapers had repeatedly speculated on whether Hyde would 'set aside the cloth cap and plus fours which he usually wears' in favour of 'morning dress and a silk hat'.[51] As late as the day before the inauguration, a spokesperson for Hyde had told the *Daily Express* that the President-Elect had 'not made up his mind today what he will wear for the ceremony'.[52] Hyde's instinct was for informality and in a widely publicised interview the President-Elect had even sought to make use of the disdain Fianna Fáil ministers had for morning suits to prepare the ground for his wearing non-ceremonial garb. *The New York Times Magazine* recorded:

> People in Dublin are wondering whether President Hyde will doff his gray homespuns and his famous tweed cap, which he pulls down at a rakish angle, when he goes into residence at the Viceregal Lodge in the Phoenix Park. Recently, when the new Senate of Éire assembled in Dublin for the first time, Dr Hyde arrived in Leinster House to take his seat still wearing what he playfully called 'that villain of a cap'. His only concession to city conventions was to lay aside his homespun plus fours for a navy suit, over which he wore a brown Irish tweed overcoat. Surely, some say who place more stress on clothes than the personal dignity of the man, as President he will wear full-dress morning clothes and a tall silk hat. When this poser was put to him he looked almost affectionately at the cap, thrown casually on a corner of his desk, and said, 'I don't think people will expect me to wear those things. I never wear a silk hat. You know, my dear fellow,' he went on, 'An Taoiseach does not wear a silk hat.'[53]

Nevertheless, on the morning of 25 June, Hyde was dressed in a waistcoat, morning suit and silk top hat. Both McDunphy and the President-Elect's daughter, Una Sealy, the wife of a Circuit Court judge, had eventually persuaded Hyde that it would be best if he donned traditional formal wear. Hyde's preference for a more egalitarian form of dress may have stemmed from his expressed desire, despite his new elevated office, that he would always be free to move among the people of Ireland in 'a bond of equality with them'.[54] Hyde's immense public popularity was founded on a lifetime's engagement with people of all classes in preserving and proselytising Ireland's cultural traditions. The President-Elect intuitively understood that this distinguished work had been central to propelling him towards high office and in all probability he would have reflected on his personal journey on the day he became Ireland's first citizen. As Ulick O'Connor speculated:

> One wonders what thoughts were in Hyde's mind on that June day. Did he think of those years when as a young man he had been a member of the class whose lives had revolved around

> viceregal life and how he had kept hidden in his heart his secret passion for the culture of the people whose cabins lay in the environs of the great estates? He had spent a large part of his life poring over manuscripts and setting down poems and stories from the people's lips so that the culture of the Gael might not perish.[55]

Behind Hyde's public pride in being chosen to be Ireland's first President, there was familial pain. Hyde's wife, Lucy Kurtz, an English-born lady from a distinguished Württemberg family, was in poor health and, according to Hyde's aide-de-camp, Lieutenant Basil Peterson of the Irish Air Corps, 'she was in no way pleased that her husband had been plucked out of his quiet retirement to go and live in the [Phoenix] Park and play a form of politics'.[56] Hyde's marriage had long been strained. Mrs Hyde did not share her husband's interest in the Gaelic revival and she had grown to resent many of Hyde's closest friends and colleagues, who (she felt) took his work for granted. She resolutely refused to leave Roscommon to live with him in Dublin and ill health also prevented her from attending the inauguration ceremony. In the days leading up to his installation, Hyde leaned closely on his only surviving child, Una, who temporarily moved into the Áras to help the President-Elect settle.

Peterson arrived punctually at the front door of Áras an Uachtaráin to escort Hyde to the ten o'clock religious service in St Patrick's Cathedral, which was preceding the installation ceremony. The aide-de-camp was resplendent in the Air Corps' full ceremonial dress uniform, which he described as having a 'Ruritanian quality' and was 'appropriately, sky blue with trimmings of scarlet and gold – not [to] mention gold wings – rounded off by a black coat with scarlet lining and a cap of an Austrian pattern'.[57] Like the President-Elect, Peterson was nervous. It was the biggest day of the 26-year-old's military career and he had been given the difficult responsibility of ensuring that the day's tightly planned order of proceedings ran on time. Hyde genially did his best to put the young Air Corps officer at ease by admiring his uniform. Peterson, however, was already privately fretting about the 'complication' caused by Hyde's late insistence that his daughter accompany him on the journey to the church service.[58] Protocol dictated that everyone should take their place in the cathedral before the President-Elect arrived and though Hyde considered his daughter's presence in the car with him 'a tidy form of delivery', for his aide-de-camp it 'really made a mess of things, for Mrs Sealy had to enter the cathedral by another door and be in her seat a quarter of an hour before Dr Hyde arrived'.[59]

Peterson, by his own admission, was 'more used to plotting aircraft routes than movements through city streets' and he was also a 'country boy' who 'had been in the cathedral only once and had no knowledge of the surrounding streets'.[60] Almost inevitably, as Hyde's limousine approached St Patrick's Cathedral and the nearby maze of small side streets in the oldest part of Dublin, with Peterson trying to keep an eye on his watch and a street map, the car took a wrong turn. At the back of the cathedral, the progress of the President-Elect's car was blocked by a Garda who had strict orders not to allow any vehicles to pass through. Despite Peterson's animated entreaties, the police officer refused to budge, stubbornly insisting that Hyde's car was 'in the wrong place at the wrong time'.[61] 'Just as time was almost up' and with the President-Elect in real danger of being late for his first engagement of the day, a Garda inspector arrived on the scene and 'whisked Mrs Sealy away' and, to Peterson's enormous relief, personally directed the presidential car to the west gate of the cathedral, where a red carpet had been laid.[62]

Hyde was welcomed by the Most Rev. Dr John Gregg, Protestant Archbishop of Dublin, and, accompanied by his aide-de-camp, he was escorted in procession into the cathedral. Peterson had been initially 'puzzled' by his appointment as Hyde's aide-de-camp.[63] Unlike Captain Éamon de Buitléar, Hyde's other aide-de-camp, who had joined the Gaelic League as a sixteen-year-old, Peterson spoke only 'minimal' Irish, but 'as he quickly recognised, his appointment was essential for another reason: he was a Protestant'.[64] As a practising Roman Catholic, de Buitléar was prohibited by his own Church from attending a Protestant service so the military authorities had specifically detailed Peterson with this task. St Patrick's Cathedral was packed and Hyde was seated in a special pew, which was formerly known as the royal pew and reserved for the Lord Lieutenant of Ireland. As a sign of national pride at the changing dispensation, that evening's *Saturday*

Herald proudly noted that 'this pew will in future be known as the President's Pew'.[65]

Much of the service was conducted in the Irish language and prayers were said for Ireland, Dr Douglas Hyde and for Christian citizenship. According to the *Saturday Herald*, the service was 'brief but beautiful in its simplicity' and 'a burst of brilliant sunshine flooded the cathedral during the singing by the choir of a translation of the moving poem of Dr Hyde's, "God be in my head and in my understanding"'.[66] For Peterson, the church service was 'an emotional occasion and made me feel that at last the Irish had come into their own' and the President-Elect, whose father had been a Church of Ireland rector and had wanted Hyde to follow in his footsteps into the clergy, also displayed signs of being moved.[67]

Included in the congregation who came to pray for Ireland's President-Elect were a number of members of old ascendancy families, including the Earl of Meath, a veteran Anglo-Irish soldier of the Boer War and First World War; the Earl of Belmore, the Deputy Lieutenant of County Fermanagh; the Earl of Wicklow, who had served briefly alongside Hyde in the Irish Free State Senate; and Lord Farnham, a serving Irish Peer in the British House of Lords.[68] The spheres of international diplomacy and journalism were most prominently represented by the Consul-General of the US, Henry B. Hatch, and the editor of *The Irish Times*, Bert Smyllie. Also present were a number of members of Seanad Éireann and an even smaller group from the judiciary.[69] In retirement, Peterson claimed that 'official representation was missing', but he seems to have been unaware that the newly elected TD Erskine Childers, who one day himself would be elected as President of Ireland, was officially representing the Taoiseach.[70]

Just over a mile away, north of the Liffey, official Catholic Ireland was on full show. His Grace, the Archbishop of Dublin, Most Rev. Dr Edward Byrne, presided at a ten o'clock Solemn Votive Mass of the Holy Ghost in the Pro-Cathedral, Marlborough Street, where 'inspiring devotional scenes were witnessed'.[71] The *Saturday Herald* reported that 'there was a large and distinguished congregation', which included de Valera and his entire cabinet; W. T. Cosgrave and most of his front bench; the Chief Justice, Timothy Sullivan; the President of the High Court, Conor Maguire and other members of the judiciary, Dáil, Seanad and public bodies.[72]

Simultaneous ten o'clock services to mark the presidential inauguration were also being held by the State's other Christian Churches. Less than half a mile north of the Pro-Cathedral, at the Presbyterian Church in Parnell Square, the Right Rev. W. J. Currie, Moderator of the General Assembly, presided over a modestly attended service.[73] The sermon was preached by Rev. R. K. Hanna, who in recognising a Presbyterian affinity with the unionist regime in Northern Ireland, said that 'many of the southern Presbyterians were born in the North and their hearts clung to the old folk in the old home'.[74] Hanna, however, was also quick to acknowledge what he viewed as an olive branch and declared that 'we see in the election of a Protestant by a community which is predominantly Roman Catholic a gesture of goodwill towards us, the minority.'[75] Drawing a contrast between Hyde's election and the political situation in other European nations, Hanna praised the tolerant ethos of the Irish state, and asked his congregation to 'think for a moment of what has happened in Russia, of what is happening in Germany and of what is threatening to happen in England. There is a widespread revolt against the Christian creed and the Christian morality.'[76]

At the same time, on the far side of the city centre, in the Methodist Centenary Church on St Stephen's Green, the Rev. R. Lee Cole preached a short sermon on the significance of the presidential installation, although he seems to have had difficulty grasping what Hyde's new constitutional title would be, as he referred to Hyde on a number of occasions as 'our new Governor'.[77] The overall sentiment of Cole's remarks, however, was hopeful and inclusive, and pledged Methodist fealty to Hyde and to Ireland. He said:

> We are thankful to Almighty God for the peace and quietness which prevails after many years of struggle and for that growing sense of unity which has shown itself in the election of a Governor by a unanimous vote of all parties in the state. We pray that this disposition to agreement may increase and deepen so as to affect all parts of our community, and that the old days of contention, hatred and bloodshed are now over.

> On Dr Douglas Hyde in his new office we pray God's blessing. Our presence here today is an assurance of our support, our sympathy and our prayers.[78]

Later on that afternoon, at four o'clock, a sermon was preached and a special prayer offered by the Rev. Abraham Gudansky, Chief Minister of the Jewish Congregation, in the Synagogue, Adelaide Road.[79] The Government was represented at this service by Bob Briscoe, a Fianna Fáil TD, who was member of the Jewish faith. Rabbi Gudansky praised Hyde as 'an Irishman to the very depths of his soul, [who] laboured unceasingly for the restoration to his people of its most precious national heritage – its language and its culture'.[80] At a time when anti-Semitism was again raising its ugly head across the continent of Europe, Gudansky praised a spirit of forbearance in Ireland and emphasised Jewish fidelity to an independent Ireland. He said:

> We who are blessed in the enjoyment of equal citizenship, renew today our wholehearted allegiance to the state, and reaffirm that, while remaining true and faithful to the ideals of Israel's nationhood, we are determined to cooperate with our fellow citizens manfully and loyally in ensuring Éire's continued progress and welfare. There is nothing inconsistent in our dual nationality. In fact, the better the Jew, the truer his patriotism to his adopted land.[81]

The burgeoning spirit of ecumenicalism reflected in the comments of various religious leaders surrounding Hyde's inauguration was not entirely universal. One letter writer to the *Evening Herald* had suggested that the 'Protestant minority show its gratitude' for the election of Hyde as President by handing over Christ Church Cathedral to the Catholic authorities. This provoked a nasty debate with correspondents to the paper arguing trenchantly in favour of and against the proposition.[82]

Back at St Patrick's Cathedral, the same sense of mild confusion that characterised Hyde's arrival at the Church of Ireland service was on display as he exited. After the benediction, the procession was re-formed and passed down the nave of the cathedral with Archbishop

Gregg and Peterson escorting the President-Elect. The aide-de-camp ruefully recalled:

> The service over, the choir moved into the aisle. We followed and the clergy followed us. It was then that I had my one encounter with the belt of a crozier or its equivalent. The choir abruptly turned to the left and we began to follow. Nobody had bothered to tell us otherwise. Suddenly I felt a jab in my back and a voice hissed 'Straight on, straight on.' I redirected Dr Hyde and we finally again reached the main door where the assembled clergy bade us farewell.[83]

Outside 'the weather was fine' and a large crowd had gathered, drawn largely from some of the worst tenements in the city, situated close to St Patrick's, to catch a glimpse of the man who would within a few hours be their first citizen.[84] The onlookers had, however, been marshalled some distance away, across the road from the cathedral and their view was further restricted by a long line of saluting Gardaí. Hyde was joined at the gates of the cathedral by his daughter and by his widowed sister, Annette Kane, his only surviving sibling. To distant applause, they walked slowly along the Garda guard of honour that extended right up to the parked limousine, but to the surprise of everyone Hyde did not enter the vehicle, but instead walked around it. With Peterson in tow and the line of Gardaí now behind him, the President-Elect crossed the road and approached the cheering crowd. Hyde spent a few moments shaking outstretched hands and he paused to sign an autograph for a barefooted boy before affectionately tousling the youngster's hair. People in the crowd roared encouragement and good wishes at the President-Elect, but Peterson found himself the subject of some good-humoured ribbing. In a memoir of that day penned over forty years later, the aide-de-camp still vividly recalled 'a somewhat outspoken crowd of Dubliners – their comments on my uniform were less than kind'.[85]

Hyde had an uneventful journey back to Áras an Uachtaráin accompanied by his sister, daughter and aide-de-camp. The President-Elect barely had time for a quick cup of tea before the Chief Justice arrived. Timothy Sullivan had close familial links to the first

Governor-General of the Irish Free State; owing to the many marital links between their two families, the late Tim Healy had been both Sullivan's double first cousin and his father-in-law. However, it was on the strength of his top-ranking judicial position, which also made him the senior member of the Presidential Commission appointed by the Constitution to exercise the functions of the President prior to the entry in office of the first President of Ireland, that Sullivan had been chosen by the Government to accompany Hyde on the journey to his inauguration ceremony.[86] In inviting people to attend or participate in the inauguration ceremony, the Government had expressed the 'hope that persons entitled to wear gowns, robes or uniforms will wear them on this occasion' – a democratic suggestion that Sullivan had taken literally, as he turned up in Áras an Uachtaráin in his austere working judicial dress of a black coat, a black Irish poplin gown with white bands and a bobbed wig.[87]

The President-Elect's limousine departed the Áras for Dublin Castle at 12.20 p.m.[88] Hyde and Sullivan were joined in the state car by Peterson and de Buitléar, the latter a 36-year-old Dubliner and career soldier, who had served as adjutant of the Third Dublin Brigade of the IRA during the War of Independence and had joined the National Army in 1922.[89] The two aides-de-camp sat in disciplined silence, but the Chief Justice and Hyde made amiable conversation as they were driven through the Phoenix Park and onto the south quays. Hyde's earlier journey to and from St Patrick's Cathedral had taken him along Watling Street, onto Thomas Street and then through the smaller streets of the Liberties. Now, on his way to Dublin Castle, Hyde's car sped parallel to the Liffey, up one of the main arteries to the city. Hyde's car was the only one in sight. Earlier in the week, the Commissioner of the Garda Síochána, Michael Kinnane, had given notice of orders to suspend all traffic and that no standing vehicle would be allowed on any of the streets along which the inauguration procession would move.[90] The newspapers had printed specific details of the route that Hyde would take to and from the installation ceremony, which was being billed 'as one of the most historic occasions' in the capital's history, and this helped to bring over 125,000 cheering pedestrians onto the streets to line the route.[91] The inauguration was taking place on a Saturday, which had also been declared a public holiday, to maximise participation. Peterson later mused that people turned out 'in considerable numbers' because they 'had had little in by way of spectacle for a number of years', but this assessment underestimated both Hyde's considerable popularity with his fellow citizens and also the sheer sense of patriotic pride at the manifestation of sovereignty involved in the creation of an Irish head of state.[92]

As a populist nationalist party, whose political appeal was embedded in championing the pursuit of the fullest measure of Irish independence, Fianna Fáil in government was keen to create an air of national celebration around Hyde's inauguration. In conjunction with the city corporation, the Government had put considerable effort into decorating the city to generate a sense of carnival and colour around the installation ceremony. In the preceding days, council workmen had been busily engaged in raising portions of the pavements to make room for vermilion-coloured poles, on which flags, preserved from the Eucharistic Congress in 1932, were flown. Streamers had also been crossed and re-crossed high above the route that Hyde's historic procession to and from Dublin Castle would take, and even Dublin's bridges had been renovated. Capel Street Bridge was decked out in pleasant green, in restful contrast with the multicoloured flags in its vicinity.[93] At the Government's request, the national flag was also flying from prominent positions at City Hall, Trinity College, the Bank of Ireland College Green, the General Post Office, the head offices of the Dublin Port and Docks Board, and other principal buildings.[94] A reporter for the *Saturday Herald* who walked the parade route observed that 'Dublin was gay with flags and banners and many streets were spanned with bunting in honour of the event, while the Tricolour flew from all public buildings and business premises.'[95] On the eve of the inauguration, a Dublin city fire engine had even been deployed to allow a corporation employee 'place artistically arranged flowers' in the high windows of City Hall.[96] *The Irish Times* also noted Dublin's inner-city residents had embraced the city decoration scheme for the presidential inauguration and that 'the citizens have cooperated with Government and civic authorities in making Dublin's streets a fitting background for the colourful procession . . . Windows on the route have been made gay with flowers, twisted papers and flags.'[97] The good weather and the enthusiasm with which Dubliners took to the streets 'to give a fitting welcome to the first President of the new Ireland' also contributed to a festive atmosphere that was described by one journalist as the whole capital being 'more or less en fête'.[98]

From his days at the head of the Gaelic League, Hyde was accustomed to being the focus of cheering crowds. In November 1905, Dubliners had lined the route from the Gresham Hotel to Kingsbridge Station to applaud Hyde, as a torchlight procession led by an advance guard of Dublin hurlers and five marching bands escorted the then President of the Gaelic League on the first stage of his journey to the United States on a fundraising tour.[99] More recently, in April 1938, there had been touching scenes when Hyde had made his first journey to Dublin after becoming the agreed presidential candidate of Fianna Fáil and Fine Gael. On his way from Frenchpark, Hyde was honoured by towns and villages on the route, and a large procession escorted him into Longford.[100] In May, large crowds gathered outside the Department of Agriculture to celebrate Hyde's formal declaration of election and only the presence of a group of Garda bodyguards prevented Hyde from being mobbed by enthusiastic well-wishers.[101] These crowds, however, paled into insignificance when compared to the thronged streets on 25 June 1938. It would have been clear to Hyde from the moment his car pulled onto Dublin's south quays that his inauguration had captured the city's imagination. The pavements were packed and, at every vantage point, a dense cheering crowd strained to see their President-to-be as he was driven alongside the Liffey towards Dublin Castle.[102] Carrying his silk hat in his hands, Hyde was clearly taken aback, but he smiled and waved to the thousands who applauded him, and at times he chatted with the Chief Justice.[103]

Closer to Dublin Castle, the sheer volume of people on Dame Street and Parliament Street had been creating crowd-management difficulties for the authorities, who had underestimated the numbers. The *Saturday Herald* reported:

> Dublin took a greater interest than was anticipated in the installation ceremonies. For a considerable time before eleven o'clock there was a trek to the entrances of the Upper Castle Yard and the streets immediately surrounding it. The crowd

> grew in dimensions every few minutes, and it was obvious that the Gardaí were going to have a great deal of work in keeping the route of the procession clear. By noon there was a dense mass of people around the Upper Castle gates, and intense interest was taken in the arrival of the various members of the Diplomatic Corps, representatives of public bodies and members of the Government. Mr de Valera was accorded an enthusiastic reception on his arrival.[104]

Just before 12.45 p.m., a burst of cheering from Parliament Street announced the President-Elect's impending arrival at Dublin Castle. At the gates of the Castle Yard, there was some dangerous crushing as 'the crowd swayed to and fro in its anxiety' to see Hyde pass by.[105]

In 1204, King John had issued a 'command' to his cousin, Justiciar Meiler FitzHenry, to build 'a strong fortress in Dublin [and] . . . to erect a castle there, in such a competent place there as you may consider to be suitable if need be for the defence of the city as well as to curb it, if occasion shall so require'.[106] For the seven centuries that followed, Dublin Castle had been the seat of British rule in Ireland. This long occupation colourfully came to an end on 16 January 1922 when members of the Provisional Government of Southern Ireland, led by Michael Collins, arrived by taxi slightly behind schedule in Dublin Castle to receive the formal handover of the Irish state. The last British Viceroy, Lord FitzAlan, reportedly chided the Irish leader on this occasion, 'You are seven minutes late, Mr Collins,' to which he received the reply, 'We've been waiting over seven hundred years, you can have the extra seven minutes.'[107] Collins himself summed up both the magnitude of the change that he had helped effect as well as the castle's connotations with British imperialism when he recorded: 'How could I have expected to see Dublin Castle itself – that dreaded Bastille of Ireland – formally surrendered into my hands by the Lord Lieutenant, in the brocade-hung Council Chamber?'[108]

The extent of the Irish people's hostility towards Dublin Castle had been such that once independence was achieved the Free State Government considered razing it to the ground, but common sense prevailed and the castle survived to witness a new era in Irish public life.[109]

Inside the castle walls, Hyde alighted from the car and was met by a warm handshake from the diminutive figure of the Tánaiste, Seán T. O'Kelly, who had been de Valera's initial favourite choice to be President. Meanwhile, Peterson detected a professional detachment in his fellow military officers standing in formation in the courtyard and he recorded that 'the infantry guard of honour came to attention but otherwise paid us no notice. Douglas Hyde was not yet their commander-in-chief.'[110] The civilian observers in the courtyard were far less reticent and Hyde's appearance provoked ecstatic clapping and cheering. *The Irish Times* noted that 'virtually every window in the Upper Castle Yard was crowded with members of the Civil Service, some of the more adventurous of whom – women among them – found vantage points on the roof. When the President[-Elect] arrived he looked faintly surprised at the enthusiasm of the welcome which he received from the waiting throng.'[111]

With cheers still ringing in his ears, Hyde was shepherded through the main door into the State Apartments by O'Kelly. In silence, followed by an entourage of soldiers and civil servants, they ascended the split staircase onto the Battle-Axe Landing, named after the weapons carried by the ceremonial guards stationed here during the Viceregal era. On the landing, Hyde paused outside the doors of St Patrick's Hall, waiting for a signal to proceed, so that the carefully choreographed ceremony would commence exactly on time. Hyde was familiar with the order of ceremonies and he had been coached assiduously by McDunphy. Nothing had been left to chance in the preparations. Two days previously, Hyde and McDunphy had met with de Valera, O'Kelly, Maurice Moynihan, the Secretary to the Government, and other senior officials at Dublin Castle, where they made a survey of the building and observed the preparations for the inauguration ceremony. So that proceedings would 'run smoothly' on the big day, the President-Elect had been taken through a rehearsal of the ceremony in St Patrick's Hall.[112]

There was no precedent for a presidential inauguration in Ireland, though Bunreacht na hÉireann did prescribe the circumstances in which the President was to enter on his office. Article 12 of the Constitution sets out the oath of office and states that 'the President shall enter upon his office by taking and subscribing publicly, in the presence of members of both Houses of the Oireachtas, of Judges of the Supreme Court and of the High Court, and other public personages.'[113] Government officials ultimately opted for a short and dignified ceremony, which was to be conducted almost entirely in Irish.

Considerable attention had been given to planning the seating arrangements for the principal dignitaries of the state. A dais had been erected at the far end of St Patrick's Hall to seat the President-Elect, members of the Government, members of the Presidential Commission and members of the Council of State.[114] To the front of the dais, on the right-hand side, seats had been reserved for the Diplomatic Corps. Altogether, diplomatic representatives from eleven countries were in attendance, including the Papal Nuncio, Most Rev. Paschal Robinson; Dr Hans-Ulrich von Marchtaler, German Chargé d'Affaires; John Cudahy, the Envoy Extraordinary and Minister Plenipotentiary of the US; and B. Cauvet Duhamel, the French chargé d'affaires.[115]

Sitting behind the foreign diplomats were the parliamentary secretaries and immediately behind them were members of the Opposition front bench, followed by other members of the Oireachtas.[116] The Fianna Fáil TDs and senators were clearly distinguishable from their Oireachtas counterparts by their less formal attire. The Opposition parliamentarians generally wore full morning attire with silk hats, but the Fianna Fáil members wore business suits.[117] Although Sinn Féin had no Oireachtas representation, as a gesture of goodwill the Government had extended an invitation to the inauguration to the party's leadership. This olive branch was not accepted. Brian O'Higgins, a member of the Sinn Féin Árd Comhairle and a former party president, said that 'no republican' would be 'present at Dublin Castle or any other place in connection with the installation of Dr Hyde as President of the twenty-six county British Dominion.' He said that Sinn Féin regarded the invitation sent to them as 'a studied insult planned for publicity and in the worst possible taste'.[118]

On the opposite side of the aisle to the Oireachtas members were the clergy from the main religious denominations in the state, including the Primate of the Church of Ireland, Most Rev. Dr Godfrey Day; the Rev. Dr T. G. Irwin of the Methodist Church; Rev. Dr W. J.

Currie, the Moderator of the Presbyterian Church; and Rev. Dr Francis Wall, the Auxiliary Bishop of Dublin and the titular Bishop of Thasus, who was representing the Roman Catholic Archbishop of Dublin, Edward Byrne.[119] The fact that the Catholic Bishop and the Church of Ireland Primate had engaged in friendly, 'animated conversation' as they awaited the arrival of the President-Elect was deemed worthy of comment in a number of newspapers.[120] Behind the clergy sat members of the judiciary, representatives of the army and the Garda Síochána, universities, civil service, public bodies and local authorities, including James Hickey, the Lord Mayor of Cork, and Alfie Byrne, the Lord Mayor of Dublin, who had flirted with the idea of running against Hyde for the presidency.[121] There was one hiccup in the protocol of seating when Domhnall Ua Buachalla, the last Governor-General of the Irish Free State, was initially seated alone at the back of the hall. Later, however, he was moved to a prominent seat nearer the dais.[122]

From noon onwards, the invited guests began to take their seats.[123] By 12.44 p.m. every seat on the floor of the hall was filled. With the ceremony just about to begin, the Government, with members of the Presidential Commission, took their seats on the dais behind the presidential chair, a newly made ceremonial blue-and-gold chair with a harp crest made by Messrs Atkinson and elaborately embroidered in beautiful Irish poplin by the Dun Emer Guild.[124] Two members of the Presidential Commission – Justice Conor Maguire and the Ceann Comhairle, Frank Fahy – seated themselves at the front, alongside the Attorney-General, Patrick Lynch, and the Taoiseach, and for a few minutes everyone seemed to be fidgeting rather nervously.[125]

On the Battle-Axe Landing, Hyde stood in contemplative silence, awaiting his cue. The President-Elect's reverie was interrupted by the Tánaiste, who gently leaned across Hyde and whispered something into his ear. Hyde and O'Kelly had known each other a long time, dating back to the turn of the century and, in 1902, Hyde had helped secure O'Kelly employment as the business manager at the Gaelic League's newspaper, *An Claidheamh Soluis*.[126] In 1915, O'Kelly had been a central figure in the IRB's takeover of the Gaelic League, which precipitated Hyde's resignation as president of the organisation and saw O'Kelly installed as the Gaelic League's General Secretary. For a period, Hyde had been embittered by this course of events, but he had long forgiven if never quite forgotten the slight he had felt. Whatever words O'Kelly had whispered on the Battle-Axe Landing, they visibly moved Hyde, who responded by tenderly rubbing the Tánaiste's face with the back of his hand. Further conversation was rendered impossible by the sudden fanfare of trumpets from the Minstrels' Gallery inside the main hall, announcing that the inauguration ceremony was about to commence.[127]

At exactly 12.45 p.m., Hyde crossed the threshold into St Patrick's Hall and the entire gathering rose to their feet.[128] The hall had been the scene of many historic events, as for generations it had hosted representatives of British Government – Lord Lieutenants and Viceroys from the time of King George II – but it was a slightly incongruous setting for the installation of an independent Irish head of state.[129] The hall had been designed by Lord Chesterfield. The ceiling, under which Hyde was to receive his seal, had been painted by Vincentio Valdre in 1783 with three panels, representing St Patrick converting the Irish to Christianity; Irish chieftains surrendering to King Henry II and, in the centre, King George III at his coronation supported by the symbolic figures of Justice and Liberty.[130] The floating banners of the Order of the Knights of St Patrick, with their dim gold and silver, adorned the walls of the hall, as they had when Prince Albert Edward, the eldest son of Queen Victoria, had been invested in the order exactly fifty-one years previously.[131]

As Hyde advanced up the centre aisle, escorted by the Tánaiste and Chief Justice and followed by his aides-de-camp, he would have surely been struck by the blaze of colour on display in St Patrick's Hall.[132] On either side of the red carpet leading to the dais under the balcony, from which a large tricolour was draped, the gold-braided uniforms of members of the Diplomatic Corps, the dove-grey robes of the Papal Nuncio, the black, scarlet and purple robes of the other ecclesiastical dignitaries, the black gowns and white wigs of judges, the dark green uniforms of senior army officers, the navy blue of senior Gardaí and the kaleidoscope of colourful robes worn by the various representatives of the universities, the trade and professional organisations and the local authorities, many of the latter bearing gold chains of office, all combined to make the setting one of striking brilliance.[133]

At the dais, Hyde was received by the Taoiseach and, after shaking hands, the President-Elect took his seat in the blue-and-gold chair in the centre.[134] Ranged behind Hyde in a semicircle were members of the cabinet. On his immediate right was de Valera and on his left 'the tall, spare figure of the Chief Justice'.[135] The Taoiseach spoke a few words of welcome in Irish and then Timothy Sullivan invited Hyde to sign the declaration of office. On a table before the President-Elect lay the wording set forth in the Constitution. Hyde leaned forward and signed the document, then rose as the Chief Justice administered the oath of office.[136] Speaking in Irish, Hyde affirmed:

> In the presence of Almighty God, I, Douglas Hyde, do solemnly and sincerely promise and declare that I will maintain the Constitution of Ireland and uphold its laws, that I will fulfil my duties faithfully and conscientiously in accordance with the Constitution and the Law, and that I will dedicate my abilities to the service and welfare of the people of Ireland. May God direct and sustain me.[137]

Outside the gates of Dublin Castle, by means of specially installed speakers, the assembled crowd listened attentively to the broadcast of the event going on inside St Patrick's Hall.[138]

Having subscribed the oath, the now President was handed the Great Seal by the Chief Justice.[139] The Taoiseach then rose and, facing Hyde, addressed him directly first in Irish and then in an English version corresponding to the Irish text. De Valera said:

> Mr President, on behalf of the Irish nation, on behalf of the living, those who dwell at home as well our kin beyond the seas, on behalf also of the dead generations who longed to see this day but have not seen it, I salute you. You are now our President, our head, freely chosen under our own laws, inheriting the authority and entitled to the respect which the Gaels ever gave to those whom they recognised to be their rightful chiefs, but which for centuries they denied to those whom a foreign law would enforce upon them. In you we greet the successor of our rightful princes, and in your accession to

> office, we hail the closing of the breach that has existed since the undoing of our nation at Kinsale.[140]

Making characteristic reference to the issue of partition, de Valera noted that 'not all the territory of Éire is at the moment under your sway, a *Uachtaráin fhiúntaigh* [worthy President], but the justice of our claim and the tenacity of the Gael in holding to what is his own are our assurance that that too will also be set right.'[141]

Lauding Hyde for the seminal role he had played in preserving the Irish language from extinction and nurturing its revival, the Taosieach said:

> We are glad to pay you honour as one worthy of the office to which you have been called. Your foresight in saving from death our own sweet language, which your work and that of your colleagues of half a century ago have made it possible for us now to restore, merits for you the gratitude of all generations of the Irish that are to come. Without our language we could be but half a nation. Thanks to you, we can, if we will, be once more a complete nation, ranking high amongst the oldest of the nations of the world.[142]

An unusually emotional de Valera then suggested to Hyde that his inauguration would provide the inspiration for a new Celtic Dawn. He said: 'A scholar, a chraoibhín dhílis, you symbolise for us the things by which our people set most store; in your person you hold up to us the ancient glory of our people and beckon to us to make the future rival the past, urging us to be ever worthy of our inheritance as a great spiritual nation whose empire is of the soul.'[143]

The Taoiseach concluded by quoting the inscription of the Annals of the Four Masters, '*Do chum Glóire Dé agus Onóra na hÉireann*' ['To the Glory of God and the Honour of Ireland'].[144] De Valera's remarks were well received, but the warm applause was truncated by the sight of the President rising to his feet.

Over the preceding fortnight, de Valera and McDunphy had engaged in discussion as to whether it would be constitutionally appropriate for Hyde to make a substantive inauguration statement.

They had rather rigidly concluded that this would not be proper. McDunphy recorded in a procedural note:

> In considering the arrangements for the installation of the first President, Dr Hyde, into office, the Taoiseach, Mr de Valera, discussed with me the questions of the President making a brief statement which would be broadcased [sic] with the other details of the ceremony. It was suggested that such a statement unless confined to a mere formality such as an expression of appreciation, would be an address to the Nation on a matter of public or national importance within the meaning of section 7 of Article 13 of the Constitution and as such would entail
>
> a. prior consultation with the Council of State, and
> b. prior approval of the Government.
>
> It was obvious that these conditions could not be fulfilled in the circumstances, and the proposal therefore that the newly installed President should make some statement on a matter of policy was abandoned.[145]

While Hyde was prepared to accept this advice, he contended that it would appear ungracious of him to depart the inauguration without expressing his gratitude. The President, thus, replied briefly in Irish. According to a reporter from the *Saturday Herald*, 'it was noticeable that his voice was clear, fresh and young. He spoke with great sincerity and every word was clearly audible in the Press Gallery at the opposite end of the long hall.'[146] Hyde's comments were translated as follows: 'Mr Prime Minister, I am very thankful to you for the kind remarks you have made. I ask God to give me grace and power to advance the good of Ireland. I ask God to give me sense and prudence and strength so that I may fulfil my duty as President of Ireland.'[147]

When Dr Hyde concluded his brief speech, the entire company rose and applauded.[148] Immediately there was another fanfare of trumpets from the gallery and then the national anthem was played by the No.1 Army Band, which in Peterson's recollection 'did its best to bring down the rafters'.[149] To renewed clapping, Hyde was escorted back down the aisle and out of St Patrick's Hall by de Valera, O'Kelly and the President's aides-de-camp. The entire ceremony had taken only fifteen minutes.[150] As the party emerged into the Castle Yard, the first of the salute of twenty-one guns, fired from the esplanade in Collins Barracks, was heard announcing to the citizens of Dublin that Ireland's first President had been installed.[151] Simultaneously, the national flag was raised over Áras an Uachtaráin.[152]

In the Castle Yard, the presidential salute was played and, accompanied by Captain O'Connor, the officer commanding on duty, the President inspected the guard of honour of an entirely Irish-speaking battalion.[153] Hyde then proceeded to his car, accompanied again by his two aides-de-camp and the Chief Justice. The members of the Presidential Commission and the Council of State stepped into a convoy of cars parked behind the presidential limousine.[154] The vehicles were preceded by a troop of cavalry in their full dress ceremonial uniform of saffron and blue. Shortly after one o'clock, the clip-clop of trotting horses heralded the commencement of the procession of the President to his residence in the Phoenix Park.[155] As the presidential car, preceded by the 24-man mounted guard, swung out through the gates of Dublin Castle, 'there was a rousing cheer from the public gathered in the vicinity'.[156] The crowd 'strained to get a better view' as the new President drove out in his open car. Silk hat still in his hand, Hyde chatted amicably with the Chief Justice, now and again acknowledging the ovation.[157] Hyde's car was closely followed by a vehicle containing the Taoiseach and Tánaiste, who were 'greeted with cheers and cries of "Up Dev"'.[158] In the third car were the President of the High Court, Conor Maguire, and a Supreme Court judge, Gerald Fitzgibbon. Then in another car came Seán Gibbons, Cathaoirleach of the Seanad, and Frank Fahy, Ceann Comhairle of Dáil Éireann. Patrick Lynch, the Attorney-General, was in the last car.[159]

As part of the military arrangements for Hyde's procession to the Phoenix Park, troops had already taken up positions lining the route from Cork Hill, where the President exited Dublin Castle, to George's Street. Troops were also situated at College Green and from the junction of Abbey Street and O'Connell Street to a point approximately 30 yards beyond the GPO.[160] At each juncture, as the procession passed them by, the troops moved to 'present arms', a ceremonial two-part drill command used to convey respect.[161]

Behind the soldiers on Dame Street, members of the public lined the pavements five and six deep and 'the whole area resounded with the cheering and joyful outbursts of the assembled gatherings'.[162] An enterprising reporter from *The Irish Times* climbed on the roof of a premises on Cork Hill to get a bird's-eye view of the procession. He noted, 'Looking down on the thronged sidewalks of Cork Hill, Dame Street and College Green, the fluttering flags, the crowded roofs and windows and lines of green clad military, one was vaguely reminded of an old print of Dublin in another era. It might have been the opening of Grattan's Parliament.'[163]

Dubliners had taken to the streets in their thousands to view an occasion that was being dubbed 'one of the most historic which the capital has ever witnessed'.[164] As the procession crossed the Liffey, Hyde looked up the capital's main thoroughfare and saw crowds on a scale that had not been seen in Dublin since the Eucharistic Congress, six years previously. Every conceivable vantage point was packed solid. A reporter for the *Evening Mail* noted that 'O'Connell Street was black with people waiting for the presidential procession.'[165]

Outside the GPO, the procession made a planned short pause for the purpose of paying tribute to those who had fought for Irish freedom in the 1916 Rising.[166] *The Irish Times* rather grandiosely described the moment in which a bare-headed President Hyde observed a two-minute silence at the site where Patrick Pearse had read the Proclamation of the Irish Republic as 'history's salute to history'.[167] It is impossible to gauge what thoughts raced through Hyde's mind at this precise moment, but his relationship with Pearse had been complex. At one stage, Pearse had been one of Hyde's closest lieutenants in the Gaelic League, but as Pearse became more immersed in militant nationalism a chasm had developed between them. Hyde had made clear to Pearse that he believed violence should not be used to achieve Ireland's nationhood unless there was no alternative, and even then, only if victory was assured.[168] Hyde had little sympathy for the notion of a blood sacrifice.

President Hyde was not the only dignitary standing to attention at the GPO who had originally harboured feelings of hostility towards the Rising. The Chief Justice, Timothy Sullivan, and the Attorney-General, Patrick Lynch, had both been supporters of the Irish

Parliamentary Party in 1916 and had viewed the Rising as regrettable, though Lynch would later embrace republicanism and join Fianna Fáil.[169] Mr Justice Gerald Fitzgibbon was from a unionist background and had been deeply opposed to Irish separatism.[170] In contrast, Éamon de Valera, Seán T. O'Kelly and Frank Fahy, who also joined President Hyde in the mark of respect for the 1916 leaders, had actively participated in the Rising and O'Kelly had actually served in the GPO as Pearse's aide-de-camp.[171]

After the few minutes of silent tribute, the cars moved on again and deafening cheers broke out, which Hyde smilingly acknowledged.[172] The procession proceeded from the GPO via Upper O'Connell Street, Parnell Square, North Frederick Street, Blessington Street, Berkeley Road, the North Circular Road and the New Cabra Road towards the Phoenix Park.[173] As the motorcade reached the suburbs, the crowds were thinner than in the city centre, but local residents had still come out in force to applaud their new President. The crowds in the suburbs were bolstered by large numbers of children gathered outside their schools, even though it was a Saturday. This sight emotionally affected Hyde.[174] Passing by St Peter's National School in Phibsborough, the President received particularly warm and boisterous greetings from the assembled pupils. Hyde had been struggling to keep his emotions in check all day; however, the enthusiasm of the schoolchildren finally caused the dam to burst. The 78-year-old President sat back and wept. Meanwhile, Hyde's car speed on towards Áras an Uachtaráin, the official residence of the President of Ireland and his home for the next seven years.

2

The Political Origins of the Presidency

Douglas Hyde was born in Longford House, Castlerea, County Roscommon, in January 1860, in the twenty-third year of the reign of Queen Victoria as monarch of the United Kingdom of Great Britain and Ireland. If the notion was remote at the time of Hyde's birth that Ireland would in his lifetime be decoupled from the United Kingdom, it would have been totally unfathomable in the mid nineteenth century to think that this youngest son of a rural Church of Ireland rector would one day replace Queen Victoria's great-grandson as the head of an Irish state.

The office of President of Ireland was born out of the tumultuous political origins of independent Ireland in the early part of the twentieth century. The thinking that gave rise to the Irish presidency evolved from the bitter and contentious events that transformed the Irish political landscape in a 21-year period from the Easter Rebellion in 1916 to the enactment of Bunreacht na hÉireann in 1937. In this period, Ireland went from being a constituent, homogenous part of the United Kingdom, under the British Crown, to being a truncated 26-county state with a republican constitution and a president at its pinnacle.

At every stage of this transformative political journey, there was strong and often rancorous debate about what the state's status should be, and integral to this was the divisive question as to what model of head of state would be acceptable to nationalist Ireland. The fact that the office of President of Ireland emerged from this disputed background yet, in its formative years, quickly obtained widespread public respect bears testament to the political skills of Éamon de Valera, the other authors of the Constitution, and to the office's early incumbents.

From a modern vantage point, with the presidency an integral institution in Ireland's democratic order, it is important not to overlook the fact that it was by no means inevitable that this office would, from the outset, attract popular support. Every other preceding form of head of state in twentieth-century Ireland had attracted significant opposition in a country that had been politically sundered by the legacy of the War of Independence and, more especially, the Civil War.

The Irish presidency, of which Douglas Hyde would become the first incumbent, emerged from and managed to transcend controversial political terrain. The career of Éamon de Valera, a central figure in Irish politics from the East Clare by-election in 1917, was integral to the creation of the office of President of Ireland. De Valera's evolving political views between 1916 and 1937 (including his controversial and – at times – torturous opposition to each successive format of head of state that existed in Ireland during this period) undoubtedly shaped the Irish presidency. Ironically, de Valera's immersion in Irish politics had stemmed from his involvement in the Gaelic League, the organisation Douglas Hyde had established in 1893 to promote the Irish language and to develop the Gaelic revival.

The question of what form of head of state was desirable had been exercising nationalist Ireland from the turn of the twentieth century. As a schoolboy at Blackrock College's Literary and Debating Society, de Valera had once argued in favour of the prevailing political orthodoxy in the early 1900s of the Irish Parliamentary Party, whose ambitions extended to a Home Rule parliament in Dublin, but not to 'breaking the link' with the United Kingdom or to having any other head of state, bar the British sovereign.[1]

It was not until the aftermath of the 1916 Rising that winds of political change would give rise to populist demands for independent statehood in Ireland. The question of what form an Irish head of state should take was one, however, which sowed confusion among advanced nationalists. Though the Rising was fought to proclaim an Irish Republic and its leader, Patrick Pearse, was alternately referred to as 'Provisional President of the Republic' and 'Commanding *[sic]* in Chief the Forces of the Irish Republic and President of the Provisional Government', the commitment to a republican president as head of state was at best lukewarm.[2] F. S. L. Lyons has noted that Pearse, Thomas MacDonagh and Joseph Plunkett were 'quite ready to envisage' a German prince being installed as King of an independent Ireland.[3]

This debate about monarchy and republicanism was part of the dynamic of Sinn Féin in the immediate post-Rising period. The party's founder, Arthur Griffith, 'accepted the sovereignty of the British monarch in Ireland, but insisted that only the King, Lords and Commons of Ireland had the right to rule Ireland.'[4] A contentious split was only avoided when, at the October 1917 Sinn Féin Ard Fheis, Éamon de Valera came up with a formula that was acceptable to both wings. He proposed that the party's aim would be to secure 'the international recognition of Ireland as an independent Irish Republic. Having achieved that status the Irish people may by referendum freely choose their own form of government.'[5]

In his presidential address to the Ard Fhéis, de Valera elaborated on this compromise yet, at the same time, he managed to make clear that he would not accept the British sovereign as Ireland's head of state.

> The only banner under which our freedom can be won at the present time is the Republican banner. It is as an Irish Republic that we have a chance of getting international recognition. Some of us would wish, having got that recognition, to have a republican form of government. Some might have fault to find with that and prefer other forms of government. This is not the time for the discussion on the best forms of government . . . this is the time to get freedom. Then we can settle by the most democratic means what particular form of government we may have. I only wish to say in reference to the last clause that there is no contemplation in it of having a monarchy in which the monarch would be of the House of Windsor.[6]

This categorical rejection of the House of Windsor is an important benchmark in assessing de Valera's core political beliefs. It is also fundamental to understanding the genesis of the office of President of Ireland. De Valera's refusal, dating from this point, to contemplate any role for the British sovereign as an Irish head of state would feature prominently in the Treaty negotiations, the subsequent Civil War and his campaign of opposition to the position of the Governor-General in the Irish Free State. The office of President of Ireland would grow out of his efforts to produce an alternative solution to the dilemma between monarchy and republicanism.

The political importance that de Valera increasingly attached to what form an Irish head of state should take was encompassed in his objections to the 1921 Anglo-Irish Treaty. He told the Dáil that his principal opposition was that he 'did not want the King as the monarch of Ireland – that was the main thing'.[7] De Valera also made clear that his objection to the Oath of Allegiance was based on the King's role as head of state in Ireland. He told the Dáil he could not support the Treaty because it: 'makes British authority our masters in Ireland. It was said that they had only an oath to the British King in virtue of common citizenship, but you have an oath of the Irish Constitution, which will have the King of Great Britain as Head of Ireland. You will swear allegiance to that Constitution and to that King.'[8]

De Valera's solution was 'Document No. 2' and the only substantial difference between it and the Treaty was that de Valera's document excluded the oath and the Governor-General. As de Valera pointed out, Document No. 2 'embodied the policy of external association, by which the internal republic would not be affected.'[9] The King would be recognised only as 'the Head of the Association', namely the British Commonwealth, with which Ireland would be associated.

Civil War in Ireland was fought not on partition, or the limits of independence, but on the political willingness or intransigence of the respective sides to compromise on the dilemma between monarchy and republicanism, which had been exercising nationalists in one form or other from the start of the twentieth century.

De Valera had previously declared himself not to be 'a doctrinaire republican'.[10] However, it soon became evident that unlike Griffith and Michael Collins, who were ultimately prepared to compromise on dominion status, de Valera was, in fact, doctrinaire in his anti-monarchism, especially in relation to the British Crown's role vis-à-vis an Irish head of state.

At this stage, de Valera's views on an Irish head of state were largely defined by what he was against rather than what he was for. Yet, external association and the related Document No.2 do mark important roadmaps in the evolution of his thinking. These related concepts were ones he would draw on again in the future. In particular, the fact that the President of Ireland had no international functions in the first decade of the office was a tortured formula of external association put into political practice. In many respects, this was turning the clock back to the sort of Treaty de Valera had wanted his plenipotentiaries to conclude in London in 1921. It was a type of compromise that meant that the President of Ireland up to 1949, in accordance with de Valera's thinking, was the head of the 'internal' (but undeclared) republic, while at the same time Irish diplomats were accredited by the British monarch as 'Head of the Association', i.e. the Commonwealth (of which de Valera had cryptically remarked that Ireland might be 'in it' but was not 'of it').[11]

In tracing the evolution of de Valera's thinking in regard to what constituted a desirable form of head of state, the events of 1921 loom large. He did not attend the Treaty talks at that time, having come to the firm belief that, because he was the President of the Irish Republic, he was the symbol of that Republic.[12] Drawing on this experience, in later years, de Valera would attach real significance to the political symbolism that could be derived from the type of head of state Ireland had. Specifically, in 1937, he would establish an office of President to signify and symbolise Ireland's republican status.

The 1921 Treaty provided for a 'representative of the Crown' who was to be 'appointed in like manner as the Governor-General of Canada and in accordance with the practice observed in the making of such appointments'.[13] In effect, the Irish Governor-General was a proxy head of state for the British monarch. The Irish Governor-General's duties were mainly ceremonial, yet the office's existence nevertheless underpinned the executive authority of the Crown in Irish affairs. As John Coakley has pointed out:

> The British Government clearly saw the Irish Governor-General, like his counterpart in other dominions, as a Trojan Horse . . . The British thus argued that in the Irish Free State, as in Canada, it would have to be a fundamental principle of

> the Constitution 'that the executive authority was vested in the Crown, that the Crown was a constituent part of the legislature and that the Crown was the fountain of justice.' The Governor-General, then, was expected to act as agent both for the British Government and the King.[14]

In light of the above, it is hardly surprising that the office of Governor-General was a major focal point for republican hostility and the subject of, at least, two attempted violent assaults during the Civil War.[15] From de Valera's perspective, it was anathema to his political beliefs that an Irish head of state should perform duties that encompassed a responsibility to serve British interests. During the Treaty debates, de Valera had set out his fear that the role of the Crown and the Governor-General would be used as a pretext for British interference in Irish affairs.[16] Though Kevin O'Higgins would subsequently assure a Dáil committee, examining the Constitution of Saorstát Éireann Bill, that the powers of the Crown had been reduced to 'the irreducible minimum', there were grounds for de Valera's concerns.[17] On 2 December 1922, Tim Healy, the first Governor-General, gave the British Government a written assurance that he would keep 'a watchful eye on Bills and Amendments or proposed Amendments to Bills which may in any way conflict with the Treaty, or may be such as may affect the relations of His Majesty with foreign states or other parts of the Empire.'[18]

The Governor-General's watching brief for the British Government was a role of which de Valera was particularly critical. John L. McCracken has pointed out that 'strong exception' was taken by opponents of the Treaty to the first Irish Governor-General paying an official visit to the British Colonial Secretary because this served to confirm the dichotomy of an Irish head of state representing British interests.[19] Though this latter role was formally abandoned in April 1927, arising from a decision taken at the previous year's Imperial Conference, this facet of the Governor-General's initial duties made a clear impression on de Valera's thinking and subsequently, in formulating the office of President, he was determined to ensure that an Irish head of state would remain totally distinct from British interests.

De Valera's difficult relationship with Healy also informed his views on what format an Irish head of state should take. Healy had been a polarising figure in nationalist politics since the split in the Home Rule Party in 1890, during which he had viciously attacked Parnell in a series of highly polemical speeches. Healy's familial links with Kevin O'Higgins, a bête noir of republicans, grounded the office in charges of nepotism and 'interested motives' from the start.[20] De Valera and Healy had previously clashed in the lead-up to the Civil War when Healy had sought to solicit de Valera's support in the event of Collins and the Provisional Government deciding to cancel the scheduled Army Convention.[21] Relations deteriorated completely when, in his first interview as Governor-General, Healy made it clear that he blamed de Valera for the Civil War and urged the American public not to give financial support to Irish republicans.[22]

Healy's frequent forays into the realms of partisan politics undoubtedly influenced de Valera's perspective that it should not be permissible for a head of state to engage in contentious political debate. At the same time, Healy's capacity for political invective did little to build support for his office or allow republicans to become reconciled to his office.

In November 1926, in the run-up to the first Fianna Fáil Ard Fheis, the Governor-General had launched a scathing attack on the new party. After paying tribute to the Cumann na nGaedheal ministers, Healy went on to declare that

> there was no practical opposition 'in this country' and that he would like to know on what grounds the members of the Government were being told that if a number of persons – 'whom we never heard of before, except in connection with explosions and assassinations' – were put into power they would have a 'regular transformation scene.' To those gentlemen who said that they would not enter into the legislature of their country because their principle forbade them to take the Oath to His Majesty, he would say in the words of Gilbert and Sullivan: 'You are curious optimists; you never would be missed.' They were quite welcome to stay out and the further out they stayed the better some would be pleased.[23]

Healy's remarks caused political consternation, with W. T. Cosgrave, head of the Cumann na nGaedheal Government, forced to distance himself from the Governor-General. In expressing regret that such a speech had been made, Cosgrave noted that it was 'plain that the office of Governor-General must be of a non-partisan character'.[24] Privately, Cosgrave noted in a letter to Kevin O'Higgins that he 'did not like "letting down the old man" but there was no other course. His own view was that the speech did them no good, did de Valera no harm and would influence no one except against them.'[25]

Though de Valera was at this point an abstentionist TD, his viewpoint was captured in a Dáil speech by Thomas Johnson that was reported in some detail.[26] The Labour Party leader vehemently argued that any form of Irish head of state should refrain from engaging in partisan politics. He stated:

> The Dáil ought not allow to pass without strenuous protest a constitutional impropriety which, if condoned, would imply a willingness to accept as nominal head of the state a political partisan, responsible to no one in this country for his actions, but free to use his privileged position to promote certain political ends . . . this House is bound to require that whosoever may hold the office of Governor-General, or any equivalent office in this country, shall not use his position to prejudice the electorate against any member of the Dáil or the claim to unbiased treatment of any party or deputy who, following the verdict of the poll, may be called upon to form a Government.[27]

This criticism did not dissuade Healy from making further partisan interventions. In the course of the general election campaign in June 1927, the Governor-General made personal comments about Countess Markievicz that drew a sharp response from de Valera.[28] Subsequently, in the final month of his term of office, in January 1928, Healy made two particularly virulent and bitter attacks on de Valera.[29]

These controversies are important in understanding the rather restrictive view that de Valera would take on the President of Ireland's freedom to contribute to public debate. The Governor-General's readiness to use his status to denigrate de Valera politically impacted heavily on the Fianna Fáil leader's subsequent thinking that a head of state should be above party politics. To militate against the head of state's position ever again being used to ferment hostility against any political group, in drafting Bunreacht na hÉireann, de Valera would insist on a protocol that mandated the President to seek the permission of Government before he could communicate with the nation.[30]

On 1 February 1928, James McNeill replaced Tim Healy as Governor-General, but there was no possibility of de Valera becoming reconciled to the office. McNeill's investiture ceremony in Leinster House was boycotted by Fianna Fáil TDs and the party kept up a steady attack on the office.[31] As Brendan Sexton has noted of this period,

> In the late 1920s [de Valera] had attacked the Governor-Generalship on three main grounds. First of all it was far too costly. Secondly, it was an 'absolutely useless office' filled by a 'rubber stamp.' Thirdly (and this was the fundamental reason for de Valera's unrelenting hostility), the office was 'regarded by the majority of our people as a symbol of our defeat and as a badge of our slavery.' The sooner it was abolished the better.[32]

The Labour Party had initially made the running on attacking the office of Governor-General on cost grounds, but, when McNeill took up office, Fianna Fáil increasingly adopted this tactic.[33] Fianna Fáil's criticisms in this period would subsequently impact on the resources allocated to the Irish presidency and also influenced de Valera's viewpoint that it would be politically prudent for the office to be low-key.

Under the terms of Article 60 of the Free State Constitution and the Governor-General's Salary and Establishment Act 1923, the Governor-General's salary was fixed at £10,000 per annum.[34] This became a cause of real resentment in the late 1920s as the global recession impacted upon Ireland. In 1929, de Valera attacked the fact that James McNeill was being paid the same salary as the Australian Governor-General, though 'Australia has a population well over twice the population of the Free State.'[35]

McNeill, who was a retired Indian civil servant, had according to one of de Valera's biographers 'brought home some memories of Dunbar splendours and attempted to give the Viceregal building something of its old status'.[36] Social gatherings at the Viceregal Lodge were frequent, large and costly affairs, with many ex-unionists being prominent guests as part of the Governor-General's 'healing efforts'.[37] As Mary Bromage has pointed out, de Valera regularly criticised the Governor-General, in populist terms, for creating 'a new kind of court-life at the Phoenix Park, and silk hats symbolised all that Fianna Fáil detested in public deportment'.[38]

By 1929, between a combination of salary, expenses and tax-free allowances, the Governor-Generalship was costing the Free State in excess of £27,000 per annum.[39] De Valera told the Dáil:

> We regard it as a crime under present conditions to squander a sum of close upon £27,000 this year, when we know there are people unemployed whose families are on the verge of starvation. We are spending on this absolutely useless office a sum of money that could be earned on an average by 200 workers in any of our industries.[40]

The damage that Fianna Fáil had inflicted on the Governor-Generalship by consistently criticising the cost of the office was not lost on de Valera when, a decade later, he had to fix the costs for the office of President of Ireland. Following the plebiscite on the 1937 Constitution, in which W. T. Cosgrave had tried to persuade the electorate that the new office would, in fact, cost more than the Governor-Generalship, de Valera moved to ensure that there could be no credible basis to undermine the presidency by citing excessive spending. President Hyde's salary was fixed at a modest £5,000, half of what the Governor-General had been paid.[41] The total cost of the President's establishment was fixed in 1938 at £15,000, which was a 45 per cent reduction on the cost of the Governor-General's office a decade earlier, even before inflation was taken into account.[42] To further insulate themselves and the office of President from criticism on cost grounds, Fianna Fáil had, in advance of fixing the figure for the President's establishment, set up an all-party committee to advise on this issue. This helped to build a consensus on the costs for the presidency, with Fine Gael's T. F. O'Higgins offering strong support for the Government's proposals.[43] It also ensured that a more frugal level of funding was provided for the new office to allow, in Finance Minister Seán MacEntee's words, 'the presidency to be fulfilled unostentatiously but, nevertheless, as befits that high office'.[44]

On 9 March 1932, Fianna Fáil formed its first government. Those who expected de Valera to move immediately to abolish the office of Governor-General would be disappointed. In fact, de Valera had moved to quell such expectations in the months leading up to the general election. In October 1931, he had told the Fianna Fáil Ard Fheis:

> To avoid legal difficulties, the office of Governor-General may have to be retained in the initial period of taking over. The ultimate aim would be to assimilate the office to that of President of the Republic. Of course, there can be no question of our continuing to provide for any period extravagant sums which are at present paid in salary and for the upkeep of the establishment.[45]

This speech is significant in signalling that de Valera had arrived at very clear views as to how he was going to deal with issues surrounding the question of head of state. Though James McNeill had shown magnanimity in coming to Leinster House to appoint de Valera formally as the new head of government, thus sparing him the embarrassment of a visit to the Viceregal Lodge, Fianna Fáil were resolved to replace McNeill's office and to constitute an office of President, which would politically signify Irish sovereignty.[46] De Valera's decision to pursue a gradualist, step-by-step approach to the diminution of the office of Governor-General would ultimately have positive ramifications for the stability of the new office of President. This choice allowed de Valera to lay a smoother path for the emergence of the presidency as part of a new and ordered constitutional framework rather than as a controversial, direct replacement for an office that had been swiftly axed.

In 1932, an immediate all-out assault on the office of Governor-General would also have intensified hostilities with the British Government, which were already simmering because of de Valera's swift action in bringing forward a Bill to abolish the Oath as well as defaulting on the payment of land annuities. De Valera had sought a mandate for these specific steps in the 1932 election campaign and he was conscious of not going beyond this by moving precipitously on the office of Governor-General.

From the outset, the Fianna Fáil Government followed a course that de Valera had outlined in 1923 of 'squeezing England out' by boycotting the Governor-General.[47] This meant politically demeaning the office to the point that it would become publicly irrelevant. The first in a series of official snubs directed at the office was delivered at a dance in the French legation less than seven weeks after Fianna Fáil had entered government when, upon the arrival of the Governor-General, two of de Valera's most prominent ministers, Seán T. O'Kelly and Frank Aiken, walked out of the legation. McNeill pressed for an apology, but instead was further insulted by the Government's determined efforts to sideline him during the Eucharistic Congress in the summer of 1932.[48]

McNeill was furious about his treatment. On 7 July, the Governor-General wrote to de Valera complaining about his 'ill-conditioned bad manners' and threatened to publish the correspondence that had passed between them, unless he received an apology.[49] De Valera declined to apologise and, ultimately, the correspondence appeared in Irish newspapers on 12 July 1932. From this moment, McNeill's dismissal became inevitable. De Valera's authorised biographers noted that:

> The whole theory that the Governor-General should act only on the advice of the Irish executive was being challenged and, however one may sympathise with McNeill's personal feelings, the episode brought into question the very foundation of the office as previously understood. To assert the authority of the Government, de Valera saw no option but McNeill's removal from office.[50]

This episode is very significant in understanding the future development of the office of President. In Opposition, de Valera had already witnessed the controversy that a head of state who immersed himself in partisan politics could generate. In government, the experience of the instability generated by the public conflict with McNeill impacted strongly on de Valera's political thinking. As President Childers' biographer has argued:

> It is probable that as he drafted the relevant Article 12 [of Bunreacht na hÉireann, which establishes the office of President of Ireland], Éamon de Valera was conscious of his embarrassing wrangle with Governor-General James McNeill shortly after he took office in 1932 . . . [that] ended with McNeill challenging the authority of the Government. Clearly any possibility of a future clash between Government and head of state was to be avoided.[51]

In the Dáil debate on the draft Constitution in May 1937, when Frank MacDermott sought the insertion of a provision allowing the President of Ireland unrestricted freedom to explain a course of action that he might take, de Valera alluded to the salutary lessons of his dispute with McNeill. He said:

> We have heard a great deal about clashes. There is no opportunity here for a clash in the ordinary sense, bringing matters before the people. The danger would lie if the President, over the head of the Government, was to make some appeal to the nation on some matter or address a message to the nation. You would immediately have two authorities, and you cannot have that. On the whole, the best course would be to make it possible for the President, in a case where he concurred and where the Government also wished it done, to issue an address. But I do not think the President ought to be permitted to enter into what might give rise to a public controversy with the Government.[52]

McNeill's appointment was finally terminated in November 1932 and de Valera then made a determined effort to consign the office of Governor-General to the pages of history. He first proposed that the Chief Justice should act in the Governor-General's place, but retreated from this proposal when the Chief Justice, Hugh Kennedy, expressed concerns about the need to maintain a separation of powers between the judiciary and the executive.[53] De Valera also flirted with the idea that he, himself, as President of the Executive Council, should assume the duties of the Governor-General, but this was rejected out of hand by the British Attorney-General as a direct contravention of the Treaty.[54]

Having failed to persuade the British to acquiesce in the abolition of the office of Governor-General, de Valera eventually acted on a suggestion passed on by Hugh Kennedy, which originated from an unnamed Englishman. In a memo to de Valera on 6 October 1932, Kennedy wrote:

> I happened, some years ago, to discuss the Office of Governor-General with an Englishman who formerly held position of great importance and influence . . . I mentioned to him one of the great objections in Ireland to the Viceregal and Governor-General position was the inevitable re-creating of the old Sham Court, gathering round it all the hovering sycophants and certain social types alien to the national life of the country . . . He said to me, 'Why should not the office be conducted as a purely formal office by a man residing in an ordinary residence in the city, say in Fitzwilliam Square, in such circumstances that nothing of that kind could arise? Then there should be no expectations created either of entertainment or social privilege, round the position. He should be an officer with a bureau for transacting the specific business with which he was entrusted, and his office would begin and end there.'[55]

This course of action, which de Valera adopted, amounted to an intensification of the strategy to demean the office of Governor-General to a point where it would become totally meaningless. The appointment of Domhnall Ua Buachalla, a former Fianna Fáil TD, as Governor-General marked the beginning of this phase. In reply to a friend who had extended congratulations to him, Ua Buachalla wrote of his appointment: 'It is a step in the direction of abolishing the post altogether. I would greatly prefer not to have to bother with it, but since it was [de Valera] who asked me to take it for the good of the country, I told him I would do what he wished.'[56]

The reason why de Valera continued at this point to chip away at the office of Governor-General rather than unilaterally abolish it has a lot to do with the politics of Anglo-Irish relations at that time. De Valera was at this stage committed to establishing an office of President, but he also recognised that this was a gradualist task that could not be achieved without a degree of British acquiescence. In late November 1932, at the time of Ua Buachalla's appointment, there were a number of checks on de Valera unilaterally getting rid of the office, including very real concerns that de Valera might be pushing the British too far. Speaking on the vote on the Governor-General's establishment in July 1933, de Valera touched on this latter point:

> If the office of Governor-General is retained today, it is because there is a fear in certain people's minds that, if it were abolished, you would have a renewal of some war. The people on the opposite side are crying out about the tariff war, and because there are people in this country who feel that if they completely and thoroughly ended the Treaty, there would be a renewal of a war of one kind or another, by a big state against ours, they are compelled in that particular way to submit to the retention of an office like this.[57]

The fact that Ua Buachalla was a political ally that he 'could trust implicitly' did, however, allow de Valera to downgrade the office, free from concerns that the Governor-General might cause a rumpus.[58] This factor gave de Valera significant political room to manoeuvre in phasing out the office of Governor-General so a space could be made for a new and more acceptable form of head of state. Ua Buachalla's role as an architect of the presidency was publicly acknowledged by de Valera when he told a rally in Dublin, on the eve of the plebiscite on Bunreacht na hÉireann in the summer of 1937, that without Ua Buachalla's work 'you would not be asked tomorrow to enact a free constitution'.[59] De Valera went on to say that Ua Buachalla had carried out his duties solely

> in the best interests of our people, so as to rid us for ever from a Governor-General . . . From the moment he got into it he was being taunted with the fact that he was a nonentity and was not appearing in public, and every effort was made to seduce him from the position from acting as we wanted him to act so as to end that office altogether . . . He did his duty so well that there will never again be a Governor-General.[60]

In accordance with de Valera's wishes to degrade the office to insignificance, Ua Buachalla had rarely appeared in public, lived in a modest suburban residence and, as Governor-General, did no more than the minimum required by law, mainly the affixing of his signature to Bills passed by the Oireachtas.[61] As the office of Governor-General retreated from public profile, on the legislative front, Fianna Fáil had engaged in a piecemeal erosion of its powers. In November 1933, the Constitution (Amendment No. 20) Act 1933, which transferred from the Governor-General to the Executive Council the responsibility for recommending financial measures to the Oireachtas, came into effect. On the same day, the Constitution (Amendment No. 21) Act 1933, which eliminated the Governor-General's right of reserving legislation for consideration in Great Britain, was also passed into law.[62]

The Governor-General's sole remaining legislative responsibility was to sign Bills presented to him by the Executive Council. The significance of such legislative measures was not missed in London. The King's Private Secretary, Lord Wigram, sent an agitated letter to the Dominions Office complaining that the office of the Governor-General was now 'practically abolished'.[63]

In May 1935, during the debate on the Governor-General's establishment, de Valera hinted that the time when he would 'abolish the office altogether' was close at hand.[64] On 17 May 1935, the draft heads of a new Constitution prepared on de Valera's instructions by John Hearne, Legal Adviser to the Department of External Affairs, referred to 'the establishment of the office of President of Saorstát Éireann, the holder of which would fulfil all the functions now exercised by the King and the Governor-General'.[65]

By June 1936, sufficient progress had been made in the new

Constitution's drafting for de Valera to send a courtesy memorandum to King Edward VIII informing him:

> a) that this Constitution would deal with the internal affairs of Saorstát Éireann;
>
> b) that amongst the provisions of the new Constitution would be the creation of the office of a President elected by the people and the abolition of the Office of Governor-General.[66]

De Valera's timetable was accelerated by the abdication crisis of 1936 in Britain. This provided de Valera with what his authorised biographers described as an 'unrivalled opportunity' to remove all references to the King and the Governor-General from the Free State Constitution with the British Government powerless to object.[67] As D. George Boyce has noted, Stanley Baldwin's Government were 'unable to use their superior power, or even to mobilise Commonwealth opinion against him. The abdication was a sensitive and complex political problem, requiring all Baldwin's dexterity; it also had the unpleasant undertones of a scandal. No British government could take a stand against de Valera's action on this issue.'[68]

By forcing the British to acquiesce in the removal of the Crown from the Irish Free State Constitution, de Valera had arrived at a position where he knew there would be no basis for British complaint or retaliation when his government introduced what Seán MacEntee had said in July 1936 would be a 'republican' Constitution.[69] Longford and O'Neill have written that de Valera saw in the abdication crisis 'a means of facilitating what he had already in mind'.[70] The crisis is significant in understanding the evolution of the office of President in that it allowed de Valera finally to pull down the shutters on the office of Governor-General unhindered, while, at the same time, opening up a political space for him to bring forward his proposals for a new format of head of state in the context of a new constitutional order.

As Edward VIII abdicated in London on 11 December 1936, de Valera, under a guillotine motion, steered the Constitution (Amendment No. 27) Bill through the Dáil.[71] With the signature of Domhnall Ua Buachalla, the office of Governor-General officially became defunct.

The following day, again under guillotine motion, the Dáil passed into law the Executive Authority (External Relations) Bill.[72] This Act authorised the British monarch to act solely in matters regarding the appointment of diplomatic and consular representatives on the advice of the Irish Government. It also finally made a political reality of de Valera's External Association formula of 1921 and settled the long-running debate between monarchy and republicanism on his terms.

The Constitution (Amendment No. 27) Act placed the state in the anomalous position, for a parliamentary democracy, of having no permanent, formal head of state. Consequently, as Keogh and McCarthy have observed, 'the creation of a new office of head of state, Uachtarán na h-Éireann, under the Constitution, assumed more urgency as a result of the events of December 1936'.[73]

It is in the realms of the 'what if' school of history as to how the office of President of Ireland might have subsequently been accepted or developed had King Edward VIII not chosen to vacate the throne. It is, however, hard to assume that, in these circumstances, the British Government would have remained silent or accepted a republican constitution that dispensed with the British sovereign and his Governor-General. In such a scenario, the new office of President of Ireland might well have been in the eye of the storm from the outset for its part in superseding the King's constitutional role.

The abdication crisis meant that this did not come to pass. De Valera deftly used the King's predicament to create a constitutional vacuum, which he could subsequently fill on his own terms with the office of President of Ireland. Stanley Baldwin's administration was left with little option but grudgingly to accept de Valera's manoeuvrings. As Owen Dudley Edwards has argued, if the British Prime Minister wished de Valera 'to cooperate in the dropping of the King, then Baldwin would have to accept the way in which he would acknowledge the next one'.[74]

By abolishing the office of Governor-General and scaling down the King's position in Ireland to merely that of 'a constitutional organ' or a 'symbol of their cooperation' with a number of associated states without provoking a major diplomatic row, de Valera neutralised in advance many causes for criticism of the Irish presidency.[75] This was a stunning political accomplishment and one that largely took the new office outside the hurly-burly of Anglo-Irish relations in the 1930s. It was also a political achievement that gave the office of President of Ireland a degree of much-needed stability from its inception.

3

The Custodian of the People's Constitutional Liberties

John M. Kelly, a leading authority on Irish constitutional law, has described the creation of the office of President as 'one of the most conspicuous innovations of the 1937 Constitution by comparison with that of 1922'.[1] In a similar manner, the political scientist Jim Duffy has argued that the office of President was intended to symbolise the 'constitutional autochthony', or indigenous nature, of Bunreacht na hÉireann.[2] Historian Dermot Keogh has observed that:

> Acutely aware of the importance of symbols in Irish life, the presidency was established at one level to emphasise the definitive removal of the King and his representative, the Governor-General. The office of the President provided the tangible evidence. De Valera's primary concern, however, was to establish an institution rooted in popular suffrage which gave the people a guardian of the Constitution.[3]

These three viewpoints are consistent and of some merit in understanding the inception of the office of President. From de Valera's perspective, the office of President was important in signalling a new constitutional order that superseded the hated 1921 Treaty. The political character of the office was shaped by de Valera's desire to highlight that the role of the King and Governor-General as the Irish head of state had been irreversibly supplanted.

As well as using the office of President as a manifestation of constitutional nationalism, de Valera sought to make the presidency, in Seán MacEntee's words, 'the custodian of the people's constitutional liberties' and the 'guardian and protector' of the people's rights.[4] In the Constitution, the office of President was given a number of powers to safeguard democracy. These powers reflect well on de Valera's democratic credentials at a time when there was a continent-wide drift towards authoritarianism.

The reaction of the main Opposition parties to the office of President was negative and, in particular, they held genuine sensitivities that the new presidency could be a staging post en route to a dictatorship. The word dictator or a derivative of it was used over 200 times in the Dáil debate on the draft Constitution with the vast majority of these references relating to the office of President.[5] Yet other critics of the office of President, such as Frank MacDermott, would point out that 'the powers of the new President are exceedingly limited . . . [and] will be a great deal less powerful than the Prime Minister'.[6] The presidency was the focal point of opposition to Bunreacht na hÉireann. De Valera, however, both faced down and, in a few cases, constructively responded to these criticisms in a manner that impacted on the subsequent evolution of the office of President of Ireland.

'We Know What a Popular Election Is'

Article 12.2.1 of Bunreacht na hÉireann states that 'the President shall be elected by direct vote of the people'. This provision was responsible for significant Opposition unease. But for de Valera, making the presidency a nationally elected office was the supreme manifestation of the fact that he was instituting a new republican dawn. The essential point for de Valera was that the new office of President would derive its authority from the people of Ireland, not the British Crown. As Faughnan has noted, 'the most characteristic feature of the presidency, namely, its elective nature, was clearly intended to be an assertion of sovereignty. The President would, unlike the Governor-General, have the people as his source of ultimate authority.'[7]

Elsewhere, however, an academic perception has emerged that de Valera only made the presidency elective in order to allay Opposition fears about the office. For example, David Gwynn Morgan has argued that for de Valera 'one way of dispelling the inevitable suspicions was to make the presidency an elected office'.[8] Morgan's contention does not, however, stand up to historical scrutiny. The reality is that from the outset, de Valera had determined that the presidency was going to be an elective office. Article 4 of the Preliminary Draft of Heads of a Constitution, prepared by John Hearne on de Valera's instructions in May 1935, stated 'the President of Saorstát Éireann (hereinafter referred to as "the President") shall be elected by the people of Saorstát Éireann'.[9] The Dáil debate on the draft Constitution also makes clear that, for de Valera, it was a fundamental principle that the President would be directly elected by the Irish people and that he would not deviate from this. He said:

> We here have always made clear that we believed in the fundamental right of our people to choose their own Government, the form of their state even, and, believing in that right, we naturally enshrined it in the Constitution. If there is one thing more than another that is clear and shining through this whole Constitution, it is the fact that the people are the masters. They are the masters at the time of an election, and their mastery is maintained during the period from election to election through the President, who has been chosen definitely to safeguard their interests.[10]

The Opposition were strongly united against the proposal that the President would be directly elected by the people. A variety of reasons were put forward, but all of them had at their core concerns that an elected President would be a vehicle for a dictatorship. Desmond Fitzgerald argued that the fact that the President of Ireland was elected by direct suffrage of the people meant that he could possibly claim a stronger mandate than the Taoiseach and this could lead to potential difficulties. Fitzgerald argued

> that you have the seeds of conflict sown, if this Constitution is passed in its present form, by reason of the possibility of conflict between the President, claiming a direct mandate from

> the people, and the Executive Council, or the Government, as it is now to be called, also claiming a direct mandate from the people. If the President happens to be a particular type of man, he will refuse to do these things or will thwart the Government in certain things.[11]

The Labour leader, William Norton, saw danger in the fact that the new President would be dependent on a political party to secure election and would in return do that party's bidding. Norton painted a picture of a scenario where

> the Government may come in here with a Bill to give additional powers to the President. He may be President by virtue of the support which he is able to get from the Fianna Fáil party. He has been, perhaps, one of their own active party men. He has been elected by the use of the Government party machine. He knows he is indebted to the machine for being President. The Government machine may feel that Parliament is a handicap and a drag upon many of the things which it would wish to do, that Parliament takes a long time to enact legislation and that there is criticism in Parliament which it is desirable to avoid. What is to prevent a Government party holding these views, coming to the House and passing a Bill designed to give the President the power to take away from Parliament the right of examination or the right of criticism which up to that it had enjoyed?[12]

In a similar vein, Fine Gael also maintained that the fact that the President would have to be elected made it unlikely the President would act in any other manner than that of a political partisan. Cecil Lavery said:

> It is useless to speak of the President in our existing circumstances as being a person above politics. That is futile. Anybody who knows the conditions in this country must realise that no man is going to secure a majority of the entire electorate of this country unless he has a powerful organisation

> behind him, unless he is a party politician in the fullest sense of the word, and unless he has the support of a political organisation. As I say, the President may hold the same views or different views from the head of the Government. In either case he may be a source of danger to the state.[13]

Building on Lavery's argument, another Fine Gael deputy, Professor John Marcus O'Sullivan, advanced a scenario where a combination of a partisan President and Government of a different political persuasion would result in Irish democracy inevitably being wiped out. O'Sullivan said:

> There may be a President in office for [say] five years of his term of office, with a Government of an entirely different policy. There you have a clash. It is useless to ignore the power that the President will have to make the work of that Government impossible. He can hold up the Government, at every hand's turn practically, in a variety of ways. Deadlocks will be the order of the day, and deadlocks can only lead to one thing in politics, a coup d'état. You are asking for it, and it has nearly always happened. When you have had divisions of power of this kind it has been very frequent that a deadlock has been reached, a coup d'état carried through, and a dictatorship established. You will find that in the history of the first French Republic, of the second French Republic, and of the recent German Republic. That is the great danger. With our political inexperience in this country we cannot hope to escape what other countries have suffered from.[14]

John A. Costello, a former Attorney-General and a future Taoiseach, offered the view that a presidential election was no safeguard to democracy because he believed that Fianna Fáil would elect either de Valera or a pliant yes-man as President to give them unfettered control. Costello said:

> You will have an equally serious situation if you have the position where the President [of Ireland] is the dominant

> personality and the Prime Minister the yes-man, and an equally serious situation if you have the Prime Minister the dominant personality and the President the yes-man. The scheme is one for dictatorial powers, come what may, to whoever is President, whether it is the present President of the Executive Council [i.e. de Valera] or somebody else. Under the proposal to have the President of this state elected by popular suffrage, it inevitably follows that the President must be the centre of political activity in the future. He must have a political party of his own or else he must be allied to one or other of the big political parties, which must subsist in this state for years to come.[15]

Desmond Fitzgerald was adamant that de Valera had created the office of President of Ireland for himself. He said 'most people in this country, having read the Constitution, recognise certain handiwork in it, and can see what it is directed towards. Most people know perfectly well that President de Valera proposes to take that office himself.'[16]

Numerous other Fine Gael speakers including T. F. O'Higgins and Patrick McGilligan, a professor of constitutional law and a former minister, also warned of the dangers of de Valera having either a yes-man or himself elected President so as to establish a dictatorship.[17] The consistent refrain of this theme throughout the Dáil debate on the Constitution undoubtedly reflected the Opposition's underlying mistrust of de Valera's motives dating from the Treaty split. This came to the surface in Professor O'Sullivan's contribution when he referred to de Valera as 'a man who has always shown supreme contempt, not merely for Parliamentary institutions, but for the Dáil itself'.[18]

It should also be noted that at least some of Fine Gael's charges that an elected President would amount to a dictatorship were clearly motivated by that party's political weakness. Leading Fine Gael TDs would have been all too aware that in this period they were unlikely to be able to match Fianna Fáil's electoral strength in a nationwide presidential election, hence their readiness to denounce such a proposal. James Fitzgerald-Kenney, a Mayo TD and senior counsel, seemed to argue that the people could not be trusted to elect the right President. He said 'but if a President is going to be elected by the people is that going to get the best President? We know what a popular election is. Think out how that is going to work. If it is anything like a close fight, is it not the man with the longest purse who is going to win?'[19]

In the Dáil debate, de Valera gave the Opposition little solace in their criticisms. He was determined that the Constitution would include the principle that the President would be directly elected and so derive his authority from the Irish people. Fianna Fáil's strength in the Dáil ensured that no amendment could be carried that watered down this key objective. In comments uncharacteristically laced with sarcasm, de Valera rejected the Opposition's argument that an elected President would not be above politics and consequently threaten democracy as follows:

> But, of course, this wonderful man, who is able to get the whole Parliament to vote him full power and is able to get the Council of State to give him full power and has nothing but yes-men in the Chief Justice, in the head of the Government, in the Attorney-General and everybody else, will be able to do as he likes. They are all yes-men, and this wonderful man, this superman who is to come upon the earth and be a President, is going to be of such a character that everybody about him is going immediately to kneel at his feet and offer him all these powers. In these circumstances, of course, if we get such a person on this earth, there would be no need of a Parliament or anything else.[20]

De Valera also gave little credence to the scenarios put forward that there might be a serious constitutional clash because a President and Taoiseach differed over who had a superior mandate or because they came from different political traditions. He maintained:

> The two persons, the President and the Taoiseach, if they carry out the spirit of this Constitution, will be working together, one may say, detached from the immediate political arena, giving, I hope, detached and wise counsel, and if you have a good man as President and a sensible man as head of the Government, they will work together for the national and

> common interest. That does not mean that you will be dragging the President into party politics, because he will be bound by the Constitution and his duty to give, in case of a change of Government, to the new Taoiseach the same advice, the same help and the general support for the common good as he was giving to his predecessor.[21]

Throughout the debate, de Valera maintained that the fact that the President of Ireland would be elected by the people was the best guarantee against a dictatorship. De Valera argued that an elected President was less likely to abuse his powers because such a President 'would lose the good opinion of the people. That is one of the checks you have on the President's powers all the time, that he is put there trusted by the people, that they expect him to carry out his trust properly, and that if he abuses it they will let him know their opinion very quickly.'[22]

Despite his vehement rejections of the notion that there was any inconceivable means by which the President could become a dictator, de Valera chose not to deny the other charge that he intended to put himself forward for President. An editorial in the *Irish Independent* from May 1937 had observed that 'even Mr de Valera's own tied organ has not denied that the post of President under the new Constitution is being created for Mr de Valera himself'.[23] On another occasion, de Valera was less than categorical in his denials and sent mixed messages about his intentions. *The Irish Times* reported that 'in relation to the suggestion that the position of the new President was intended for himself, Mr de Valera said no one had a right to occupy the post unless elected by the people. "If the Irish people choose to elect me," he added, "I will have a right to take it, but I want to say that where I am is the place where I can do most work."'[24]

According to an account deliberately left for posterity by Frank Gallagher, one of de Valera's most trusted political associates, the Fianna Fáil leader made a calculated political decision not to answer this accusation in order to ensure the Constitution's safe passage. Gallagher's extraordinary account states:

> In 1937 de Valera brought one of his dreams to fulfilment when he carried the new Constitution through the Dáil and

> later the country. It was stubbornly fought all the way. Some of its principal clauses were represented as providing a post for himself as President. The accusation was flung at him a score of times in the Dáil discussions: he did not answer it. It was used again in the election campaign of 1937 in which the Constitution was made law by popular vote. Again it was not answered. The Constitution came into force on 29 December 1937. De Valera broadcast on it that night and I was in the studio during his talk. Before the signal to begin, he said 'And now my job is to find a President.' 'Good heavens,' I said, 'are you not going to be that yourself?' 'No,' he smiled. 'Then why did you let them get away with suggesting that you would be?' 'Ah,' he said, 'if I had contradicted that they would just have chosen some other and perhaps more hurtful ways in which to attack the Constitution.'[25]

De Valera's hard-nosed approach to the Dáil debate on the draft Constitution was tempered somewhat by the performance of Hugo Flinn, Parliamentary Secretary to the Minister for Finance, who led for the Government on a significant proportion of the debate. Flinn's approach was constructive and genuinely conciliatory. In his opening contribution, he explained his approach to the Dáil:

> I think, in listening to the speeches, however intolerant, however exaggerated, and, in certain cases, however mad they may be, upon this subject, that it is our business to look behind the exaggerations and madnesses [*sic*] of them, to discount all the political prejudices of them, and as far as is humanly possible, to attempt to get out of them all the value we can in constructive criticism in relation to the Bill.[26]

Flinn sought to reassure the Opposition and explain away their criticisms of the presidency. He also admitted to seeing some validity in the concerns of Fitzgerald and others in regard to the President claiming a superior mandate to the Taoiseach in the event of a row between these two constitutional officers. Flinn even gave weight to this argument when he set out a scenario whereby a President who had fallen out with a Government on a particular issue resigned, but sought re-election to the office. Flinn argued that a President who received such a mandate would create a 'real risk' and a 'position of difficulty', and this aspect of the Constitution 'certainly' required 'to be considered'.[27]

De Valera, however, remained unmoved and the provision in the Constitution by which the President is elected remained unchanged. Flinn's warnings about the potential for conflict with the Government arising from a President who has resigned and then seeks a fresh mandate also went unheeded. It is worth noting that almost forty years after Flinn's postulating of such a scenario a number of Dublin City and Community Councillors ran an ultimately unsuccessful 'Draft Ó Dálaigh' campaign, which was an effort to persuade Cearbhall Ó Dálaigh, in the aftermath of his resignation as President, to nominate himself for re-election and to seek a mandate to ensure that 'the integrity of the presidential office be kept intact and clear of party politics'.[28]

Flinn's foresight and his political equanimity was not the norm in a debate that was often tribal and venomous. For Fianna Fáil, it was essential that the President be an elective office deriving its authority from the people. For the Opposition, it was essential that such an office not be supported because it could potentially lead to a dictatorship.

In the debate on the Constitution, de Valera refused to compromise on his position. But, as will be explored later, the prevailing anxiety and fears of the main Opposition parties were such that de Valera would, following the Constitution's ratification, revisit their concerns.

MacDermott's Bar

Article 12.3.2 of Bunreacht na hÉireann states that 'a person who holds, or who has held, office as President, shall be eligible for re-election to that office once, but only once'. In the same article, de Valera set the President's term of office at seven years.

As part of his core belief that the Irish people should be free to elect their own President, de Valera's original intention had been not to put any restriction on a President's right to run for re-election. Hearne's preliminary heads from May 1935 simply stated that the

President 'shall be eligible for re-election'.[29] The draft Constitution that was brought before the Dáil in May 1937 also placed no limit on the number of times a President could be re-elected.[30]

In contrast, Fine Gael and Labour sought to place an absolute bar on a President's right to seek re-election. John A. Costello had already in the debate made clear his belief that a directly elected President was a threat to democracy; however, he argued that by preventing a President from seeking re-election this risk could be reduced as there would be less incentive for a President to stray into partisan politics. Costello moved an amendment to this effect. He told the Dáil it was 'human nature' that a President would conduct himself with an eye towards 'securing re-election' and 'his actions will be directed to his own political advantage. The only way we can minimise the evil effects which will result if this system of direct vote for the President is persisted in, is by providing that there shall be only one term of office for each individual.'[31]

Costello's amendment was supported by William Norton, who accepted the view that a President with no restriction on his right to run for re-election might be unduly influenced in performing his functions by a desire to achieve re-election.[32] De Valera's response underlined the very different perspectives between the main parties on how the presidency would develop. Fianna Fáil maintained that the best way to ensure the independence of the office was by allowing the President to seek re-election because a serving President would, thus, be slow to stray into partisan politics and risk damaging his standing with the electorate. He told the Dáil:

> Remember that to be re-elected the President has to get the support of the people. He is answerable to them. They will judge his actions during his first period of office by his conduct in that office and, consequently, if a man has proved satisfactory, I see no reason why he should not be allowed to go forward again for re-election. Those who will oppose his re-election, if they have any reason for it, will put forward as a ground: 'Well, he has not acted in such wise,' or 'he is no longer suitable for the office,' or some other reason of that kind.[33]

Despite this assertion of his position, de Valera eventually grudgingly accepted an amendment sponsored by the then independent TD Frank MacDermott, who had been a prominent and constructive contributor to the debate on the Constitution. He astutely pitched his motion as a halfway house between the Government's draft Constitution, which allowed a president to seek re-election for an infinite number of terms, and Fine Gael and Labour's position, which said a President should not be eligible for re-election. MacDermott told the Dáil:

> I do think that seven years is a long term, and fourteen years, it seems to me, is an altogether inordinate term under this Constitution. In fact, the term may be twenty-one years. There is really no limit to what it may be, and I am of opinion that there ought to be some limit. That is why I put down an amendment suggesting five years, and a further amendment suggesting that the new President could not be re-elected more than once . . . there should be the opportunity of one re-election. I think a man would probably conduct his post all the more worthily for knowing that he has got that opportunity of testing the feelings of the Irish people again.[34]

De Valera refused to budge on changing the length of the seven-year term of office, but he reluctantly declared himself open to compromise by limiting a President's right to seek re-election to only one occasion. De Valera said it remained his personal belief that if the people wished to elect a President for an infinite number of terms, that was their democratic right. He did, however, offer the intriguing analysis, which may raise some eyebrows given de Valera's subsequent long tenure as Taoiseach in particular, that an individual in office too long could become stale. On that basis, de Valera said he was reluctantly open to restricting a President to two terms:

> If a man is held by the people to be suitable for the office [of President of Ireland], there does not seem to be any good reason for what I might call artificially excluding him. The only argument that I can think of is that sometimes after a prolonged period of office, a man is not active. He does not

> bring as fresh a mind to his work as a new man going into the office. There might possibly be a suggestion that if a man had held office for two periods – a comparatively long period in a person's life, fourteen years – he might have got stale but we must remember that his functions are those of a judge rather than those of an executive . . . It may arise in the case of the proposed re-election of a particular individual and the people may say: 'Very well, this man is getting a bit old, it is better to get a fresh man.' My own view is that the less we put in the Constitution in the way of restrictions of that kind, the better. The people will have to be the judges themselves and if they do not think that a person is suitable to be elected as President, it may be assumed that they will not vote for him. However, if there is any strong view held that, after two periods of office at least, there should be a break, I am quite willing to concede that but my own instinct is against it. I think you should put no artificial barriers at all there.[35]

MacDermott ultimately moved a motion that a President be eligible for re-election 'once but only once'.[36] De Valera, who had not conceded ground on any of the President's functions and duties throughout the debate, chose to accept the motion.

The political significance of this aspect of the debate was that it showed once again that the views of Fine Gael and Labour were diametrically opposed to Fianna Fáil's. De Valera firmly believed in the principle that people had the right to keep on electing the same President if they believed him to be doing a good job. Fine Gael and Labour believed a President who could be re-elected at all was a danger to democracy. Ultimately, de Valera accepted MacDermott's amendment, which gave a veneer of reasonableness to his attitude in the debate while, at the same time, not giving any quarter to the main Opposition parties. In reality, though, as de Valera hinted at in the debate, this compromise was hardly a compromise at all. Using the analogy of the French presidency, de Valera predicted that it was 'likely to be the position' that no Irish President would want to serve a third term.[37] This political forecast has proved to be a fairly astute assessment.

Four Irish Presidents, to date, have served two terms. Both President O'Kelly and President de Valera would have preferred to retire on completion of their respective first terms. In more modern times, as the end of his first term approached, President Hillery privately told the leaders of Fine Gael, Labour and Fianna Fáil that 'all I want is out'.[38] He was eventually prevailed upon to serve a second term. Bertie Ahern has confirmed that President McAleese, in 2004, was 'very keen' to go forward for a second term.[39] Whether she would have wished to continue for a third term had there not been the Frank MacDermott-inspired constitutional bar is, however, a matter of conjecture.

In 1937, though MacDermott had effected some restriction on the number of terms a president could serve, the fact that a president would be able to seek re-election to a second term remained a great concern to the Opposition parties, who believed that this factor would inevitably push the office into the sphere of partisan politics. While de Valera gave little credence to the Opposition's concerns during the debate on the draft Constitution, the choice of first President would ultimately do much to dispel the fear that the incumbent would conduct his responsibilities with a narrow focus on securing electoral advantage.

Appointing University Visitors or Creating a Dictator?

Article 13.10 of Bunreacht na hÉireann states that 'subject to this Constitution, additional powers and functions may be conferred on the President by law'. This provision caused more unease and more antagonism than any other provision in Bunreacht na hÉireann. It went to the very heart of the Opposition's dictatorship fears. Throughout the Dáil debate on the draft Constitution, de Valera argued that it was 'foolish to talk of a dictatorship in connection with the President' and he would stoutly maintain that the President's functions were 'not of a dictatorial character'.[40] Yet despite these constant assurances, Opposition fears remained intact.

It is an extraordinary feature of the debate on the draft Constitution that many of the criticisms of the President's role related to matters extraneous to the text of the document. As will be explored later in this chapter, the Opposition's criticisms of the powers actually conferred on the President in the draft Constitution were more muted or, at least, less sensational than their projections of what the office of President might evolve into. Their focus was not so much on what was in the text as on what might happen next. Article 13.10 was the focus for much of this concern as well as some undoubted scaremongering.

In the Dáil, the Opposition trenchantly complained that new presidential powers would subsequently be created under Article 13.10 that would not be regulated by the Constitution or have been ratified by the people in a referendum. James Dillon accused de Valera of creating a device by which 'you can give the President any power you like by law'.[41] John Marcus O'Sullivan argued that 'every power that man can get that is not prohibited by this Constitution can be given to the President . . . If you had a subservient Dáil, and the President wants to get power into his hands and has a subservient party in this house, what is to prevent him getting it?'[42]

John A. Costello argued that Article 13.10 meant that a President could be given additional powers that would not be exercisable on the advice of the Government. He maintained that this would cause 'a very serious menace in the future'.[43] Desmond Fitzgerald saw in Article 13.10 a scheme by which de Valera could 'legislate with his majority to give any additional power he likes to that functionary, then he can proceed to walk into that office to exercise those powers'.[44] James Fitzgerald-Kenney suggested the purpose of Article 13.10 related to 'smoothening [*sic*] the road within the Constitution for a dictatorship'.[45]

Such an analysis was strongly supported on the Labour benches. William Davin said in regard to Article 13.10 that he was 'suspicious of giving any additional powers to the President of this state except such additional powers are to be given to him by way of referendum'.[46]

According to Ward, de Valera regarded such concerns as absurd.[47] He foresaw only very limited uses for Article 13.10. He viewed it as 'a sort of omnibus clause' to enable certain things to be done such as, for example, the 'appointment of visitors to a university'.[48] Hindsight would prove that this was precisely the sort of appointment for which de Valera envisaged this power being used. Under Article 13.10, Ireland's first President would, on the advice of the Government, appoint council members and senior professors of the Dublin Institute for Advanced Studies, appoint the Governor of the Central Bank and take up position as the ex officio President of the Irish Red Cross

Society.[49] Yet, in the context of the political landscape of the late 1930s, and in the course of an often contentious debate, the Opposition were convinced that Article 13.10 was a device, in the words of William Norton, for a presidential 'invasion of the rights of Parliament'.[50]

The debate shows that de Valera was clearly bemused by this line of thinking. He told the Dáil that it was inconceivable to him 'why a Government should hand over to somebody else powers which they could exercise themselves'.[51] The tenor of the debate, however, saw de Valera eventually move to try and assuage the Opposition's concerns. Acting on a suggestion received in a private memo drafted on 21 May 1937 from James Douglas, who had sat on Michael Collins' Constitution Committee in 1922, de Valera decided that a qualifying provision would be added into the draft Constitution to make it clear that Article 13.10 could not be used to give the President extraordinary additional powers in the future.[52]

On 25 May, Hugo Flinn informed the Dáil that de Valera would move the following amendment that 'no power or function conferred on the President by law shall be exercisable or performable by him save only on the advice of the Government'.[53] This amendment became, word for word, Article 13.11 of Bunreacht na hÉireann. Flinn explained the thinking behind this move to the Dáil. He said:

> When that amendment is incorporated in the Constitution it means that any power whatever which is given to the President will be exercised by the continuous authority, and under the continuous control, of this Dáil. The Dáil has no power to give an authority that it has not got itself. It cannot do more through the President than it can do itself directly. Any power which it delegates under the clause as it now is it delegates under its continuous control.[54]

In effect, Article 13.11 not only slammed, but bolted the door shut on any remote possibility of a presidential dictatorship. By way of this article, de Valera ensured that any additional powers conferred on the President could not give enhanced political influence or dominance to the office, as such powers could only be exercisable on the say-so of the Government. However, the Opposition remained unconvinced. Even after the Constitution had passed through the Dáil on 14 June 1937, Fine Gael continued to attack the office of President as a threat to democracy. As Keogh and McCarthy have pointed out, during the course of the plebiscite campaign, Fine Gael alleged that the Constitution was a sinister plot by de Valera to establish himself as a dictator.[55] For similar reasons, the Labour Party opposed the Constitution, citing the presidential powers as a threat to democracy.[56] Throughout the campaign, de Valera was constantly forced to defend the office of President. In a meeting in Carlow, he described the attacks on the presidency as 'contemptible' and was reported as saying 'it was a lie to suggest in the Constitution the new President was given dictatorial powers'.[57]

In the run-up to polling day, the *Irish Independent* ran a number of editorials that focused its criticism on the presidency. On 23 June 1937, the paper stated that 'this Constitution, we repeat, contains the seed of dictatorship in the Nazi-like powers to be conferred upon the President'. On 29 June, in spite of Article 13.11, the *Irish Independent* editorial said:

> Every citizen who does not want to gamble with the future of his country and his family will vote against the draft Constitution on Thursday next because . . . it enables the legislature to confer additional and unlimited powers upon the President. The powers which this Constitution proposes to confer upon the President are capable of being utilised to create a dictatorship.

The dictatorship genie was well and truly out of the bottle. In pondering the question of who would be Ireland's first President, de Valera would surely have reflected on how he could get this genie back in the bottle.

The Crisis of Democracy in Europe

From today's perspective, it would be easy to dismiss as fanciful the Opposition's obsession that the office of President of Ireland was a route to a dictatorship. However, such a viewpoint pays scant regard to the international climate of the time.

By 1937, most heads of state in Western Europe were either hereditary monarchs, fascist dictators, or were elected indirectly, most commonly by the national parliament. The notion of a presidency elected by universal suffrage was definitely going against the political grain. In western Europe, at this point in time, there were few concrete examples of directly elected Presidents. In 1935, the Portuguese President, Oscar Carmona, was directly elected by the people. Yet, the election was a sham and Carmona was a mere figurehead. From 1932, António de Oliveira Salazar had, in effect, been the dictator of Portugal.[58] The fact that there was no credible comparative office to equate to the President of Ireland in European politics at the time of its creation undoubtedly contributed to the scepticism of the Opposition parties.

These concerns were intensified by the accelerating collapse in democracy throughout the continent. At the time of the Dáil debate on the draft Constitution, Poland, Lithuania, Yugoslavia, Austria, Estonia, Germany, Bulgaria, Latvia, Greece, Italy and Spain had all succumbed to dictatorship.[59] The debate on the draft Constitution shows that TDs were very much in tune with developments on the continent. The manner and frequency in which popularly elected politicians on the continent and further afield had seized power was cited in arguments deployed against the office of President of Ireland. Norton said:

> I have seen nothing during the past fifteen years, particularly in eastern European countries, which justifies me in assuming that the President we are going to elect here is going to be a paragon of virtue, seeing that with prototypes the experience of many other countries has been the opposite. We may, in this Constitution, drawn in this way, find that particular powers are given the President, and new functions created, which, in the course of time might mean tyranny and dictatorship. I want to be assured that there is no possibility of that happening.[60]

Patrick McGilligan cited the fact that, in the three Baltic states and in Poland, heads of state that were largely ceremonial had established dictatorships.[61] T. F. O'Higgins referred to the fact that countries with popularly elected Presidents had shown a tendency to metamorphose into 'dictatorial countries'.[62] James Fitzgerald-Kenney referred to the regimes in Italy and Germany as a warning in regard to the President of Ireland's powers.[63] Similarly, William Davin warned about 'continental precedents' from 'countries which are now governed in a very anti-democratic way', where powers were 'stolen' from the President.[64]

The spread of fascism on mainland Europe generated considerable unease about the President of Ireland's powers in regard to the Defence Forces. Though de Valera consistently maintained that these powers were only nominal, John Marcus O'Sullivan accused him of complete ignorance of political events on the continent. O'Sullivan said:

> [De Valera] is living in the twentieth century – I often wonder if he does live in the twentieth century – and he calmly tells us that the representatives of the people will never give control of the Army to the President [of Ireland]. Does he know that such a place as Europe exists? Will the President [of the Executive Council] get it into his head that there are places other than Great Britain in the world? He finds it difficult to do that. There are places on the continent in which the representatives of the people have given that power over to the President.[65]

Similarly, Norton told the Dáil:

> I dislike the idea, in the era through which we are now passing, of placing the control of the Defence Forces in the hands of a single person, because we have had many examples in Europe of the manner in which armies, controlled by a single man, have been used for the disruption and destruction of democracy, particularly in recent years.[66]

The Opposition's thesis that the presidency could be used to establish a military dictatorship highlighted not just suspicion, but a massive gulf in political interpretation arising from events on the continent. Fianna Fáil strongly refuted the claim that the office of President had anything to do with the establishment of a dictatorship and argued, on the contrary, that given the prevailing atmosphere in Europe, the office was necessary to prevent such an eventuality. Frank Aiken told the Dáíl:

> Instead of the President under this draft Constitution being a dictator, he is, in my opinion, a person who will guard the rights and liberties of the people against any attempt to set up a dictator by either the Executive Council or the two Houses of the Oireachtas. I was myself very anxious to see that there should be a functionary of that sort above ordinary or everyday politics who would be specially sworn and specially charged and who would in an especial way pledge himself to look after the constitutional rights of the people and be their guardian against any internal dictatorship.[67]

Despite Fianna Fáil's insistence on such democratic credentials, Opposition suspicions were not alleviated by a subliminal recognition that de Valera and his co-authors had engaged in a spot of constitutional plagiarism in regard to the office of President of Ireland. A number of constitutional experts, including Forde, have pointed out that the model for many of the features of the Irish presidency was the presidency of the German Weimar Republic.[68] The influence of Weimar Germany on the Irish presidency is hinted at in drafts of a constitution drawn up by de Valera in May 1935 on squared copybook paper. In this so-called 'squared paper draft', Weimar was mentioned in the context of the presidency with what Hogan has described as the 'somewhat cryptic note' in which de Valera wrote 'Page 187 – German Pres TFA'.[69] As Hogan also observes, apart from the undoubted reference to the German presidency, it is not clear what the other letters refer to.[70] Kelly has undertaken a short comparative study, which shows, at the very least, many superficial similarities. Kelly wrote:

> The office and functions of the President, which had to be devised from scratch in 1937, exhibit so many secondary resemblances to the office and functions of the President of the Weimar Republic under the Constitution of 1919 that a direct importation must be suspected . . . The German President had

> a seven year-term (Article 43 [of the Weimar Constitution]), it required a two-thirds majority of the Reichstag to remove him (Article 43), he might not be a member of the Reichstag himself (Article 44), he had the supreme command of the armed forces (Article 47) and the right of pardon (Article 49), and he appointed the Chancellor and, on his recommendation, the Ministers (Article 53). Every German citizen who had completed his thirty-fifth year was eligible for the office.[71]

Apprehension that the office of President of Ireland was being modelled on an office that had given way to Nazism were vocalised in the Dáil debate, although not in a targeted manner. De Valera's defence of the Irish presidency was interrupted at one point by Norton's rejoinder of 'We saw what happened in Germany.'[72] Labour's Patrick Hogan mentioned the election of 'Rudolph Hitler' [*sic*] and expressed concern that Ireland could also succumb to becoming 'a totalitarian state like Germany'.[73] Outside the Dáil, the *Irish Independent* criticised de Valera for not using a British constitutional model. Commenting on the President's specific functions, the paper editorialised that 'these powers are far in excess of those exercised by the ruler of the British Empire; they flavour more of Fascism or Hitlerism than of a "democratic state" which Éire is declared to be.'[74]

On this point, the office of President of Ireland had an unlikely defender. Frank MacDermott rubbished any suggestion that similarities between the Weimar presidency and the Irish presidency meant a dictatorship would follow. MacDermott, in fact, believed that the Irish presidency was deserving of more powers and that the risk of an Irish dictatorship was negligible. He said:

> If Hindenburg had more power, or if he had not been a very old man, he might have prevented the dictatorship of Hitler. For many years Hindenburg was regarded by the German nation as the main barrier left in the way of a dictatorship . . . And as to the suggestion that this draft Constitution is tending in the direction of a dictatorship by the President, I suggest it

> would be a tendency more in the direction of a dictatorship by the Taoiseach. But I do not think that it is tending in the direction of a dictatorship at all.[75]

The main reason that the Weimar argument did not gain traction was that, although there were similarities between the Irish and German presidencies, these were more similarities of form rather than of substance. De Valera was too astute a politician not to have taken heed of the mistakes of the Weimar presidency. German democracy had been significantly damaged by controversies arising from the President's direct involvement in government formation, by the President's power to rule by decree in a crisis and by the platform presidential elections gave to extremist groups.[76] None of these features were replicated in Bunreacht na hÉireann.

Significantly, de Valera ensured that Irish procedures for government formation differed substantially from those of Germany in two areas, namely the requirement that the Parliament, and not the President, formally selected the head of Government, and that the head of state was excluded from exercising any choice over cabinet appointments. De Valera stressed the former point before the Dáil:

> You will notice that it is the President who will appoint the head of the Government or the Taoiseach. He appoints him; he does the formal act called appointment, but it is not the President who selects the head of the Government. The head of the Government under this Constitution will be selected by the Dáil in the future, as the head of the Government was selected by the Dáil in the past.[77]

Article 48 of the Weimar Constitution allowed the President to rule by emergency decree should he consider this necessary. The overuse of this power was one of the key factors in the destabilising of the Weimar democracy.[78] Bunreacht na hÉireann did not make the same mistake. In the draft Constitution that went to cabinet in October 1936, de Valera had included a diluted version of the German Article 48. Article 8.10 of this draft stated that 'the President may, at the request of the Council of Ministers and with the concurrence of Dáil Éireann, become

Chairman of a national Government during a period of national crisis or emergency whether internal or international'.[79]

It is significant that this Article is crossed out in de Valera's copy of this draft of the Constitution. Furthermore, this article did not survive into later drafts. A decision was clearly taken not to place the office of President into the executive realm of government in any circumstances. The above article was scrapped and latterly replaced with the more anodyne provision that 'the Taoiseach shall keep the President generally informed on matters of domestic and international policy'.[80] In respect of this constitutional provision, de Valera made it clear that he saw a President's role as being one in which he could offer only private, constructive criticism. De Valera said:

> He will give advice to the Taoiseach, saying to him: 'My view is so and so,' but the other man is free not to take it. There is no division of responsibility. There is the direct responsibility of the Government from day to day for governmental policy. The President has nothing to do with policy except as an adviser in the background. He is supposed to be experienced and to give to the man in the turmoil the view that the hurler on the ditch can get of the game looking at it from the point of view of the national interest.[81]

This was far removed from the power of German Presidents in ruling by decree.

A further important point of divergence between the office of President of Ireland and its German prototype was that de Valera took a much more cautious approach to the nomination process for candidates in presidential elections. The German nomination process was regulated by law rather than the Constitution and allowed a very open-ended nomination process, so much so that candidates who had not stood in the first round of elections could enter the campaign in the second round.[82] German presidential elections were divisive affairs with numerous candidates and extremist groups using them as a platform to promote their agenda. In 1932, the Nazi Party leader, Adolf Hitler, had run against the incumbent President, Paul von Hindenburg. Though Hitler had no chance of winning, the election gave him the opportunity to expound his views and helped build further support for the Nazi Party.

In drafting the Constitution, de Valera was aware of the potential dangers of small, extremist groups using a presidential election as a means of getting themselves attention by running their own candidate. To avoid this danger, he resorted to what one political scientist has described as 'the politics of illusion'.[83] Article 12.4 of Bunreacht na hÉireann ensures that any prospective President, other than a retiring or former President, must be nominated by at least twenty members of the Oireachtas, or by four county councils. In effect, de Valera ensured that no one could reach the starting blocks in a presidential election without the backing of one of the main parties, or some combination of the smaller ones. In more modern times, this nomination process has been criticised across the political spectrum as too restrictive.[84] In the Ireland of the 1930s, with examples of what had happened in Europe fresh in their minds, members of the Dáil took a different view.

In the debate on the draft Constitution, the only criticism of this provision, which would give leading Irish politicians a gatekeeping role on presidential nominations, was from deputies concerned that de Valera had not gone far enough to ensure spurious or extremist candidates could not get on the ballot paper. Éamonn O'Neill, a Fine Gael TD from Cork West, was critical that it only required the nomination of twenty Oireachtas members or four county councils to run for President of Ireland. He felt that it was quite possible that 'some person of straw, or some disreputable character, might get himself nominated'.[85] However, de Valera received support on this issue from an unlikely quarter by way of a backhanded admission from James Fitzgerald-Kenney. The Mayo TD said he accepted that 'a man taken from any party in the Dáil or Seanad who could not get twenty members willing to nominate him would be eminently unsuitable for the position'.[86]

In the same debate, de Valera, in rejecting an Opposition amendment to debar prisoners and certain other categories of people from running for President, hammered home the vetting powers contained in the nomination procedure for the office of President. He pointed out that, in reality, the electorate would only be able to choose a President from a list created by a political elite. He told the Dáil:

> First of all you have to get the people who are going to be candidates nominated by a number of councils or by a number of members of one or other House of the Oireachtas and then they have to go forward for election by the people. In what circumstances is it likely that a person who is undergoing a term of imprisonment is going to be nominated by twenty members of the Oireachtas and put forward for election by the people? If there was any chance of that happening then I would be inclined to think that there was something strange about the imprisonment.[87]

The nomination process of twenty Oireachtas members or four county councils was designed as a bulwark against anti-democratic or undesirable forces using a presidential election for their own ends. The fact that Opposition TDs wanted de Valera to go further with this safeguard reflects the concerns about dictatorship that dominated the Irish body politic.

Trust in the new office was not helped by a problem of nomenclature. In an Irish context, the term President had previously been deployed in regard to the role of the Head of Government. At the time of the debate on the draft Constitution, de Valera's official title was President of the Executive Council. In a previous constitutional arrangement, he had served as President of Dáil Éireann. In an international context, Irish parliamentarians would have been deeply conscious that the presidency in the United States and elsewhere in Europe was the focal point of political power. The similarities between the new office of President of Ireland and the Weimar presidency, which had already been superseded by Hitler's dictatorship, only served to exacerbate Opposition fears.

The Fianna Fáil Government was no less conscious of events in Europe. They were determined to introduce a new republican constitution that would underpin Irish democracy. The presidency was central to this plan and a number of Fianna Fáil ministers emphasised in the debate that this new office, with, in MacEntee's phrase, 'a solemn duty to safeguard and secure the liberty of every citizen irrespective of party', would make it more difficult for a continental-style dictator to emerge.[88]

A fixation with preserving democracy and preventing dictatorships was prevalent in Irish politics in the late 1930s. This crystallised in the debate that centred on the role of the office of the President in the new Constitution. Both the Government and the Opposition thought that they were on the side of the angels and that the approach being advocated from the other side of the Dáil would lead to a totalitarian state. It is from the perspective of this turbulent and fear-ridden era in European history that the emergence of the office of President and specifically its powers can best be understood.

The 'Substantial Powers'

De Valera argued that it was essential that the President of Ireland would be elected because of the significant powers the Constitution bestowed on the office. He told the Dáil: 'Nobody would propose getting the whole people to elect a person unless it was proposed to give him substantial powers, and consequently if those powers are in any way to be exercised in connection with legislation it is only right that a person who had got the authority definitely from the people for doing certain things should exercise it.'[89] Though James Fitzgerald-Kenney complained that the draft Constitution was 'giving most extraordinary powers to a President', he and other Opposition members largely chose to ignore the President's discretionary powers.[90]

An extraordinary feature of an extraordinary debate was that the Opposition spent much of their time extrapolating dangers in regard to the presidency not from the provisions actually defined in the Constitution, but from those that they believed might be conferred on the President at a later date. Bunreacht na hÉireann gives the President a number of key discretionary powers, which are highly political and serve to act as a reserve power to uphold democracy. A significant portion of the genesis of these powers is to be found in the wider turmoil of European politics in the 1930s. In 1934, in an attempt to maintain democratic freedoms on the continent, de Valera proposed to the League of Nations that it should agree on 'a convention to universalise those sacred rights of the individual which should not be taken from him under any pretext by any majority whatever'.[91] As T. P. O'Neill points out, it was not until after the Second World War that such an international convention was adopted; nonetheless, on the domestic front, de Valera incorporated such principles into his Constitution. O'Neill wrote:

> His instructions to his principal legal adviser in regard to the preparation of the draft show the importance to him of this aspect of his work. As John Hearne noted at the time, his orders were that: 'The draft was (a) to contain certain basic articles guaranteeing fundamental human rights, (b) to place the said articles in a specially protected position, i.e. to render them unalterable save by the people themselves or by an elaborate constitutional process.' The President and the Supreme Court were given the task of protecting these rights.[92]

In his opening statement in the Dáil debate on the draft Constitution, de Valera stressed the importance of the presidency as a pillar to defend democracy. He maintained that a president exercising his constitutional powers would be 'acting on behalf of the people who have put him there for that special purpose. He is there to guard the people's rights and mainly to guard the Constitution.'[93]

The Constitution gives the President what de Valera described as six 'substantial powers'[94] – Article 13.2.2, Article 13.2.3, Article 22.2, Article 24.1, Article 26, Article 27 – all of which are ultimately exercisable on the President's own initiative, independent of Government, and are designed to protect the people's interests. To fulfil this role, de Valera's stated view was that a President should stay 'away from party politics' but be 'interested in the broad politics as far as the state as a whole is concerned'.[95] At a meeting in his Clare constituency, two days before he opened the Dáil debate on the Constitution, de Valera stressed the 'non-party character' of the Constitution, particularly in regard to the status of the presidency.[96] In order to 'aid and counsel the President', a Council of State was established under Article 31. It was de Valera's intention that this body would ensure that a President would receive a broad range of views before exercising his discretionary powers.

Fine Gael did not take a benign view of the Council of State. John A. Costello claimed that the Council of State's 'only practical function in the Constitution is to declare the President an idiot'.[97] Patrick McGilligan dismissed the Council of State as the President's 'own bodyguard of yes-men' and he mistakenly claimed that the entire Council could 'be appointed or dismissed by the President until he gets a group who will agree with his viewpoint'.[98] McGilligan felt if the Council of State was to serve 'any useful purpose' it should 'have the assistance of the Archbishop of Armagh and his colleague in Dublin'.[99]

De Valera strongly rejected the suggestion that the Council of State would be partisan or purposeless. He said it was wrong to paint 'a picture of the President of the Supreme Court, the President of the High Court, ex-Presidents and other people all being yes-men'.[100] For de Valera, the objective in creating the Council of State was to ensure that a President would get impartial advice so he could exercise his discretionary powers in the interests of the common good. He also suggested that where one of the larger parties did not have an ex officio presence on the Council of State, a President should address this in the appointments he could make at his own discretion, 'making the Council of State as representative as possible'.[101] This was a viewpoint that Douglas Hyde would prove to be in tune with as, when he did eventually get round to making his appointments to the Council of State in January 1940, he appointed James Dillon, Richard Mulcahy and Senator Michael Tierney of Fine Gael, William Norton, the leader of the Labour Party, Senator Sir John Keane, widely seen as the voice of ex-unionists, and Senator Robert Farnan of Fianna Fáil.[102] Michael McDunphy, who was Secretary to the President during the tenures of the first two office holders, in his usual fastidious style, even kept tables documenting how Council of State membership was proportionately shared between the political parties.[103]

De Valera's vision of a representative Council of State helped to establish the presidency as a politically independent office. It also ensured that a President would have, in de Valera's own words, 'a body competent to advise and warn him of any dangers and of all the facts of the situation' in exercising his powers impartially.[104]

The Power of Dissolution

As it happens, the first of the six substantial powers that the Constitution bestows upon the President is the only one exercised without consulting with the Council of State. Article 13.2.2 of Bunreacht na hÉireann states that 'the President may in his absolute discretion refuse to dissolve Dáil Éireann on the advice of a Taoiseach who has ceased to retain the support of a majority in Dáil Éireann.' The crucial importance of this power was recorded by Michael McDunphy. He wrote: 'This power is unique in the Irish Constitution. It is the only case in which the President has an absolute and unquestionable right to act in direct opposition to a constitutional request from the Head of the Government, to reject an advice which in other matters is equivalent to a direction, which must be complied with as a matter of course.'[105] Under Article 28.10 if the President does refuse to grant a dissolution, the Taoiseach concerned must resign, and the Dáil would then have the opportunity of nominating a successor.

De Valera said he viewed Article 13.2.2 as a 'very fundamental power' and he made it clear that the political purpose in putting this provision in the Constitution was to protect democracy. In regard to this power, he said 'the wise exercise of it by the President may mean that he is maintaining the supremacy of the people at a time when it is vital that the people's supremacy should be maintained.'[106]

The Opposition did not focus unduly on this provision in their scrutiny of the Constitution, but T. F. O'Higgins and McGilligan did note that Article 13.2.2 constituted a shift from the position in the 1922 Constitution.[107] The latter argued for the maintenance of the 1922 position and said that 'I think the present position, in which there is an absolute prohibition against the head of an Executive Council who has lost the support of the majority in Dáil Éireann getting a dissolution, is the correct position.'[108]

De Valera believed that the people, not Parliament, should be 'the ultimate court' to adjudicate on issues. He believed that if a Taoiseach was defeated in the Dáil on an issue of grave importance, rather than having to resign, it was more democratic that an election would decide the issue. He told the Dáil:

> If [the Taoiseach] goes to the President, and the President agrees with him that the situation is one in which the people ought to be given an opportunity to decide the question, he can say: 'Very well, you prepare the proclamation and I will sign it, and we will dissolve Parliament.' Then there is an election on that issue, and the electors will settle whether the

> Taoiseach, when he comes back, has a majority to carry on, or whether he is in a minority. What that simply means is that we are making provision in the Constitution for the possibility of referring a question of primary importance, on which the Government has been defeated, to the people for a decision.[109]

Michael McDunphy, who was a key member of the committee charged with drafting the Constitution, later noted, in explaining his understanding of Article 13.2.2, that 'it must be assumed that the President would be slow to refuse a dissolution except for very adequate reasons'.[110] De Valera did, however, acknowledge that there were a limited number of scenarios in which a defeated Taoiseach should not receive a dissolution and the role of the President was to act as an 'arbiter'.[111]

Though de Valera did not use the Dáil debate to spell out the exact circumstances in which a President should refuse a dissolution, Gallagher has put forward a number of undemocratic situations against which the drafters of the Constitution may have seen Article 13.2.2 being deployed. Gallagher wrote: 'One can envisage improbable scenarios – a request from a Taoiseach who has been ousted from his party, who no longer commands any support in the Dáil but has not yet been defeated there, and who now seeks to bring his party down with him, or, even more unlikely, from a Taoiseach whose party has just lost a general election but who has not yet been replaced by the Dáil.'[112]

It is certainly arguable that the 'improbable scenarios' that Gallagher suggested, writing in 1988, may have seemed far more plausible in the hothouse atmosphere of European politics in the 1930s when democracy was under siege. Indeed, given the historical context, it is almost certainly the case that de Valera saw the President's role in regard to the creation of Article 13.2.2 as a democratic reserve to safeguard against a head of government who might seek to subvert the spirit of the Constitution.

The Power to Convene the Oireachtas

Article 13.2.3 of Bunreacht na hÉireann states that 'the President may at any time, after consultation with the Council of State, convene a meeting of either or both of the Houses of the Oireachtas'.

Writing in 1992, Ward argues that 'it is difficult to imagine a contingency in which the President would summon either house without advice, or what might be accomplished in such a session'.[113] In the 1930s, however, when dictators were marching on the continent and parliaments were being proscribed or forcibly shut down, the reasoning for such a power might have been more apparent.

For de Valera, Article 13.2.3 was an important democratic safeguard to cover a situation where the Oireachtas was in recess and the appropriate authorities failed or were unable to reconvene Parliament. Again this power received only passing scrutiny from the Opposition, though McGilligan did query the necessity of giving a President the power to convene an Oireachtas meeting.[114] De Valera, however, emphasised that this power could be of crucial democratic significance if a government sought to escape parliamentary scrutiny on a contentious issue or, in a worst-case scenario, set up a dictatorship by suspending the Oireachtas indefinitely.[115]

Closely related to Article 13.2.3, the Constitution also gives a President the power, again after consultation with the Council of State, of sending a message to or addressing either the nation or the Houses of the Oireachtas on 'any matter of national or public importance'.[116] The Constitution, however, insists in Article 13.7.3 that a President must have received the approval of the Government before proceeding with any such message or address.

For de Valera, the sole purpose for granting a President this power of communication was that he believed it would enable a government to present an important message to the people in a non-partisan fashion.[117] While de Valera did not specifically clarify the circumstances in which such an address might be made, it is hard not to assume that he viewed this power as a contingency to be used in extraordinary circumstances only. He seemed to suggest to the Dáil that there would be an 'advantage' in having the calming fallback of such an address or message in a possible national crisis 'because it came from the President, [it] would be listened to by the people, who might not listen to the Government of the day'.[118]

De Valera, however, was also keen to emphasise his view that such an address or message would only be appropriate with Government concurrence. He maintained that it would be a 'danger' and 'unwise' to allow a President to act in this regard on his own initiative.[119] In Chapter 2, it was explored how de Valera's clash with the Governor-General had influenced his views on a head of state's right to communication. In the debate on the draft Constitution, de Valera touched upon this before going on to reject as 'highly undesirable' a suggestion that a President should be allowed to make use of an address or message to the nation to explain the manner in which he had exercised one of his discretionary powers.[120] In wider circumstances, de Valera took an equally rigid view and he told the Dáil that 'I do not think it right that the President should be allowed to make any statement or give any address which would be contrary to the policy or the views of the Government of the day.'[121]

Gallagher has criticised the existence of Article 13.7.3 as one of a number of examples of 'rather draconian restrictions placed on the President' reducing him to 'a rather demeaning dependence on the Government's grace and favour'.[122] This criticism does not take account of de Valera's need, in the late 1930s, to ensure that Bunreacht na hÉireann's constitutional balance would be maintained and could withstand the test of some future, aspirant dictator. Article 13.7.3, thus, militates against a President becoming a fulcrum for opposition to the government of the day and using his office to turn public opinion against a democratically elected government.

Referral to the Supreme Court

Article 26.1.1 of Bunreacht na hÉireann states:

> The President may, after consultation with the Council of State, refer any Bill to which this Article applies to the Supreme Court for a decision on the question as to whether such Bill or any specified provision or provisions of such Bill is or are repugnant to this Constitution or to any provision thereof.

Though Article 26.1.1 is the discretionary power that has been most invoked by Presidents down the years, it received scant attention from the Opposition in the debate on the draft Constitution. It was Seán MacEntee who articulated the fundamental importance of this presidential power in ensuring that Irish democracy works. He said:

> If the state is to develop and if the law is to be accepted and the whole machinery is to work, people at any rate must have a reasonable assurance that the laws under which they live are valid laws and will prevail. That difficulty has been faced in this Constitution in this way, by the power which is given to the President and by the duty and responsibility which are imposed upon him before he signs a law of being reasonably certain in his own mind that it is not contrary to the Constitution. It does put the President undoubtedly in a position of great power, but I think no less power and no less authority is necessary if the democratic regime is going to survive in this country.[123]

In respect to this power, the presidential sobriquet of 'guardian of the Constitution' is eminently justified.

'The Umbrella in the Closet'

The three remaining discretionary powers – Article 22.2, Article 24.1 and Article 27 – were designed to maintain the constitutional balances in Bunreacht na hÉireann. These powers are a contingency to cover a major disagreement between both Houses of the Oireachtas. De Valera explained the role of a President in this regard as 'simply a medium' to ensure such a dispute would be resolved in an orderly and democratic fashion.[124]

To date, none of these powers has been used and throughout the debate on the draft Constitution, de Valera maintained that this was likely to be the case. By making a Government majority in the Seanad very likely, de Valera reduced dramatically the prospects of a major political conflict between the Dáil and Seanad. The political scientist Morley Ayearst has likened the arbiter powers given to a President, in the unlikely event of such a clash, as akin to the reserve powers of a colonial governor – an 'umbrella in the closet' to be used in emergencies only.[125]

Article 22.2 of Bunreacht na hÉireann enables a President, after consulting with the Council of State at the request of one third of the Seanad, to refer the question of whether a Bill is or is not a money Bill to a Committee of Privileges, consisting of an equal number of members of the Dáil and of the Seanad, with a judge of the Supreme Court as chairman. For discussion of money Bills, the Seanad has only twenty-one days, although it has three months for the discussion of an ordinary measure. De Valera explained that 'to prevent any fraud upon the Seanad by compelling them to discuss within twenty-one days and practically not to interfere with the Bill, which they would have a perfect right to discuss if it came in the guise of an ordinary measure, and to prevent the possibility of mistakes by the chairman of the Dáil, there is an appeal to the President against a certificate of the Ceann Comhairle.'[126] De Valera stressed that a President's power in this regard was one that would normally lie dormant and that 'when an emergency of that kind can be provided for, it is wise to do it'.[127]

Article 24.1 provides that at the request of the Taoiseach and the Dáil, the President, after consultation with the Council of State, may, in the interests of 'public peace and security' or 'a public emergency', curtail the period provided for in the Constitution for the Seanad to consider a Bill. De Valera explained that a President's role in this regard would be that of 'an umpire, so to speak, to see that the Lower House acts in accordance with the spirit of the Constitution'.[128] De Valera emphasised that this power was again intended for use only in extraordinary circumstances in which national security might depend upon making a rapid decision.[129]

De Valera's concept of the President's role in regard to Article 24.1 was of a contingency reserve who in 'rare cases' might conceivably be asked to intervene to exercise 'a power of check' in a dispute between both Houses of the Oireachtas.[130] Though the Opposition was largely silent on this provision, de Valera was keen to stress the President's function was solely that of an important democratic reserve and that 'it would have to be a clear and an obvious abuse of power before the President would interfere. If he were to interfere unnecessarily he would be a very foolish man, indeed.'[131]

The final substantial power of the President occurs under Article 27, which allows a petition to be addressed to the President by a majority of senators and at least one third of the members of the Dáil, requesting him not to sign a Bill until it has been approved by the people either at a referendum or at a general election. The President, after consulting with the Council of State, then decides whether or not the Bill 'contains a proposal of such national importance that the will of the people thereon ought to be ascertained'.

This provision applies to Bills that have been passed in accordance with Article 23.1 of the Constitution without the consent of the Seanad. De Valera outlined such a scenario to the Dáil:

> Suppose you had a situation where there was a fundamental matter of national importance and that it was passed in this House by a single vote and rejected almost unanimously in the Seanad; that the President was satisfied, and it was obvious from the expressions of public opinion that he noticed, that this was a matter on which there was a considerable difference of opinion in the country, then the President would weigh up the situation and say to himself, 'Does my duty compel me to send it to the people? Do the differences that exist warrant that the people should be put to the expense either of an election or a referendum?' If he comes to the conclusion that the people's will should be obtained upon it, he tells that to the Head of the Government who has presented the Bill to him, having listened, before he made up his mind, to the advice of important people in the state, namely, those who are in the Council of State.[132]

Where the President accepts a petition, the Bill cannot become law until it has been ratified by the people at a referendum, or by resolution of the Dáil, passed after a general election.

De Valera suggested that future presidents should be very cautious about exercising this power. But he also maintained that this presidential power was another important democratic reserve that allowed the will of the people to be ascertained on a crucial issue on which the Oireachtas was badly divided.[133]

This provision was attacked by W. T. Cosgrave, not on democratic but on cost grounds. He suggested that 'every Bill that in the exercise of his functions and of his discretion [the President] submits to referendum will cost the country £100,000'.[134] This was a line of attack that Cosgrave would continue to repeat in the course of the plebiscite campaign and the irony was surely not lost on either de Valera or

Cosgrave that de Valera had used similar populist tactics to undermine the Governor-Generalship.[135] Though de Valera argued, accurately as events would prove, that Article 27 would be used sparingly, if at all, and that the costs being cited were 'nonsense', Cosgrave's criticism fed into other lingering suspicions about the office of President.[136] This suspicion was something that de Valera would continue to try to assuage in the period immediately following the ratification of the Constitution.

The Super Governor-General

The suspicions about the presidency were ironic because, beyond the Opposition's disdain for de Valera and their concerns born out of events on the continent, many of the functions of the office of President constituted little more than a republican repackaging of the Governor-Generalship and other features in the Free State Constitution. John Marcus O'Sullivan touched on this point in the Dáil debate when he referred to the President of Ireland on a number of occasions as 'the super Governor-General'.[137] De Valera did obliquely admit that there was some basis for this contention. He told the Dáil:

> One set of critics say that we are creating a dictatorship, and another set of critics say that we have made no change at all. There is no truth in the statement that we are creating a dictatorship. To a certain extent, there is truth in the statement that we have used, and propose to use in the new Constitution, methods which we have used here and found satisfactory in the past. I think there is wisdom in that. In any case, wishing to get this through the Dáil, and wishing to get it to the people and accepted by the majority of the people, I was anxious, naturally, that the things that we were satisfied with should remain: that we should not have change simply for change's sake.[138]

De Valera's problem with the Free State system was its British monarchical trappings. These he replaced with a constitution that was republican in character. De Valera had no difficulty with the checks and balances that regulated the relations between the government, parliament and people and which underpinned the Free State system of democracy. These he preserved or adapted to fit his new Constitution.

The President's role as part of the democratic checks and balances in Bunreacht na hÉireann was, in many cases, a direct descendant from the 1922 Constitution. For example, according to Article 22.2 of Bunreacht na hÉireann, the President, if so petitioned, is empowered to set up a Committee on Privileges to solve a dispute between the Dáil and the Seanad over whether a Bill is a money Bill. There was, however, nothing original in this power and de Valera simply rebranded an earlier procedure contained in Article 35 of the 1922 Constitution.

Duffy has pointed out that a comparison of both articles suggests that de Valera simply modified the provisions of the old Constitution vis-à-vis the creation of a Committee on Privileges so as to allow for the inclusion of the new President. Instead of the parliamentary process functioning in such a way as to bring about the automatic creation of a Committee on Privileges, the process under de Valera's text is augmented by the inclusion of the President.[139] Casey has shown that the 'new' presidential power in Article 27 of Bunreacht na hÉireann is, in fact, little more than a repackaged version of a provision deployed in Article 47 of the 1922 Constitution.[140] Ward, meanwhile, has highlighted that in regard to the President's powers of dissolution, de Valera had adapted a proposal from the 1927 Amendments to the Irish Free State Constitution Committee.[141]

De Valera's drawing on the Free State precedent is also to be found in the President's principal duty to act as the state's Chief Appointments Officer. The President, like the Governor-General of the 1922 text, has no scope for personal initiative. With the exception of his selection of seven members of the Council of State, the President in this role can exercise no choice, the persons being appointed having been selected by another authority. Thus, for example, on the nomination of Dáil Éireann, the President appoints both the Taoiseach and the Comptroller and Auditor-General.[142] De Valera very deliberately stressed the President's lack of power over appointments and, in an unsuccessful effort to slay the dictatorship myth, he even drew parallels with the Governor-General:

> It is true that it is his signature that will go to a number of appointments, but he has himself nothing to do with the selection of the people who are to be appointed. Now, clearly you have not much power if you have to put your signature to something and to accept something which has really been done by somebody else . . . The President's powers of appointment are confined, as I said when speaking in Irish, to putting his name to a paper, to performing the sort of ceremony that was performed [by the Governor-General] when I was first elected [in 1932] and congratulated on my appointment. Seeing, therefore, that the head of the Government is chosen by the representatives of the people, it is foolish to talk of a dictatorship in connection with the President in that matter anyhow.[143]

The somewhat curmudgeonly manner in which de Valera responded to the Opposition's concerns over the presidency reflected his bemusement and frustration at the dictatorship charge. From his perspective, he had every conceivable opportunity to establish a dictatorship, but had chosen instead to bring forward a democratic constitution. However, the Opposition refused to accept his bona fides. Europe's slide towards totalitarianism in the late 1930s undoubtedly influenced these perceptions. Indeed, the extent to which Government and Opposition were watching with trepidation unfolding events on the continent is palpable from much of the Dáil discussion that moulded early impressions of the presidency.

The Opposition parties focused on anxieties that the President might seize power in a variety of ways or become head of a junta, that anti-democratic powers would be conferred upon the President in a post-plebiscite scenario or that the process of directly electing a President could actually pave the way for an authoritarian leader. The Fianna Fáil Government, meanwhile, was intent on ensuring that the nomination procedures did not allow extremists to promote their views, that the office be established as a symbol of democracy and that the President be given tangible powers that would act as a reserve to prevent a dictator emerging or democratic order breaking down.

Certainly, in the context of the 1930s, the discretionary powers conferred on the President in relation to the dissolution of the Dáil, convening a meeting of the Oireachtas and requesting the Supreme Court to validate the constitutionality of legislation, as well as his role as a medium in any dispute between the Dáil and Seanad, would have placed real hurdles in the path of any aspiring Irish dictator had one ever emerged. These factors were largely ignored by the Opposition in their criticisms of the new presidency.

Though de Valera had engaged in some constitutional plagiarism in regard to the office of President, this too serves to highlight his democratic credentials. The fact that de Valera took on board large tracts of the Weimar presidency, while excluding the clauses that had undermined its democracy, is hardly coincidental. Similarly, de Valera's near admission that the checks and balances in the Free State Constitution had worked well – and his actual retention of some of these provisions in the new format of the President of Ireland – suggested that a commitment to constitutionalism was now at the core of Fianna Fáil's politics.

For the Opposition, their unyielding focus on continental dictators may have been a missed opportunity. In nakedly political terms, the fate of Weimar was unlikely in this period to have aroused the passions of the Irish electorate as much as the charge that the new President might actually be a Governor-General in disguise. Yet, there is no doubt that the scale and venom of the Opposition's attacks on the new office of President created real public unease about the merit and nature of the office, which did not dissipate on the ratification of Bunreacht na hÉireann. In order to establish popular support for the office of President of Ireland, de Valera would have to take such underlying discontent into account when the time came to put forward a candidate for this post.

4

The Successor of Our Rightful Princes

Douglas Hyde was inaugurated the first President of Ireland on 25 June 1938. This was not just a landmark day in his life, but a seminal moment in Irish constitutional and political development. The Irish newspaper coverage was unanimous in recording a day of fanfare, ceremony and celebration of national advance.[1] For the Fianna Fáil Government, it was an opportunity to showcase the measure of political independence that had been achieved. Maurice Moynihan, the Secretary to the Government, subsequently noted of the inauguration day: 'Save for partition, the work of peacefully replacing the Treaty settlement with one more acceptable to national feeling was then complete. For de Valera, who had shown so much patience and firmness of purpose in pursuing this goal, the occasion was one of very special significance.'[2]

Behind de Valera's soaring rhetoric on the inauguration day were many months of complex political manoeuvrings, which propelled a supposedly apolitical retired academic into the role of the first President of Ireland. There has long been an accepted wisdom that Hyde's transition to the presidency was a seamless process that was preordained from the moment the office of President was conceptualised in the draft of Bunreacht na hÉireann. This, however, is a misconception. It was only as a result of some significant shifts in the political landscape in the latter half of 1937 and early 1938 that the notion of an agreed candidate became an increasingly likely proposition.

It was only against such an emerging backdrop, in which party candidates became undesirable, that Hyde's candidacy became viable.

Though Douglas Hyde's candidacy was ultimately the result of a late political compromise between the two main political parties, Hyde was, nonetheless, an inspired choice who neatly underlined consensus and a broad commitment to a number of key political objectives, including the national language, partition and non-sectarianism.

Consensus was not a word associated with the office of President during the debate on the draft Constitution in spring 1937. The Opposition parties' loud and vocal criticisms of the new office centred on the suspicion that de Valera would either have himself elected President or install a pliant yes-man in the post to give Fianna Fáil unfettered control. The Opposition's fears were not diminished by de Valera's near insistence during the debate on the draft Constitution that the presidency would be filled following a party contest. On 26 May 1937, he told the Dáil: 'We have got to face the possibility of having an election for the office of President, and, in my view, the times when you are going to have an agreed election will be very, very few, indeed. From my experience, I should say that the chances of getting agreement and an uncontested election are going to be very slight.'[3] The process of de Valera's conversion to the merits of an agreed candidate filling the first presidency only commenced following disappointing results, from Fianna Fáil's perspective, on the plebiscite on the Constitution and the 1937 general election, both of which took place on 1 July that year. Fianna Fáil lost eight seats, leaving de Valera dependent on the support of the Labour Party. Meanwhile, the Constitution was adopted by a margin of 56.5 per cent in favour versus 43.5 per cent against, which was not the overwhelming majority de Valera might have hoped for.[4]

The qualms about the nature of the new presidential office had been a major theme of the campaigns and had undoubtedly cost Fianna Fáil votes. Even after the election, the Opposition continued to express concerns in this regard and de Valera began to view it as a political necessity to defuse this persistent charge. De Valera realised the best way to do this was to ensure that the first President was somebody who was independent of party politics and whom the electorate would not believe could emerge as a dictator.

Seán T. O'Kelly had been de Valera's original choice for the office of President. During the debate on the draft Constitution, his candidacy was facetiously alluded to by a number of Opposition TDs.[5] McMahon's research also points to the fact that at the time of this debate, de Valera had confided in Alfred Smith, the former Governor of New York and the Democratic candidate for the US presidency in 1928, that he viewed O'Kelly as 'best qualified' to take on the role of the new President.[6]

Michael McDunphy, who was designated for appointment as Secretary to the office of President in November 1937, was a very interested observer of the process that would determine who would be the first President. McDunphy, who remained a senior civil servant in de Valera's own department up until the coming into effect of the Constitution on 29 December 1937, noted subsequently that there was a widespread impression that Seán T. O'Kelly would be nominated by Fianna Fáil.[7] McDunphy also noted that Frank Fahy, a Fianna Fáil TD for Galway East and the serving Ceann Comhairle since 1932, was also 'frequently mentioned as a candidate'.[8]

O'Kelly and Fahy's respective candidacies became politically more difficult for Fianna Fáil in the aftermath of the 1937 election. The extremely tight parliamentary arithmetic meant that a Dáil vacancy, which would be created by a Fianna Fáil TD being elected to the office of President, would put further pressure on the Government's precarious majority. A further compelling argument, given the close connection of O'Kelly and Fahy with de Valera, was that either of their candidacies would have further amplified the dictatorship charge.

These circumstances did not, however, immediately encourage the Taoiseach to embrace Hyde. De Valera instead gave serious consideration to the merits of two distinguished Irish public servants, Seán Lester and Robert M. Henry.[9]

Lester was born and raised in Carrickfergus, County Antrim. Though he came from a Protestant and unionist background, Lester joined the Gaelic League in Belfast and subsequently, in 1908, he joined the IRB.[10] In 1923, he took up employment in the fledgling Irish Free State Department of External Affairs. Since 1934, Lester had held the high-profile position of the League of Nations High Commissioner to the Free City of Danzig.[11] Lester's name reached the newspapers as a potential president and though he officially declined to comment, he was sceptical of his own chances. Lester wrote in his diary in November 1937 that 'it was published in the Dispatch and Daily Mail that I was talked of in Belfast and Dublin as a "probable". A non-political President is rather unlikely. Dev himself, or Seán T. O'Kelly with Alfie Byrne (!) opposition candidate.'[12]

Professor R. M. Henry, the Belfast-born son of a Plymouth Brethren preacher, was an internationally recognised classical scholar and influential administrator at Queen's University Belfast.[13] Henry had been associated with the separatist movement during the War of Independence and in 1920 he had authored *The Evolution of Sinn Féin*, the then definitive account of the party's rapid growth. Henry's candidacy was promoted by Bernard Duffy, a well-known barrister, novelist and playwright from Carrickmacross, and P. J. Little, the Government Chief Whip.[14] Duffy, in a letter to Little in January 1938, which was passed on to de Valera, advocated Henry as President.[15] He argued that such a choice would help Fianna Fáil and 'the lost ground might be regained and much added to it if a really admirable gesture were made in the election of President'.[16]

Though ultimately the prospective candidacies of both Lester and Henry came to nothing, it is important to observe that the common denominator of both individuals was that they were Northern Protestants with nationalist backgrounds. In giving consideration to both of these individuals, de Valera surely recognised that the choice of President could be used to send a symbolically powerful message.

De Valera would also have been conscious that sentiment in the nationalist community in Northern Ireland placed a strong emphasis on the new President coming from the partitioned area. This viewpoint was encapsulated in a statement issued, on 12 January 1938, by the abstentionist MPs for Fermanagh and Tyrone, Patrick Cunningham and J. A. Mulvey, under the banner of the Northern Council for Irish Unity. This statement spoke of the desirability of choosing as President of Ireland 'a patriotic figure' who would embody in his person 'the whole of Ireland'.[17] This statement went on to maintain:

> The choice of a distinguished Irishman from the six counties would be a pledge to the people of that area that they are

> regarded as equal citizens of Ireland, and that the unity of Irishmen of all creeds, clans and classes is sincerely desired . . . The presidential office is the only institution which can provide a link between North and South at this stage, since at present the Dáil and Senate cannot operate for the whole country. A President of Northern origin will emphasise the de jure unity of Ireland, which Ireland's enemies deny.[18]

If the choice of President was important to signal the priority attached to ending partition, for de Valera it was also crucial that it underlined the state's commitment to the Irish language.

In his conversations with John Cudahy, the American Minister to Ireland, de Valera made a strong association between the presidency and the language. Cudahy reported to the US State Department that

> in their conversations on the subject [of the presidency] de Valera often had emphasised to him 'the importance of language in the survival of nationalism' and had told him that while of course he could not predict the outcome of the election (a qualifier Cudahy accepted with tongue in cheek), 'he would not consent to any candidate who did not speak Irish fluently and . . . insist upon the importance of the Irish language movement.'[19]

Intriguingly, there may have been a deeper level of meaning to the exchanges between de Valera and Cudahy on the Irish presidency. Cudahy's father was born in Kilkenny, making the American Minister eligible to take out Irish citizenship, and there is evidence to suggest that Cudahy may have tried to get himself nominated as an agreed candidate.[20] Certainly an approach was made to General Mulcahy on Cudahy's behalf.[21] De Valera's commitment to the Irish language was undoubted, but the emphasis he placed on it in his conversations with Cudahy may also have served as a convenient and diplomatic way to make clear to the American Minister that he would not entertain his presidential ambitions.

The press, especially some English newspapers, threw up some other unlikely candidates for President. Count Edward Taaffe, a grandson of a former Austrian Prime Minister, who had moved to Ireland from Prague in 1937, declared his candidacy in the *Liverpool Daily Post*, but this story and his campaign to become President went no further.[22]

McDunphy recorded that a number of English papers had mentioned Count John McCormack, the Athlone-born tenor, but the Secretary to the office of President noted that McCormack's candidacy 'does not appear to have been regarded seriously in Ireland'.[23] In any case, McDunphy suggested that McCormack was 'ineligible' for election because he had previously taken out American citizenship, a factor that did not prevent Dana Rosemary Scallon from contesting presidential elections in 1997 and 2011.[24]

Another potential candidate in 1938 was the well-known linguist and former Gaelic League President Lord Ashbourne, who McDunphy privately noted was 'regarded with favour in many circles'.[25] Ashbourne, however, was lukewarm on the job and made it clear he would only allow his name to go forward in certain circumstances. He said: 'I would only accept if the two parties, supporting Mr Seán T. O'Kelly and Ald. Alfie Byrne, respectively agreed to my nomination, but that, I think, is impossible. Moreover, I detest politics and I detest writing, and there would be nothing else to do but sign papers.'[26] It is very doubtful whether Taaffe, McCormack or Ashbourne were seriously entertained as prospective presidents by the main parties.

There is no official record as to when de Valera came to the view that the Gaelic scholar Douglas Hyde would be a good choice for President. In an academic paper in 1988, Janet Dunleavy claimed that

> it must have been late 1936 or early 1937 when de Valera spoke to Hyde about the presidency. Although the prospect was attractive, the decision could not have been easy for Hyde to make. On the one hand there were reasons to hesitate. His wife, Lucy, was chronically ill. He himself, although still healthy and hearty, already had exceeded the biblical age of three score and ten . . . At the same time, it was difficult for him to resist the chance to be once more a maker of modern Ireland. By early summer, 1937, it was evident that de Valera had prevailed.[27]

In their subsequent joint biography of Hyde, Janet Dunleavy and Gareth Dunleavy, who were both Professors of English and Comparative Literature at the University of Wisconsin-Milwaukee, expanded on this unlikely timeline and made the extraordinarily dubious suggestion that even before the Constitution had come into effect, de Valera had encouraged Hyde to engage in a public relations operation of a literary bent so as to ensure universal approval for his imminent selection as an agreed president.

Dunleavy and Dunleavy state:

> Circumstantial evidence and other documentation, however, leave little doubt that the two men [Hyde and de Valera] were regularly in touch and had in fact collaborated on the scenario that developed. There were, for example, Hyde's two major publications in 1937. After having concentrated for ten years on scholarly editing, folklore, literary, historical and linguistic studies, and translating from the Irish, suddenly he dusted off, reviewed, revised and saw through the press *Mo Thuras go h-Americe* (My Voyage to America), his account of his 1905–1906 lecture tour, and *Mise agus An Conradh* (Myself and the League), his diary of his years as president of the Gaelic League. Published in 1937 (therefore prepared for publication beginning at least a year or two earlier), neither of these books has the objectivity of a backward look; both present Hyde as a strong, wise, and effective leader and ambassador.[28]

The willingness of Hyde's biographers to equate the republication of two of Hyde's books in 1937 to his subsequent elevation to the presidency is a case of reading history backwards. It ignores the fact that de Valera leaned heavily in the Dáil debate on the draft Constitution towards the desirability of a presidential election. It also fails to take into account the strong belief in government and political circles that Seán T. O'Kelly would be the Fianna Fáil candidate. It neglects to mention that de Valera only began to back away from a party candidate as a result of lingering public suspicion in the aftermath of the plebiscite on the Constitution. It also fails to take account of the fact that de Valera actively considered potential non-party candidates other than Hyde.

In support of their speculative theory that Hyde's presidency was a long time in gestation, Dunleavy and Dunleavy also cite the fact that a biography of Hyde was published in the same year he became President. They wrote: 'In 1938 Diarmuid Coffey published *Douglas Hyde: President of Ireland* (a revision of his *Douglas Hyde: An Craoibhín Aoibhinn*, published in 1917); like *Mo Thuras go h-Americe* and *Mise agus An Conradh*, it had to have been in preparation before Hyde's nomination. All three of these books are the kind produced to rouse public interest in a political figure or otherwise further public relations.'[29]

In fact, the new edition of Coffey's book did not appear in print until some months after Hyde's inauguration. This new edition contained an updated final chapter to bring the biography up to the point of Hyde's elevation to President, but apart from this and a new subtitle, the text was largely the same as the 1917 publication.[30] The book bears all the hallmarks of a publication rushed out to cash in on Hyde's new status, a point that Coffey, in his author's notes, all but confirmed when he stated that 'when he [Hyde] was elected President, the Talbot Press asked me to bring out a new edition'.[31] The notion put forward by the Dunleavys that a publishing house was secretly aware for months that Hyde was going to be President and was discreetly beavering away on a new biography, while nothing leaked out, is hardly credible.

The known facts in regard to how Hyde's candidacy emerged are far more prosaic than the slick public relations campaign imagined by Dunleavy and Dunleavy. Hyde's candidacy was first mooted in *The Irish Times* in May 1937. On 26 May 1937, Hyde and W. B. Yeats had been presented with the prestigious Gregory Medal by the Irish Academy of Literature. The following day, *The Irish Times* comprehensively reported on this event and the paper also contained a letter and an editorial advocating Hyde as President. The letter, signed by a correspondent who took the pseudonym 'Fianna Gael' and who in all likelihood was an *Irish Times* staff member, read:

> It is vital that the first President should be a man who will command general respect and support. He ought to be a man above all party politics – with no political 'record'. Otherwise

> there will be a contested election, with a great deal of public linen washing. Is there such a man in Ireland today? I believe that there is, and his name is Douglas Hyde . . . the nomination of Dr Hyde by Messrs de Valera and Cosgrave, acting in concert, would transform at a single stroke the whole complexion of our political life. Is there any man in Ireland who has done the state such service as Douglas Hyde? Is there anybody so remote from the hurly-burly of political controversy? Is there any other candidate whose name is held in such general esteem?[32]

The suspicion that this letter was orchestrated from within *The Irish Times* is heightened by the fact that the paper devoted an entire editorial to endorsing the plea of a purportedly anonymous letter writer. Under the editorial heading 'A Great Irishman', *The Irish Times* advocated Douglas Hyde being 'elected unanimously to be the first occupant of the presidential office' and continued: 'The fact that the new constitution can be promulgated in Irish is the result of his life work and he has the supreme advantage of being "above the battle". We have little doubt that the suggestion made by our correspondent will be received with enthusiasm. The crowning honour then would be placed upon a magnificent career of national service.'[33]

It would be wrong to assume that this editorial marked the beginning of a bandwagon that propelled Hyde into the presidency. Hyde's private reaction was 'to be amused, rather than interested' by this suggestion that he should be the first President.[34] The editorial was written in the context of the Dáil debate on the draft Constitution, in which Fianna Fáil had made clear their preference for a presidential election. Furthermore, up to the turn of 1938, de Valera was still mulling over whether he should put forward a Fianna Fáil candidate. In October 1937, he crossed swords with *The Irish Times*, which continued to advocate an agreed candidate. The paper had continuously argued from the time of the publication of the draft Constitution that the presidency should not be a party matter. While recognising that a president should not act in a party political manner, de Valera used the platform of his party's Ard Fheis to stoutly defend Fianna Fáil's right to put forward a party candidate. He said:

> If *The Irish Times* thinks we will have no interest in the person who is going to be the first head of this Irish state, *The Irish Times* is making a mistake. We shall do everything to give to the Irish state a head that will be worthy of the Irish state; and when he has been elected by the people in a free election we hope that all parties will give him the loyalty and reverence which are due to the man who will be chosen to represent Ireland . . . That ought to be good enough for *The Irish Times*. And if it is not good enough, they can do their best to get a majority in the other direction.[35]

By the end of 1937, Hyde's name was one of a number of undeclared, potential non-party candidates in the political ether. However, at that point, an election fought along party lines still seemed the most likely option. This was underlined by *The Irish Times* on 29 December 1937, the day Bunreacht na hÉireann came into effect, when it reported that 'it now appears to be certain that the official [presidential] candidate of the Government will be Mr Seán T. O'Kelly, the Tánaiste'. The game changer was a sermon in Armagh delivered by Cardinal MacRory on 2 January 1938. It was this factor more than any other that brought about the decisive shift towards an agreed non-party candidate for President, which would ultimately benefit Hyde. *The Irish Times* reported:

> His Eminence made an eloquent plea for agreement among the parties regarding the election of the first President of the new Ireland. The Uachtarán, he said ought, if possible, to be agreed upon without an election. 'It would be a very fine thing if this could be done.' The President, continued His Eminence, will be expected to be outside, and above, all parties, but if he should be a nominee of a party, there will always be a danger of suspicion that he will favour that party. If on the other hand, an agreed candidate could be found, 'it would be an object lesson in unity, and might have far-reaching results'.[36]

MacRory's statement altered the political landscape. Within less than a week of his sermon, it was reported that the Cardinal's appeal for an agreed candidate had 'made a deep impression on the party leaders'.[37] The political correspondent of *The Irish Times* said in the wake of MacRory's appeal that 'the Fianna Fáil parliamentary organisation already has discussed the matter at some length, and is virtually unanimous in its desire to discover a non-controversial candidate. Machinery has been created within the organisation whereby Mr de Valera, with or without the assistance of two other plenipotentiaries, will be authorised to choose a candidate in consultation with the other party leaders.'[38]

On 10 January, the Irish Press reported that Oscar Traynor, the Minister for Posts and Telegraphs, had told an annual Dublin Fianna Fáil Smoking Concert in the Red Bank Restaurant that 'every member of this organisation would like to see the first President of Éire the unanimous choice of a united people' and that Fianna Fáil would put 'no barriers' in the way of attempts to bring about such 'a happy event'.

At a Fianna Fáil Parliamentary Party meeting on 7 April, this position was formalised. The minutes show that it was agreed that 'it would be desirable to get an agreed candidate' and that 'in the event of an agreement being arrived at between the two main parties so as to avoid an election . . . full power to make a decision in this matter would be left to the Taoiseach'.[39]

Fine Gael, too, were quick to stress that they 'entirely agreed with his Eminence', but their scepticism of de Valera also shone through.[40] While making it clear that Fine Gael were willing to engage with Fianna Fáil in an effort to achieve consensus on the presidency, James Dillon expressed doubts that de Valera 'would consent to the appointment of anybody who was not a creature of his own' and in such a scenario there would be 'a pretty vigorous' election.[41]

Fianna Fáil's conversion to the merits of an agreed candidate had a number of good political reasons to advance it. Firstly, there was the Opposition's sustained criticism of the President being 'a partyman' and the fears that this had generated about a possible presidential dictator. This had impinged on Fianna Fáil's support.

Secondly, Fianna Fáil felt that there was a real danger that if two candidates – a pro-Treaty and an anti-Treaty one – should contest the election, the voting might be uncomfortably close, and the resulting President might not be accorded the respect due to the office by the minority who had voted against him.[42] In such an eventuality, the new office of President might have been irreparably damaged.

Thirdly, Fianna Fáíl may have viewed a contested presidential election in 1938 as an untimely distraction given that the Government had agreed to enter into important Anglo-Irish negotiations with Neville Chamberlain's Government. These talks ultimately opened on 17 January 1938 and Fianna Fáil ministers knew that the negotiations would see key players bogged down in talks for an extended period, leaving little time to take to the hustings.[43]

Fourthly, Fianna Fáil's precarious Dáil situation may also have influenced the party against a presidential election in 1938. Fianna Fáil had no parliamentary majority and the Labour Party had begun to criticise strongly Fianna Fáil's industrial policy and failure to deal with emigration.[44] Two cabinet members, Lemass and Traynor, had already dropped hints about another election and the party may well have seen it as prudent to save scant resources for a general election.[45]

Despite the compelling reasons outlined above, it was the Cardinal's statement – which received a strong degree of public approval – that finally prompted Fianna Fáil to embrace the prospect of an agreed president. MacRory's plea may have given Fianna Fáil a convenient excuse to retreat from the position they had taken since the Dáil debate on the draft Constitution that there should be a presidential election, but it also says something significant about the power of the crozier in Irish politics in the late 1930s.

Although the Cardinal's intervention had effected a decisive shift towards an agreed candidate, Hyde was still far from certain to be Ireland's first President. In particular, Robert Henry's candidacy – as a non-party figure – had its advocates in Fianna Fáil. On 9 April 1938, a very favourable account in the *Irish Press* of Henry's career, coupled with the announcement that he was soon to retire from the Chair of Latin in Queen's University Belfast, raised expectations that he was being lined up by Fianna Fáil for the presidency.[46]

It seems that in this period the leadership in Fianna Fáil may well have been taking an each-way bet on a number of acceptable potential candidates. That de Valera had settled on Hyde as a potentially strong option for President is underlined by the fact that, on 31 March 1938,

Hyde was selected as one of the Taoiseach's eleven nominees to the newly reconstituted Seanad Éireann. With hindsight and the knowledge that a higher office would ultimately beckon for Hyde, it is hard not to contend that Hyde's Seanad appointment was an effort to raise his profile and possibly even a subtle attempt to tie him in some way in the public consciousness to Fianna Fáil.

At twelve noon on 21 April 1938, P. J. Ruttledge, Minister for Justice, and Gerry Boland, Minister for Lands, met in conference with two Vice Presidents of Fine Gael, James Dillon and T. F. O'Higgins, in de Valera's rooms in Leinster House. The initiative for this meeting had been taken by Fianna Fáil, who had invited representatives of the main Opposition party to meet with them, and Fine Gael had readily accepted this invitation, in the interests of securing 'a candidate who would be above and apart from party politics'.[47]

The extent to which Fianna Fáil had only grudgingly accepted that a consensus approach to the presidency was desirable is evident from the absence of the Labour Party. With thirteen TDs and only two senators, Labour – unlike Fine Gael – did not have sufficient Oireachtas strength to nominate a candidate. The fact that Labour could not force an election meant that getting their agreement was deemed unnecessary. Fianna Fáil did not invite Labour to the talks on an agreed presidential candidate and this met with no protest from Fine Gael. At this point, seeking a genuine cross-party consensus on who would be the first President seems to have been less important to the two main parties than protecting their own political hegemony.

Fianna Fáil's lukewarm conversion to an agreed candidate is also evident from the fact that in the opening session of the talks, Ruttledge and Boland strongly advanced the cases of Fahy and O'Kelly as the agreed candidate, even though O'Kelly had privately made it clear to de Valera that his preference was to remain a minister.[48] The names of both O'Kelly and Fahy were vetoed by the Fine Gael representatives, who suggested 'that if any agreement was to be possible members of the present Dáil should be ruled out and a strictly non-party candidate chosen'.[49] Fianna Fáil also put forward the name of Conor Maguire, who was a serving member of the Presidential Commission and the President of the High Court. Though at this point Maguire was an independent member of the judiciary, he had a strong Fianna Fáil pedigree, having formerly been a Fianna Fáil TD and de Valera's first Attorney-General.[50] He too was vetoed by Fine Gael.

Dillon and O'Higgins were then invited to submit possible nominees.[51] After adjourning to consult with W. T. Cosgrave, the Fine Gael representatives returned and submitted three names – Dr Richard Hayes, Cahir Davitt, and Professor Denis Coffey.[52] The names put forward by Fine Gael reflect their viewpoint that the first President should be a non-party person, yet from Fianna Fáil's perspective these names may also have suggested a Free State bias.

Hayes was a well-known medical doctor and a director of the Abbey Theatre. He had fought under the command of Thomas Ashe and Richard Mulcahy in Ashbourne during the 1916 Rising and had served as a TD from 1918. He had firmly supported the Treaty and had been a member of Cumann na nGaedheal until he resigned his seat in 1924 to concentrate on medicine and scholarly interests.[53]

Cahir Davitt was a son of the famous Land League leader and had been a circuit judge for Dublin city and county for over a decade. Davitt had publicly supported the Treaty and during the Civil War he had been appointed the first Judge Advocate General of the national army.[54]

Coffey was the first President of UCD and held that post from 1908 until 1940. He had been 'an intimate friend of John Dillon', the late father of one of the Fine Gael plenipotentiaries, and UCD under his stewardship was not regarded as a Fianna Fáil-friendly institution.[55]

Each of the names put forward by Fine Gael was rejected by the Fianna Fáil plenipotentiaries.

According to *The Irish Times*' report from the day after the conference, 'several names were under consideration, including those of prominent public men who were at one time or another a popular choice for selection as a candidate. These, however, were ruled out one by one for one reason or another and by one side and the other. Eventually there was unanimity on the selection of Dr Hyde.'[56]

The *Catholic Herald* strongly suggested that Hyde's selection just shaded it over Robert Henry on the basis that Hyde was better known in the south. The paper's Dublin correspondent wrote:

> There was a wish among northerners that a patriot from the six counties should be chosen – also a Protestant and a noted scholar

> – and I believe that his name was among those which were discussed when the two parties conferred. His election would have established, what we still lack, a concrete bond between the two parts into which Ireland has been divided, but I believe that it was felt that the new President must be one well-known to the larger area.[57]

In a number of interviews, former Taoiseach Liam Cosgrave has said, based on conversations with his father W. T. Cosgrave, that Hyde's name was first proposed by the Fine Gael plenipotentiaries.[58]

Throughout 21 April 1938, the talks on an agreed president adjourned on a number of occasions to allow consultations with the respective party leaders. At 7 p.m., the Fianna Fáil and Fine Gael plenipotentiaries eventually convened a press briefing in Leinster House to inform members of the media that Hyde would be their joint nominee for President.

A file from the Department of the President of the Executive Council shows a shambolic approach to the protocol and news management of this event.[59] This file, coupled with contemporary newspaper accounts, also contains further evidence to undermine the Dunleavys' theory that Hyde's nomination was a done deal for a long time before it came to pass.

The official file shows that though the plenipotentiaries briefed the press on the evening of 21 April that Hyde was the choice of the Fianna Fáil/Fine Gael conference, the parties had not made preparations to get word formally to the selected candidate. Hyde would only officially get word that he was to be offered the nomination by Fianna Fáil and Fine Gael the following day, which suggests the opposite of advanced coordination in relation to his selection.

Hyde's sister heard the announcement from Leinster House on the radio on the evening of 21 April and gave him the news.[60] His reaction, significantly, was one of surprise. The general consensus of the reporters, who had quickly begun to arrive that evening at his house in Frenchpark, Roscommon, was also that Hyde was astonished by the news.[61] While he made it clear that he would be honoured to accept the nomination, he had been clearly caught off guard. He told *The Irish Times* and the *Irish Press* that he had not the 'faintest idea' that the parties would choose him and he was 'anxious' to see the statement the parties had issued on conclusion of their talks.[62] Hyde's family were also stunned by what had transpired. Hyde's daughter, Una Sealy, told a reporter who called to her Donnybrook home of her 'surprise' at the selection of her father; however, she claimed she was probably aware of the news before Hyde, as the decision of the Fianna Fáil/Fine Gael conference had been immediately conveyed to her over the telephone by one of the plenipotentiaries, James Dillon. Sealy expressed the belief that her father would make an ideal president because 'as a man of culture and learning he could meet all classes of the people equally well'. She did, however, raise a potential difficulty in Hyde accepting the role when she said that her mother 'dislikes any form of publicity and would be furious if her photograph appeared in the press'.[63]

Even the following day, Hyde still seemed bemused by events, telling reporters that the news had been unexpected, even wondering aloud when he might receive official confirmation. Hyde's Roscommon home had no telephone. *A Daily Express* correspondent, who called to Hyde's home on 22 April, quoted him as saying: 'I had as little notion as the man in the moon that they would ask me. I don't know even now that I have been asked, except that I have just been reading about it. I suppose I'll receive an official invite, maybe in a day or two.'[64]

In fact, Hyde would get official confirmation later that day. The official file notes that at 2.15 p.m. on 22 April a letter was forwarded to the 'translation staff' in Leinster House with a request to have 'it translated into Connaught Irish with the least possible delay (within the next half hour if at all possible)'.[65] A handwritten note on the file also recorded that the Fianna Fáil whip, P. J. Little, and the Fine Gael whip, Peadar Doyle, 'left Dublin by car for Frenchpark around 5 p.m. this afternoon' to convey the letter of invitation to Hyde.

The last-minute nature of the rush to get this letter finalised again suggests that there was no advance knowledge of Hyde's nomination as the Dunleavys have claimed. The letter to Hyde, signed by the Fianna Fáil and Fine Gael plenipotentiaries, stated in English: 'On behalf of the Fianna Fáil and Fine Gael parties we cordially invite you to accept nomination to the office of President of Ireland. We should be glad if you would favourably consider this invitation and inform us of your decision as soon as you may find it convenient to do so.'[66]

The official file also contains further evidence of a disdainful attitude to the Labour Party. Though Labour had been excluded from the conference to select an agreed presidential candidate, the party, on hearing of Hyde's selection, decided within less than a day to support this choice.[67] De Valera appeared to have consented to the Labour leader William Norton's request to be part of the official invitation to Hyde, but this did not ultimately happen. Seán Murphy, a Department of External Affairs official, noted that after Norton had expressed his support for Hyde's candidacy, the original intention had been 'to send to Dr Hyde a telegram signed by the Taoiseach, Deputy Cosgrave and himself [Norton]. He had agreed to this course before leaving Dublin.'[68] The fact that the official invitation was issued solely in the names of the Fianna Fáil and Fine Gael plenipotentiaries was breezily dismissed by de Valera as 'a misunderstanding' caused by Norton (and Cosgrave) being 'not available'.[69]

Little and Doyle finally arrived at Hyde's residence at close to 10 p.m. on 22 April, over twenty-four hours after the announcement had been made in Leinster House. Hyde was then given the plenipotentiaries' letter officially requesting him to accept the nomination of Fianna Fáil and Fine Gael.[70] Though Hyde graciously accepted the offer in front of a number of journalists who were present, in an aside to Little and Doyle he hinted at some qualms. Hyde privately said he had decided to accept the nomination on the basis that he felt the parties might find it difficult to reach a consensus on another name should he decline. An *Irish Press* reporter noted that he had overheard Hyde say to the two whips in Irish that 'I was thinking of not accepting the position but I thought then, that it was a wonderful thing that both parties came together. I thought that maybe if I did not accept it they might not come together on any other name. That is why I accepted.'[71]

The previous evening, Hyde had also expressed doubt to an *Irish Times* reporter, stating that his 'one objection' was that he was 'so old'.[72] Hyde had also displayed some uncertainty to the *Irish Independent*'s reporter, who wrote that Hyde 'wondered if it had been difficult to select a non-political candidate and if there was anyone else in the running should he not accept the position'.[73] The very real qualms Hyde vocalised again sit uneasily with the Dunleavys' notion that de Valera and Hyde had long conspired to ensure Hyde's elevation to the presidency.

In his conversation with the press at Hyde's home, P. J. Little showed more political sensitivity to the Labour Party than de Valera had. Little stressed to newspaper reporters that all parties in the Dáil were happy for Hyde to be nominated and he said 'Labour is very pleased.'[74] Unlike de Valera, who was unperturbed by Labour's non-inclusion in the official invitation to Hyde, Little was prepared to share a morsel of credit with the Labour Party. The Fianna Fáil whip was conscious of the need to keep Labour on board to avoid an election, with the popular Lord Mayor of Dublin, Alfie Byrne, still hovering in the wings.

Byrne's name had been associated with a presidential run going back as far as the debate on the draft Constitution and in December 1937 he had declared that he would be a candidate.[75] McDunphy later recorded his belief that Byrne would have been 'a very strong candidate'.[76] Byrne's electoral record was that of a formidable vote-getter. In the 1932 general election, he had received the highest vote in the country in his Dublin North constituency.[77]

Byrne's background was in the Irish Parliamentary Party, but, though nominally an independent, he was closely associated with Fine Gael. He was elected Lord Mayor of Dublin every year from 1930 to 1939 in an arrangement whereby he voted first with Cumann na nGaedheal (and subsequently Fine Gael) in the Dáil in exchange for their support for his candidature on Dublin City Council.[78]

Byrne's presidential ambitions had initially been encouraged within Fine Gael. It was widely accepted that if Fianna Fáil had insisted on putting forward Seán T. O'Kelly or any other party candidate that Byrne 'would have [had] the support of the Cosgrave party throughout the country'.[79] In such a scenario, Byrne's candidacy would have made sense for Fine Gael, especially given that they had argued that the first President should not be 'a party man' and that Byrne would be a formidable candidate who would not give Fianna Fáil a free run.

Following the change in the political dynamic in the wake of MacRory's sermon, Byrne and his election agent, Louis Lemass, a cousin of the Fianna Fáil minister, intensified their efforts to ensure that Byrne would be a candidate for President.[80] A prominent Election

Committee meeting was hosted by Byrne in the Mansion House at the beginning of April.[81] When Fianna Fáil and Fine Gael entered into conference on who should be their agreed nominee for President, Byrne hinted that there would be an election unless he was the agreed candidate. He told reporters that if de Valera or Cosgrave emerged as the agreed candidate he would not contest the presidential election, but 'he did not see why he should be asked to stand aside for anybody else'.[82] Byrne's suggestion that he would not readily get off the pitch may have been an attempt to make the plenipotentiaries believe that the only way they could avoid a presidential election was by agreeing on his nomination. However, Byrne was surely conscious that Fianna Fáil was unlikely to acquiesce to his nomination given that he was only one step removed from being a Fine Gael candidate.

Byrne also sent an overt message to the Labour Party as the Fianna Fáil-Fine Gael conference progressed. He told *The Irish Times* that 'I cannot understand why Mr Norton, the leader of the Labour Party, was not invited to the conference in this matter. An agreed candidate should be chosen by all parties in the Dáil.'[83]

Byrne's comments were a calculated attempt to benefit from Labour's dismay at not being invited to the Fianna Fáil/Fine Gael conference to select a presidential candidate. With Fine Gael out of the picture, Byrne's last hope of securing a nomination was to obtain the support of the Labour Party and a handful of other Oireachtas members. Norton, however, did not take Byrne's bait and had quickly indicated that he would back Hyde. Little's comments in Roscommon, in crediting Labour's support for Hyde, were politically astute. His words were designed to ensure that Labour TDs and senators would not desert Hyde and assist Byrne's efforts to gather the twenty Oireachtas signatures necessary to secure a nomination to contest the presidential election.

Byrne had already been outmanoeuvred in his efforts to secure a nomination by way of the county councils. The *Sunday Independent*, on 17 April, had reported that nominations would close in the presidential election on 4 May 1938.[84] This order had been promulgated by Seán T. O'Kelly, the Minister for Local Government, the previous week and Byrne argued that it made it almost logistically impossible for him to put his case to the councils for a nomination. He said: 'The arrangements for the elections afforded very little opportunity to an independent candidate to secure his nominations. The county councils will not hold their monthly meetings until first week in May and any intending candidate wishing to be nominated by four county councils would require to be at work immediately to have the matter on the agenda for these meetings'.[85]

Though Fianna Fáil and Fine Gael dominated all the councils and Byrne was unlikely to get the requisite support, the Lord Mayor maintained that he had been 'jockeyed' out of the race by Fianna Fáil. He wrote angrily to the *Irish Press,* complaining that

> it was suggested to those of us in public life that we should not make speeches, comments, or indulge in any kind of criticism or talk which might injure, in any way, the negotiations in London. We all faithfully, I believe, kept that pledge. It will seem therefore had I indulged in any kind of presidential election campaign I might have been accused of interfering with such negotiations. I am still of the opinion that the short notice is unfair to candidates who may think of contesting the election and decide to visit the constituents.[86]

With the county council route a non-starter, Labour's decision to back Hyde effectively ended what was by then an outside chance of anyone else securing a nomination through the Oireachtas. Byrne waited a day before making any statement, but when it became clear that Labour would stick with Hyde, the Lord Mayor bowed out of the race.[87]

Hyde's selection at the Fianna Fáil/Fine Gael conference was received with surprise, but also widespread acclaim. The *Catholic Herald*, putting another nail in the Dunleavys' claim, reported that 'certain ceremonial arrangements had been completed on the assumption of a Catholic President's election, which have been cancelled at the last moment – showing that the decision was sudden and unexpected".[88] *The Irish Times*, the *Irish Independent* and the *Irish Press* all ran glowing editorials praising the choice of Hyde.[89] His selection was almost universally welcomed by public figures, religious leaders and civic leaders across the state. Even Alfie Byrne, who at this stage was still holding out for a nomination, praised Hyde as a 'charming, cultured Irish gentleman'.[90]

In Northern Ireland, the Northern Council for Unity welcomed the choice of Hyde on the grounds that it demonstrated Thomas Davis's words that 'we heed not race nor creed nor clan'.[91] In a variation on this theme, the *Catholic Herald* suggested that Hyde's Protestantism made him a 'natural choice' because 'his selection is a signal to the people of the North-East that the majority in Ireland does not identify religion with nationality. This destroys the pretence that the patriotic movement is what (for want of a fitter word) we call sectarlare.'[92]

The powerful political symbolism of a Protestant President of Ireland in the late 1930s had certainly not been lost on de Valera. He had actively considered Seán Lester and Robert Henry, both of whom were members of the Protestant community. Hyde's religion mattered because it allowed the parties, especially Fianna Fáil, to stress the ecumenical character of the Irish state both for its own sake and as a means to rally against partition.

Intriguingly, despite the widespread acclaim for Hyde's selection and the boost it was perceived to give the anti-partition cause, there was a small pocket of internal dissent on this issue within Fianna Fáil. Minutes of the Fianna Fáil Parliamentary Party dated 25 April 1938 record: 'Deputy Micheál Ó Cleirigh proposed and Deputy Ó Briain seconded a resolution heartily approving of the action taken in reference to the presidency and the choice by agreement with the Opposition made of Dr Douglas Hyde as the President-Elect. The Resolution was passed – three voting against.'[93]

On 4 May, when nominations for the office of President of Ireland closed, Hyde officially became President-Elect. This resulted in another round of hugely positive press for Hyde.[94] *The Irish Times* editorialised: 'Dr Hyde is not the choice of a party, but, in effect, the choice of the whole people and as such, he will symbolise the state in a true sense. We salute our new President, and we congratulate the political parties that sank their differences to perform a task, which above all others, called for unity.'[95]

How deep these differences were actually sunk is debatable given the fact that Labour was not invited to sign Hyde's nomination papers.[96] At the ceremony that marked the close of nominations, in the boardroom of the Department of Agriculture, no Labour politician was present, though Hyde was escorted to and from the event by the respective Fianna Fáil and Fine Gael whips. Subsequently, the President-Elect visited Government Buildings and met with a number of prominent members of the two main parties.[97] Fianna Fáil and Fine Gael may have been prepared to bask in the public goodwill for a president above and beyond party politics, but this did not mean they were going to share the spoils with the Labour Party.

This point was largely missed by or mattered little to the public, who were very enthusiastic about Hyde's election. Cheering crowds gathered outside the Department of Agriculture to greet the new President-Elect on the close of nominations and there was an even bigger public turnout on Hyde's inauguration day.[98]

From the outset, Hyde's immense popularity gave the office of President a high public standing, which individuals like the divisive Tim Healy and the largely unknown James McNeill could never have delivered for the preceding office of the Governor-General.

There is some irony in the fact that the supposedly apolitical Douglas Hyde became President because of blatantly political factors. Though Hyde was a compromise choice, his candidacy, in the end, neatly covered a number of political imperatives. Most pertinently, Hyde's candidacy allowed a veil to be drawn over the political charge that the presidency was a vehicle to a dictatorship. As *Dublin Opinion* noted of Hyde, in May 1938, it was not possible to 'imagine the old gentleman marching into Leinster House at the head of his troops'.[99] The choice of Hyde also reflected well on the Irish state's democratic credentials abroad. The prestigious *New York Times Magazine*, in May 1938, described Hyde as 'the antithesis of a continental dictator' and, in a very positive feature on Ireland's President-Elect, wrote:

> At a time when dictators and strong men are the fashion in Europe, such a selection of such a man to become ceremonial head and first citizen of Éire is a happy achievement. This gentle Gaelic savant, poet and man of peace symbolises Irish ideals and native culture rather than the ranting, bellicose nationalism so prevalent on the continent . . . During the debate on the Constitution in the Dáil it was suggested that the powers given to the President would make him another dictator. When the speeches were recalled to 'An Craoibhin', he

> ejaculated, 'Bless my soul!' with a look of perturbed amazement and then hastily added, 'I am sure I should never be anything like that.'[100]

For both Fianna Fáil and Fine Gael, Hyde's career profile ticked all the key political boxes. His religion was a positive to bolster the anti-partition cause, to refute unionist arguments of Rome Rule and to highlight the non-sectarian nature of the Irish state.[101]

As a leading Gaelic scholar, Hyde commanded widespread respect as the 'most persuasive apostle' of Ireland's cultural renaissance.[102] His election underlined official commitment to the cause of the language revival.[103] It is no exaggeration to say Hyde's earlier work with the Gaelic League had inspired the Irish revolution – as well as many of the revolutionaries who now led the state's two largest parties. Hyde was therefore a unifying figure, which was important in building up popular support for his new office.

Hyde's non-partisan career meant he was a nationalist 'Adam before the fall' figure, who 'had not been involved in the bitter internecine struggle of the Civil War and so carried no weight of guilt, in the eyes of either of the contesting parties'.[104] To both sides of the divide, Hyde underscored Ireland's distinct nationality, but in a non-contentious, inclusive manner. In an emerging nation whose politics was badly divided, predominantly on the issue of how the fullest measure of Irish sovereignty could be achieved, Hyde's candidacy was political manna.

In his memoir, David Gray, the American Minister to Ireland, dismissively suggested that Hyde's elevation to the presidency was 'a case of the candidate who had no enemies', but this does not negate the fact that he was also, in the words of Ó Tuathaigh, 'an inspired and inspiring choice'.[105] Hyde was a non-polarising figure; he was hugely respected across the political divide; his elevation pointed to an indigenous Gaelic restoration and, from the very outset, he gave the new office a sense of dignity and stability that was crucial to its popular acceptance by the Irish people.

In essence, then, the selection of Douglas Hyde got the Irish presidency off to a good start.

5

The Foundations of Presidential Precedence

The broad consensus on Hyde becoming Ireland's first citizen underlined the deep affection in which he was held in Irish society. Hyde's high public standing was such that he – rather than the largely despised or ignored Governor-Generals – had been frequently called upon to give national benediction to landmark projects. In September 1931, at de Valera's request, Hyde penned a 'Message to the Nation' in the first edition of the *Irish Press* urging people to 'Speak the Irish.'[1] Over half a decade previously, on 1 January 1926, Séamus Hughes, a former Cumann na Gaedheal General Secretary, who had been appointed the first announcer at the Irish Free State's first radio station, 2RN, invited Hyde to inaugurate the new service formally.[2] Deliberately paraphrasing Robert Emmet's famous words from the dock, Hyde used the advent of Irish radio to champion the cause of a Gaelic Ireland. 'Our enterprise today,' Dr Hyde said, 'marks the beginning not only of the New Year, but of a new era – an era in which the nation will take its place among the other nations of the world'. A nation, he continued, could not be made by act of Parliament or by a treaty. It was made from 'inside itself'. It was made 'first of all by its language, if it has one, by its music, songs, games and customs'. Hence, while not forgetting what other countries had to offer us, 'we desire to especially emphasise what we have derived from our Gaelic ancestors – from one of the oldest civilisations in Europe, the heritage of the Os and Macs who still make up the bulk of our country'.[3]

Hyde's ancestors were neither Os nor Macs. The family had originated in Berkshire, south-east England, and had been granted land in Cork by Queen Elizabeth during the sixteenth-century plantation of Munster.[4] A junior branch of the family had produced a long line of Church of Ireland clergymen. In 1867, Hyde's father became rector of Tibohine, County Roscommon, and the family moved to nearby Frenchpark. Though Hyde was from a privileged Anglo-Irish background, as a child growing up in an Irish-speaking area, he developed a love of the native songs, stories and customs of the local people. He learned Irish by speaking to his neighbours and keeping a notebook in which he phonetically transcribed words and expressions.[5] Hyde grew into an accomplished linguist. He became fluent in a wide range of languages, including German, Hebrew, Latin, Greek and French. However, when asked by a fellow university student what his first language was, Hyde famously replied 'I dream in Irish.'[6]

In 1877, Hyde joined the Society for the Preservation of the Irish Language; in 1878, he joined the Gaelic Union; and, in 1880, aged twenty, he entered Trinity College, Dublin. In this period, he befriended the old Fenian John O'Leary, as well as W. B. Yeats and T. W. Rolleston. With the latter two in particular, Hyde shared an interest in Irish folktales, which he began to translate into English. Hyde was already prolifically writing Irish-language poems, often published in the quasi-separatist weeklies *The Shamrock* and *The Irishman*, under the pen name 'An Craoibhín Aoibhinn', originally a Jacobite phrase meaning 'the pleasant little branch'. Some contemporary commentators interpreted this nom de plume as being chosen to represent a new shoot on the old branch of the nation.[7]

In 1892, Hyde became president of the National Literary Society. His inaugural address, 'The Necessity for De-Anglicising Ireland', delivered on 25 November, argued that the serious decline of the language had left the Irish people culturally deficient and impoverished. He urged that 'every Irish-feeling Irishman, who hates the reproach of West-Britonism, should set himself to encourage the efforts which are being made to keep alive our once great national tongue. The losing of it is our greatest blow, and the sorest stroke that the rapid Anglicisation of Ireland has inflicted upon us'.[8] If this did not happen, Hyde argued that Irish people would lose forever their identity and 'we will become what, I fear, we are largely at present, a nation of imitators, the Japanese of Western Europe, lost to the power of native initiative and alive only to second-hand assimilation'.[9]

This speech was the catalyst for the establishment of the Gaelic League in July 1893 by Hyde, Eoin Mac Neill and Fr Eugene O'Growney. Hyde was the first President of an organisation that quickly became a social phenomenon. As McGarry has observed:

> It [the Gaelic League] was an immediate and runaway success. Its constitution declared that 'no matter of religious or political difference shall be admitted into the proceedings'. Its aim was the revival of the Irish language, of Irish literature, music and dances. Hyde, as he often said, was not attempting to make Irish the language of everyday speech but wanted to prevent it dying out. People of all creeds and classes joined. 'It gave Protestants,' he said, 'an opportunity to identify themselves with a great national interest.' A considerable number of unionists joined, he noted, possibly because they saw the League 'as a means of meeting their Nationalist compatriots on a neutral ground'. Branches of the League opened all over the country. Regarded as chic and fashionable, people turned to it in droves. Its success was also helped by the repugnance which had swept the country towards constitutional politics following the split in the Irish Party and Parnell's death. It was an exciting, romantic time in the League. People agitated successfully for the right to address letters and parcels in Irish. Hyde went to London and had this cleared with the Post Master General. Irish classes sprung up in every small town in the country. Feiseanna were organised to encourage, singing, dancing and Irish music. People set up Irish dramatic societies.[10]

Hyde's energetic leadership was a huge factor in the soaring growth of the Gaelic League. In 1899, Hyde claimed there were over ninety-two Gaelic League branches, ranging in membership from 50 to 400. Others claim that by 1904 the League had grown to 600 branches with a membership of over 50,000.[11] The League's mass membership and the Irish public's goodwill towards the Gaelic revival caused Hyde to lift his ambitions beyond saving the language from extinction. Hyde and the enthusiasts of the Gaelic League were now largely stimulated by the success of the Czechs in restoring their language – almost dead at the beginning of the nineteenth century – to its place as the predominantly spoken language of the Czech people by the time that century closed. In Ireland, as the century turned, Hyde won a decisive victory for the Irish language in the education curriculum. In 1899, the Palles Commission on Intermediate Education inquired into the viability of Irish as an examination subject. Two Trinity academics, John Pentland Mahaffy, a prominent classicist and future Provost of the college, and Robert Atkinson, a professor of comparative philology, maintained that Irish was a language of no intrinsic academic value and they spearheaded a campaign to have Irish excluded as a subject for the Intermediate examination. However, as Moore notes:

> They came up against a formidable opponent in Hyde who, whilst remaining courteous and dignified throughout the very public debate, dissected their arguments by producing evidence from many eminent Celtic scholars throughout Europe. Scholars from universities in Leipzig, Greifswald, Berlin, Liverpool, Copenhagen, Rennes and Oxford provided citations supporting the Irish language as well as demonstrating its measures as a language with a deep scholarly history. It was a resounding success for Hyde and the League with Irish being accepted as a subject on the curriculum, and Hyde receiving the plaudits from a public now firmly behind him.[12]

In 1900, Hyde's popularity was such that John Redmond offered him the choice of any one of sixteen safe seats in the House of Commons, but Hyde declined the offer as he did not wish to embroil himself or the League in party politics.[13] In November 1905, Hyde set out on an eight-month fundraising tour of the United States, on the Gaelic League's behalf, which was organised by John Quinn, a wealthy Irish-American lawyer, patron of the arts and subsequently one of Hyde's closest confidants. Hyde brought his message of 'a self-reliant, self-controlled, self-sufficient Ireland' to fifty-two American cities and he also addressed crowds in Harvard and Yale.[14] He had two very amicable meetings with President Theodore Roosevelt in the White House and the US President agreed to appeal to Irish-Americans to fund chairs of Irish in American universities. Hyde recorded that Roosevelt had spoken 'a great deal about Irish saga and the ancient Irish epics, and drew a most interesting comparison between them and the Norse saga. He struck me as being a scholar of the very broadest sympathies.'[15]

Hyde won widespread praise for his generosity in the immediate aftermath of the San Francisco earthquake of April 1906. This disaster occurred only shortly after Hyde had visited the city and he immediately donated the £5,000 he had collected in San Francisco to the earthquake relief fund.[16] He still managed to return to Ireland in June 1906 with 'the then phenomenal amount of £11,000 for the League' and, in Dublin, he received 'a hero's welcome with crowds thronging O'Connell Street' to pay tribute to his work.[17] Further acclaim followed that year when he was awarded the freedom of the cities of Dublin, Cork and Kilkenny. A poll in late 1906 ranked Hyde as the fourth most popular living Irishman; only the Catholic archbishops of Armagh and Dublin and the nationalist leader John Redmond ranked higher.[18]

Following the establishment of the National University of Ireland in 1908, Hyde faced stringent opposition, most notably from the Catholic bishops, to Irish becoming a compulsory matriculation subject for the new university. Hyde, however, once again proved to be a doughty campaigner and he was not afraid to use the power of public demonstration. More than 100,000 people attended a pro-Irish rally in Dublin in September 1909. The campaign for compulsory Irish for matriculation culminated in a triumph for Hyde in 1910, when the Senate of the National University of Ireland announced that Irish would be obligatory for entrance from 1913.[19]

In 1909, Hyde was appointed as the first Professor of Modern Irish at University College Dublin, a position he happily served in until his retirement in 1932. His tenure as President of the Gaelic League had been marked by his determination to pursue a policy of conciliation and to keep the League free from politics. However, this approach began to come under pressure from those who saw the League as a convenient vehicle for militant nationalism. In 1913, in an article entitled 'The Coming Revolution', Patrick Pearse directly articulated the case for physical force. Pearse wrote: 'Whenever Dr Hyde, at a meeting which I have had a chance of speaking after him has produced his dove of peace, I have always been careful to produce my sword; and to tantalise him by saying that the Gaelic League has brought into Ireland "Not Peace but a Sword".'[20]

By the time of the Gaelic League Ard Fheis in Dundalk in July 1915, the League had become heavily infiltrated by members of the IRB, who succeeded in having a series of motions passed to dilute the non-political status of the League. In protest, Hyde resigned as President of the Gaelic League and ceased to be involved in the organisation. Though he was in favour of an independent Ireland, he strongly rejected the use of physical force and he was deeply unhappy that the League had been taken over by those immersed in revolutionary politics. In the aftermath of the 1916 Rising, he kept his counsel, but he was not supportive of the rebellion, which had prominently involved many of those central to the coup against him in the Gaelic League.[21] Hyde's true feelings were on display in a letter to John Quinn on 12 October 1916, in which he wrote that the 'League had been steered on the rocks by fools' and that the general outlook in Ireland was 'as black as can be'.[22]

Both Aodh de Blácam, a journalist and propagandist who worked closely with Arthur Griffith, and W. M. Crook, a friend of Hyde from his Trinity days, claimed that the name of the political party Sinn Féin, founded in 1905, was derived directly from poetry that Hyde had penned in the 1880s and 1890s.[23] Hyde never joined the party, but culturally, economically, socially and politically he was a believer in the 'ourselves alone' philosophy and he once remarked: 'We want to go for nothing outside the four seas that can be possibly secured at home.'[24] Following Sinn Féin's triumph in the 1918 general election, winning 73 of Ireland's 105 Westminster seats, the party's elected representatives convened a separatist parliament in the Mansion House on 21 January 1919. During his tenure as President of the Gaelic League, Hyde had been careful not to express any political preference, but he now publicly declared his support for 'our Dáil Éireann'.[25] Hyde was, however, disturbed by the violence of the Anglo-Irish war. He was privately critical of the behaviour of the British authorities, but he also recognised that the IRA shared responsibility for the breakdown in law and order in the country. Though again refraining from any public comment, he strongly supported the Treaty. In December 1921, he wrote to John Quinn that 'we seem to have really hammered out a measure of real freedom . . . So far as I can see, we have got almost everything we want under the new treaty . . . I think we got the very most we could have got without war, and war is too awful to contemplate again.'[26]

Hyde abhorred the Civil War and he played no part in it. In February 1925, at a time when republicans were still boycotting the institutions of the Irish Free State, Hyde accepted a co-option to Seanad Éireann. He served for less than ten months as an independent member and conducted himself in a strictly neutral fashion. He spoke only twice in the chamber, both times on non-contentious matters.[27] Hyde lost his seat in the Seanad election in September 1925. He had been targeted in the campaign by the Catholic Truth Society, which urged voters to oppose Hyde on account of his alleged support for divorce, something he denied.[28]

In 1935, following Hyde's retirement as Chairman of the Folklore Institute of Ireland, a reception presided over by Eoin MacNeill took place in the UCD Council Chamber, Earlsfort Terrace, to honour Hyde's services to the Gaelic revival. De Valera was the keynote speaker. In lauding Hyde, he said: 'I think that no more suitable man than you was ever chosen as leader, head or guide.'[29] De Valera also told Hyde that 'the Gaels of Ireland would not be satisfied to let Dr Hyde retire without having an opportunity of expressing their respect and affection for him'.[30]

Hyde's retirement was abruptly interrupted by de Valera appointing him to the newly reconstituted Seanad in March 1938. By the time the Seanad convened for its first meeting on 27 April, Hyde had been chosen as the Fianna Fáil/Fine Gael candidate for the presidency. This inaugural meeting of the Seanad was the only sitting that Hyde attended before vacating his seat on his formal election as President of Ireland on 4 May. Hyde sat on the Government benches in the Seanad, but his independence was underlined when he voted against the Fianna Fáil nominee for the Cathaoirleach of the Seanad, Seán Gibbons.[31]

The choice of Hyde as President, with his stellar, non-partisan career, was a strong indicator of the intended nature of the office, a point underlined by John Cudahy in his diplomatic reports back to Washington. Cudahy wrote that Hyde's candidacy reflected the actual conception of the office held by the framers of the new Irish Constitution as 'one of permanence, a symbol of Ireland, one of dignity and representation far removed from the tumult and hurly-burly of political strife'.[32]

Protocols and Precedence

Duffy has argued that de Valera visualised the presidency in terms of 'a kind of home-grown king' and certainly at Hyde's inauguration the Taoiseach's comments about 'our rightful princes' and 'the closing of the breach that has existed since the undoing of our nation at Kinsale' had echoes of an indigenous Gaelic restoration.[33] De Valera would subsequently note that he attached significant political importance to the office of President because it was both 'the symbol of the independence we have achieved' and 'the most obvious symbol of our status as a sovereign state'.[34] For de Valera, it was therefore a matter of considerable political priority that Hyde was treated with respect and the deference due to a head of state. The individual he charged with the day-to-day responsibilities of this task was Michael McDunphy. Keogh has accurately observed of this appointment that 'de Valera demonstrated the importance of the office of President by transferring one of the most senior members of his own department, Michael McDunphy, to serve as Secretary to the new President and run his office at Áras an Uachtaráin'.[35]

In the office's formative days, McDunphy and de Valera operated at an official and political level a zero-tolerance approach to those who did not treat the office of President with respect or give it the precedence the Constitution attached to it. McDunphy kept detailed files cataloguing individuals who made 'offensive' and 'disrespectful' references to the President and these slights were invariably followed up.[36] For example, in April 1939, McDunphy noted approvingly that he had taken issue with the editor of *Dublin Opinion* over an inappropriate reference to the President, only to find that the Taoiseach had beaten him to the punch. McDunphy noted: 'In conversation today with Mr P. Montford, who is associated with *Dublin Opinion*, I learned that the Taoiseach had already spoken to him in regard to the importance of avoiding any disrespectful references to the head of state. This conversation had taken place in January 1939. Mr de Valera had made it clear that his sole concern was for the head of state, who was above party politics and should be above controversy.'[37]

In Fianna Fáil, in particular, an intensely negative attitude had quickly developed towards those who would say anything even mildly disparaging about the President. An *Irish Press* journalist, Anna Kelly, was reprimanded, after complaints from Fianna Fáil members, for writing a light-hearted account of one of Hyde's first garden parties in Áras an Uachtaráin, in which she was reputed to have compared the President's moustache with 'certain inhabitants of the next door zoo'.[38]

In October 1939, Fianna Fáil councillors staged a walkout from Dún Laoghaire Corporation when an independent councillor, William Rollins, referred to Hyde as 'an old cod who resided in the Phoenix Park and drew a salary of £15,000 a year while people in Dublin were starving'.[39] McDunphy, meanwhile, in his file in the Áras, noted of Councillor Rollins that 'it is obvious that this man is of a type who should not be included in the guest list for any presidential social function'.[40]

It would be inaccurate to leave the impression that McDunphy's sole modus operandi was to blacklist anyone who criticised the presidency. McDunphy brought his vast experience as a senior civil servant to the establishment of the office. In many ways, he was ideally suited to the job. As an Assistant Secretary in the Department of the President of the Executive Council, one of McDunphy's responsibilities had been to be the liaison official with the office of Governor-General.[41] This gave him immense experience in the area of protocol and the voluminous collection of files from the office of President are an extraordinary testament to McDunphy's workload in drawing up the precedents and ground rules designed to uphold the dignity of the President's office. For example, McDunphy, unhappy that President Hyde was not received with sufficient standing at the All-Ireland Football Final in 1938, drew up a detailed set of protocols which, by and large, still apply today, to underline the President's status upon visiting Croke Park. McDunphy wrote:

> Arrangements should be made in future to ensure that the President's arrival at such events will be marked in a more fitting manner. He should be conducted to his seat in such a way that: 1. His arrival is visible to the spectators . . . 2. An appropriate announcement should be made over the loud speakers in Irish and in English so that the people are aware of his arrival. 3. The National Anthem should be played as soon as he appears. 4. In addition, a separate enclosure should be provided for the President where he may be free from troublesome attention.[42]

In an explanatory note of his own duties as Secretary to the office of President, McDunphy noted that in order to establish the decorum of the office in its formative years, he essentially became a gatekeeper for the President. He wrote:

> Many hoped and still hope to use the President for personal or party ends, including personal friends, political enthusiasts, cranks and devotees of various types. Secretary has to deal firmly but courteously with these . . . Secretary receives all visitors to the President and arranges their appointments, where desirable. He decides in all cases whether a person should or should not be received, and how.[43]

McDunphy went on to note that the 'Secretary must have an exact and detailed knowledge of the Constitution and of constitutional procedure. Latter in fact must be created by him. He must have judgement and political acumen and be familiar with diplomatic procedure, privilege and precedence.'[44]

McDunphy's previous experience would have stood him in good stead. As well as being a qualified lawyer, in his previous role as Assistant Secretary in the Department of the President of the Executive Council, he had been closely associated with the operation of the 1922 Constitution and with the framing of Bunreacht na hÉireann.[45]

Indeed, McDunphy was one of a small group of four key civil servants, hand-picked by de Valera, to work on the draft of the 1937 Constitution.[46] He, therefore, would have had a keen understanding of de Valera's thinking in creating the office and a unique insight into how it was intended the office should develop.

As Secretary to the office of President, McDunphy's commitment day in, day out to establishing defined structures, his adherence to protocol, his fastidiousness, his experience of government and his understanding of ceremonial matters, combined with Hyde's judgement and genial nature, built a sense of dignity around the new office and, more importantly, kept it largely removed from controversy. This work, which the files of the office of President show was often mundane, nonetheless was politically important in building credibility and respect for the office across the political spectrum, which had been distinctly lacking in relation to the office of Governor-General.

McDunphy's appointment was an astute political decision. *The Irish Times* welcomed the selection of 'an able, courteous and efficient civil servant' and, allied to the choice of Hyde, the esteem with which McDunphy was held helped to alleviate suspicions of the office of President.[47] McDunphy's background was one of nationalism and public service. He had entered the Department of Agriculture in 1911 as a Second Division Clerk, but was dismissed from duty for refusing to take the Oath of Allegiance in October 1918.[48] During the War of Independence, he had served in the Dublin Brigade of the IRA, but was more actively engaged as a prominent civil servant of the First Dáil.[49]

Prior to his appointment as Secretary to the office of President, McDunphy had been Assistant Secretary to successive Governments from the setting up of the Provisional Government in January 1922.[50] Significantly, he had worked closely with W. T. Cosgrave during the latter's period as President of the Executive Council and there was an enduring respect between both men. As Head of Government, Cosgrave had once even decisively intervened in McDunphy's favour against his own Minister for Finance in a dispute about McDunphy's salary.[51] McDunphy's ongoing good relations with Cosgrave played an important role in establishing Fine Gael's trust in the office of President, especially as Cosgrave would have intuitively understood that McDunphy would never consent to be a dictator's sidekick.

For de Valera, McDunphy's appointment was a convenient solution to a simmering staffing problem in his own department. Making McDunphy Secretary to the office of President allowed him to promote a capable official who had been severely disappointed in the past. In 1932 and 1937, McDunphy had seen first Seán Moynihan and then Maurice Moynihan promoted over his head to fill the vacant position of Secretary to the Government.[52] McDunphy's relationship with Maurice Moynihan was prickly, but he remained on good terms with de Valera. McDunphy and de Valera had worked very closely together during the drafting of the Constitution and subsequently, after McDunphy had moved to the Áras, their dealings with each other appear to have been constructive and warm. The Taoiseach insisted on maintaining a direct line of communication with McDunphy in his new role. He was receptive to hearing McDunphy's views, often on matters that went beyond McDunphy's area of responsibility, including wider issues concerning neutrality.[53] De Valera was also usually solicitous in acting on McDunphy's requests pertaining to the smooth running of the office of President, in one instance even accepting McDunphy's analysis over the formal views of the 1940 Constitution Review Committee.[54]

Further evidence of the mutual respect between de Valera and McDunphy was that when McDunphy was moving to the Áras, the Taoiseach sensitively recognised McDunphy's understandable concerns about his status. De Valera pointed out to McDunphy that his new role as Secretary to the office of President was akin to being a Departmental Head, a position that McDunphy had been disappointed not to achieve on the two occasions referenced earlier. McDunphy subsequently noted that

> when the writer of this memorandum, who has held that post since its creation in December 1937, was selected by the Government for appointment, he was informed by the then Taoiseach that, while his office would not, of course, be a Department of State within the meaning of the Ministers and Secretaries Acts, he would, for all purposes, rank as a Secretary of a Department, in no way responsible or subordinate to the Secretary of the Department of the Taoiseach, or any other

> department, and that in the discharge of his duties he would be responsible directly to the President, subject only to a general definition of his duties by the Government.[55]

This memo goes to the kernel of the complex set of relationships that did much to shape the development of the office of President. It also sheds light on the dynamic that saw the office of President carve out a more independent status than may originally have been envisaged within the machinery of government. This would, however, ultimately reflect positively on the office's public standing.

In November 1939, an extraordinary row developed between McDunphy and Moynihan over a relatively minor procedural matter concerning the time limit for the President's signature of Bills under Article 25.2.1 of the Constitution. Both McDunphy and Moynihan were strong-willed and shared a tendency towards truculence. When Moynihan arbitrarily dismissed McDunphy's concerns, McDunphy, believing that the office of President was not being taken seriously, sought to bring the Taoiseach into the fray. He wrote to Moynihan:

> As Secretary to the President I regard it as my duty, independent of any departmental viewpoint, to bring to the notice of the Taoiseach any doubt or difficulty, actual or potential, whether in law or in practice, which in my considered opinion has any bearing on the constitutional functions of the head of the state. From your letter under reply it is not clear that the present question has in fact been before the Taoiseach, but rather that a decision has been taken departmentally to dismiss it without consideration.[56]

Moynihan's reply was far from diplomatic and clearly not designed to soothe McDunphy's sensitivities. On 15 December, Moynihan wrote, 'the general tone and attitude adopted in your official minute of the 21 ultimo are unwarranted and in certain respects not far short of being offensive. Beyond that, I do not propose to discuss the matter.'[57]

When McDunphy took the opportunity to raise his concerns about the interpretation of Article 25.2.1 with the Taoiseach when de Valera called to the Áras to undertake his monthly briefing of the

President, this provoked another angry missive from Moynihan. On 23 December, he wrote:

> I note your statement that you availed of the Taoiseach's presence at Áras an Uachtaráin on the 19 instant to discuss this matter with him. I assume that the discussion was initiated by you, and, on that assumption, I am obliged to point out that the submission of such a question to the Taoiseach is a matter for this department. It should not have been raised by you in conversation with the Taoiseach and your action in raising it on the occasion of a visit by him to the President was grossly incorrect.[58]

Moynihan's next move was to complain to de Valera. Clearly wishing to exercise control over the office of President, and especially McDunphy, Moynihan sought to cut off McDunphy's direct access to the Taoiseach. Moynihan wanted de Valera to issue an instruction that the secretariat in the Áras should route all their communications with the Taoiseach's department through himself. It is significant that de Valera refused to comply with this request, which would have severely restrained the independence of the office of President. Letting Moynihan down lightly, de Valera assured him that he would refer any communications from McDunphy to the Secretary to the Government. However, he was not prepared to put in place a formal rule in this regard. Moynihan noted on 10 January 1940 that 'he [the Taoiseach] feels that the circumstances may arise in which direct communication by the Secretary to the President to himself may be unavoidable'.[59]

In conversation with McDunphy, de Valera subsequently made it clear to the Secretary to the President that he had the Taoiseach's authorisation to raise any official matter he wished with him. McDunphy noted: 'In the course of a conversation which I had with the Taoiseach today on the occasion of his visit to enquire after the President's health we touched upon a number of semi political matters as well as official matters. Before referring to the official matters I asked him whether he had any objection to my speaking to him in person on such subjects. He replied that if he listened to me, that in itself constituted full authority.'[60]

On another occasion, when Moynihan learned that McDunphy and de Valera had a discussion arising from the President's decision to refer a Bill to the Supreme Court, this provoked another acrimonious exchange between the two senior civil servants. McDunphy, who by this stage was minuting every conversation he had with Moynihan, indicating how seriously he viewed the deterioration in their relationship, noted:

> The Secretary to the Government informed me on the telephone . . . that he had been informed by the Taoiseach that I had spoken to him at his home the previous evening. I said that was correct. He informed me that the Taoiseach wished him to inform me that he was adopting the view that I had put forward, and that an official communication to that effect would be sent me in due course. He then said words to the following effect – 'By the way, I am surprised at your speaking to the Taoiseach directly in this manner in view of our recent conversation.' I replied, speaking slowly, in a manner which left no doubt as to my attitude, 'I am not going to discuss that matter with you. It is not a matter in which you have any jurisdiction.'[61]

In regard to Moynihan's objections to the Secretary to the office of President having the right to directly consult with the Taoiseach, McDunphy noted 'the immoderate language in which the Secretary to the Government had addressed himself to me on the subject, language which seems to suggest that, through some peculiar process of reasoning, he is under the impression that the Secretary to the President is a subordinate officer of his Department.'[62] McDunphy's refusal to bow to this impression and the vigorous manner in which he fought his corner was an important marker in establishing the actual independence of the office of President. The crux in the relationship between the Taoiseach's department and the office of President was the bad blood between McDunphy and Moynihan. The mutual respect between de Valera and McDunphy meant that the office of President was cooperative with the Government and always respectful of the Taoiseach's position. It is very unlikely that Hyde would have tolerated any alternative. However, the difficulties between McDunphy and

Moynihan meant that administratively the office of President sought, as much as possible, to paddle its own canoe. McDunphy's sensitivity about his status, combined with an ongoing turf war with Moynihan, saw the office of President consistently seek to underpin its independence in its earliest years. The extent with which this took root can be seen from the fact that, in the presidency's early years, it would become accepted that it was against the rules of parliamentary debate to comment favourably or unfavourably on the President's conduct.[63] Yet had a less single-minded Secretary to the office of President consented to Moynihan's efforts to make the office of President an adjunct of the Department of the Taoiseach, this would surely have had a debilitating impact on the presidency. It would have resulted in the office being seen as somewhat less than independent and potentially have had a polarising effect on the public's perception of the office.

McDunphy deserves credit for his resilience in upholding his office's independence, but de Valera's unwillingness to give succour to Moynihan's empire-building tendencies was also clearly significant. Though in his battles with Moynihan in regard to the office of President, McDunphy was arguably more sinned against than sinning, his zeal in defending and seeking to build up credibility for the office of President was a cause of regular frustration for his colleagues.

McDunphy had taken umbrage in March 1939 when a statement about the President inviting school children to the Áras, as part of an effort to promote the Irish language, had not topped the news headlines on the state broadcasting service.[64] This caused McDunphy to write in complaint to Moynihan. The Secretary to the President was critical of the fact that 'a statement regarding the President was given after a resumé of a speech by the Minister for Industry and Commerce on commercial development' and insisted that the matter be raised with the Director of Radio Éireann.[65] McDunphy appeared to believe that any broadcast from the President should automatically lead the news, irrespective of its news value. This was an argument that Thomas Kiernan, the Director of Radio Éireann, angrily dismissed in a letter to Moynihan on 15 April 1939, in which he described McDunphy as 'very unhelpful'.[66] In order to buttress his case, McDunphy prevailed upon a reluctant Joseph Walshe, Secretary to the Department of External Affairs, to ascertain from Irish diplomatic staff abroad what the position was in regard to the primacy of broadcasts from heads of state in other countries.[67] The results were at best a mixed bag in terms of McDunphy's purposes, but this did not stop him from subsequently insisting later in 1939 that External Affairs conduct research into the position and duties of aides-de-camp in the residences of other international Heads of States.[68]

McDunphy was keen to ensure that the protocol surrounding the President of Ireland matched best international standards, but his penchant for minutiae could grate with colleagues, especially the under-resourced officials working in the Irish diplomatic service abroad. Michael MacWhite, the Minister Plenipotentiary in the Irish legation in Rome, wrote to Frederick Boland, Assistant Secretary in the Department of External Affairs, scathingly criticising the fact that 'it would appear as if the Áras an Uachtaráin is rapidly outdistancing other government departments in the incubation of red tape. If our prehistoric ancestors had devoted their time to the discovery of precedents for their guidance I am afraid our generation would still be wielding Palaeolithic instruments instead of fountain pens.'[69]

The British Connection

McDunphy's greatest concern in upholding the precedence of the presidency was in countering any suggestion that the President of Ireland was inferior to or connected in any way to the British sovereign. Notwithstanding his background in the independence movement, the confusion sown by the External Relations Act, and the general fixation in Irish politics in the late 1930s and 1940s with the British connection, McDunphy's gusto for this task could, at times, border on the fanatical.

In 1942, the High Court ruled in favour of the Government in a case dealing with a prerogative formerly exercised by the King of England to dispose of monies left to charity when a trustee was not appointed. McDunphy approvingly noted:

> Although it has always been clear to impartial jurists that the President of Ireland, whose office was created by Article 12 of the Constitution of 1937, was the head of a sovereign,

> independent state, as defined by Article 5, there has been a constant endeavour on the part of certain pro-British partisans to create the impression that the President is merely a sort of successor to the former Governor-General as representing the King of England in Ireland. In the course of a case before the Irish High Court on 23 April 1942, the Attorney General stated that 'The President was the creation of the new Constitution, and the President was not in any sense the successor of the King of England.'[70]

On the same file, McDunphy would note a few months later, with a clear sense of annoyance, that 'there apparently exists a belief, based probably on wishful thinking, that the office of President is in some way the continuation of [the] Governor General and of [the] Lord Lieutenant, and that the President is in a sense a representative of the King of England. This of course is quite incorrect.'[71] The complexities of the External Relations Act undoubtedly contributed to an initial, popular misconception that the office of President of Ireland was in some way connected to the British Crown. In one of his first newspaper interviews as President, Hyde was asked by a journalist from the *Sunday Chronicle* what relation his office 'bears to the King of England'. The President assured his questioner that there was 'absolutely none'.[72]

There had been considerable apprehension in Government circles about what might transpire at the special religious service in St Patrick's Cathedral that Hyde attended on the morning of his inauguration. Specifically, there was a concern that the British national anthem might be played, as it was known to feature at some social and even religious functions involving the Church of Ireland at this time.[73] McDunphy was determined that the presidency would not be associated in any way in the public mind with Britain. He contacted the Dean of St Patrick's, Rev. David Wilson, about the service arrangements and made it 'abundantly clear' that the British National Anthem should not be aired.[74] This instruction was observed and McDunphy noted that the Dean of St Patrick's had been 'very courteous and showed a complete appreciation of national susceptibilities in the matter'.[75]

The outbreak of the Second World War resulted in the appointment on 3 October 1939 of a 'British Representative to Ireland' for the first time since independence. This was a diplomatic posting created 'in view of [the] special war problems' on the initiative of Chamberlain's Government, but it served to accentuate sensitivities in official Irish circles that the office of President might be perceived as being subordinate or linked to the British Crown. De Valera and Hyde were determined to uphold the presidency as a symbol of Irish independence. From the moment Sir John Maffey set foot in Ireland, there was a determined effort made to counter any impression that the British Representative might outrank the President in precedence.

Maffey first came to Áras an Uachtaráin in October 1939 to pay his respects to Hyde. Prior to his meeting with Hyde, Maffey was given an extraordinary warning by McDunphy, which a senior civil servant would hardly have given without political cover and presumably the approval of both the President and the Taoiseach. Further evidence that McDunphy was acting on orders can be gauged from the fact that he made a detailed report of this exchange for de Valera's attention. McDunphy wrote:

> In conversation with Sir John and afterwards with his Secretary, I said that I thought it well to mention that owing to the peculiar historic relations between Ireland and England it was inevitable that for some considerable time the British Representative, whoever he would be, would become the focal point of attention of people who were not willing to accept the new status of Ireland and would be anxious to regard the British Representative as a sort of successor to the Lord Lieutenant and that in fact an attempt would be made to make him the centre of a pro-British, anti-Irish party in Ireland. I said that if this were allowed to develop it would operate fatally against the success of the mission of any British diplomat who would permit it to occur.[76]

While a subsequent chapter will examine the interaction between the office of President and Maffey in terms of its impact on the policy of neutrality, it is important at this point to look at the dogged manner in which the office of President, strongly supported by the Taoiseach, was determined to guard the standing of the presidency against any perception that Hyde's office was of lesser status than that of the British Representative. In a fledgling independent state, this was politically important to underline sovereignty and to show that the old colonial masters no longer ruled the roost.

McDunphy was fervent in his commitment to not allowing the presence of a British Representative in Ireland in any way to upstage the President. He kept an especially watchful eye on the activities of Lady Maffey, Sir John's wife, and her increasing prominence in Irish society.[77] According to McDunphy, the Government took 'a serious view' of Lady Maffey's conduct in adopting 'the role which the anti-Irish element here wishes to give her, that is as a sort of successor to the Lady Lieutenant of Ireland, a position which is completely incompatible with the present status of the country'.[78] What McDunphy termed the outstanding example of 'objectionable activity' on Lady Maffey's part occurred in April 1940, in connection with a proposed visit of President Hyde to Punchestown Races.[79] This case shows the importance that the office of President would attach to the politics of protocol in its formative years. It also highlights that the Government were prepared to row in behind the presidency and that, when it came to upholding Hyde's precedence, this was not a trifling matter.

McDunphy noted his belief that the members of Punchestown Committee were 'indisputably anti-national' and, thus, was immediately suspicious of the committee's attempts to induce the President to attend the races as a private citizen.[80] McDunphy reported that 'every obstacle is being placed in the way of his [President Hyde] attending officially as head of state'.[81] On further investigation, McDunphy discovered that Lady Maffey was to be given a place of first prominence at the race meeting and was, in fact, to be treated as hostess of the day.[82] This caused consternation in the Government, with de Valera also taking very seriously the reluctance of the Punchestown Committee to fly the national flag, as was the proper protocol, to coincide with the President's appearance.[83] McDunphy held further consultations with two other cabinet ministers, Gerry Boland and P. J. Ruttledge, the latter also being a member of the Irish Turf Club, before confronting the Chairman of the Punchestown Race Committee. McDunphy stressed the Government's anger and made it clear that a situation would not be allowed to arise where the wife of the British Representative would take precedence over the President.[84] Faced with this official broadside, the Punchestown Committee backed down and it was agreed that Hyde would attend the meeting and that full presidential protocol would be observed. Ultimately, however, Hyde did not attend the event because he suffered a stroke just days before the race meeting.

Hyde's subsequent physical incapacity limited his public appearances and this only served to increase unease about Lady Maffey's prominence in Irish society. McDunphy clearly believed that Lady Maffey's presence as the official guest at numerous functions and events was undermining or usurping the President's role. This was not a lone view and both the Taoiseach and Joseph Walshe, the Secretary of the Department of External Affairs, had raised this issue with John Maffey. In June 1942, McDunphy noted with a sense of triumph that Lady Maffey's activities had been curtailed and that Walshe had 'spoken to Sir John Maffey on a number of occasions' and McDunphy understood that 'a promise was given that there would be an improvement'.[85] Yet, later that month, after a public notice appeared in *The Irish Times* that Lady Maffey would perform the opening of an Easter fete in Grangegorman, following communication between the Áras and External Affairs, McDunphy noted that this would 'form the subject of further representations' from the Department of External Affairs to the British Representative.[86]

The office of President's susceptibilities to any association with Britain was also evident in Hyde's attitude to the artworks on display in Áras an Uachtaráin, most of which were remnants from a time when the occupant of the house was a British viceroy. In December 1938, McDunphy noted that 'the majority of the pictures in the portion of President's house accessible to the public consist of portraits of members of British Royal families and of Lord Lieutenants'.[87]

On 5 December, Hyde led George Furlong, Director of the National Gallery, and his assistant, Brinsley MacNamara, on an inspection of the paintings in the Áras. At the President's request, the officials from the National Gallery were charged with making a valuation of the pictures in the Áras and drawing up recommendations for their replacement; however, Furlong cautioned that 'there were considerable doubts as to the powers of the National Gallery to loan pictures to any Government Department or service'.[88] The reluctance of the National Gallery to loan paintings of specifically Irish themes to the President and the unwillingness of Office of Public Works to remove portraits without having anything to replace them with meant that, to Hyde's frustration, there was a considerable delay in replacing the imperial art.

In April 1939, McDunphy complained to Moynihan that the portraits of British sovereigns and viceroys were 'frequently the subject of adverse comment by visitors, particularly Irish Americans, and sometimes of equally embarrassing approval by persons of a different outlook. From the beginning, I have regarded them as misfits, which should be removed as soon as suitable replacements could be arranged'.[89] The delay in replacing the portraits was further exacerbated by a proposal from the poet Rupert Strong that the paintings in the Áras be 'offered' to the British National Gallery 'in exchange for the Lane Pictures'.[90] Hyde, McDunphy and Moynihan were in agreement that this proposal was 'ludicrous' – however, it contributed to ongoing delay. By February 1942, Hyde's patience had worn thin and McDunphy, with President Hyde's full approval, used the course of the war to give impetus to the de-anglicising of art in Áras an Uachtaráin. In one especially colourful memo, McDunphy argued:

> Certain recent developments have led me to the conclusion that the retention on the walls of the Áras of pictures of former English monarchs and Lord Lieutenants and other British functionaries is regarded in some quarters as an expression of attachment on the part of the President to the British Crown, and as a negation to some extent of the policy of strict neutrality adopted by the nation in the present European war.[91]

McDunphy went on to state: 'I have discussed the matter with the President, and he agrees that the replacement of these pictures is long overdue, and that it should be commenced as soon as possible, proceeding gradually until the process is complete. Both from the political and artistic point of view the first step should be the removal of the portrait of Lord Chesterfield which hangs in the hall.'[92]

In September 1942, McDunphy contentedly noted that 'all the portraits of British Sovereigns and Viceroys have now been removed from the walls of the Áras and have been set aside'.[93] While Hyde and McDunphy's purging of imperial art from the Viceregal Lodge might seem churlish in today's climate, it must be remembered that, in its time, it was in no way a unique occurrence in the context of a new state still attempting to stake out its separatist origins. Indeed, the low-key manner in which Hyde insisted this task should be conducted had a quiet dignity far removed from the unceremonious dumping of Queen Victoria's portrait outside the Mansion House in 1939 by the new Lord Mayor, Kathleen Clarke, or Alfred O'Rahilly's boasting in 1934, as President of University College Cork, that he had decided to 'erase the vestiges of British sovereignty' from the campus when he had Queen Victoria's statue removed.[94] Furthermore and positively, Hyde's perseverance saw Áras an Uachtaráin emerge as a significant public depository for Irish art. In response to Hyde's patient promptings, the National Library eventually agreed to loan some valuable Irish landscape paintings to the Áras permanently and, during the remainder of his tenure, Hyde established 'a collection of Irish historical pictures' in the President's house by encouraging emerging Irish artists to donate such works.[95]

At times, the office of President could take its concerns about the British connection to extremes. There are few extenuating circumstances for McDunphy's performance in relation to a wedding he and Hyde's sister, Annette Kane, were invited to in Lucan House in early 1942. The bride was Molly O'Connor from Lucan and the groom was Luke Teeling, an RAF flight lieutenant. Many of the groom's guests were colleagues of his in the British military, which worried McDunphy. He wrote:

> I was concerned to ensure that no attempt would be made by these officers to do what had been done recently on a number of festive occasions, viz. to avail of the opportunity to stage a pro-belligerent demonstration either by toasting the King of England and/or the singing of the British national anthem. If such a thing were to happen at the wedding reception I, as Secretary to the President, could not possibly honour such a toast or anthem and would leave immediately.[96]

McDunphy, though he had been invited to the wedding in a private capacity, rather pompously decided to contact the bride and told her that any pro-British display would not be acceptable. The bride told McDunphy such a display would not be in accordance with her own views and she undertook to talk to her fiancé and his best man, Edward Chichester, the Marquess of Donegal, to ensure that there would be no potential snub to the presidency. After the wedding, which passed without any incident, McDunphy recorded: 'Whether there was or was not any original intention to demonstrate, the indication to so many people from the Secretary to the President that such an action was not to be tolerated, was of itself a useful indication of the state viewpoint.'[97]

McDunphy's action, which in many ways was inappropriate, particularly as the wedding was not a public event and also given that the President himself was not going to be present, is, however, illustrative of the lengths to which he was prepared to go to defend the primacy of the presidency. McDunphy's intolerance, even at a private wedding, of a toast to the King (rather than to the President) and his belief that the singing of 'God Save the King' might convey the impression that the British monarch remained the head of state shows a compulsion to ensure that the President of Ireland would be universally recognised as Ireland's first citizen. McDunphy's action also underlines a then common fixation with the British connection (and a tendency to define Irish sovereignty by being not pro-British), while his very use of the phrase 'pro-belligerent' highlights a readiness to take advantage of the wartime situation to justify a high-handed approach to uphold the President's precedence.

At the end of 1942, the war was also used as a convenient excuse to stop the British Representative getting literally too close to the President. Maffey had wanted to move his official residence in Dublin from Dundrum to the Phoenix Park and he wanted to acquire the tenancy of a building that was formerly part of the presidential grounds.[98] McDunphy was adamant that this should not happen and he was strongly supported in this view by the Government. McDunphy wrote, on 15 December 1942:

> I think it is very undesirable that in the present circumstances any branch of the Diplomatic Corps, particularly one

> representing a belligerent state, should be housed in what is in essence an annexe of the presidential estate. The fact that the President's house was formerly the residence of the British Viceroy, and late of the Governors-General, both of whom represented the British King, renders it undesirable that any position should develop in which it might appear to the uninformed that this position still obtains.[99]

Though McDunphy suggests that the war – and the need to maintain the appearance of neutrality – was the main reason for his objection to Maffey taking up a residence in the Phoenix Park, this is undermined by McDunphy's own admission in the same memo that 'the President's near neighbours in the Park, the Nuncio and the American Minister, make occasional calls in an informal manner because of their personal friendship with the President'.[100]

The fact that David Gray, the American Minister, who lived across the road in the Phoenix Park, could drop into the Áras as he pleased, although the United States had entered the war a year previously in December 1941, suggests that McDunphy was, in fact, less concerned with perceptions of neutrality and more concerned with blocking the British. McDunphy's reasoning for this was the by now familiar theme of ensuring that the British connection did not impinge in any way on the presidency. McDunphy noted: 'There are many people in this country who pretend to believe that the President is merely a successor in the post of Governor-General and anything which would help to foster that view must be avoided. A clear break away from that position is essential. Apart from the actual proximity of the residencies, this would lead in time to personal contacts which might be interpreted as a form of British influence on the President.'[101]

The sensitivity that the President might be seen as an underling of the British Representative was not just a foible of McDunphy's. It was clearly a concern that permeated through the office of President. In 1944, Hyde's aide-de-camp, Captain Thomas Manning, wrote a memo complaining that the British Representative had sought to lead the procession of official mourners following the funeral of Sir John Lumsden, the founder of the St John Ambulance Brigade of Ireland, at Christ Church. Manning noted:

> I noticed Sir John Maffey's car on the off-side of the road facing the same direction as the cortege, Sir John Maffey seated in the back. As the cortege moved off his chauffeur pulled across the road with the intention of getting in front of the President's car, but a member of the Garda[í] stepped forward and stopped him, signalling to the President's driver to pass Sir John's car on the outside, which he did, thence getting into the original position in the rear of the chief mourners.[102]

Making it clear that he viewed this incident as more than a mere accident, but rather as a slight against the President's precedence, Manning pointed out that a similar event had occurred at the funeral of Professor William Thrift at Trinity College and that

> while waiting for the remains in the quadrangle near the College Chapel an attendant approached the President's car and informed me that our position in the funeral cortege was in the rear of the British Representative's car. I informed him that as I was the President's representative I was taking precedence over all the Diplomatic Corps, and that the President's car would follow the chief mourners. I instructed our chauffeur to this effect.[103]

Manning's report was sent to the Department of the Taoiseach for further attention. Though it is unclear whether it prompted follow-up action, the report does serve to highlight the determination of the office of President at every level to defend vigorously the President's precedence as well as a susceptibility to any British encroachments in this area.

The President versus *The Irish Times*

A determination to uphold the President's status, combined with a resolve to counter an implication that the President was of an inferior rank to British royalty, is central to understanding the prolonged campaign the office of President waged against *The Irish Times*.

On 24 September 1938, McDunphy contacted Moynihan asking him to bring to the Taoiseach's attention his specific concerns regarding a social diary in *The Irish Times*. McDunphy wrote:

> *The Irish Times* has a column entitled 'Court and Personal' surrounded by the British Royal Arms, in which social notes are published each day. It is the invariable practice of that paper when publishing news about the King in this column to give it precedence over any reference to the President. This of course is contrary to the spirit of Section 1 of Article 12 of the Constitution, which provides that the President shall take precedence over all other persons in the state. At the moment I do not think it is worthwhile taking any action in the matter but I think it is no harm that the Taoiseach should be aware of the position.[104]

On 17 October, McDunphy followed up on the above correspondence with a further complaint about the 'Court and Personal Column'. McDunphy noted that in the listing of social engagements, which invariably was led by the British King's itinerary, reference to the President was 'subordinated to one about the Crown Prince of Denmark. It is obviously the policy of the paper to treat the head of state as somebody inferior to anybody connected with Royalty of whatever country.'[105]

On 28 October, Moynihan telephoned McDunphy on de Valera's behalf. Moynihan said that the Taoiseach had asked him to pass on to McDunphy that the Taoiseach 'would take the earliest opportunity of setting right the matter' with *The Irish Times*.[106] However, de Valera also intimated that he would proceed cautiously. The Taoiseach was clearly intent on raising the matter with *The Irish Times*, but he may have considered that a direct intervention would be perceived to be somewhat immoderate. Moynihan noted in the file he kept on this issue that 'in the event of his [the Taoiseach] seeing Mr Smyllie [Editor] of *The Irish Times* in regard to any other matter, the Taoiseach wishes that this file be brought to his notice'.[107]

Moynihan's file suggests that de Valera did, in fact, actually meet Smyllie in late October 1938 and *The Irish Times*, for a brief period, changed tack, with the 'Court and Personal Column' giving precedence to the President in its listing of social engagements, but this did not last.[108] By 26 March 1939, McDunphy, in correspondence with Moynihan, wrote:

> You will observe that the objectionable practice adopted by *The Irish Times* of subordinating information regarding the President to news regarding the King or other members of the royal family continues. I feel we cannot continue to permit this . . . The whole matter is stamped with the outlook that the President is an inferior personage vis-à-vis not only the King but members of the royal family, and this of course should not be officially connived at.[109]

In July 1939, de Valera sent his trusted secretary, Kathleen O'Connell, to see Bert Smyllie. Moynihan noted that the Taoiseach had said that 'the best course would be to ask her [O'Connell] to mention the matter to Mr Smyllie. In the Taoiseach's view the best solution to the difficulty would be to remove the items relating to the President from the 'Court and Personal Column' and to publish them in a separate column.'[110] O'Connell's intervention also had little impact, but McDunphy clearly saw an opportunity in the outbreak of the Second World War to put *The Irish Times* in its place. In September 1939, McDunphy wrote to Moynihan, for the Taoiseach's attention, regarding *The Irish Times*' continued subordination of the President's status, pointing out that 'in normal circumstances this is bad enough, but under present conditions when the States of which the British King is Head, are at war with a country with which this state is at peace, I would suggest that the matter is sufficiently serious'.[111]

As if to underpin the gravity of his argument, McDunphy said that the use of the Royal Coat of Arms in a newspaper published in the capital of a neutral state was improper and 'a source of offence to the people of Ireland'.[112] McDunphy also pointed out that the practice of *The Irish Times* was growing more objectionable and that on a number of occasions information concerning the President's activities was given lesser prominence than that of ministers of the Northern Ireland Government and the Governor of Northern Ireland.[113] McDunphy's strident tone implies that he had at least the President's tacit support in persisting on the matter and it is unlikely that a senior civil servant like McDunphy would have adopted such an insistent tone without the support of his political master. McDunphy's correspondence elicited a favourable response from de Valera on 8 December, in which the Taoiseach again suggested that *The Irish Times* should be encouraged to print details regarding the President's itinerary in a separate column while, at the same time, authorising McDunphy to consult with the editor of *The Irish Times* to try to come to such an arrangement.[114]

A meeting took place later that month and McDunphy seemed to have reached agreement with the newspaper. On 19 December 1939, McDunphy reported to the Taoiseach that he had now arranged with *The Irish Times* that any information about 'the President published in that paper shall not appear in the column "Court and Personal"'.[115] At this point, it looked like the matter had been amicably resolved and that *The Irish Times* would be mindful of any perceived slight to the President's precedence in the future, but this is not what transpired. By February 1940, the issue had flared up again. McDunphy wrote to de Valera that 'after a period of two months in which *The Irish Times* honoured the arrangement referred to in my note of 19 December last, they again today reverted to their objectionable practice of including a news item regarding the President in the column "Court and Personal" in a position subordinate to an item regarding the King of England.'[116]

McDunphy embellished his chagrin at *The Irish Times*' refusal to recognise the President's precedence with concerns regarding the neutrality of the state. He stated: 'The personal attachment of the proprietors of *The Irish Times* to the British Royal family, and matters imperial generally, projects itself at times into the columns of the newspaper in a way which is entirely out of keeping with its position as an Irish newspaper. This trait is particularly objectionable at a time like this when the country is neutral and Great Britain is one of the belligerent countries.'[117] McDunphy's pointed correspondence again had an impact. De Valera handed the matter over to Frank Aiken, the Minister for Coordination of Defensive Measures, who was the minister responsible for wartime censorship. According to McDunphy's records, Aiken hosted a meeting in Government Buildings on 6 August 1940 attended by the Controller of Censorship, Joseph Connolly; Joseph Walshe, the Secretary of the Department of External Affairs; Padraig Ó Cinnéide, Assistant Secretary to the Government; and McDunphy himself.[118] The subject of discussion was, McDunphy noted, 'the objectionable practice of *The Irish Times* in featuring a special column headed "Court and Personal" bearing on top a replica of the British Coat of Arms and giving prominence to the British royal family'.[119] The result of this meeting was that *The Irish Times* never again put information about the President in the 'Court and Personal' column and details pertaining to the President appeared elsewhere in the paper. While minutes of the meeting in Government Buildings do not exist, it is likely that *The Irish Times* was threatened with having to submit each issue in full for censorship if its representatives did not acquiesce. This was the standard practice of the wartime censorship operation to ensure compliance and one that *The Irish Times* had been threatened with a number of times previously in relation to other issues.[120] Ultimately, as relations deteriorated further with *The Irish Times* over censorship, the 'Court and Personal' column was discontinued from 14 March 1942. McDunphy noted of this: 'I was informed by Mr Walshe, Secretary Department of External Affairs, that this discontinuance was the result of a direct order from the Government.'[121]

The final round in the bout with *The Irish Times* over the President's precedence took place in April 1944. By this stage, each issue of the newspaper had to be submitted to the censor before publication and Bert Smyllie, who had become the press censor's 'most troublesome customer', would surely have been a prime suspect when leaked information on the Government's censorship policy vis-à-vis *The Irish Times* was utilised by the Opposition during a Dáil debate.[122] Aiken, as a result, came under sustained attack from Fine Gael TDs for his attitude towards the paper and especially for insisting that *The Irish Times*, in its notices, could only refer to the Dún Laoghaire Presbyterian Church and not, as it had always been called, the Kingstown Presbyterian Church.[123]

Aiken rallied by vehemently defending his negative view of *The Irish Times* and he maintained this was justified particularly because of the disrespectful manner in which *The Irish Times* had previously ignored the President's precedence. He told the Dáil:

> I do object to somebody for a political purpose trying to push an English name down my throat when the people have adopted legally the Irish name for it . . . I want to say this. It is not a new thing as far as *The Irish Times* is concerned. We

> are frankly at daggers drawn. They have a different outlook from the outlook of the vast majority of the Irish people on many things. Take, for instance, the completely insulting manner in which they were alluding to the President before we entered in. Whether anybody agrees with the Constitution or not, the Irish people have a right to make their own Constitution and to say what person will take precedence over all others in the state. In the Constitution, in Article 12, I think it is, it was enacted by the Irish people that the President shall take precedence over all others. What does *The Irish Times* do before we took steps to stop it? They did not give him precedence over all other persons in the state. He sometimes came after every hyphenated person in the country. I have one instance of it here where the only precedence he gets is over an advertisement for corsets in one of the downtown shops. He is put in at the bottom of the list in the social and personal column.[124]

In essence, Aiken's parliamentary tactic was to invite the Opposition to hit him while he held the President in his arms. It was a tactic that worked well. This debate is important in that it shows the respect for the presidency that had grown across the political divide in the Dáil. Aiken's highlighting of *The Irish Times*' 'insulting' treatment of the President caused Opposition deputies to retreat from defending the newspaper. T. J. Murphy of the Labour Party subsequently criticised *The Irish Times* for 'a stupid policy' and T. F. O'Higgins criticised both the 'petty vendettas of Minister Aiken and *The Irish Times*'.[125]

The Irish Times was bruised by Aiken's assault and clearly felt compelled to reply. In an editorial two days later, *The Irish Times* was at pains to stress its loyalty to Hyde, stating that 'we cannot permit him [Aiken] to accuse us of any kind of disrespect for the President. Dr Hyde is a man whom we hold in the highest esteem as a man, as a scholar and as the nation's first citizen.'[126]

The Irish Times unwisely sought to explain away the suggestion that it had sought to demean the President's precedence by claiming a one-off, inadvertent error. The paper claimed: 'The alleged insult to the President, of which the Minister complains, exists only in Mr

Aiken's imaginations. The fact that on one occasion President Hyde's name appeared after certain other names in our "Social and Personal" column was purely accidental – a mistake such as happens in every newspaper office every night of the week.'[127]

Aiken, however, was not prepared to let *The Irish Times* off the hook by way of such a disclaimer. He had Thomas Coyne, the Director of Censorship, contact McDunphy looking 'for fuller information regarding the attitude of *The Irish Times* towards the President'.[128] Though McDunphy expressed reservations about the President being brought 'into the limelight as the subject of controversy', this did not stop him giving Coyne chapter and verse on how *The Irish Times* had denigrated the President in their social column.[129] The following day, in a letter to the paper, Aiken made reference to 'the sixty-one other occasions from May 1938 to December 1941, on which the President did not get his constitutional precedence'.[130] Though Smyllie responded by stating that *The Irish Times* did not have as much leisure time as the Minister and that the paper therefore had not managed 'to verify the mathematics', Aiken had driven home his point.[131] After wartime censorship was lifted, *The Irish Times* did not revert to subordinating details of the President's engagements in its social columns.

The persistence of McDunphy, and subsequently Aiken, on this issue was central to the outcome. An important and hard-fought principle had been established. From this point forth, the President's precedence was accepted by all national newspapers and this helped to further strengthen the foundations of the office in its formative years.

The GAA Red Cards the President

The most wounding attack on the President's precedence occurred when Hyde became the unlikely victim of the wrath of the Gaelic Athletic Association.

Douglas Hyde had a long and close relationship with the GAA. He had been a friend and long-time associate of the GAA's founder Michael Cusack and was also a great admirer of the GAA's role in reviving native games. Hyde saw this as a significant step towards the de-anglicisation he had called for in 1892.[132] In 1902, Hyde had been made a patron of the GAA in recognition of his work with the Gaelic League and for an Irish-Ireland.[133] However, on 17 December 1938, the GAA Central Council revoked the patronage of the President of Ireland, following a complaint made against Hyde by the Patrick Pearse Club in Derry.[134] The GAA also made it clear that whether President or not, Hyde would never again be asked to attend an All-Ireland Final.

The background to this extraordinary decision by the GAA was that, on 13 November 1938, President Hyde, accompanied by the Taoiseach and Oscar Traynor, the Minister for Posts and Telegraphs and a patron of the Football Association of Ireland, attended the Ireland versus Poland soccer match in Dalymount Park.[135]

Hyde's attendance at the soccer match was deemed by the GAA to be in direct violation of Rule 27, the ban on 'foreign games'. The 'foreign games' ban stipulated that members of the GAA could not play or attend any event organised by the sports of soccer, rugby, cricket or hockey.[136]

Prior to the President's attendance at the soccer game, it was clear that his action could provoke a response from the GAA. Hyde's attendance had been flagged in advance and newspapers had speculated on what implications this would have for the ban.[137] Cormac Moore's research into the GAA's removal of Hyde suggests that the President's attendance at the soccer match was a result of a conscious judgement and that Hyde may have wished to underpin his credentials as a President for everyone, not just advocates of an Irish-Ireland. Moore argues:

> A decision to attend was made regardless of the consequences as soccer was seen by the President, according to McDunphy, as being a popular sport amongst 'a very large section of the Irish people, a big number of whom are and have been earnest workers in the National Movement'. McDunphy also expressed the view that the President did not want 'to ally himself with the narrow parochial outlook of those who regard it as an offence against nationality to play or even look at any healthy game of which they do not personally approve'. It is hard to see how the President could have come to any other conclusion.

Leinster House, 27 April 1938: Douglas Hyde *(left)*, who had recently accepted the nomination of Fianna Fáil and Fine Gael to run for the presidency, is photographed with Alfie Byrne, the Lord Mayor of Dublin. Byrne had flirted with the idea of opposing Hyde, but by this point had dropped out of the race. (NATIONAL LIBRARY OF IRELAND)

St Patrick's Cathedral, 25 June 1938: President-Elect Douglas Hyde departs from a special religious service, accompanied by Dr John Gregg, Church of Ireland Archbishop of Dublin, and his aide-de-camp, Lieutenant Basil Peterson. (INDEPENDENT NEWS AND MEDIA)

ublin Castle, 25 June 1938: 'Mr President, on behalf of the Irish nation, on behalf of the living, ose who dwell at home as well our kin beyond the seas, on behalf also of the dead generations ho longed to see this day but have not seen it, I salute you.' – Éamon de Valera directly ldressing Douglas Hyde at his inauguration. (INDEPENDENT NEWS AND MEDIA)

Dublin Castle, 25 June 1938: Immediately after the inauguration ceremony, President Hyde stands alongside the berobed Chief Justice, Timothy Sullivan. To Hyde's right is the Taoiseach, Éamon de Valera, and the Tánaiste, Seán T. O'Kelly. In later years, first O'Kelly and subsequently de Valera would succeed Hyde as President of Ireland. (INDEPENDENT NEWS AND MEDIA)

O'Connell Street, 25 June 1938: The presidential procession pauses at the General Post Office to pay tribute to those who lost their lives in the 1916 Easter Rising. Hyde is seated in an open-top car alongside the Chief Justice. Members of the Blue Hussars, a mounted cavalry guard that escorted the President of Ireland on ceremonial occasions, are also seen in the picture. (INDEPENDENT NEWS AND MEDIA)

Nelson's Pillar, 25 June 1938: People on O'Connell Street strain to catch a glimpse of the new President. The scale of the crowds in Dublin city centre rivalled those in attendance at the Eucharistic Congress in 1932. (INDEPENDENT NEWS AND MEDIA)

Dublin Castle, 25 June 1938: At a state reception in Dublin Castle on the evening of his inauguration, President Hyde is congratulated by the Taoiseach and his wife. In 1902, Mrs de Valera had acted opposite Hyde in a production of his play, *The Tinker and the Fairy*. Hyde's aides-de-camp, Basil Peterson *(left)* and Éamon de Buitléar *(right)*, are also visible, as is the Taoiseach's eldest son, Vivion de Valera *(far right)*. (INDEPENDENT NEWS AND MEDIA)

Áras an Uachtaráin, 8 January 1940: At a Council of State meeting are *(back row, l–r)* Attorney-General Patrick Lynch, Senator Seán Gibbons, Senator Dr Robert Farnan, General Richard Mulcahy TD, Senator Sir John Keane and William Norton TD; *(front row, l–r)* Tánaiste Sean T. O'Kelly, Taoiseach Éamon de Valera, President Douglas Hyde, Michael McDunphy, Chief Justice Timothy Sullivan, Mr Justice Conor Maguire. Present but not captured by the photograph: James Dillon TD, Frank Fahy TD and Senator Michael Tierney. (NATIONAL LIBRARY OF IRELAND)

Pro-Cathedral, Marlborough Street, 15 February 1940: President Hyde attends the funeral of the Roman Catholic Archbishop of Dublin. (INDEPENDENT NEWS AND MEDIA)

Áras an Uachtaráin, 17 January 1942: On the occasion of his eighty-second birthday, President Hyde views messages of good wishes with Michael McDunphy, Secretary to the office of President, and his sister, Annette Kane. (INDEPENDENT NEWS AND MEDIA)

Áras an Uachtaráin, c. 1944: A rare photograph of President Hyde in a wheelchair taken after a reception for members of the Diplomatic Corps. Also pictured are Éamon de Valera (to his right), Seán T. O'Kelly, Mrs Kane (both to his left) and members of the Irish Defence Forces. (INDEPENDENT NEWS AND MEDIA)

St Patrick's Cathedral, 14 July 1949: Members of the Defence Forces carry Douglas Hyde's coffin. The Taoiseach, John A. Costello, stands with his hat in his hand in the right of the photo. Catholic Church doctrine made participation in Protestant ceremonies a reserved sin. With the exception of Noël Browne, cabinet members did not attend Hyde's funeral service. (BRITISH PATHÉ)

> Did the GAA expect the President of the state to refuse every invitation received for every event organised by one of the 'foreign games' for his seven years as President? For the President to do so would have been a gross dereliction of his duties. He could not have called himself impartial and above politics.[138]

The GAA's decision to expel Hyde was hugely controversial, but it actually reverberated positively on the office of the President. Hyde's removal generated a media storm, which was generally condemnatory of the GAA's action. In its editorial, the *Irish Press* castigated the GAA, stating that 'the President is the head of the whole state and not of any section in it. He owes an equal duty to all citizens whatever views they may hold, or whatever form of recreation they may indulge in'.[139] *The Irish Times* also rushed to Hyde's defence. In its editorial, *The Irish Times* described Hyde's removal as patron of the GAA as 'cant of the worst kind' and went on to say that 'the loss will be to the GAA. Misplaced zeal cannot go farther; the zealots, at least, might have the decency to feel ashamed. Their little victory over President Hyde will be Pyrrhic, because the head of the state will continue to be the representative of all the people, and not of any clique, however large it may be.'[140]

The Roscommon Herald, from Hyde's home county, was incandescent, stating that 'Hitler and Mussolini might do that sort of thing; the GAA should not try to do it. The serfs of the dictators have no choice but to obey, but the people of Ireland have fought to free themselves from serfdom. We say that the GAA has covered itself with ridicule by "banning" the President of Éire.'[141]

Almost en masse, the country's provincial and national newspapers editorialised strongly against the GAA's action. Letters to the newspapers, diligently clipped out and saved by McDunphy, show that the public's sympathy was also largely with Hyde.[142] This was amplified by the dignified manner in which the President dealt with the controversy. He wisely decided not to drag his office into a running battle on the matter and chose to remain silent, declining all media requests for a statement.[143]

The GAA's decision to revoke Hyde's patronage undoubtedly

boosted Hyde's popularity. The President was seen as a victim of an injustice and what one commentator described as 'uncouthness and boorish behaviour', yet Hyde was perceived to have conducted himself with decorum.[144] The standing of the President and his office was also enhanced by a widespread impression that, the senior echelons of the GAA apart, Hyde had acted in a proper and impartial manner in attending the soccer game and in refusing to favour one sporting organisation over the others. This impression was further reinforced when, in February 1940, Hyde, undeterred by the GAA's previous action against him, attended a prominent rugby fixture.[145] In his own unassuming fashion, Hyde was determined to be a President for all Irish people and the political reaction to the GAA's move against him underlined that this was widely appreciated.

In many ways, the response of the political parties to the GAA's refusal to accept Hyde's right as head of state to attend any function he wished is significant in again highlighting how quickly the presidency had gained acceptance across the political spectrum. Fine Gael and Labour, who had both expressed outright hostility to the office in the debate on the draft Constitution, were genuinely appalled by the treatment of Hyde. Richard Mulcahy sought a meeting with the President with a view to discussing proposals 'for the termination of the absurd position in which it was not possible for the head of the state to be Patron of a body which was founded for the promotion of National Games'.[146] Though Hyde appreciated this offer, he declined the request for a meeting because he did not wish to involve his office in any action in which 'there were bound to be differences of opinion'.[147]

In the Dáil, William Davin gave expression to Labour's anger when, on the second stage of the Offences Against the State Bill, he inquired 'if the Gaelic Athletic Association, who were recently responsible for expelling our President from the office of patron of that body, could be brought under the powers contained under Section 7 of the Bill, charged and found guilty of intimidating the President in the exercise of his normal duties?'[148]

In Fianna Fáil, the attitude was one of controlled fury. De Valera had wanted to take the GAA to task immediately following Hyde's expulsion, but the President, not wishing to inflame matters further, prevailed upon the Taoiseach not to make any public response.[149] De Valera acquiesced in maintaining a silence, but his position was that 'no single organisation had any right either to approve or bar the presence of the President of Ireland at any public function'.[150] It was a point of principle in relation to which de Valera would bide his time, but ultimately return with a vengeance. In the meantime, a public glimpse of the Taoiseach's annoyance may well have been on display in a motion, passed by the Fianna Fáil Cumann in Ennis, which protested at the GAA's behaviour towards the President. This motion, emanating from de Valera's own constituency, received national publicity and was unlikely to have been made public without de Valera's sanction.[151]

The GAA's treatment of Hyde set in train a rapid deterioration in relations between Fianna Fáil and the GAA. Prior to this event, there had been a sense of affinity between two organisations, which shared an underlying nationalist credo.[152] The aftermath of Hyde's expulsion saw a degree of sniping between Fianna Fáil and the GAA, which, while never touching directly on the action taken against the President, had its roots in this controversy. For example, at the 1943 Fianna Fáil Ard Fheis, Oscar Traynor described the ban on foreign games as 'an attempt to divide one section of the people against the other'.[153] At the same Ard Fheis, de Valera angrily remarked that 'the GAA were making a mistake' in criticising the Government's stance in opening up the Irish Army to sports other than Gaelic games.[154]

Though de Valera had remained silent at Hyde's request, it was clear that he viewed the GAA's action against Hyde as a direct assault on the President's precedence. In August 1945, following Hyde's retirement, de Valera finally got his opportunity to make his views forcefully clear to the GAA's top officials. This occurred when the President of the GAA, Séamus Gardiner, and the GAA's General Secretary, Padraig Ó Caoimh, wrote to Seán T. O'Kelly requesting a meeting with the new President of Ireland to pay their respects.[155]

O'Kelly had been a cabinet member at the time of Hyde's expulsion and would have been well aware of de Valera's annoyance with the GAA. O'Kelly also had the benefit of McDunphy's views on the matter, which were not tolerant of the GAA's position.[156] The upshot of this was that rather than getting an invite to the Áras, the GAA officials received an unexpected summons to meet with the

Taoiseach in Government Buildings for the purpose of establishing the reason for their request to the office of the President, given the action taken against President Hyde.[157] This meeting took place on 10 August 1945 and the Taoiseach, in the presence of the Assistant Secretary to the Government, Padraig Ó Cinnéide, subjected the two most senior officials from the country's leading sporting organisation to a verbal dressing-down.[158] At the outset, de Valera emphasised that the GAA's treatment of President Hyde was unwarranted and would not be tolerated in the future. Ó Cinnéide noted that 'in the case of Dr Hyde, the Taoiseach said that when he entered upon his office and his name was being continued as a patron of the GAA, his permission should first have been sought and his attention drawn to the possible implications of the "foreign games" rule, if that rule was to apply to him'.[159]

De Valera further expressed the view that the acceptance of a position as patron of an organisation did not necessarily imply membership of that organisation and that 'Dr Hyde, as patron, was in quite a different category from the ordinary members of the GAA and that the organisation was not bound to apply and need not have applied the "foreign games" rule to him.'[160]

De Valera also expressed the view that the President should be invited to the GAA's principal functions, such as the All-Ireland Finals, irrespective of what other functions he attended. De Valera added that if President O'Kelly should now choose to receive representatives of the GAA, or accept an invitation to any function held under its auspices, the President would do so subject to the clear understanding that he did not condone in any degree the action of the GAA in regard to Dr Hyde.[161]

Reinforcing his point, de Valera stressed that should President O'Kelly at any point accept any invitation from the GAA, the Association needed to understand that this did not carry any implication whatsoever that the President would restrict himself in the exercise of his discretion in regard to the acceptance of invitations from other athletic and sporting bodies.[162] According to Ó Cinnéide's valuable minute of the meeting, the Taoiseach said that in all probability the President would receive and might accept such invitations from these bodies and that it was completely proper that he should do so.

De Valera emphasised that, in extending an invitation to the President to attend any of their annual functions, the Central Council of the GAA should realise that in the ordinary course of events the invitation should be repeated for 'all future similar events and should not be withheld as a mark of disapproval by the GAA of anything the President had done or had not done in his relations with other bodies'.[163]

De Valera also insisted that the GAA's Central Council should take steps to prevent any public criticism by GAA members of the President acting in accordance with the principles he, as Taoiseach, had just outlined, but which GAA members might consider to be in conflict with their rules. Concluding his tour de force defence of the President's precedence, de Valera said that the GAA must understand that 'the President is President of all sections of the community and cannot in any circumstances put himself in such a position as to seem, by implication or otherwise, to discriminate against any section of the community'.[164]

Following a meeting of the GAA's Central Council Executive Meeting on 17 August 1945, the GAA fully assented to all of de Valera's stipulations.[165] On 2 September 1945, President O'Kelly attended the All-Ireland Hurling Final, which was the first GAA fixture attended by a President of Ireland since Douglas Hyde had been present at the 1938 All-Ireland Football Final.

O'Kelly's attendance ended a stand-off between the office of President and the GAA on terms favourable to the presidency. De Valera's insistence that the GAA bow to the President's precedence and his unique position as head of state meant that an intolerable situation was brought to an end whereby future Presidents would or would not be welcomed at Croke Park – especially for national events, such as All-Ireland Finals – depending on their willingness to boycott other sporting bodies. De Valera's firmness on this point ensured that the office of President was able to transcend the petty politics of the ban. This was an important victory for the standing of the presidency in Irish life and helped it to develop into an office that was seen as truly representative of the entire community. This had been Hyde's intention in initially accepting an invite to a soccer match, and his courage and dignity in not acceding to the GAA's pressure to use the presidency as a tool in their efforts to ostracise other sporting organisations deserves to be recognised as politically astute and laudable.

Hyde and de Valera had viewed the GAA's removal of Hyde's patronage as an attempt to place a veto on what functions the President might attend. Their refusal to acquiesce in this was a staunch defence of the President's precedence. Furthermore, de Valera's ultimate success in making the GAA recognise that the President, in the course of his official duties, would and should attend other sporting events was a victory over the narrow politics of the ban and a defining moment in the presidency being perceived as a truly national office.

6

A Healing and a Gaelic Presidency

During Douglas Hyde's tenure, the office of President was comprehensively engaged with the big political issues of the day. A number of political themes became synonymous with Hyde's presidency and while, appropriately, these themes were not party political, they encapsulated important issues on which there was a broad consensus.

Hyde's presidency was a healing one. He had come into office at the tail end of a tumultuous and fraught decade in Irish politics. Prior to his taking up office, public debate remained poisoned as a repercussion of the rancorous Treaty division and all too frequently descended into insult and a readiness to question the democratic bona fides of political opponents. As President, Hyde made a determined effort to take the bitterness out of Irish politics and to foster better and more harmonious relations across Irish society.

Hardly surprisingly, a key theme of Hyde's presidency was the Irish language. Hyde's tenure coincided with the high-water mark in Government efforts to restore the language. However, despite their shared objectives on the language, this issue became a point of political division between the Fianna Fáil Government and the President.

A Healing Presidency

From the outset, Hyde placed the theme of healing Civil War bitterness at the heart of his presidency. An interview in *The New York*

Times in the run-up to his inauguration recorded that Hyde 'expressed pleasure at the thought that his choice as President should have brought the two big parties in the Dáil together. His face was suffused with earnestness when he said, "I hope my small influence will always help toward a better understanding among the parties."'[1] Although initially reluctant to take the presidency, Hyde was conscious that the parties had come to an unprecedented agreement. He confided to P. J. Little and Peadar Doyle, the respective whips of Fianna Fáil and Fine Gael, that he 'thought that maybe if I did not accept it they might not come together on any other name. That is why I accepted.'[2]

Hyde was not suffering from an exaggerated sense of duty or self-importance when he expressed concern that should he not take the post, the parties might not be able to agree upon another name. The fact that Fianna Fáil and Fine Gael had actually come together even to discuss an agreed presidential candidate was in itself considered groundbreaking and there was no expectation, such was the animosity between the parties, that the conference would actually produce a positive result.[3] The sense that something out of the ordinary had happened in Irish politics when the two parties ultimately came to a consensus on Hyde was underlined by a Fianna Fáil TD, Bob Briscoe, in his memoirs, when even twenty years after the event, he described the choice as 'a unanimity unparalleled among Irishmen.'[4]

In its time, the agreement reached on Hyde's candidacy was heralded as a rare, even unique, moment of engagement and co-operation between two parties that had emerged from opposing sides in the Civil War. Significantly, in its editorial on 22 April 1938, the day after this agreement, *The Irish Times* said it hoped that it would mark a 'fresh start' and bring an end to 'the bitterness of the Civil War', which had caused Irish politics to be 'bedevilled by personal grudges'.[5]

Hyde's commitment to use his influence to bring about 'a better understanding among the parties' was undoubtedly populist, but given his status, from his days in the language movement, as a respected old mentor to individuals who had ended up as leading figures on both sides of the Civil War divide, it was also something that he was almost uniquely placed to do.

The optimism that Hyde's selection might pave the way for a new era of more temperate politics was further augmented by the Fianna

Fáil and the Fine Gael whips travelling to Roscommon in the same car to extend the offer of the presidency and subsequently, following Hyde's formal election on 4 May, by James Dillon, Peadar Doyle and T. F. O'Higgins accepting an invitation to a luncheon in honour of the new President-Elect, hosted by the Taoiseach, Éamon de Valera, in Leinster House and attended by a number of Fianna Fáil ministers.[6] While in today's climate no more would be read into such events than the normal course of political courtesies, in the context of their time, these interactions were recognised as new departures and as a thawing in relations. In its editorial published the day after the above mentioned luncheon, *The Irish Times* observed that 'the feeling between the two chief parties is better than it ever was before . . . And the readiness in which they collaborated in the choosing of a President has helped, as we think, to establish a new code of political conduct . . . Is there any reason why these good relations, now that the ice has been broken, should not be maintained?'[7]

By 1938, formal party rules, which had first been adopted by the Fianna Fáil Parliamentary Party a decade earlier, strictly stipulating against 'fraternisation under any circumstances' with members of Cumann na nGaedheal/Fine Gael in Leinster House, had begun to wither on the vine. Nevertheless, a culture of bitterness was still all too prevalent.[8] For example, since the 1922 split, Cosgrave and de Valera only spoke to each other across the floor of the Dáil chamber and feuds were commonplace among the leading personalities of both parties.

As President, Hyde set out to tackle this bitterness between the parties. In an early summation of his own role, McDunphy wrote that one of his primary duties was to assist Hyde in making the Áras 'a place where persons of every creed, class and shade of politics could meet on equal terms'.[9] The Herculean task that Hyde had set himself was underlined by a meeting the President-Elect had with the Fine Gael leader W. T. Cosgrave and his colleague Richard Mulcahy the day prior to his inauguration. McDunphy noted:

> In the course of conversation, both during and after lunch, Dr [*sic*] Cosgrave stated that his chief object in asking to see the President was to assure him both on his own behalf and on behalf of the Fine Gael party of whom he was the leader, that

> they would give unreserved loyalty both to the institution of the presidency and to the present occupant of it, Dr Hyde. He felt it particularly necessary to stress this in person because of certain circumstances which he then proceeded to develop.[10]

These circumstances were that Cosgrave had received a letter from de Valera informing him that, as an ex-officio member of the Council of State (by virtue of Cosgrave having previously served as President of the Executive Council), a place had been reserved for him on the dais for the presidential inauguration.[11] Cosgrave was, however, determined not to engage under any circumstances with members of the Government party outside of the Dáil, in spite of Hyde and McDunphy's efforts to dissuade him of this approach. McDunphy recorded for his file that Cosgrave

> informed the President that he did not intend to accept this invitation but would take his place among the other members of the Oireachtas in the body of the hall. He asked the President to accept his assurance that by this action he intended no disrespect whatever to the President or to his high office. He felt that his presence at the ceremony, in this capacity as a member of the Dáil, would prove the contrary. It was clear from the discussion that Dr Cosgrave's decision had no relation either to the presidency or to occupant thereof, and that he was most anxious that the President should not misunderstand his action which clearly arose from some other reasons, apparently of a political nature.[12]

Despite entreaties from Hyde and McDunphy that his absence from the dais would be taken as an indication of disunity, at the inauguration Cosgrave insisted upon sitting with a group of Fine Gael TDs rather than being seated in close proximity to a number of prominent Government members on the dais.[13]

Despite Cosgrave's attitude at the inauguration, Hyde made further efforts to bring the Fine Gael leader together with members of the Government in a non-politically charged atmosphere. In April 1939, Cosgrave was one of the guests invited to the 'first official dinner of a general nature' hosted by the President in the Áras.[14] This dinner was attended by a selection of Government members, Oireachtas members, heads of Government Departments, and civic and religious leaders.[15] Cosgrave declined the invitation. McDunphy noted:

> Dr Cosgrave wrote me a personal note in which, while expressing sincere appreciation of the honour conferred on him by the President's invitation, he regretted that he could not accept, the reasons being those which motived his absence from the dais on the day of the Installation of the President. He would prefer in existing circumstances if he were not invited to presidential functions of a general nature which would involve his meeting members of the Government.[16]

McDunphy's note gave Cosgrave's regrets a diplomatic varnish, but in reality Cosgrave was very blunt in pointing out that he would not accede to any attempt by the President (or anyone else) to get him to interact with the Fianna Fáil ministers outside of his parliamentary duties. In a letter to McDunphy on 20 April 1939, Cosgrave wrote: 'they [Government Ministers] only have courtesy when "on top". I have had no contact with them and desire none. I bear them I hope and believe no malice. Lest it would be a mockery of courtesy and sheer hypocrisy for me to do anything else than to keep away from any social contact with them.'[17]

Despite Hyde's persistence, Cosgrave's disdain for members of the Government extended beyond removing himself from social engagements that they might attend. On the two occasions during Hyde's presidency that the Council of State met, Cosgrave declined to attend.[18]

Though Hyde's healing intentions did not get very far with Cosgrave, the President's efforts were more generously reciprocated by Richard Mulcahy. When Hyde made his personal appointments to the Council of State in January 1940, Mulcahy was one of six individuals chosen by the President.[19] McDunphy compiled a note on the President's thinking in appointing Mulcahy. He wrote that 'in selecting General Mulcahy for appointment regard was had to the fact that he was (a) An Ex-Minister; (b) a prominent member of the Fine Gael or Opposition Party in the Dáil led by Mr William T. Cosgrave'.[20]

Mulcahy, unlike Cosgrave, carried out his responsibilities to the Council of State with a solemn sense of duty. Although he had been pilloried by republicans from the time of the Civil War for the Free State's policy of reprisals, he did not allow this to prevent him from sitting around the same table as a Fianna Fáil Taoiseach and Tánaiste at the Council of State during Hyde's presidency. Subsequently, despite his personal distaste for O'Kelly and especially de Valera, Mulcahy would accept appointment to their respective Councils of State, such was his respect for the office of President.[21]

Hyde, with de Valera's encouragement, used his Council of State appointments to demonstrate that his presidency was inclusive. McDunphy noted that the selection criteria Hyde used was 'from the point of view of making the Council of State as a whole as representative as possible of the political views of the various parties in Parliament'.[22] In May 1938, in a conversation with McDunphy, de Valera had expressed the hope that the President-Elect would, when the time came, appoint to the Council of State 'members of parties in the Dáil not already represented e.g. the Labour Party'.[23] McDunphy's file suggests that de Valera had a direct hand in Hyde's appointments. McDunphy wrote that 'it may be taken that any President would consult with the Head of the Government before making such appointments'.[24] As Bertie Ahern has confirmed, this precept has not been observed in recent times.[25] McDunphy's belief that a President and Taoiseach should consult before the President would make his appointments to the Council of State is, however, significant. In the context of Hyde's presidency, it serves to highlight the political importance that was attached to getting these appointments right so as to underpin the inclusive nature of the office of President.

Hyde used his social itinerary to further the inclusive and healing aspects of his presidency. Prior to his stroke, the President hosted a busy list of engagements and took a constructive approach to bringing people of different political persuasions together under the auspices of the Áras.[26] Hyde was especially solicitous in extending the hand of friendship to those who might not have been easily reconciled to the new constitutional order of the Irish state. James McNeill, the former Governor-General, had also refused an invitation to sit on the dais at Hyde's inauguration, but he was subsequently a welcome guest at the Áras.[27] Sir John Keane, a member of Seanad Éireann, a former aide-de-camp to the Lord Lieutenant of Ireland and, in McDunphy's words, 'generally regarded as representing the ex-unionist view in the country', accepted Hyde's appointment to the Council of State and was a regular guest of President Hyde at the Áras.[28]

The most spectacular example of Hyde's efforts to use the Áras an Uachtaráin as a venue to bring people together was a garden party that he hosted in the Áras in the summer of 1939. This event was attended by over 2,000 guests, 'representative of every side of social life in Ireland'.[29] The guests included nearly every member of the Oireachtas irrespective of political affiliation, although W. T. Cosgrave was the most notable absentee. However, the photographs of literally dozens of Fine Gael and Fianna Fáil TDs intermingled on the lawns of the Áras were a visible demonstration that the era of 'non-fraternisation' was being consigned to the dustbin of history.[30]

Mary McAleese's presidency, in particular, has been praised for the manner in which she made use of presidential engagements in the Áras to bring people from sometimes divergent political viewpoints on Northern Ireland together as part of a peace-building exercise.[31] In a similar vein, though it has been given scant attention by historians, the quiet diplomacy that Hyde sponsored in the Áras was significant in creating a space where people who had fought on different sides could meet in a non-politically charged atmosphere. After the years of bitterness and turbulence which characterised Irish politics in the post-Civil War era, Hyde's efforts were not just necessary, but an important bridge-building initiative of this time.

Despite Hyde's best efforts, a number of groups in Irish society remained unmoved by his healing agenda. Militant republicans, in particular, chose to effectively boycott the President. De Valera had hoped in the aftermath of the ratification of the Constitution that the IRA would accept this vote as an act of self-determination by the Irish people and abandon their non-recognition of the state. As a gesture, on the advent of new Constitution, the Fianna Fáil Government released twelve republican prisoners on 14 December 1937.[32] On 4 May 1938, the day Hyde was declared elected, in a further gesture to the IRA, the Government released six Military Tribunal detainees. *The Irish Times* reported 'the amnesty given last evening is assumed to be intended to mark the auspicious occasion of the election of the first President of Ireland in the person of Dr Douglas Hyde, as well as recognition of the generally peaceful condition of the country'.[33] These gestures went unreciprocated and the attitude of IRA supporters to Hyde was one of disdain.

At the Sinn Féin Ard Fheis in November 1938, the party's president, Margaret Buckley, said that a new label had been put on the office of Governor-General, 'but Douglas Hyde is successor to all the Lords Lieutenant, and is, as they were, the King of England's representative in this British dominion now called "Éire"'.[34]

In an unwarranted personal attack on the new President, Buckley also said: 'Dr Hyde is the right man in the right place; he has always been a staunch and consistent supporter of the British connection, and it is not surprising that when closer relations with the British Empire were contemplated, a figurehead acceptable to that empire should have been selected.'[35]

Hyde's attempts, as President, to reach out to militant republicans were met with a contempt that suggested it was a calculated policy to underline their rejection of the new constitutional order. McDunphy, who had a very close relationship with Hyde, had tried to shield the President from some of the worst excesses in this regard. Dunleavy and Dunleavy wrote:

> Only once, in the recollection of Éamon de Buitléar [an aide-de-camp to Hyde], did sparks fly between Hyde and McDunphy: in spring 1939, Hyde had arranged a reception at Áras an Uachtaráin for a number of members of the Gaelic League, most of them Hyde's former associates and old friends. It was not until the event was half over that Hyde realised that not everyone invited had accepted – in fact, some of the refusals, he learned, had been insulting if not hostile. These McDunphy had withheld from the ritual review of the daily mail on the day they had been received. Hyde insisted that henceforth all letters addressed to him be opened before him.[36]

Subsequently, in the summer of 1939, the extent of republican hostility to the office of President was brought home to Hyde when he received a stinging rebuke from his old friend Maud Gonne MacBride, in response to an invitation to attend a presidential function. The veteran republican pointed out her unhappiness with the Offences Against the State Bill 1939, which would provide for the internment without trial of IRA members. Apportioning political blame to the President, Gonne MacBride wrote to Hyde on 8 June 1939 that 'I regret I cannot come to your party because of the horrid coercion Act to which you have or are about to have to append your signature. We who used to dream of a Gaelic Ireland, loving justice for its beauty, know that such Acts will put that dream further than ever from reality, and is a deep disgrace to Ireland.'[37]

Such hostility intensified when the Second World War broke out and militant republicans accused Hyde of complicity in de Valera's actions against the IRA.[38] In early 1940, 'an anti-Hyde pamphlet' entitled 'Imaginary Happenings', distributed by the Irish Book Society, implicitly criticised the President 'for remaining silent and inactive when Gaelic Leaguers who are Republicans were imprisoned for their separatist activities, and even when they were at death's door in a hunger strike for justice'.[39] A satirical pamphlet published later that year by the Irish Book Bureau, a company run by the Sinn Féin activist Joe Clarke, was entitled 'Political Bombshell! Dr Hyde Refuses to Sign A Bill'.[40] The Dunleavys have observed that this was

> more direct in its attack on Hyde, through the old technique of the imaginary interview. The occasion for the interview . . . was his 'point blank' rejection of legislation . . . 'that seeks to make it a crime to think for more than 32 seconds at a time about the restoration of the Republic of Ireland; every other conceivable form of offence being already provided for in the other Coercion Acts'. The 'interviewer', the reader is told, caught 'His Excellency' at the back entrance of the 'Viceregal Lodge' (such terms were employed by disaffected nationalists to communicate their conviction that de Valera and Hyde had sold out to the British) as he was slipping out with his caddy, McDunphy, for 'a quiet game of golf' on his private course. 'The President of Ireland (less six counties) Hyde' (as the writer labels his subject) defended his decision by declaring it, in an imaginary quote, 'consistent with every action of my public life for the last forty years'.[41]

The criticism and ridicule of the President by militant republicans, their spurning of Hyde's early overtures of goodwill, as well as their upsurge in activity following the outbreak of the Second World War, led to over fifty years of non-engagement between the office of President and militant republicans. This position, which had its roots in the IRA's disrespectful treatment of President Hyde, very quickly became the accepted status quo. It was a position that would not be seriously challenged until President Mary Robinson's controversial decision to shake hands with Gerry Adams on a visit to West Belfast in June 1993.[42]

Hyde's efforts to reach out to both communities in Northern Ireland were also stymied by intransigent attitudes. In June 1938, the President and Taoiseach had wished to attend the unveiling by Cardinal MacRory of a statue of St Patrick in Downpatrick, but as a memo drafted by one of the senior officials of the Northern Ireland Minister for Home Affairs, Sir Richard Bates, noted, the Stormont Government 'viewed with grave concern the proposal that Mr de Valera and Dr Hyde should attend' the ceremony.[43] The memo suggested that the proposed visit was 'an attempt to place the Northern Ireland Government in an embarrassing and invidious position' and ultimately, recognising that they were not going to be welcomed by the six-county authorities, de Valera and Hyde decided not to pursue their intention to travel.[44] Any hopes that Hyde's presidency would mellow Ulster unionist attitudes to the southern state may well have received a rude awakening at this point. Though Hyde came from the same religion as the majority in Northern Ireland, this had no impact on the views of the Stormont Government, possibly because of a hard-line perception, in D. H. Akenson's phrase, that 'Douglas Hyde really did not count as a Protestant north of Newry.'[45]

Hyde made a further attempt to visit Northern Ireland in 1940, but, on this occasion, it was his own Government that was the cause of him not travelling. Hyde had sought permission under Article 12.9 of the Constitution to leave the state to attend a ceremony in Belfast to mark the centenary of the unification of the Presbyterian Church.[46] This was the only actual request Hyde, who was an Anglican, made of the Government to leave the state during his presidency and it was undoubtedly motivated by reasons of ecumenicalism and a desire to be inclusive. However, the politics and protocols of partition worked against Hyde's intentions. When the Government learned that the Governor of Northern Ireland would also be present at the ceremony, they advised Hyde not to travel because, they felt, he would not be treated with equal respect. Hyde subsequently withdrew his request to travel.[47]

This, in fairness, was probably a wise decision, and it would have been brought home to Hyde in April 1940 that the unionist administration in Northern Ireland was determined not to interact with his office. At this time, to mark Denis Coffey's retirement from the presidency of UCD, Hyde intended to host a dinner in honour of his old colleague and saw this as an ideal opportunity to bring together under the one roof representatives of all the universities of Ireland, including Queen's University Belfast.[48]

McDunphy, accordingly, asked the Provost of Trinity, Professor William Thrift, to sound out what the attitude would be to such an invitation north of the border. Thrift wrote to the Pro-Chancellor of Queen's, Lord Chief Justice James Andrews, who was also a member of the Trinity College Dublin Northern Ireland Association, to ascertain his views.[49] Andrews was the brother of the then Stormont Minister for Finance John Andrews, and he was intimately acquainted with unionist politics. He gave the cold shoulder to Thrift's overtures on behalf of the President and McDunphy disappointedly noted that the response was that 'in the present unfortunate situation they could not accept an invitation to the proposed dinner to be given by the President in Dr Coffey's honour. The reluctance to participate in presidential functions is confined entirely to those associated with politics in the North.'[50]

Despite this rebuff, the office of President became embroiled in another attempted initiative involving Trinity College and a senior legal figure in Northern Ireland. In this case, it was McDunphy who unilaterally pulled the plug on a form of rapprochement that offended his core nationalist beliefs, although the President appears to have acquiesced with his Secretary's view. In August 1942, McDunphy noted a conversation he had with Thrift's successor, Dr Ernest Alton, and recorded that 'in the course of our conversation he referred to his recent accession to the post of Provost and he said he intended to do all in his power to make Trinity College a truly national college and to prevent any developments within the College of an anti-Irish nature'.[51]

McDunphy had strong anti-partition views and his interest was aroused when Alton, who was a close friend of Hyde, told him of a potential initiative to advance the cause of Irish unity. McDunphy noted:

> In particular, he [Alton] was anxious to secure the return of the North into the frame of a united Ireland. He had recently had a letter from Lord Justice Sir Anthony Brutus Babington of the Northern Court of Appeal who was a friend of his. In his letter Sir Anthony had stated that in his opinion the present condition of severance between the two parts of Ireland could not continue, that it was the duty of all Irishmen to work for early unification and that in his opinion Trinity College was a very appropriate place in which the first move should be made.[52]

This news would have been seen by McDunphy as an extraordinary development, especially as Babington had been a member of the Northern Ireland Parliament and James Craig's Attorney-General up until as recently as 1937.[53] McDunphy took the liberty of briefing the Taoiseach and, in November 1942, when Alton came to see Hyde in the Áras, McDunphy quizzed him on progress. To McDunphy's consternation, it emerged that he and Alton were previously at cross purposes and that Babington's conversion was not as absolute as McDunphy might have wished. McDunphy wrote 'it soon became clear that the united Ireland contemplated by Mr Justice Babington of the Northern Ireland Judiciary was one within the framework of the British Commonwealth of Nations, involving recognition of the King of England as the Supreme Head, or as Dr Alton put it, the symbol of unity of the whole system'.[54]

McDunphy, as has earlier been explored, was extremely sensitive to any suggestion of the British monarch ranking above the President and, before Alton had even got in the door of the President's study, McDunphy had castigated his point of view. McDunphy wrote:

> I pointed out that this in essence was Dominion Status, that it was a retrograde step which would not be in accord with the spirit of the Constitution under which Ireland was a sovereign independent state with a President at its head, and that it would be definitely contrary to the wishes of the Irish people.

> Surely he must realise that independence gained after such a long and costly struggle would not be lightly abandoned, and that no true Irishman would for a moment consent to the subordination of the President of Ireland to the head of any other state.[55]

McDunphy noted that 'Dr Alton seemed disappointed',[56] but it is unknown whether the Provost proceeded to raise the issue with Hyde. If he did, it came to nothing and McDunphy's firm rejection of the 'Babington initiative' seems to have scuppered any chance this proposal may have had to achieve progress.

One further healing initiative involving Hyde and McDunphy, which was very much ahead of its time, was a move to bring about better relations between Trinity College and the Catholic Church. Since the late nineteenth century, the Church had been opposed to Catholics attending Trinity College, but John Charles McQuaid 'was the first Irish bishop expressly to forbid Catholics to study at TCD, a move followed by the rest of the hierarchy'.[57]

On 3 July 1942, shortly after Dr Ernest Alton had become Provost of Trinity, McDunphy, acting with the President's imprimatur, wrote to Archbishop McQuaid's Secretary, Fr Glennon, with a view to brokering a meeting between the Archbishop and the Provost. McDunphy told Glennon that he had recently met with Alton and that the Provost 'was anxious to pay a courtesy call on His Grace the Archbishop, but was not quite sure how he should proceed, or whether in fact the proposal would be acceptable'.[58] That McDunphy was acting with Hyde's full sanction was clear from the fact that he followed up this correspondence with a phone call to Glennon on 21 July suggesting that the Áras could be used to facilitate such a meeting.[59] Glennon's reply on McQuaid's behalf was, however, uncompromising and it would have served to scupper any notions the President may have had that he could promote better relations between the Church and the college, which might lead to the ending of the ban on Catholics attending Trinity. Glennon wrote to McDunphy:

> I am asked by His Grace Archbishop to say that he has read your letter of 3 July and heard your further explanations given today by telephone concerning Áras an Uachtaráin as a

> platform or meeting place for members of different religions . . . I am requested by His Grace to answer that if Dr Alton as Provost of Trinity College wishes to pay a courtesy call on the Archbishop of Dublin, the Archbishop will, as the normal course of Christian politeness requires, receive Dr Alton, but Dr Alton will kindly understand that, in view of the existing law of the Catholic Church concerning attendance at Trinity College by Catholics, the Archbishop may not return the courtesy call at Trinity College.[60]

It was not until the beginning of the academic year in 1970, over a quarter of a century after Douglas Hyde's retirement as President of Ireland, that McQuaid finally rescinded the ban on Catholics attending Trinity.[61]

As President, Hyde displayed generosity and foresight in trying to bring together disparate strands in Irish society. However, despite the fact that more often than not his healing efforts fell on stony ground, they were distinctly ahead of their time. Hyde made a noble attempt to kick-start a normalisation process in Irish politics. For over a generation, the Civil War had soured debate and contributed to a mean-spirited and nasty political atmosphere. Douglas Hyde set out to tackle this by making reconciliation a cornerstone of his presidency. He helped to create a space for a new civility to grow in the relations between Fianna Fáil and Fine Gael. Though the President's attempts at healing brought about some gradual improvements, the Fine Gael leader W. T. Cosgrave, in particular, shunned Hyde's healing work. Hyde's goodwill agenda was unsuccessful in achieving rapprochement with both northern unionists and militant republicans, as well as in trying to broker a new understanding and engagement with Trinity College in Irish society. Though each of these gestures ultimately failed, the olive branches Hyde proffered underlined both the progressive instincts of his presidency and the bridge-building potential that his office possessed.

A Gaelic Presidency

In his initial response to reporters' queries, Hyde put the development of the Irish language as a central aim of his presidency. He said: 'I hope in the coming days to be able to do everything that lies in my power for my country and the language.'[62] In a letter in Irish to Hyde, in the immediate aftermath of his agreeing to be the candidate of the two big parties, de Valera showed that he too envisaged that the objective of the language revival would be synonymous with Hyde's presidency. On 23 April, de Valera wrote: 'As long as I hold my present position as An Taoiseach, it will be my duty to work with you side by side for the two objectives of Ireland Gaelic and Ireland free. I am certain that we will solve our problems splendidly together. May God prosper our labours.'[63]

Both de Valera and Hyde were determined that the presidency would be perceived as a bastion of Irish culture. Hyde had requested that, to the extent that it was consistent with obtaining qualified individuals, those appointed to his staff should be Irish-speaking.[64] By 1939, every member of staff in the Áras spoke Irish fluently, with the exception of the butler because it had proved impossible to procure an Irish-speaking butler.[65] Due attention was also given to the naming and location of the President's residence. Initially the Government had been reluctant to use the premises of the old Viceregal Lodge, given its previous imperial associations. De Valera had planned to convert the Viceregal Lodge into a folk museum.[66] The Taoiseach's intention had been to house the new President in the Phoenix Park residence occupied by the American Minister, which had been known during British occupation as the Chief Secretary's Lodge. An alternative place suitable for an American legation near Dublin could not be found, however, and this plan had to be abandoned. Consideration had also been given to housing the first President in St Anne's in Raheny, Ashtown House in the Phoenix Park and South Hill in Milltown, but each of these proved for one reason or another to be unsuitable.[67] With no feasible alternatives, the Government was eventually forced to revert to the old Viceregal Lodge, but decided that it should be officially renamed. McDunphy recalled, in a light-hearted letter in 1969 to President de Valera, that Hyde was central to this process and had insisted on an Irish name. McDunphy wrote:

> Dr Hyde was not interested in the political connotations of that name, but he was concerned that the new name should be an Irish one. He suggested the title 'Brú na Life' (Liffey

> Mansion) but I pointed out that to English speakers the pronunciation would be 'Brew na Liffey' [and] would almost certainly be interpreted by humourists as an advertisement for the products of the famous Dublin Brewery, Arthur Guinness and Co. Ltd, which was situated a [short] distance away on the Liffey. Dr Hyde laughed heartily at this and agreed that that would not do, and after some thoughts he suggested the name 'Áras an Uachtaráin' (Residence of the President) and that name was officially adopted and now remains.[68]

Initially, the Government's intention was that the building now renamed Áras an Uachtaráin would be used only on a temporary basis. In May 1938, Hugo Flinn had confirmed to the Dáil during a vote on exchequer funding for the Office of Public Works that the Government intended to build a new presidential residence.[69] These plans were, however, scuppered by the lack of budgetary funding and the outbreak of the Second World War. Instead of building a brand-new residence, it was ultimately decided to renovate the Áras as funding permitted. In a memo dated December 1940, McDunphy noted:

> Due to the outbreak of the European War, it seems extremely unlikely that there is any early prospect of a new residence being provided for the President. The present residence, apart from its great age which has resulted in the roof being defective to the point of being dangerous and other evidences of senile decay, the general layout of Áras an Uachtaráin (formerly known as the Viceregal Lodge) is entirely unsuitable for modern requirement. There is something however to be said for using certain portions of the nucleus, provided of course that the foundations are sound. The whole of the ground floor including the entrance hall, the reception room, the ballroom, the President's study, the Secretary's office and the staff room are all lofty and dignified in appearance.[70]

Hyde was less concerned with the internal renovations of the Áras and more focused on what the building would be known as to the outside world. In November 1938, while driving through the Phoenix Park,

President Hyde had displayed uncharacteristic anger when he spotted signposts bearing the redundant name of the Viceregal Lodge. Hyde instructed McDunphy to write to the Government with a request that offending signs be 'at once . . . removed'.[71] This was a request upon which the Government quickly acted. On 28 November 1938, McDunphy had also written to Maurice Moynihan informing the Secretary to the Government that 'the President has expressed the wish that the name of the official residence to be inscribed on any new signposts, etc., should be in Irish only, namely Áras an Uachtaráin'.[72]

Hyde's presidency coincided with, and was complementary to, intense Government efforts to revive the Irish language. In the immediate post-independence period, there was ironically a significant decline in spoken Irish. Both Brown and Fanning suggest that the sense of urgency to restore the language that had been present under the British administration may have been lost.[73] Hyde's presidency was very much about giving impetus to a second wave of the Gaelic revival, but his modus operandi was very different from that of the Fianna Fáil Government. Under the Fianna Fáil Minister for Education, Tom Derrig, 'the drive for Irish was intensified', but it also began to include a large element of compulsion.[74] In 1934, Irish was made a compulsory subject in secondary schools.[75] In 1937, competence in Irish became compulsory for entry to the Civil Service and the Garda Síochána.[76]

These methods were not Hyde's methods and, from his earliest days in the Gaelic League, as Tim Pat Coogan has pointed out, Hyde maintained that he wished to 'win Ireland's nationality', as he referred to the struggle to revive the language, 'by persuasion and democratic means'.[77] In a letter to *The Irish Times* in 1954, A. M. Sullivan, a leading Irish lawyer who had been involved with Hyde in the Gaelic League, claimed that 'Douglas Hyde foresaw what has since come to pass – that resentment at the compulsion of "coercion Irish" would destroy all the interest and affection for Gaelic that the League had built up.'[78]

An analysis of Hyde's speeches as President shows that he never expressed support for the Government's policy of compulsion. Hyde was vocal as President in encouraging people, especially schoolchildren, to speak Irish, but he did so on the basis of promoting the language for its cultural and patriotic values.[79] President Hyde frequently hosted Irish-language-related events in the Áras; for example, in March 1939, he held a reception for 600 schoolchildren involved in the Cumann Drámaidheachta na Sgol.[80] On receiving the Freedom of Galway City on 31 August 1939, Hyde used the occasion to urge people to speak Irish in everyday life and he also sought to dispel any stigma surrounding the language:

> I will never forget the events of the day and I hope that the children who are looking on will not forget, either, but that as a result, they will show increased interest in their native language by speaking it in all places . . . The persons who occupy the highest posts in the state – An Taoiseach, An Tánaiste, and myself – never speak to each other in any language but Irish. When we can discuss difficult complicated matters in Irish, is it not possible for the people of Galway to use the language for ordinary everyday conversation?[81]

The Áras also became a regular venue for Gaelic League receptions, which underlined the status of the language revival movement in Irish life. Hyde's position as President of Ireland was also seen as extremely apt when the Gaelic League celebrated the fiftieth anniversary of its foundation. This anniversary received significant attention in Irish society and, in anticipation of it, a number of Irish and English newspapers had run photo essays on Hyde.[82] The Department of Posts and Telegraphs also issued two stamps depicting Hyde's image in honour of the anniversary. This was the first time that a living person had appeared on an Irish postal stamp and, indeed, up to the mid 1990s, this protocol was breached on only two subsequent occasions, most prominently in 1979 to mark the visit of Pope John Paul II to Ireland. That Hyde was head of state for the Gaelic League anniversary conveniently allowed Irish-language enthusiasts to draw attention to the fact that the Gaelic League had paved the way for the Irish revolution and that one of the purposes of independent nationhood was to create an environment in which the language could flourish. In October 1943, at the landmark state reception held in Dublin Castle to celebrate the League's establishment, Hyde's failing health prevented him being present, but the propaganda value of having the leading

Irish language revivalist as President was still evident. *The Irish Times* reported on proceedings:

> As a substitute for the President, the guests heard a recording made by him a few weeks [*sic*] ago of a short address of welcome, in which he expressed his deep regret that his cold prevented him from being present. His voice came through clearly, but there was a heavy tremor in it when he said that his age weighed heavily on him, though he felt the years falling from him again when he thought of the friends gathered there that day. Then, with a note of pleading in his voice, he repeated a phrase that he had used again and again in the old days: 'A nation without a language is like a soldier without a weapon.' The assembly, whose numbers had risen to their feet for this address, remained standing while Mr de Valera read his own address . . . He expressed the gratitude of the Government to the people who had worked for the language in the past and whose work had not only saved the language, but had also brought about self-government.[83]

Though the President and Government had a mutually strong desire to revive the Irish language, it was also ironically the issue that created the greatest tensions between Hyde and the cabinet. This arose in the context of the question of compulsory Irish, and Hyde's decision to refer the School Attendance Bill 1942 to the Supreme Court for a decision on its constitutionality. Section 4.1 of the Bill stated: 'A child shall not be deemed for the purposes of this Act to be receiving suitable education in a manner other than by attending a national school, a suitable school, or a recognised school unless such education and the manner in which such child is receiving it have been certified under this section by the Minister to be suitable.'[84]

The controversy surrounding this section of the Bill was a slow burner. On the second stage in the Dáil, only Professor John Marcus O'Sullivan expressed any doubt about the constitutionality of the Bill. He suggested that Section 4 of the Bill might impinge on Article 42 of the Constitution, which, while guaranteeing every child's right to receive 'a necessary minimum education', recognised that the parents should not be obliged to send their children 'to any particular type of school designated by the state'.[85]

By the time the Bill reached the Seanad, however, opposition to it had crystallised. A number of non-Fianna Fáil senators, most prominently Sir John Keane and Michael Tierney, were convinced that the purpose of Section 4 of the School Attendance Bill 1942 was to make parents who sent their children to school abroad – in essence, mostly members of the Protestant community, who had a tradition of sending their children to Great Britain or Northern Ireland – liable to prosecution for failing to have their children taught Irish.[86]

Though Derrig had given an assurance that, as long as he was minister, he would operate under the assumption that a child was receiving a proper education if the child was attending a recognised school, public or otherwise, outside the state, his failure to accept a legislative amendment, proposed by James Douglas, on this basis suggested that the Government at a future stage might use this legislation to prevent children from being educated outside Ireland.[87] Derrig's assurance of moderation was not given credence by the comments of some of his party's allies in the Seanad. Liam Ó Buachalla, a Fianna Fáil senator and language enthusiast, and William Magennis, one of the Taoiseach's nominees, both spoke trenchantly in favour of measures to compel parents to educate their children in Irish.[88]

The progress of this debate had been monitored closely in Áras an Uachtaráin and undoubtedly alerted the President that the Bill was very contentious.[89] The debate had received a lot of publicity and was even the subject of a hard-hitting *Irish Times* editorial, focusing on Tierney's colourful claim that the School Attendance Bill was analogous to the Penal Laws, which had made it an offence for parents to have a child educated abroad.[90]

Had the President needed any further confirmation that the School Attendance Bill 1942 was now a political hot potato, this duly arrived by means of correspondence signed by six senators and two TDs on 15 February 1943, a full three days before the Bill passed through the Oireachtas.[91] The letter was the brainchild of the independent Senator James Douglas and was also signed by the three independent Trinity senators, Ernest Alton, Joseph Johnston and Robert Rowlette; by two Fine Gael TDs, John Marcus O'Sullivan and Richard Mulcahy; and by two Fine Gael senators, Michael Hayes and Michael Tierney.[92] John A.

Costello's papers show that this letter was actually drafted by Costello, a Fine Gael TD, senior counsel and a very close friend of Douglas.[93]

The letter, though lengthy, was cleverly pitched and did not lose sight of the fact that it was not the President's role to adjudicate on policy disputes. It did not get bogged down in the merits or demerits of the Bill regarding the revival of the language or the treatment of minorities, though these two issues had ultimately dominated Oireachtas discussion. Instead, the letter maintained that 'in our opinion Section 4 of this Bill introduces new principles which may be held to be repugnant to Article 42 of the Constitution, and we respectfully suggest that it would be desirable to have the question of the repugnancy or otherwise of this Section submitted to the Supreme Court before the Bill became law'.[94] The letter continued:

> Section 4 of the Bill provides that it shall not be a reasonable excuse to show that a child is receiving a suitable education within the meaning of the Act in a manner other than by attendance at a National school, a Suitable school or a Recognised school unless such education and the manner in which such child is receiving it has been certified by a minister to be suitable . . . The final decision as to the school would rest with the Minister and not with the parent, which would appear to be repugnant to Article 42 of the Constitution.[95]

The Oireachtas members' tactic of writing to the President before the Bill had passed all stages in the Oireachtas made it more difficult for the President, if it had been his intention, simply to sign the Bill and leave the matter of challenging it in the courts to individuals if they saw fit. Though Senator Douglas and the other signatories did not disclose their letter publicly, there was no guarantee that this would not happen if the President refused to act. On 22 February 1943, it was announced that Hyde had decided to convene a meeting of the Council of State to consider the School Attendance Bill.[96] This meeting took place in Áras an Uachtaráin three days later.[97]

A procedural note that McDunphy subsequently wrote makes clear that the Council of State meeting was subject to some political manoeuvring. McDunphy noted:

> At the request of one of the members of the Council of State, and with the consent of the President and the other members of the Council, a letter signed by six senators and two deputies under date of 15 February was read at the meeting of the Council of State on 25 February. Before the meeting the President had considered the question of whether copies of this document should be circulated, but had decided that it would be better not to do so as the communication was in the nature of advocacy of a particular point of view. He felt that it was better to leave the case to be made at the meeting itself. To circulate one document of this nature would possibly invite requests for the circulation of documents developing or countering the arguments contained in the first one, and this I think should be avoided.[98]

While McDunphy's memo is deliberately vague, the identity of the member of the Council of State who made 'the request' that the Oireachtas members' letter be read at the meeting was most likely either Tierney or Mulcahy, both of whom were signatories of the actual letter. This manoeuvre, in getting the contents of this lengthy legal letter considered at the Council of State meeting, was undoubtedly an attempt to ensure a particular viewpoint was fully ventilated and could be construed as a none-too-subtle attempt to put pressure on the President to refer the Bill to the Supreme Court.

A further memo by McDunphy hints at a lively Council of State meeting with intense discussion. McDunphy noted that at the first Council of State meeting in 1940 (which will be examined later), Hyde had 'expressed a wish that references to political situations and legal arguments should be avoided' and this had resulted in a stilted discussion. However, in February 1943, 'in relation to the School Attendance Bill, the President decided to relax both these restrictions. The result was that the discussion was much freer, fuller and more informative.'[99] The meeting lasted an hour and a half.[100]

The day after the Council of State meeting, Hyde took the decision to refer Section 4 of the School Attendance Bill to the Supreme Court for a ruling on its constitutionality.[101] On 25 March 1943, when arguments opened in the Supreme Court, one of the barristers assigned by the Court to argue against the Bill was Costello.[102]

On 15 April 1943, the Supreme Court advised the President that Section 4 of the School Attendance Bill 1942 was repugnant to the Constitution. The judgement delivered by the Chief Justice Timothy Sullivan said that the Bill was an unwarranted intrusion. He stated: 'The state is entitled to require that children shall receive a certain minimum education. So long as parents supply this General Standard of Education we are of opinion that the manner in which it is being given and received is entirely a matter for the parents and is not a matter in respect of which the state under the Constitution is entitled to interfere.'[103]

As a result of the Supreme Court decision, President Hyde was then bound by the Constitution to decline to sign the Bill. This was the first time that the Supreme Court had advised against the constitutionality of a measure referred to it under Article 26, and the *Irish Press* explained to its readers that this meant that 'the Bill becomes "dead"'.[104] This was a political embarrassment for the Government, which had strenuously argued, both in the Oireachtas and, via counsel for the Attorney-General, in the Supreme Court, that the Bill was desirable and constitutional.

For the President, this Bill and the controversy that surrounded it was undoubtedly a political minefield, yet Hyde managed to navigate a way through it with some dexterity. The main political opposition to the Bill had zoned in on concerns regarding compulsion in the teaching of Irish and how this might impact on parents, mostly from minority religions, who wished to send their children abroad to be educated. Hyde's background, both as a champion of the Irish language (although he was at best lukewarm on the policy of compulsion) and as a Protestant, meant that these were sensitive issues for him to deal with. However, the President resisted any temptation to enter into the debate or justify his actions. It was surely a difficult personal decision for Hyde to delay, and even potentially be party to preventing, the enactment of legislation designed to promote the revival of the Irish language. However, the President put his constitutional duties first. Despite the political machinations surrounding the passage of the Bill, which were also in evidence even at the Council of State, Hyde did not let his personal views interfere with his overriding duty to guard against legislation which he believed to be repugnant to the Constitution. For this, the President deserves strong praise.

Morgan suggests that, on the contrary, Hyde's action was the subject of belated criticism from Fianna Fáil as the President prepared to vacate his office. Morgan claimed 'in 1945, President Hyde was subjected to some criticism by the Government during the election campaign for his successor because he had used his Article 26 power to refer the School Attendance Bill 1942 to the Supreme Court'.[105]

In making this claim, Morgan cited in support a truncated quote from de Valera that was covered in *Round Table*, a British Commonwealth political journal.[106] The full context of de Valera's remarks were carried in *The Irish Times* on 14 June 1945, which reported:

> Mr de Valera, in a reference to Dr Douglas Hyde, said that they were most fortunate in their first President. In him they had a man of culture, a scholar, a man who had devoted himself to the nation. Dr Hyde was a man whose character was such, whose dignity was such, whose understanding was such that it was always a pleasure to have dealings with him. They wanted somebody to replace him who would be able, in the same way, to inspire the affection of the people and the confidence of all who had to deal with him. In the ordinary way, Fianna Fáil would be the Government of the country for the next four years, dealing with the head of the state, and they should try and ensure that there would be no friction, no time lost in settling up difficulties that should not have arisen. Did anybody think a more appropriate person could be got to continue the work that was to be done than Mr Seán T. O'Kelly? asked Mr de Valera.[107]

Taken on their own, de Valera's remarks about 'no friction' and 'no time lost' could be construed as a criticism of Hyde, but given the Taoiseach's praise for the outgoing President, it is still quite a leap to link these comments to the issue of the School Attendance Bill two years previously. An alternative, benign interpretation is that in the context of the first contested presidential election, de Valera had simply moved on from praising the first President to making the legitimate political point that the Fianna Fáil Government would work better with O'Kelly than any of the other candidates hoping to succeed

Hyde. Hyde's decision to send the Bill to the Supreme Court to test its constitutionality was totally vindicated by the Supreme Court ruling that elements of the Bill were, indeed, unconstitutional. This very fact should have insulated the President from any criticism. Hyde had done his duty and done it well. Put simply, the President had made the right decision. It is unlikely, therefore, that given de Valera's protective stance on the presidency, he would have been minded to criticise Hyde's action in this instance.

Hyde's presidency occurred against the backdrop of a tail-off in support for the language revival movement. However, he remained unceasing in his efforts to encourage people to speak Irish, but this did not extend to voicing support for the Government's policy of compulsion. The School Attendance Bill 1942 put the President in an invidious position. Though Hyde was not enthusiastic about compulsion, his background would have made it hard for him to be party to a process that would ultimately lead to the striking down of legislation designed to foster the growth of the Irish language. Hyde understood the concerns in the Protestant community about legislation that could potentially be used to debar parents from having their children educated abroad. The President was also aware of the political manoeuvring surrounding the Bill, but did not allow himself to be distracted by it. Hyde kept his sole focus on his constitutional responsibilities and, correctly deducing that the Bill was unconstitutional, he did his duty in referring it to the Supreme Court.

7

The Politics of Neutrality

Hyde's presidency coincided with the Second World War and it was the politics of neutrality that determined that he remain in office. Without the Second World War, Hyde would have undoubtedly retired from the presidency, on the grounds of ill health, without completing his full term. However, with the day-to-day threat of invasion especially real in the period prior to Hitler invading Russia in the summer of 1941, the need to avoid the instability that might arise from a resignation and a possible presidential election was viewed as vital, and Hyde bravely soldiered on.

Neutrality, which had popular public support, was a major theme of Hyde's presidency. The office of President played an integral part in the national effort to keep Ireland out of the Second World War. As part of the state's diplomatic offensive, Hyde established extremely cordial relations with representatives of the Allied and Axis powers based in Ireland. On a deeper level, the office of President became an important listening post during the war. McDunphy, in particular, played a valuable role in information gathering, which was used to keep the Taoiseach apprised of the attitudes of representatives of the belligerent countries.

Hyde's health had been robust for the first two years of his presidency.[1] However, on 12 April 1940, while enjoying a round of golf in Áras an Uachtaráin with McDunphy, the President took ill and 'had to be carried to the House and put to bed immediately'.[2] The

President's doctor, William Boxwell, 'diagnosed it as a slight stroke, which would necessitate the President's remaining in bed and keeping absolutely quiet until further notice'.[3] To McDunphy's grave concern, Boxwell was 'unable to say whether the President would be well again in a week or three months'.[4]

In an effort at news management, McDunphy informed the media organisations that 'President Hyde is slightly indisposed and has been ordered by his doctor to keep to his room for the present'.[5] This statement appeared verbatim in a number of national newspapers without any further information, speculation or commentary, which suggests that official muscle was being deployed from the outset to play down concerns regarding the President's health.[6] This did not prevent rumours sweeping the country that Hyde was dead. On 19 April 1940, David Gray, the American Minister, wrote to inform President Roosevelt that 'in confidence, we have been told that the President, Douglas Hyde, has had a stroke. He will probably make a partial recovery, but it is feared he is through.'[7]

Hyde's serious medical condition emerged at the worst possible time for the Government. On 9 April 1940, three days before Hyde suffered his stroke, Germany invaded Norway and Denmark, bringing the so-called phoney war to an explosive end. This began a period of heightened national concern that Ireland too might fall victim to invasion. In May 1940, Hitler invaded Belgium, Holland, Luxembourg and France, and at the same time Winston Churchill, a virulent critic of the Irish Government's refusal to hand over port facilities, became Prime Minister in the United Kingdom. Later that month, there was panic in Government circles when a raid on the house of a German national, Stephen Held, yielded a quantity of money, maps, coded messages and a Luftwaffe parachute.[8] Fears that the Germans were making behind-the-lines preparations for an invasion of Ireland were coupled with concerns that the British would use the pretext of German spies in Ireland to justify their own military intervention. On 1 June, British intelligence passed information on to the Irish Government that an IRA-supported German invasion was imminent.[9]

It was against this background of intense fears of invasion that the crisis over the President's health played itself out. In the fraught international climate of the time, the Government was anxious to avoid anything that could breed instability or create a vacuum. It was for this same reason that later in the war, as the Dáil came close to running its full course in 1943, a provision was made under emergency legislation for a general election to take place separate to a dissolution. However, had Hyde chosen in 1940 (or subsequently) to resign because of ill health, or had he died, a presidential vacancy, in a best-case scenario, would have been a serious distraction for a wartime Government and, in a worst-case scenario, could have created real divisions between Government and Opposition at a time when it was important to show a united national front.

McDunphy's file makes clear that de Valera attached significant political importance to issues arising from Hyde's health concerns. The Taoiseach was 'informed each day of the President's condition'.[10] On 22 April 1940, arising from a prior meeting with the Taoiseach, McDunphy obtained for the Government's attention a medical report on Hyde's condition. McDunphy's cover letter to the Government Secretary in forwarding this report gives an indication of the seriousness (and obtrusiveness) with which the Government were treating the matter. McDunphy wrote: 'I enclose herewith copy of a confidential report on the President's health, which I have received from his medical adviser. The report has been furnished at my request in order that the Government may be aware of the actual position. The information therein has not been disclosed either by the doctor or myself to the President's relatives.'[11] Dr Boxwell's report set out in stark terms for the Government how ill Hyde was. The report stated: 'The President of Ireland is suffering from a partial hemiplegia . . . At the moment there is no immediate threat to his life, but a cerebral haemorrhage in this particular situation is always serious. Any extension or recurrence might prove rapidly fatal. Should the haemorrhage not recur, the President, in my opinion, might live for some years. But it is doubtful that he will ever resume full physical activities.'[12]

The real doubts that the President would survive were evident from a McDunphy memo dated from the same month, which mentioned that the state would buy a coffin in the event of Hyde's death, but that 'consultation with the relatives would of course be necessary'.[13] In the same memo, McDunphy also drew up a checklist, which he entitled 'Actions Immediately on Death'.[14] On 18 May

1940, McDunphy attended an interdepartmental meeting in Military Headquarters in Parkgate Street to discuss arrangements in the event of the death of the President.[15] León Ó Broin, a Department of Finance official who was a member of this interdepartmental committee, wrote that news of Hyde's death 'was expected hourly'.[16] By this stage, McDunphy had 'ascertained' that it was the wish of the President to be buried in Frenchpark, Roscommon, and he subsequently discussed funeral arrangements with the Church of Ireland Archbishop of Dublin, Dr Arthur Barton.[17] McDunphy also consulted with de Valera and Moynihan in regard to putting in place procedures to deal with a situation, should it arise, of the President's 'temporary or permanent incapacity'.[18]

It was, however, considered politically astute to play down any public concerns about the President's condition. A statement issued from the Áras on 15 May 1940 said 'the doctor has advised that although the condition of President Hyde's health gives no cause for anxiety, it will be some time before he will be well enough to leave his room'.[19] On 27 May 1940, the *Irish Independent* reported that 'President Hyde's indisposition will cause him to remain indoors for a further week . . . Although confined to his room, he is carrying on his duties as normal.'[20]

Hyde's speech and intellectual capacities were not affected by his stroke and though he later made a partial recovery, he was confined to a wheelchair. After his stroke, Hyde did not appear in public for five months and thereafter was less publicly prominent than he had been in the early years of his term.[21] Hyde's determination to remain in office, despite his declining health, had much to do with the need to avoid political upheaval during a period of national crisis. David Gray, in his memoir, wrote:

> The truth about [Hyde's] condition was concealed from the public because of the critical international situation and its repercussion on the Irish internal situation . . . The last thing that Mr de Valera wanted with the 'hot water' flaring up again and the IRA on his hands, was the death of Douglas Hyde and the opportunities for rebellion provided by a general election. Fortunately President Hyde convalesced to such a degree that

> he could receive visitors in bed and dispense sweet Manhattan cocktails to Americans. He liked them himself.[22]

On 27 June 1940, de Valera, accompanied by Joseph Walshe, Secretary of the Department of External Affairs, called to the Áras to enquire in person as to the President's health.[23] De Valera spent a short time privately with the President and this was the first time Hyde had been able to talk to the Taoiseach since his illness. It was clearly a significant meeting. From this point forth, it became clear that Hyde would remain literally *in situ*. In July, building work commenced on a new air-raid shelter at Áras an Uachtaráin. The existing air-raid shelter had been deemed unsuitable, yet Hyde's doctors had advised that he should not be moved outside the Áras unless it was absolutely necessary.[24] Moynihan and McDunphy were subsequently both involved in drawing up plans for the President's evacuation by ambulance and his continued safety in the event of an invasion, with Dargle Cottage, Enniskerry, being the favoured location.[25] Moynihan wrote:

> The Taoiseach's general view is that if emergency conditions make it necessary for the President to move from his present residence and to take up quarters elsewhere, his whereabouts should be known to the smallest possible number of persons. In order to achieve this, it would be necessary that he should assimilate his way of living as much as possible to that of a private citizen. The Taoiseach appreciates, of course, that it will be necessary for Mrs Kane [his sister, Annette] and a nurse or nurses to be in attendance. In the Taoiseach's opinion the President's Secretary should also be in touch with him. It is desirable that the number of servants to be employed should be reduced to a minimum and that the residence chosen should be on the small side and that elaborate furnishings shall be avoided.[26]

The lack of adverse press coverage about the President's illness was assisted by stringent wartime press restrictions. A very effective censorship operation was deployed to quell all reports of uncertainty in regard to Hyde's position. McDunphy was at the forefront of this work. In July 1940, McDunphy brought the rigour of the press censor down on the small-circulation *Wicklow People*, while at the same time establishing a marker that he wanted applied to the national papers. McDunphy wrote:

> The Wicklow People, a weekly journal, contain[s] suggestions that the President might, as a result of his illness, be inclined or induced to resign the presidency. There is no foundation, however, for these suggestions. At the same time, comments of this type are apt to have an unsettling effect on the people and are particularly objectionable at a time of crisis like the present when the country faces the possibility of being involved in the European War. I asked Mr Knightly, the press censor, to put a curb to this type of comment. He informed me that he has instructed that in future these articles are to be submitted to him before publication and that he will put an effective check to unsettling comment of this type.[27]

Knightly was as good as his word. Although the *Wicklow People* on a second occasion in October 1940 wrote a speculative piece on the President's health and Eoin O'Duffy had in June 1940 made reference to Hyde's ill health and possible resignation in the *Sunday Press*, this was as bad as it got.[28] In 1943, following Hyde's presence at the unveiling of a statue, *The Irish Times* did hint at a long-term health struggle.[29] In general, however, the national papers were scrupulous in not writing anything destabilising about the President's health and took almost all of their copy directly from McDunphy's highly anodyne updates. As will be subsequently explored, Hyde's health was controversially brought into public discourse by some Opposition TDs unhappy at the President's decision to grant de Valera a general election in 1944. However, over the course of Hyde's term, there was no official announcement on the President's serious medical condition until, at Seán T. O'Kelly's inauguration in June 1945, the Taoiseach obliquely stated that Hyde was too ill to attend.[30] Two days later, in a more clear-cut fashion, James Dillon told the Dáil: 'During the tenancy of the presidency by Dr Hyde, circumstances were such that his health interfered with his minor activities, and so it fell out that a great many formal acts were done by other officers of the state rather than burden him with an unnecessary amount of detailed work.'[31] By this stage the war in Europe was over, the threat of invasion had passed and reports of the President's grave ill health were no longer considered likely to undermine national security. Hyde had doggedly seen his term through in the country's best interest, with a selfless sense of duty.

Despite Hyde's poor health, the office of President played a big role in supporting the official policy of neutrality. This followed a rather shaky beginning to the relationship between the President and Taoiseach on foreign policy matters. Prior to the outbreak of war, de Valera had strongly supported the policy of appeasement pursued by the British Prime Minister Neville Chamberlain.[32] It soon became apparent that President Hyde was sceptical about this policy. In November 1938, Hyde, in addressing the Cumann Gaedhealach in UCD, made what he described as 'his first political reference in public' as President.[33] Hyde's comments amounted to a suggestion, which proved to be prescient, that the Munich Agreement and appeasement could not last. The President said: 'There is one nation in Europe that those interested in the trend of European affairs may watch carefully. That nation is Romania. That country has within its borders three-quarters of a million Germans, a million Magyars, thousands of Russians, and many Slavs and Jews. In the light of recent events in Czechoslovakia, a nation such as that could not retain its peace for long. The problem begun over Czechoslovakia is not finished yet.'[34]

Though Hyde's assessment, particularly in regard to the fate of Romania, would ultimately be vindicated, the President's comments caused concern in the Government at the particular time when they were made.[35] In the course of a subsequent conversation that McDunphy had with the President, Hyde 'agreed that in future it would be wise to omit from public statements any reference of a specific nature to politics, particularly those involving the names of individual countries, except on the advice of the Government or the Taoiseach'.[36]

In private, though, de Valera was keen to hear the President's views on international politics and Hyde's voice was an influential one. Hyde, along with John Cudahy, the then American Minister in Ireland, played a key role in persuading de Valera to cancel a scheduled anti-partition tour of America in the spring of 1939.[37] Hyde, who had himself undertaken an extensive tour of America in 1905 on behalf of the Gaelic League, had warned de Valera that the trip could accomplish little because Irish-American public opinion would be focused mainly on the gathering war clouds in Europe.[38] When war did break out in September 1939, McDunphy took the unusual step for the Secretary to the office of President of attending the Dáil and observing, from the Distinguished Visitors' Gallery, the first debate on the Emergency situation. This was seen as a signal that the office of President was determined to work closely with all the departments of state in support of the policy of neutrality.[39]

As head of state, Hyde had an important diplomatic role in maintaining cordial relations with the Axis and Allied representatives in Dublin, and ensuring that both sides perceived that they were being treated with equal courtesy and friendship. This was a job to which the genuinely genial Hyde was well suited. However, there were some teething difficulties, especially in regard to the British Representative to Ireland, John Maffey. In October 1939, the Government's determination not to allow anything to infringe on the policy of neutrality, especially when it came to the President, was made very evident. Hyde had accepted an invitation to speak at a Historical Society meeting in Trinity College, but the nature of the event changed when Maffey, in his first month in Ireland, had himself added to the panel of speakers. McDunphy noted: 'It was clear to me that an organised effort was being made to create an atmosphere in which the British representative as principal speaker would receive special attention and that the President would be expected to act as protagonist of his country's point of view [i.e. on neutrality].'[40] McDunphy further noted that the addition of the provision regarding orders and decorations on the invite was intended 'obviously to lend a further British colour to the meeting'.[41]

After consulting with the Government, Hyde withdrew from the event and, according to *The Daily Telegraph*, this was because de Valera was not prepared to 'risk a possible demonstration if Dr Hyde appeared in that loyalist stronghold with the King's representative'.[42] But this was not the end of the matter, as McDunphy was determined to have the last word. On learning of Maffey's late addition to the panel of speakers, McDunphy noted that he had 'immediately sent for the Auditor [of the Historical Society] and explained the matter to him without mincing words. I told him that I took strong objection to, firstly, the discourtesy to the President and secondly, the attempt to associate him with a setting completely out of harmony with the declared policy of neutrality of the country.'[43]

McDunphy insisted upon and received a public apology to the President, from the Society and from the Provost of Trinity, Dr Thrift, for 'a misunderstanding' in announcing that the President would attend the debate.[44] While McDunphy's action may be construed as overly robust, the incident was illustrative of the determination of the office of President to adhere strictly to the policy of neutrality and not to allow Hyde to be compromised in any way in this regard.

McDunphy's personnel file shows that the Secretary to the office of President played a significant role both in wartime intelligence garnering and as an advocate in support of Irish neutrality.[45] On his departure from the office of President in August 1954, McDunphy presented the then Taoiseach, John A. Costello, with a booklet comprised of a series of extraordinary memorandums that he had written in 1940 and 1941. McDunphy said that he felt the 'proper place' for this booklet was 'in the custody of the Government as historic documents'.[46] These memos were records of conversations that prominent Allied diplomats had with McDunphy. In a cover note that McDunphy wrote in August 1954, he said 'these conversations were, in every case, reported by me personally to the then Taoiseach, Mr de Valera, the text of the notes recorded by me being used for that purpose'.[47] McDunphy's contemporaneous annotated notes on these memos also underlined this point. On one memo, McDunphy had written in his own hand 'Conversation reported by me verbally to the Taoiseach Mr de Valera. The text of this note being read by me for that purpose. March 1941.'[48]

McDunphy's booklet of memos makes it clear that the office of President was at the cutting edge of Irish diplomatic efforts during the Second World War. These memos were not the handiwork of an exuberant civil servant trying to involve himself in the action or superfluous information that never reached the Taoiseach's in tray. The very fact that de Valera, who was struggling with his sight, took the time to have McDunphy verbally brief him or, in some cases, had him read his memos to him word for word underlines the political seriousness with which McDunphy's work was viewed.

A fascinating memo from July 1940 places the Secretary to the office of President on the high wire of wartime diplomacy. McDunphy noted that he had attended a social function in the British Representative's residence at which Maffey's Secretary, M. E. Antrobus, a British Foreign Office official, had 'practically monopolised my attention during the function'.[49] Antrobus was clearly engaged in an intelligence-gathering operation, but, as he sought to quiz McDunphy on the intricacies of Irish politics, McDunphy used the lengthy exchange to give the British diplomat a lecture on Ireland's resolve to uphold neutrality. McDunphy noted:

> Mr Antrobus doubted if this country fully realised the danger of becoming involved in the European War. I said we realised it very fully; that the country was united on the question of defence as it scarcely ever was before in history. There was only one recent parallel and that was on the occasion of the threat of conscription by the British Government in 1918. His view was that there was no prospect of this country being able to defend itself without aid. I replied that be that as it may, we were determined to face whatever came. He said that the only proper thing for us to do was to ask for the help of the British army, which would be given at once. I said that no Government of this country would dare to do such a thing. An invitation to the British Government to send soldiers to this country would be bitterly resented, would lead to revolution and would hurl any government from office.[50]

When Antrobus asked McDunphy would the Irish Government see it as their 'duty' to call in the British in the event of a German invasion, McDunphy fudged the question, but warned Antrobus that any British invasion 'under the guise of protection would not be any more acceptable than open aggression'.[51] McDunphy then gave a very exaggerated assessment of the country's military capacities, no doubt hoping the British official would communicate this to his superiors. McDunphy wrote:

> As regards our power of resistance I said that while the army of a few months ago was small in numbers, we could now put up a resistance which no power, even a first-class one, could afford to regard lightly. Perhaps we might be defeated in the field within a few weeks – Mr Antrobus interrupted me to say that in his opinion there was no doubt that we could hold out much longer than that. I added that in the purely military sense we might meet defeat, and in this we must bear in mind that the French army of several millions had held out for only five weeks, but that the country as a whole would not be defeated within a year and would be a thorn in the side of any power which tried to occupy it. He said that he felt certain of that.[52]

McDunphy was also unequivocal in presenting a unified national position. He recorded:

> [Antrobus] suggested that the present unity between Mr de Valera and Mr Cosgrave was a 'mere façade'. This is the exact phrase he used. I assured him that Mr Cosgrave, whatever his political views, was a man of unimpeachable honesty, and that at a time like this any statement of rigid neutrality on the national policy by him could be taken at its full face value; that his determination to stand with the nation against invasion from any quarter was no less than that of Mr de Valera. He seemed rather surprised and in fact disappointed. He then said, 'What about General Mulcahy? Do you think he is equally strong in this matter?' I said that the same thing applied to him. He then said, 'What about Mr Dillon; don't you think he is somewhat of a "windbag"? Again I use his own word. I said that I could not associate myself with any disparaging remarks about any public representative.[53]

McDunphy was adamant that Antrobus's questioning was 'a very engineered piece of probing'.[54] Though his memo for de Valera may have been influenced by fears of invasion, which were at their height in Government circles at this time, McDunphy arrived at stark political conclusions as to the purpose of Antrobus's queries. McDunphy wrote: 'The object apparently was to ascertain whether there was any chink in the national armour which could be utilised by the British in the event of an invasion, with particular reference to the possibility of finding some prominent public leader who would associate himself with a demand for, or at least a tacit acceptance of, the entry of British troops into this country on a pretext of protecting us from Germany.'[55]

In August 1940, McDunphy authored another fascinating memo based on a conversation he had in the Áras with Captain Lauriston Arnott, Managing Director of *The Irish Times* and a former officer of the British Army. McDunphy's conversation with Arnott centred on the Local Security Force (LSF), which acted as a wartime auxiliary to the Defence Forces.[56] Arnott, who was a First World War veteran, held a prominent position in the LSF unit based in Howth, serving alongside Dan Breen, a Fianna Fáil TD and one of the most celebrated IRA leaders during the War of Independence. Unknown to McDunphy, this was a fact that would subsequently be brought to Churchill's attention in a British intelligence report that made reference to 'Dan Breen, a notorious gunman of former days, who now . . . commands one of the Dublin Divisions of the Security Force with an ex-British officer as his second in command'.[57] Arnott's conversation with McDunphy suggests that there were simmering tensions across the LSF – Arnott told McDunphy that Breen 'had announced his intention of severing his connection with it' – arising from diverging attitudes to a British invasion.[58] Arnott told the Secretary to the office of President, unaware that McDunphy would pass the substance of their conversation on to the Taoiseach, that he would personally feel conflicted if a British invasion came to pass. McDunphy noted:

> He mentioned that, while of course he was prepared to do his utmost to repel a German invasion, he felt that he could not be expected to take any part in defence in the event of a British invasion. He had brothers and friends in that army. He felt that if the tragedy of a British invasion were to occur he would like to be able to stand aside, and attend as a private citizen to his ordinary business . . . When discussing his general attitude towards an invader he said that if Germany were to invade any

> part of Ireland, and the British came to drive them out he would at once cooperate with the British. When I asked if this applied even if the British came uninvited, he seemed somewhat confused but thought that it would not alter the situation. His idea apparently was that in any case, whether the British were invited or not he would cooperate with them against the Germans.[59]

Arnott's viewpoint provoked a very sharp rebuke from McDunphy who, irrespective of Hyde's instructions to make the Áras as accommodating to all political viewpoints as possible, took offence at what he saw as a betrayal of the state that he had served for many years as a senior civil servant. McDunphy wrote:

> I asked him if he realised that an invasion would be an act of hostility against every single individual in the community. If his brothers and friends were in the invading army they ipso facto would be enemies of every citizen of this state. If he, Captain Lauriston Arnott, at present a member of a branch of the Defence Forces, were to stand aside at such a time because of personal friendships, this could only be construed as an attitude of benevolence towards the invader and an act of hostility towards the state. Did he realise that he was a member of a force raised by the Government and on which the Government was relying to take part in the defence of the country; that his proposal to defect in case of an invasion by a particular belligerent was not only an act of personal treachery in time of war, but would introduce a very serious factor of disorganisation and demoralisation at a vital hour?[60]

In the course of a politically charged conversation, Arnott suggested to McDunphy that he had 'positive knowledge' that a British invasion had been scheduled to take place the previous month, 'in the second week in July', but 'for some reason it had been called off'.[61] McDunphy, meanwhile, used the conversation to repeat his forceful mantra that any assault on Irish neutrality would be met head-on. McDunphy recorded:

> I said that if the British entered this country uninvited whether under the open guise of aggressive invasion, or under the dishonest pretext of protection, this country would fight to the bitter limit. He seemed surprised at this; he thought that British help would be welcomed whether it was asked for or not. He asked me if Sir John Maffey was aware of the country's intensity of determination to this affect. I said that I presumed he was . . . I cannot remember his exact words at this point but he seemed to think that this depth of our determination was not fully realised in Britain. I said that the point could not be too emphatically or too frequently emphasised. He said that he would be seeing Sir John Maffey shortly and would earnestly stress this point to him.[62]

Arnott's claims that he had knowledge of an aborted invasion plan, that he was in contact with Maffey, and that, despite his senior position in an auxiliary Defence Force, he would not act against a British invasion, not surprisingly, set alarm bells ringing for McDunphy. The Secretary to the office of the President summed up his concerns to de Valera by stating that he was left with the impression:

> 1. That there are groups within the Local Defence who hold this view;
> 2. That the members of these groups regard themselves, not as owing allegiance to Ireland, but as auxiliaries to the British forces in case of a German invasion of this country;
> 3. That they are definitely not to be relied on in case of a British invasion;
> 4. That on the contrary they will be ready in such case to help the British against us;
> 5. That they are well organised among themselves and that there is some form of collaboration between them and those whom they wish to serve.[63]

In the midst of the Second World War, the information that McDunphy passed on to the Taoiseach could only be classified as high-level intelligence and it undermines the commonplace view that during the war years the Áras was a remote government outpost far removed from the big political issues of the day.

McDunphy's strong views on Irish neutrality would also, in the course of the war, be analysed at the highest levels in the British cabinet. Although McDunphy was a career civil servant, the wide latitude that Hyde and de Valera gave him and the roving diplomatic role he performed was an important component in maintaining the policy of neutrality. In December 1940, McDunphy met with an unofficial British emissary, Captain Noel Fitzpatrick, who had flown to Dublin with the imprimatur of the British War Office to seek the Irish Government's views on a proposal that Fitzpatrick had advanced of raising an Irish-American legion in the United States to defend Ireland.[64] De Valera had politely rejected Fitzpatrick's plan, claiming that there were 'enough men' in Ireland to defend the state.[65]

After meeting with the Taoiseach, Captain Fitzpatrick also met with President Hyde and McDunphy at Áras an Uachtaráin. Fitzpatrick's report made it clear that de Valera and Hyde were on the same wavelength, but 'Mr McDunphy gave a more forceful definition of Irish policy. He told Fitzpatrick that it would be illogical and unreasonable to expect Ireland to abandon her neutrality until Britain put Ireland's armed forces in a position to repel German reprisals.'[66]

McDunphy also stressed that

> Irish troops would not be intimidated by British troops if any British politician was so stupid to urge this as a last resort. Neither was Ireland frightened by the 'bogey' of her fate if Germany overran Britain. It would need more than half a million first-class troops and equipment to take Ireland. It would be suicide if Germany tried it; there were several thousand Irishmen serving with the British forces and 30 million Irish-Americans who would demand a well justified explanation. The power that attempted to seize Ireland would automatically lose the war.[67]

McDunphy went on to say that 'if Britain were reconciled to a stalemate she could at least be assured that Ireland would do nothing to worsen the situation. Ireland had shown a very real desire to help Britain in its war against tyranny and atheism.'[68]

McDunphy's views, along with those of the Taoiseach, reached the British War Cabinet, which considered Fitzpatrick's report. Lord Cranborne, the Dominions Secretary, who was a strong advocate of economic sanctions to force Ireland to give up the Treaty Ports, was annoyed by the lack of progress from the British emissary's engagement with the Taoiseach and the office of President. He wrote to Churchill: 'I think that we were thoroughly justified in our distrust of Captain Fitzpatrick as an emissary. He seems to be a simple soul who has been swallowed whole by Mr de Valera and Mr McDunphy.' Cranborne continued, hinting at his frustration with the Irish Government, that 'at the present moment it is perhaps symbolic that the President of Ireland is paralytic and the Prime Minister blind'. Churchill's handwritten comment, at the bottom of Cranborne's memo, simply said 'I agree.'[69]

While, as Secretary to the office of President, McDunphy played a role in wartime Anglo-Irish relations, his booklet of memos gives no indication of any contact with German diplomats, although the same booklet also documents his conversations with American representatives.[70] This omission seems all the more odd given the fact that all the available evidence suggests McDunphy enjoyed very good relations with the German legation. McDunphy, who was a keen hiker, had regularly holidayed in Germany and Austria, as well as Switzerland, from the 1920s and, as a result, spoke very competent German.[71] From the mid 1930s on, McDunphy was also a regular guest at social events hosted by the German legation.[72] Shortly after the announcement that McDunphy had been appointed Secretary to the office of President, he was the most senior Irish civil servant to attend a German Christmas celebration in the Gresham Hotel, where 'with right arms raised in the Nazi salute, the gathering sang "Deutschland Uber Alles" [the then German national anthem], the "Horst Wessel Lied" [the official marching song of the Nazi Party] and "The Soldier's Song" [the Irish national anthem].'[73]

That the booklet containing memorandums of McDunphy's wartime conversations from 1940 and 1941 does not touch upon relations with Germany may simply suggest that McDunphy did not meet any German officials in this period. However, this is unlikely given that the German Minister, Eduard Hempel, was a regular visitor to the Áras.[74] It may also simply suggest that Hempel and his colleagues said nothing of interest for McDunphy to catalogue or, more likely, McDunphy, in compiling the booklet in 1954, with an eye on history, may have been embarrassed by memoranda which showed a close or sympathetic relationship with the Germans and decided to discard these memos.

Hyde, Professor Pokorny and Irish Reactions to the Holocaust

Certainly, from the point of view of posterity, the response in the Áras to the treatment by the Nazi regime of Professor Julius Pokorny, a friend of Hyde, was ungenerous and motivated by a desire, first and foremost, not to do anything that would cause the Germans offence. The case of Pokorny is worth examining here because it shows an extremely rigid adherence to neutrality in the Áras, even when it came to issues of personal and humanitarian concern, which went far beyond the behaviour of other Government departments. Pokorny was ultimately assisted in his plight by the intervention of the Taoiseach, Éamon de Valera. Dermot Keogh has argued that Pokorny's case is illustrative of 'the willingness of de Valera's Government to help scholars who found themselves the victims of Hitler's racial laws',[75] but the case also highlights a disappointing inflexibility in attitudes in the Áras.

Julius Pokorny was born on 12 June 1887 in Prague, but he was brought up in Austria. He was appointed 'Lektor' in Irish in Vienna University in 1912 and became 'Dozent' in Celtic Philology in 1914. In 1920, he was given the Chair of Celtic at the University of Berlin.[76] Pokorny was a leading academic authority on Old Irish and he developed political sympathies with the Gaelic League and Irish nationalism. He had first visited Ireland in 1908 and had befriended Douglas Hyde.[77] In that same year and again in 1910, he taught courses in the School of Irish Studies in Dublin, where he 'acquired the nickname "Póigín" ["Little Kiss"] from his fondness for the affection of young ladies'.[78] Pokorny was subsequently a translator of Patrick Pearse's work, he was mentioned as a character in Joyce's *Ulysses* and, in 1925, he received an honorary doctorate from the National University of Ireland.[79] According to Pokorny's biographer, Ó Dochartaigh, from 1920 until 1935, he was 'arguably the most important figure in Celtic Studies on the European mainland, as well as a propagandist on Ireland's behalf'.[80]

Though Pokorny was a Roman Catholic and 'a German Nationalist who had little difficulty with Nazism', in 1935, after the passing of the Nuremberg race laws, he was dismissed from his professorship in Berlin because of his Jewish ancestry.[81] Pokorny's difficulties had begun in 1933 within months of Adolf Hitler becoming Chancellor. In a letter to Douglas Hyde, on 5 May 1933, Pokorny wrote:

> You know I have always been a good German patriot, from my Christian parents and educated in a Benedictine convent. This Easter I got a form from the Government, asked to give particulars about my grandparents. To my astonishment, my father informed me that my mother's father had not been 'Aryan'. He had died long before I was born and I had never known it. According to a new law, everybody, one grandparent of whom is a Jew, is looked upon as Jew and to be dismissed from his office, except if he has fought in the war or been in office before August 1914. Though a lecturer since April 1914, I have been suspended from office.[82]

Pokorny continued by informing Hyde:

> Mr MacCarty [official in the Irish legation in Berlin] has written to Dublin, full particulars, in order to bring about a diplomatic intervention on my behalf, pointing out that my person was an important link between Ireland and Germany. I have given your name as a reference. Perhaps you could help me with the Foreign Office. But please remember that any anti-German propaganda may ruin me. When writing to me, please do so through the Irish legation in Berlin.[83]

On the same date, Hyde wrote in almost identical terms to Richard Irvine Best, the Director of the National Library of Ireland.[84] Pokorny was clearly living in fear. It is unclear what steps Hyde or Best took – if any – but, by the end of 1933, Pokorny had been restored to his position. In a subsequent letter to Best, he attributed his job being saved to 'the intervention of the Irish Government'.[85] This was, however, to be a short reprise.

Despite the precarious nature of his own position in 1933, Pokorny had shown immense moral courage in speaking out against the imprisonment of a colleague from the University of Berlin, Ernst Lewy, a Professor of Comparative Linguistics. Though this brought unwanted Nazi attention on Pokorny and he became the target of police investigations, he continued to support Lewy publicly and helped to secure his release in early 1935.[86] Following the adoption of the Nuremberg Laws in September 1935, Pokorny was once again suspended from the University of Berlin in November before being formally removed from his position that December.

Following his dismissal from his academic post, Pokorny chose to remain in Berlin and lobby the Nazi authorities for his reinstatement. Lewy, upon his release, had chosen a different course. He had quickly left Germany for England and in 1937 he settled in Ireland.[87] In 1938, de Valera sought Lewy's assistance in the establishment of an Institute of Celtic Studies in Dublin and the Taoiseach personally intervened to ensure that Lewy's daughter was granted a visa for admission to Ireland.[88] It is likely that Lewy also availed of his relationship with de Valera to offer assistance to Pokorny. In May 1938, de Valera made efforts through the Department of External Affairs to have Pokorny reinstated to his post in Berlin.[89]

Pokorny may also have been heartened at this time by the fact that his friend of thirty years' standing was about to become President of Ireland. On 15 June 1938, ten days before his inauguration, Hyde wrote to Pokorny from his Roscommon home, pledging his support. Hyde wrote: 'I am very sorry to hear so bad an account about you, and you may be certain that I shall do all I can to get the matter remedied. But I am not President yet, and shall not be, until I take the oath, at the close of the month, and then I must wait until "I find myself", like Kipling's ship, for I shall be new to everything, but I expect I shall be seeing the foreign minister [de Valera, the Taoiseach and Minister for External Affairs] soon, and then will be my time.'[90]

Pokorny's biographer has observed of this letter that 'whether Hyde did indeed speak to de Valera on this matter is not recorded.

There is no written documentation relating to the twelve months after Hyde sent this letter to Pokorny.'[91] In fact, a hitherto unseen file maintained by McDunphy sheds far more light on Hyde's dealings with Pokorny and shows that, in office, Hyde gradually distanced himself from Pokorny's plight.[92]

Prior to the outbreak of war in 1939, Hyde did make some efforts to assist Pokorny, but subsequently he ignored Pokorny's increasingly desperate pleas for assistance. At the same time, the available evidence shows that de Valera, who did not share the same personal bonds with Pokorny, was much more flexible in his approach and that the Taoiseach's assistance ultimately saved Pokorny's life and secured his escape from Germany in 1943.

On 24 June 1938, the day prior to Hyde's inauguration, Pokorny wrote to him from Berlin detailing the deteriorating anti-Semitic situation in Germany. In this letter, which McDunphy put on file in Áras an Uachtaráin, Pokorny noted:

> [My] prospects here become worse and worse. It is proposed to confiscate 'Non-Aryan' property and to force 'Non-Aryans' to live only in Jewish houses. This would mean everybody would know one's descent at once. So far I have had in spite of everything a comparatively easy life, since nobody suspects my descent I can move socially wherever I like. Fact is, I have very little 'Jewish blood' in me, but according to the law I am reckoned as a Jew . . . In the last year, I have come by inheritance into some money, so I could live quite comfortably together with my pension – but the new measures threaten confiscation of my property since I am looked upon by law as a Jew.[93]

In a direct plea to Hyde to intervene on his behalf, Pokorny also intuitively recognised the Nazi sympathies of Charles Bewley, the Irish Minister in Berlin. Pokorny wrote:

> If there would be a way in which the German Government could be induced to let me live in peace and to treat me as an ordinary Christian and German, I could go on working and should be quite satisfied . . . Foreign opinion is the only thing

> that matters to them, and since I am politically beyond reproach, it is only my grandparents that stand against me. I am quite sure you could help me, if some personal action from your side could be added to those of President [*sic*] de Valera. If you would allow me a suggestion, it is my opinion that Mr Bewley is not enough personally interested in my fate and that any action through the Berlin ambassador alone would be perhaps too colourless and impersonal.[94]

There is no record of Hyde replying to this letter; however, in September 1938, in a letter to John Glyn Davies, the retired head of the Department of Celtic Studies at the University of Liverpool, President Hyde alluded to a rather tepid appeal he had made on Pokony's behalf. On 16 September 1938, Hyde wrote: 'Many thanks for your kind letter about Pokorny. I am very sorry for him. I took occasion when the German Ambassador called on me the other day to mention his name as if accidentally, and to say that we appreciated his work here in Ireland.'[95] Davies' original letter to Hyde, on 11 September, had recognised, given the treatment of the Jews in Germany, that Pokorny's life was in danger. Davies wanted to create a refuge for Pokorny under the auspices of the University of Liverpool, as a lecturer of Irish, and asked for Hyde's help in getting the Irish Government to support this initiative. Davies wrote:

> I can see that he stays in Germany at his peril, and my feeling that something should be done for him in Great Britain prompted me to ask him to let me suggest one scheme to you. Eighteen months ago I discussed with the late Professor Garmon Jones the possibility of getting Pokorny to Liverpool. Garmon Jones, one of the shrewdest men in the University, thought my plan feasible, if it was backed by the Government of the Free State [*sic*]. I have set forth my views in the enclosed statement.[96]

Hyde's reply to this proposal was stunning in its insensitivity and does his reputation little credit. Oblivious to or ignoring the threat Pokorny's continued stay in Nazi Germany posed to his safety, Hyde's reply was rooted in academic politics, it was dismissive of Pokorny's abilities as an Irish teacher (even to the extent of suggesting another individual for the post) and it crucially gave no undertaking to attempt to source funding from the Irish Government. Hyde wrote:

> All the same, do you think he would be a man who would bring in students to Manchester or Liverpool? I don't think he could enthuse the Irishmen, and I am afraid they want to be enthused. If Father Kelleher could attract fifty or sixty students, I do not think Pokorny could do the same. I really don't know what to say for I don't know anyone now in Liverpool or Manchester, and have no knowledge of where to go to look for money. Of course, I understand the Government in Germany never took Pokorny's salary from him. I think he branched off into a number of un-Celtic avenues which would hardly arouse enthusiasm.[97]

Later in the same month in which Hyde and Davies had corresponded, Pokorny briefly visited Dublin. On 21 September 1938, he was received by President Hyde at Áras an Uachtaráin. Pokorny's focus was still on remaining in Germany and being restored to his position in the University of Berlin. Pokorny presented President Hyde with a personal memorandum which suggested that

> perhaps a personal, non-official intervention, such as a letter from An t-Uachtarán or An Taoiseach to the Secretary of Foreign Affairs in Dublin, would be of immense value. I would add that I have proved to the German Government that I had myself been an active fighter for their present nationalistic principles since 1916, being particularly active in fighting the Czechs in Sudetenland. All I want is to be left in peace in order to be able to continue my research work into the Celtic Past, which of course is very difficult under the present circumstances, not having any citizen's rights whatever. I can do so only if I get exempt from all repressive measures against the Jews, to whose community I do not belong, myself and my parents being Catholics.[98]

McDunphy's note of this meeting was curt and hardly sympathetic. He recorded:

> The President saw Prof. Pokorny today. The latter was anxious that the President should assist him in some way, either to get him restored to his former post of Professor in the Berlin Unvy. [*sic*] from which he had been removed on the grounds that he was of Jewish ancestry, and/or to get restored to him his property in Germany of which he had been dispossessed for the same reason. The President told him that he could not interfere in this matter affecting the internal administration of another country.[99]

Hyde had moved quite a distance from his promise to Pokorny, made shortly prior to his inauguration as President, that he would do all he could. Whether Hyde felt constrained by his office or whether McDunphy was exerting influence on him is a matter of conjecture, but, with the President a political greenhorn, the Secretary to the office of President was very much the power behind the throne in the Áras. Hyde heavily relied upon his Secretary, who was a talented and experienced civil servant, had previously served as an Assistant Secretary in the Department of the Taoiseach, and had played a key role in the drafting of Bunreacht na hÉireann. McDunphy took a very conservative view of the President's role and he saw his own function as being about building a sense of dignity around the new constitutional office and, more importantly, keeping it largely removed from controversy.[100]

McDunphy appears also to have enjoyed very good relations with the German legation, but this should not be taken as an indication that he had any sympathy for the Nazi regime, and in a long career he served the Irish state with ability and integrity. Irrespective of the harmonious relations between the Phoenix Park and Northumberland Road (the site of the German legation), there may also have been a feeling in the office of President that with the clouds of war hovering – and Irish neutrality well flagged in advance of the hostilities commencing – that nothing should be done by the head of state that could put him at odds with any foreign Government. Certainly,

McDunphy's attitude to Pokorny's difficulties was defined not by any trace of empathy, but rather by a strict sense of strict protocol and bureaucratic propriety. This was very evident in April 1939 when Liam Gógan wrote to the Secretary to the office of President, presumably with a view to McDunphy briefing the President on the up-to-date position with Pokorny.

Gógan, like Pokorny, was a scholar of Old Irish and he was the keeper of the Art and Industrial Division in the National Museum.[101] In his letter on 1 April, Gógan explained that a friend of Pokorny's had visited Dublin to obtain letters from other scholars requesting a reconsideration of Pokorny's case.[102] Gógan said that these letters would form the basis for an 'approach through a Reichsminister not unfavourable to such cases' and that, in this instance, it had been decided that letters from the President and Taoiseach were 'not actually requisite'.[103] Gógan's letter did not request anything from Hyde bar discretion. Gógan wrote that Pokorny 'regards it of great importance that neither the German Ministry here nor the Nazi group should know anything about these démarches'.[104] This particular request seemed to draw McDunphy's hostility and he annotated beside it, on 4 April 1939, that 'Mr Gógan apparently suggests that the President should be associated with activities in regard to a German citizen, of which the accredited representative of the German Govt in Ireland would not be prepared to approve.'[105] This comment was clearly a reference to a phone call McDunphy had received from Gógan on 3 April, following up on his earlier letter. In this conversation, Gógan asked McDunphy to ensure that Hyde received a Mr Lisner, an Attaché of the German Foreign Office in Berlin, who Gógan must have believed was well disposed towards helping Pokorny.[106] A memo McDunphy wrote on 4 April 1938 regarding the requested Lisner meeting said: 'The object of the suggested interview was that the President should make some representations or take some other action which would move the German Government to reinstate Prof. Pokorny in his former post, or restore him to his property.'[107]

Despite the previous warning that nothing about Pokorny should be disclosed to the German legation in Dublin, McDunphy's memo of 4 April 1939 indicates that this was exactly what he did. This memo also seems to underline that in this matter at least, McDunphy leaned more favourably towards the German authorities than those trying to help Pokorny. McDunphy noted:

> I informed Mr Gógan that it would not be proper for the President to intervene in a matter of this nature. I pointed out moreover that I understood it to be the wish of the German legation here that any German seeking to be received by the President should be introduced by the German Minister. It was a matter of surprise to me that with an official of the German Government such a procedure should be overlooked. Mr Gógan informed me that he had anticipated my reply and that he has already caused Dr Eoin MacNeill to speak to the President on the same matter. I must say that I found Mr Gógan lacking in a proper sense of respect due to the President.[108]

MacNeill was another venerable Gaelic scholar, a former Government Minister and a lifelong friend of the President, yet his intervention did not move Hyde. Lisner was not received at the Áras and, instead, on 12 April, McDunphy sent a sharp warning to Gógan that 'you do not appreciate that it would not be proper for the head of state to do anything which might, even in the remotest manner, be capable of being construed as interfering in the internal affairs of another country'.[109] Gógan's efforts had so irked McDunphy that he noted on 20 April, 'there is a personal file for Mr Liam Gógan, who as will be seen from the attached file has endeavoured to get the President to intervene on Prof. Pokorny's behalf. While Mr Gógan's activities in this regard are perfectly legitimate, his attitude to the head of state is so peculiar and so irresponsible that I have made it the subject of a separate note on his file.'[110] In effect, what this meant was that Gógan was being blacklisted by the Áras.

As the effective decision makers in the office of President, Hyde and McDunphy may have genuinely believed that it was prudent not to intervene in Pokorny's case given the state's policy of non-alignment in the fraught international situation in the run-up to the war. However, their actions (or lack thereof) contrast with those of de Valera, the main architect of wartime neutrality, who was prepared to temper this policy with compassion for Pokorny's predicament. On 17 August 1939, with war now almost inevitable, Joseph Walshe, Secretary to the Department of External Affairs, wrote to the Department of Justice making it clear that de Valera wanted Pokorny to be issued with an Irish visa. Walshe wrote: 'Although Professor Pokorny is of Jewish origin, the Minister for External Affairs [de Valera] feels that in view of his outstanding position in the world of Celtic studies the legation at Berlin should be authorised to grant a visa to Professor Pokorny at any time he desires to visit this country.'[111]

In January 1940, the Irish legation in Berlin was authorised to issue a visa to Pokorny. Pokorny, however, seemed reluctant to leave his home in Germany. His biographer has noted: 'Pokorny's behaviour in this period is still contradictory. On the one hand, he acquired an Irish visa, suggesting that he wished to leave the country. On the other hand, he continued his academic research, trying for all the world to behave as if nothing had changed.'[112]

In August 1940, Pokorny again featured on the radar of the office of President when McDunphy received correspondence from Frederick Boland, the Assistant Secretary in the Department of External Affairs. In an effort to prevent himself being taken away from his academic research and forced to work for the Nazi war effort, Pokorny wanted the Irish legation in Berlin to furnish him with a letter saying that he was working on an important Celtic research project at President Hyde's request. On 2 August 1940, Boland wrote to McDunphy:

> Dr Julius Pokorny, formerly Professor of Celtic Studies at Berlin University, has informed [the] legation at Berlin that, at the request of An Uachtarán, whom he saw during his last visit to Ireland in 1938, he is at present compiling a Celtic etymological dictionary. He has asked the legation to give him confirmation of this, in writing, for presentation if necessary to the German authorities. Professor Pokorny's purpose in asking for some such document is that he thinks that it would be of some use to him should, as is sometimes suggested, all persons who are not of full 'Aryan' descent be forced to work in munition factories, particularly those who are not already otherwise engaged in important work.[113]

Boland continued by asking McDunphy to ascertain Hyde's views on this matter while, at the same time, managing to both downplay Pokorny's concerns and to suggest that, in any case, there was little Irish officials could do to help him. It was a diplomatic washing of hands from which the office of President would ultimately take its lead. Boland wrote:

> I would be glad if you would be good enough to inform me at your earliest convenience, whether or not An Uachtarán actually did request Dr Julius Pokorny to prepare a dictionary. I am to add, for your private information, that the legation is of opinion that Dr Julius Pokorny's fears of being sent to work in a factory are based entirely on rumour. Work of that kind would be a great hardship on him, but in spite of his services to Irish learning, the legation does not see how it could assist him.[114]

As Pokorny's biographer has noted, Boland's suggestion to McDunphy that Pokorny's fears might be exaggerated was stunningly inaccurate. Ó Dochartaigh wrote: 'On 4 March 1939 the president of the Nazi Employment Office, Friedrich Syrup, had decreed that unemployed Jews could be press-ganged into heavy work in factories. This practice had begun immediately. It seems impossible that the Irish legation in Berlin was unaware of this nearly eighteen months later. As a "Jew" without work, Pokorny was eligible. Contrary to Boland's assertion, the threat of forced labour was very real indeed.'[115]

This threat became even more menacing when, in October 1941, the deportation of German Jews from Berlin commenced. By this stage, the Irish legation had largely lost sight of Pokorny and he was most likely living an underground existence in Berlin.[116] Pokorny had not been ultimately helped by Hyde in his ruse – to keep the Nazi authorities off his back – that he was working on a Celtic dictionary at the behest of the President of Ireland. McDunphy's response to Boland's query, while not hostile, refused to bend the truth to fit Pokorny's perilous position. McDunphy's letter, dated 7 August 1940, read: 'While it would not perhaps be strictly accurate to say that the President commissioned or even definitely requested Dr Pokorny to compile a

Celtic etymological dictionary, a proposal to this effect was discussed by the Doctor with the President and was then, and still is, regarded by the President as a commendable project. The President has a high regard for the services rendered by Dr Pokorny to the Irish language.'[117]

In Hyde's defence, it should be pointed out that, given Boland's less than critical assessment of the danger to Pokorny, the President may not have felt morally obliged to tell a white lie to assist Pokorny. The President's refusal to confirm that he was the instigator of Pokorny's research project put paid to any hopes that Pokorny may have harboured that letters from distinguished Irish friends would save him from the Nazis. Two days after McDunphy's response to Boland, the Department of External Affairs drew up a memo noting that it would not be true to say the President had commissioned Pokorny's research and instructing that 'the legation should inform Dr Pokorny that it is not possible to comply with his request'.[118]

Though Pokorny must have felt let down by his old friend, Hyde, he would have reason to be grateful to the Irish Taoiseach. Pokorny was, in the words of his biographer, 'one of those [German Jews] who held out in what they saw as their own country until they finally had no option but to flee (or were deported to a death camp)'.[119] In September 1942, Pokorny had reappeared at the Irish legation in Berlin looking for his visa to be renewed. In October 1942, the Taoiseach sanctioned the renewal of Pokorny's Irish visa and, following a subsequent tip-off that the Gestapo were looking for him, Pokorny eventually managed to escape out of Germany.[120] De Valera's generosity played no small part in securing Pokorny's safety. Ó Dochartaigh wrote that 'this visa probably saved his life: when he fled to Switzerland in July 1943, the Swiss authorities were turning back thousands of refugees and only a valid visa for a third country was likely to secure legal entry'.[121]

As a refugee in Switzerland, Pokorny's position was uncertain and he was financially destitute. On 21 September 1943, Liam Gógan wrote to McDunphy that Pokorny was 'badly out of funds', trying to make his way to Ireland and asking Gógan 'to convey his greetings and kind regards to the President'.[122] Hyde's response was a shameful abandonment of Pokorny to his predicament. McDunphy was on holiday when Gógan wrote his letter, but on his return he wrote in relation to it: 'Seen. President has also seen. No action necessary.'[123] On 16 January 1944, Pokorny again appealed to his old friend, the President, for financial support. In a telegram addressed to 'Douglas Hyde President of Éire Dublin,' Pokorny wrote 'Am refugee at Berne please send money through Irish legation Switzerland.'[124] This telegram may have pricked Hyde's conscience because McDunphy was given instructions to contact the Department of External Affairs for advice on the matter. McDunphy, however, was clearly unhappy with the Pokorny telegram. The following day, he wrote by hand on Pokorny's telegram, 'this is very indiscreet. Spoke to Boland, Asst Sec. Ex Affairs. He will wire today to Irish legation at Switzerland for a report.'[125] Ultimately, it was Joseph Walshe who advised on the Pokorny telegram. Walshe had already earlier that month heartlessly rejected an appeal from Gógan for funds for Pokorny. Walshe had written: 'It is quite clear that Pokorny has no friends here and we have no benevolent society for the relief of foreign professors of Celtic Languages. The general feeling seems to be that as foreigners take up Celtic languages as a study subject, and a means of livelihood, there is no reason why they should be supported by us as if they were Irishmen.'[126]

Walshe gave similarly callous advice to McDunphy in regard to Pokorny's telegram. On 15 February 1944, in a memo that McDunphy entitled 'Wire of 16 January not to be answered', the Secretary to the office of President noted: 'I consulted with the Secretary [of the Department of External Affairs] on the matter today and he expressed the opinion that it would be better to take no action on the wire, and in fact to ignore it. Prof Pokorny has made similar appeals to others in Dublin, and addressing this appeal to the President in a time of crisis like the present, is a type of indiscretion which should be rigidly discouraged.'[127]

McDunphy's memo betrays a concern with the President not being seen to do anything of which the German Government might disapprove, and this clearly ranked far ahead of Pokorny's welfare. Hyde chose to take Walshe's advice. He never responded to Pokorny's telegram, which appears to have been the last ever communication between the two men. It is likely than Pokorny felt let down in his time of need by Hyde. However, his appeals to others in Dublin appear to have borne some fruit, particularly in the case of the

Taoiseach. Pokorny was given 'special treatment' in the Swiss refugee centre after being furnished with a letter of introduction from de Valera.[128] Pokorny was subsequently granted asylum in Switzerland and he maintained thereafter that this was because of the efforts of de Valera. Pokorny lived a long and productive academic life, teaching in universities in both Zurich and Berne. He died in Zurich in 1970, aged eighty-two, after being involved in a road traffic accident.[129] President de Valera was represented at Pokorny's funeral by Frank Biggar, the Irish Ambassador to Switzerland. Biggar reported that the eulogy at Pokorny's funeral was delivered by Professor Hubschmidt, who in his remarks 'attributes to the intervention of President de Valera the decision of the Swiss Government to grant asylum to Professor Pokorny'.[130]

In the case of Pokorny, it is hard not to arrive at the conclusion that de Valera, irrespective of the constraints of neutrality, showed much more flexibility and decency than President Hyde. Douglas Hyde is an underrated, but outstanding figure in Irish history. As an academic and an activist, he played a phenomenal role in preserving the Irish language. As President, he was an unassuming and popular first citizen whose personality did much to secure broad acceptance of his office. However, Hyde's churlish treatment of Professor Pokorny, a victim of the Nazis' racial laws and an individual desperately struggling to escape the horrors of the Holocaust, is an ugly blot on an otherwise distinguished record of service to Ireland.

Hyde and Irish-German Relations

The office of President did play a central role in Irish-German relations during the Second World War. At the outset, de Valera had explained to the German Minister, Eduard Hempel, that Ireland wished to remain neutral and maintain friendly relations with Germany, but for trade and political reasons his Government would have to show a 'certain consideration' for Britain.[131] Aengus Nolan has noted that the German Foreign Office ordered Hempel to 'keep a close eye on Government officials, public comment and common rumour for any signs that may indicate anything less than committed neutrality'.[132] At Áras an Uachtaráin, Hempel would have had nothing to complain of, as Hyde was meticulous in ensuring that the German Minister was accorded the same respect as the Allied representatives in Dublin.[133] Hempel was a welcome guest at the Áras during the war and personal relations between Hempel and Hyde also appear to have been particularly good.[134] Both men shared an interest in literature, regularly exchanged books and Hempel wrote of 'the unfailing friendly kindliness' Hyde always displayed towards him.[135]

The goodwill between Hempel and Hyde may explain the German Minister's unwillingness to immerse Hyde in a controversy that would have had wartime diplomatic reverberations. Just prior to the outbreak of war, the Irish Government had decided to replace the Irish Minister to Germany, Charles Bewley, as 'his Nazi predilection' was causing serious disquiet in the Department of External Affairs.[136] Thomas Kiernan was appointed as his successor and Hempel gave the German Foreign Office a glowing assessment of Kiernan's capabilities.[137] Matters were complicated by the outbreak of war because Kiernan's appointment had not been effected by this stage. Because of the External Relations Act, de Valera had a sensitive judgement call to make as to whether he should, in Fisk's words, 'risk British apoplexy' by requesting the King to sign credentials addressed to Hitler at a time when Britain and Germany were at war.[138] The British Dominions Secretary, Anthony Eden, personally made his Government's sensitivities on this issue known to de Valera and the Taoiseach concluded that it would be 'unwise to pursue the matter'.[139]

Hyde was brought into the equation because the German Foreign Office was keen to have the issues surrounding Kiernan's accreditation resolved and suggested that either de Valera or President Hyde should sign the accreditation.[140] Hempel, who was more familiar with Irish constitutional arrangements than his own Foreign Office, recognised that the proper protocol would be for Hyde to sign the accreditation before the Führer could receive Kiernan. Hempel, however, was also familiar with Irish political realities and doubted that 'de Valera or Hyde could or would sign, as this would disturb the Commonwealth link'.[141] Hempel did not make an issue of this, even though he knew that the Irish Government was deliberately foot-dragging, while maintaining a pretence of wanting full accreditation for Kiernan. As a result, William Warnock, who was twenty-seven years of age at the outbreak of hostilities, ran the Irish legation in Berlin for almost the entire war.[142] Though Hempel expressed concerns about the disparity in representation, a German Minister as against 'a young secretary acting as Irish representative', he did not push the matter.[143]

Had Hempel sought to force the issue, Hyde and the de Valera Government would have had to make the unenviable and controversial decision of whether the President should refuse to sign the accreditation, risking a breach in diplomatic relations with Germany in the midst of a war, or whether the President should sign the accreditation, thereby bypassing the External Relations Act and undoubtedly provoking British ire at a particularly delicate time. Instead of insisting on a definitive decision, Hempel quietly suggested to the German Foreign Office that it might be just as well to let the matter drop as Warnock was doing a good job.[144] This action helped Hyde and de Valera to slide off the hook with the German Foreign Office.

Such acts of good grace on Hempel's part contributed to him becoming a popular figure in Irish Government circles. In 1974, nearly thirty years after the end of Hempel's mission to Ireland, Seán MacEntee fondly recalled him and insisted 'Hempel was not a Nazi, he was an honourable man.'[145] In 1972, in a letter to Hempel's widow, President de Valera described the former German Minister as 'a friend who always understood Ireland's position'.[146]

De Valera always maintained that it was this personal respect for Hempel, as well as a proper adherence to the protocols of neutrality, that influenced one of the most controversial actions of his career – his decision to visit the German Minister on the death of Hitler.[147] Similar reasons motivated what has only in recent times come to be seen as one of the most controversial aspects of Hyde's presidency – his decision to extend his condolences to the German Minister.

The background to this controversy was Hitler's suicide in Berlin on 30 April 1945. After this news reached Ireland, on 2 May 1945, de Valera, accompanied by Joseph Walshe, visited the German Minister. The following day's main newspapers all reported that the Taoiseach had 'called on Dr Hempel, the German minister, last evening, to express his condolences'.[148]

In 2005, a story claiming that President Hyde had also visited Hempel upon Hitler's death made international headlines.[149] It was claimed that presidential protocol records newly released at this time, for the years 1938 to 1957, suggested that Hyde had personally called to Hempel's residence and that this event occurred on 3 May 1945, the day after the Taoiseach's visit.[150] These protocol records state that the President did not send an official letter because 'the capital of Germany, Berlin, was under siege and no successor had been appointed'.[151] The records, however, make clear that it was the Secretary to the President who called upon Hempel on 3 May 1945. The protocol records in relation to the death of Hitler state:

> Call on Diplomatic Representative of State Concerned.
> (a) Representative of the President – Secretary to the President
> (b) On whom he called – His Excellency the German Minister, Dr Hempel
> (c) Date of call – 3 May 1945
> (d) Response to call, with date – The German Minister called on the Secretary to the President on 3 May, 1945.[152]

These records plainly show that it was McDunphy, not Hyde, who called on Hempel and that Hempel returned the courtesy, on the same day, by calling to the Áras. The more sensationalist story that Hyde actually visited Hempel is based on a misunderstanding or a misrepresentation of these protocol records by a news syndicate service. Contemporary newspapers also attest that it was McDunphy, on the President's behalf, who called on Hempel and this meeting took place not in Hempel's residence, as the 2005 news story suggested, but at the German legation. *The Irish Times* on 4 May 1945 reported that 'Mr McDunphy, the Secretary to the President, called on the German Minister yesterday to express condolence on behalf of the President.'[153] This story was also reported in almost identical wording in the *Irish Independent* and *The Irish Times*, suggesting that the information had come from Government sources and had been cleared by the censor.[154] McDunphy's records show that this visit was part of a carefully choreographed affirmation of the state's position. McDunphy noted in May 1945 that 'after consultation with the Government and acting on the authority of the President, I called today on the German minister, Herr Eduard Hempel, at the legation in Northumberland Road, and on behalf of the President expressed condolence on the death of the Führer and Chancellor of the German Reich.'[155]

The actual timing of McDunphy's visit to Hempel is also of considerable significance. McDunphy passed on Hyde's condolences with the Government's full knowledge, the day after de Valera's sympathy visit to the German Minister and at a time when the adverse international reaction to the Taoiseach's move was making its first waves. As Keogh has noted, 'de Valera had an opportunity to think about his action overnight and had decided not to change his course despite the instantaneous negative reaction in the international press and media'.[156] Keogh has also suggested that this 'indicated the Government had no second thoughts on this matter'.[157] But, in fact, that is not the full story.

The Government had initially viewed de Valera's visit to Hempel, followed by that of the Secretary to the office of President, as a proper manifestation of neutrality and unhesitatingly publicised both events. However, when the initial wave of criticism did not subside, but rather intensified, a shift occurred in Government thinking. International newspapers, particularly in the United States, had been vehement in their criticism of the Irish condolences and the Irish legation in Washington and consulates in other major cities received a huge volume of protest correspondence.[158] This definitely had an effect and it was McDunphy who first perceived and then chronicled a rowing-back of the Irish position. McDunphy noted that, following the German surrender, Hempel had called on the Taoiseach on 8 May 1945 to announce the termination of his mission as German Minister.[159] The Government Information Bureau had issued a terse statement arising from this, announcing that Hempel was 'vacating the legation premises' and that the Irish Government would 'take charge' of the properties.[160] On 9 May, the day after Hempel had handed over the keys of the German legation, he contacted McDunphy with a view to paying a farewell visit to the Áras. McDunphy recorded that 'this morning, Dr Hempel asked me for permission to call on me as Secretary to the President, and said that if it were possible he would like also to be received by the President'.[161] Despite Hyde's long-standing amicable relations with Hempel, McDunphy hesitated and kicked to touch. McDunphy was deeply conscious of the furore that his visit and the Taoiseach's visit to Hempel had generated and sought political cover before allowing Hempel to come to the Áras. He wrote: 'In view of the situation I consulted with the Secretary, Department of External Affairs, and he informed me that the view of the Taoiseach, who was also Minister for External Affairs, was that, if the President were willing to receive Dr Hempel it would not in any way conflict with general state policy. He thought, however, that there was no need to publicise the visit.'[162]

This direction from de Valera constituted a shift in the Government's approach and, though the Government was still happy to treat Hempel with due courtesy, an anxiety now existed about being seen to do anything that would generate further negative international publicity. Hyde willingly agreed to meet Hempel, but this was done under the radar. McDunphy noted 'in the afternoon Dr Hempel called at the Áras and was received by the President . . . No notice was issued to the press.'[163]

The covert nature of Hempel's final visit to the Áras showed how badly the Government had been stung by international criticism of the de Valera and McDunphy visits to the German representative. It was a lesson that was not forgotten in the Áras even after the departure of Hyde. In July 1945, McDunphy wrote:

> Ireland was neutral in the world war 1939–45 and this fact led to a considerable amount of hostility in the English press and in the press of other countries, directed against Ireland, in the course of which, allegations, completely unfounded, were made that the Irish Government were actively assisting both Germany and Japan against the allies. The essential courtesies extended by the President and by the Irish Government on the death of Herr Hitler, Chancellor of the German Reich, were distorted into acts of discourtesy to the allies. On the downfall of Germany this campaign of hostility was concentrated on the representative of Japan in Ireland.[164]

In the same memo, McDunphy recorded that the Áras had first postponed the courtesy call to President O'Kelly by the Swedish Consul Nils Jaenson in July 1945, and then stifled any publicity surrounding this visit to the Áras for fear this 'would be followed by an application from the Japanese Counsel for a similar courtesy, and that compliance with the request would undoubtedly lead to an accentuation of the hostile press campaign'.[165] Jaenson, however, completely unaware of this background, believed that he was being treated in a 'not very agreeable way' and, in an angry letter to McDunphy on 9 July 1945, he indicated that he was going to ask his Government to transfer him out of Ireland.[166] Another diplomatic own goal was only averted when O'Kelly, in the company of the Minister for Agriculture, Jim Ryan, met Jaenson in the Áras and the President disclosed his concerns about Ireland being portrayed as Axis sympathisers. McDunphy noted: 'The President had a frank conversation with Mr Jaenson and explained the circumstances which motivated him cancelling the first visit and omitting publication of the second, with special reference to the complication which would ensue if the Japanese Consul were to seek an audience. Mr Jaenson said he fully appreciated the position and the President is satisfied that the "incident" may be regarded as at an end.'[167]

The Swedish Consul incident highlights that, despite de Valera's public assertions to the contrary, the Government and the Áras were badly bruised by the fallout from the Hempel condolence visits. De Valera would later staunchly defend his visit to Hempel in the Dáil on 19 July 1945 when he was criticised by James Dillon.[168] Dillon did not, however, extend his criticisms to the office of President and McDunphy's visit to Hempel attracted hardly any negative publicity domestically. Yet the officials in the Áras were clearly conscious of the damage that had been done to Ireland's international reputation. The undiplomatic manner in which the Swedish Consul – a representative of a friendly, neutral nation – was treated, as part of an ill-conceived strategy to stave off contact with the Japanese, suggests almost a desperation not to bring any more odium down on Ireland's standing.

Hyde and Irish-US Relations

By the end of the war, one person who was intent on tarnishing Ireland's international reputation was the American Minister, David Gray. He had replaced John Cudahy in the American legation in April

1940 and was perceived to be close to President Roosevelt, given that he was married to Eleanor Roosevelt's favourite aunt. He viewed his mission as primarily one of helping President Roosevelt to give as much aid as possible to the British to defeat the Nazis. He made numerous stringent efforts to persuade or force the Irish Government into abandoning neutrality. The deterioration in relations between Gray and de Valera has been well documented. In the words of Joseph Walshe, he was 'persona non grata to the Irish Government'.[169] Gray's relationship with the Áras became equally tempestuous.

Gray had arrived in Ireland at the time of Hyde's stroke and initially he and McDunphy had got on well. On 18 April 1940, with the President still seriously ill, McDunphy noted in his file that the American Minister had been 'particularly kind' in sending a personal letter and flowers to the President.[170] However, as Gray failed to make progress in his efforts to persuade the Irish to make port facilities available to the British, his frustration began to mount. With the President unwell in the early part of Gray's mission, when the American Minister visited the Áras he was invariably sat down to tea with the President's sister, Annette Kane.[171] McDunphy also availed of these occasions, much to Gray's chagrin, to lecture the American Minister and his diplomatic colleagues on the solidity of Irish neutrality.[172] In a conversation on 22 March 1941, McDunphy warned Vincent Chapin, Secretary to the American legation, that should the US enter the war its bonds of kinship with Ireland would not influence the hard-headed realities of neutrality. McDunphy's notes of the meeting record:

> A good deal of play had been made of the fact that the Irish people had many relatives and affiliations in America, and the idea was being fostered and broadcast that pressure from America would be regarded not as the pressure of an enemy but the persuasion of a friend and would consequently be yielded to. I said this was a type of specious argument which convinced no one in this country . . . I said that America's participation in the war no matter what side it chose was a matter for decision by the American people alone. It would be unfortunate however, if one of the factors governing that decision were to be a mistaken impression that Ireland would

> grant America the use of our ports or bases, or would in any way facilitate her in a war in which Ireland was determined to keep absolutely neutral.[173]

At the end of this memo, McDunphy has written by hand 'Mr Chapin informed me later that he had reported very fully on our conversation to his Minister, Mr Gray.'[174] McDunphy also recorded that the Taoiseach was fully briefed on this conversation.

McDunphy's conversation with Gray on 5 May 1941 was notable for Gray hinting to the Secretary to the office of the President, six months before the attack on Pearl Harbor, that America would ultimately enter the war and that Irish and US 'national interests' were likely to 'clash'.[175] McDunphy's contempt for Gray is recorded in scathing terms. McDunphy wrote: 'I am aware from certain things which I have heard that Mr Gray has the reputation of being rather more indiscreet in his criticism of Ireland's neutrality than is proper to a man holding a high diplomatic post such as he occupies, and that generally speaking he seems to regard himself as charged with a mission of bringing this country into the war on the side of Britain.'[176]

Gray's view of McDunphy was equally unflattering and, according to the American Minister, McDunphy was generally regarded as 'an officious ass'.[177] Hyde (and de Valera) fared little better in the abrasive American's assessment. In a letter to Roosevelt in November 1943, Gray wrote disparagingly:

> Your friend Mr de Valera is continuing to ignore those little events of history which in spite of him keep occurring. He is in fact too busy attending meetings celebrating the revival of the Gaelic League to give his attention to such matters. It is fifty years since Douglas Hyde, the Protestant Anglo-Irish squire from the west, founded the Gaelic League. He now has his reward in being the paralysed, dummy President of a country which would have seen Britain overrun by Hitler with a degree of satisfaction and without lifting a finger to prevent it . . . If I go nuts, can you blame me?[178]

Gray's remarks about Hyde being a 'paralysed, dummy President' were most insensitive, especially as Roosevelt himself was partly disabled.

Roosevelt sent a temperate reply to Gray's report expressing sympathy for Hyde, 'a fine and scholarly old gentleman. If you get a chance tell him how deeply I regret his indisposition and express the hope that someday he and I will have a chance to meet each other.'[179]

By the end of the war, Gray's relationship with de Valera was on the floor. Gray was determined to discredit de Valera, especially in the eyes of the American public, and he had no compunction about drawing the Irish presidency into this row. Having failed to persuade President Truman to withdraw US diplomatic representatives from Dublin in the immediate aftermath of de Valera's condolences to Hempel, Gray now zoned in on McDunphy as part of his overriding strategy to embarrass the Irish Government.[180] Nolan has noted that 'Gray was not keen to let de Valera off the hook on this issue. Having explored his recollection, he identified another possible insult towards the US Government. The issue concerned the conduct of Michael McDunphy, the Secretary to the Irish President, who had offered his condolences to the German Minister on Hitler's death. From his research, Gray found that McDunphy had made no call to him following the death of Roosevelt.'[181] Gray wrote in June 1945 that 'examination of our records at the time of the death of President Roosevelt disclosed the fact that although Mr de Valera, Mr Walshe, Permanent Secretary for External Affairs, and leading members of the Government and Opposition had called to this legation, the Secretary to the President did not call.'[182]

On 22 June 1945, Gray wrote to Joseph Walshe in External Affairs complaining about McDunphy's conduct.[183] In his memoir, penned in 1960, Gray wrongly claimed that McDunphy had acted 'without authorisation from his master', but in the summer of 1945 his complaint had been consciously made, knowing it had the potential to attach the stigma of Nazi sympathiser to the Secretary to the office of President, to the outgoing President Douglas Hyde, and to the incoming President Seán T. O'Kelly.[184] Gray justified raising the matter at this point, over seven weeks after McDunphy had called on Hempel on Hyde's behalf, because he had previously been under the impression that McDunphy was merely 'Hyde's Secretary' as he regularly contemptuously referred to him in his reports back to Washington.[185] When Gray learnt that O'Kelly would not pick a new

Secretary, but that McDunphy would remain in situ, he told Walshe he had to raise the issue. Gray wrote: 'I have said nothing to you about this before as I was under the impression that the new President would presumably obtain the appointment of a Secretary of his own choice and the matter could be ignored, but as apparently Mr McDunphy is to stay on and as all our Mission are aware of the fact that Mr McDunphy did not call here but did call on the German legation, I feel that I must informally take the matter up with you.'[186]

Gray strongly suggested that McDunphy, and by extension both Hyde and the de Valera Government, had acted in an insulting manner because McDunphy had not called upon the American Minister on the death of Roosevelt, but had called upon Hempel following Hitler's death. Gray wrote to Walshe:

> As you may or may not know, when the Taoiseach, yourself, and most of the members of the Government called to this legation to offer condolence on the death of the late President Roosevelt, the Secretary to the President did not call. I was informed that a message in the name of the President [Hyde] was sent direct to Washington. However, when Hitler's death was reported, the Secretary did call on the German Minister to offer condolence. Whether an affront to my Government was or was not intended, it was evident that one practice was followed in one case and another in the other case. If it was considered appropriate to send a message to the foreign government, the head of which was deceased, why would the Secretary to the President not have followed the same procedure in the case of Hitler?[187]

Walshe was undoubtedly exasperated by Gray's spoiling for a row. Walshe had accompanied de Valera on his visit to Hempel. He had advised McDunphy, on the Taoiseach's behalf, in regard to Hempel's visit to the Áras. He had also cabled Robert Brennan, the Irish Minister in Washington, some eleven days prior to Gray's letter, on 11 June, inquiring if he could 'talk strongly to some influential [US] politician who would put an end to Gray's career'.[188] Walshe was never going to give Gray any succour and he 'simply decided not to send a reply' to the American Minister's letter.[189]

In an attempt to raise the stakes further, Gray had contacted Seán T. O'Kelly shortly after he succeeded Hyde with a threat to boycott the Áras. It was not a threat that seems to have worried O'Kelly unduly because it took him at least a week to even broach the matter with McDunphy. When the new President did so, he gave McDunphy his unequivocal support.[190]

McDunphy, on his official file, made a strong case for the different protocol procedures that had been involved in the respective deaths of Roosevelt and Hitler. He defended not calling on Gray and argued that international courtesies had been respected. On 4 July, McDunphy wrote:

> The circumstances of the two cases were entirely different. Following the death of President Roosevelt on 12 April 1945, the Taoiseach as head of the Irish Government and as Minister for External Affairs cabled a message of sympathy to the American Secretary of State, while President Hyde as head of the Irish state cabled a message of sympathy to President Roosevelt's successor in office, President Truman. The text of the President's message was agreed to by the Taoiseach before issue . . . With such direct communication between the heads of the two Governments and the heads of the two States, international courtesies were fully observed, and for the Secretary to the President to call on behalf of the President on the American Minister would in the circumstances have been not only an act of supererogation but possibly an anticlimax.[191]

McDunphy argued that in the case of the Hitler condolences, the German leader was accorded far less respect than Roosevelt. He also suggested that the visits to Hempel had taken place only out of necessity because the chaos in Germany at the end of the war had hampered other forms of communication. McDunphy noted:

> Herr Hitler was both head of the German state and head of the German Government and with his death the joint post became vacant and was not immediately filled, the capital of Germany, Berlin, being then in the military occupation of the Allies.

> There was consequently no one with whom the head of the Irish state or the head of the Irish Government could communicate directly, as was done in the case of the United States. Messages of sympathy were accordingly conveyed personally to the German Minister by the Taoiseach on behalf of the Irish Government, and by the Secretary to the President on behalf of the head of the state, these necessarily limited courtesies being in fact of a lesser degree than those accorded three weeks previously in the case of the United States.[192]

Significantly, despite Gray's best efforts to stir the pot, the Truman administration accepted that there was no evidence of any Irish disrespect towards the US Government. Walshe's non-reply to Gray's letter, as well as the lack of impact the American Minister's complaint made on O'Kelly, had caused Gray to suggest again to the US State Department that the matter warranted his withdrawal from Dublin. The Acting US Secretary of State, Joseph Grew, 're-examined all the steps taken by the Irish Government on the deaths of President Roosevelt and Hitler', but recommended no action.[193] Grew had accepted the line emanating from the Irish Government that Hyde had no one to telegram in Berlin and noted that 'we should not attach too much importance to the failure of his secretary to call upon Mr Gray'.[194] In August 1945, Gray ended his self-imposed ban on the Áras. On 25 September, McDunphy triumphantly noted:

> On 13 August, Mr Gray wrote to the President asking if he might be permitted to call upon him, and asking permission for his wife to call on Mrs O'Kelly. The President duly received the Minister and his wife on the 14 August. No reference was made to the complaint. On Monday 24 September Mr Gray and his wife were again visitors at the Áras . . . I think that the incident may now be regarded as closed. Presumably Mr Gray has now come to realise that he, and not I, was in the wrong.[195]

If McDunphy saw this as a victory, it was a narrow one. As Keogh has noted, earlier US State Department correspondence deplored the de Valera and McDunphy visits to Hempel and, in this regard, the draft of a telegram sent to Gray on this issue even contained the phrase 'will not readily be forgotten', although these words were subsequently crossed out.[196] In correspondence arising from the Hempel visits, the US State Department noted that their policy was one of 'leaving Ireland severely alone'.[197] While Gray did not succeed in his overall objective of creating an embarrassing international incident for Ireland by having US representation withdrawn, his efforts still managed to inflict long-term damage on US-Irish relations. Irish neutrality had already prejudiced views within the US administration, but Gray's vociferous claims to the State Department that leading Irish public figures, such as Hyde, de Valera, Joseph Walshe and McDunphy, had behaved in a manner sympathetic to Nazism in May 1945 created a long-lasting suspicion and coolness. This may have been brought home to the office of President in June 1945 when President Truman pointedly did not send a message of congratulations to O'Kelly on his election. The US State Department had advised Truman against sending such a message; although they acknowledged this would be 'normal procedure with a friendly nation', they counselled that it was now 'general policy that Ireland has missed the boat during the war and that we should do the minimum towards her.'[198]

8

Playing the Game or Blowing the Whistle

Douglas Hyde came to the presidency with little political experience and was forced to learn on the job. In a nostalgic letter to President de Valera on the day of the fiftieth anniversary of the first Dáil, on 21 January 1969, McDunphy fondly recalled that Hyde and he had lunched together on the day Hyde had been declared elected as President of Ireland in 1938. McDunphy's letter highlights Hyde's genial nature, his natural inquisitiveness and, at the outset, his total lack of knowledge of the President's role. McDunphy wrote:

> He invited me to lunch with him in the Gresham Hotel, Dublin, and scarcely were we seated than he asked me what were his powers as President of Ireland. It was not a question to be answered briefly, amid the din of a public restaurant and to a man who had no previous interest or experience in politics but I did my best to the detriment of the meal. I told him that apart from ceremonial duties involving no authority the powers and duties conferred on him by the Constitution were to be exercised by him on the advice of the Government, although there were a limited few which he could exercise in his absolute discretion, and I told him what they were. In general his position in the government of the country was somewhat akin to that of a referee on a football field. There were rules by which the game should be played, and the referee

> should not interfere unless he saw an infringement of those rules.[1]

McDunphy continued: 'He [Hyde] was delighted with that tabloid summary of his presidential powers, and he never forgot it. From time to time after that during his seven-year term of office, even during his severe illness, which kept him confined to bed, he would ask me – in Irish or in English – with a twinkle in his eye "do you think I should get out the whistle?" showing that he was keeping in touch with political developments.'[2]

During Hyde's presidency, de Valera made a point of keeping Hyde regularly briefed on government policy, in accordance with Article 28.5.2 of the Constitution. De Valera established a practice of calling to the Áras, usually on the first Friday of every month, for this purpose.[3] During the debate on the draft Constitution, de Valera had said that such regular briefings would ensure that 'the Government ought to be able to persuade him [the President], giving him all the inner knowledge that they may have about the situation'. It was de Valera's view that a Taoiseach who was negligent in this regard could not complain if a President, not having the full benefit of the Taoiseach's views, took a decision that the Taoiseach did not agree with, and chose to refer legislation to the Supreme Court or, in extraordinary circumstances, to the people.[4]

Despite his bad health, Hyde was quite active constitutionally and set a number of important precedents. Chapter 6 has already dealt with his decision to refer the School Attendance Bill 1942 to the Supreme Court, but of even greater significance was his earlier decision to do likewise with the Offences Against the State Amendment Bill 1940. This was the first occasion that the President had exercised his powers under Article 26 of the Constitution and Hyde took this decision at a politically sensitive time when concerns about the security of the state were prevalent.

Hyde's first constitutional intervention came about as a result of de Valera's policy towards the IRA in the context of the Second World War. The Government had hoped that Bunreacht na hÉireann would mark a fresh start as far as political violence was concerned, but these hopes were quickly dashed against the backdrop of a progressively worsening domestic and international situation. After an ultimatum to the British Government in January 1939, the IRA commenced a bombing campaign in Britain, which lasted for the rest of that year. The Offences Against the State Bill 1939 was introduced into the Dáil on 2 March 1939 and was signed by the President on 14 June 1939.[5] According to Fanning, 'the very title of the act underlined the significance which de Valera attached to the 1937 Constitution as justifying his taking the most draconian powers to deal with the IRA' – however, this legislation, when enacted, quickly ran into difficulties.[6]

On 1 December 1939, the High Court held that Part VI of the Act was unconstitutional and ordered the release of an IRA detainee on whose behalf a case had been taken.[7] Though the state attempted to appeal the decision, the Supreme Court held that it had no jurisdiction in habeas corpus matters and the Government was forced to release fifty-three other IRA prisoners.[8]

This turn of events must have caused some introspection in Áras an Uachtaráin, given that the President had signed the 1939 Act into law, despite the doubts that had been expressed about its constitutionality. During the Dáil debate, the Labour Party had been particular vocal in casting doubt on the validity of the legislation, suggesting that it placed an overemphasis on curbing civil liberties and was 'certainly reactionary'.[9] Though Fine Gael had supported the passage of the Bill, John A. Costello had expressed his personal opinion that elements of the Bill were unconstitutional.[10] Any embarrassment that the Áras may have felt that the President had ignored these warnings was, however, lost in the furore over what many of the released IRA prisoners were alleged to have done next.

On 23 December 1939, de Valera suffered his 'greatest humiliation at the hands of the IRA' following a raid on the Magazine Fort in the Phoenix Park.[11] The IRA escaped with over a million rounds of ammunition in thirteen lorries, leaving the country 'virtually defenceless'.[12] A serious political crisis followed and the Oireachtas was recalled early at the start of 1940.[13] On 3 January 1940, the Minister for Justice, Gerry Boland, made clear that the released IRA internees were among the main suspects. He said that he was 'satisfied that had it not been for the decision of the courts . . . that raid would not have occurred'.[14] The Government's political response to the IRA was the

Offences Against the State Amendment Bill 1940, which was rushed through the Oireachtas by 5 January 1940.

This time the office of President was following the Oireachtas debate intently. In opening the second stage of the Offences Against the State Amendment Bill 1940 for the Government, the Minister for Local Government and Public Health, P. J. Ruttledge, said 'this Bill is practically the same as the measure that was passed some months ago by the Oireachtas'.[15] Fine Gael again supported the Government legislation on the basis that it was an issue of national security, but James Dillon told the Dáil that the main Opposition party believed the Government measures for tackling the IRA should go further. He said 'our attitude is that we will give the Government the powers they ask for. We will give them this Bill, but the powers of this Bill are not enough.'[16]

The new Bill contained only a number of small changes, with the objective of making it constitutional and primarily sealing the loophole by way of which the IRA prisoners had obtained freedom. The Government obviously wished to avoid an embarrassing rerun of what had happened with the original legislation and used the Dáil to send a none-too-subtle signal to the President that he should refer the Bill to the Supreme Court. On 3 January 1940, the Taoiseach made it very clear in what manner he expected the President to act in regard to the Offences Against the State Amendment Bill:

> The view of the legal advisers of the Government is that, in view of all the circumstances and the situation as a whole, the proper line to take is, if possible, to re-enact Part VI of the Offences Against the State Act, giving an opportunity of having it referred to the Supreme Court for a decision as to whether internment is within the Constitution. In this matter, any more than any other matter, I cannot presume to know what attitude the President may take, but again, asking ourselves what anyone here was likely to do in the circumstances, we would say to ourselves that the President is likely, having seen a decision of the judge of the High Court to the effect that this Act as it stood originally was unconstitutional, and being possessed of the power, before signature, to refer a Bill to the

> Supreme Court, we would say that he is likely to refer it. As I say, he will have to form his own opinion upon that after consultation, in accordance with the Constitution, with the Council of the State. But we believe, on the grounds that I have stated, that it is likely that the President will do this.[17]

Although the decision to refer a Bill to the Supreme Court is one that a President makes in his 'absolute discretion', on this occasion de Valera was almost at pains to tell Hyde where his discretion should logically lead him. Later on, in the same Dáil contribution, de Valera reiterated that 'in view of the decision that was taken, and the opinion expressed by the High Court judge in his judgement, we believe that the President will feel constrained more or less to submit this question for decision. He will, probably, say: "Very well, this Bill does not seem very different from the other Bill, and consequently it is my duty to have the Supreme Court express its opinion upon it."'[18]

Fine Gael took a contrary view, believing that the Offences Against the State Amendment Bill 1940 should be immediately signed into law, so that the Gardaí could get on with rounding up IRA suspects without delay. John A. Costello argued that if the President referred the Bill to the Supreme Court and that the Bill was not to pass a Supreme Court adjudication, the Government would have created an unnecessary vacuum. He said: 'The net result will be that, in three or four weeks, this Government will find itself not merely without any powers but in a position never again to be capable of getting or exercising the powers which they say they require to deal with the situation with which they are at present confronted. I do not know how they can get a decision of the Supreme Court on this Bill.'[19]

The Dáil debate gave rise to an unusual and ironic difference in political emphasis. Fianna Fáil said that the Offences Against the State Amendment Bill was necessary to 'stamp out' the IRA, which was 'a danger to the country', yet took the almost unprecedented step for a government party of using the Dáil discussion to advocate that the validity of their own Bill be tested by the Supreme Court.[20] This stance was influenced by a desire in the cabinet to show that the stringent measures encompassed in the Bill were constitutional. Fine Gael, on the other hand, took the rare position for a parliamentary

Opposition of standing more firmly behind the Government's legislation than the Government itself.[21] This stance was influenced by Fine Gael's determination to show that the party stood strongly for the security of the state and also because they felt far less compunction in cracking down on militant republicanism.

Following the passage of the Bill through the Dáil and the Seanad, the diverging attitude among the main parties as to whether the Bill should or should not be immediately signed into law by the President was still being played out. On 6 January, when presenting the Offences Against the State Amendment Bill 1940 to Hyde for signature, de Valera, whether as a point of constitutional propriety or in a political move to ensure that the President was aware of his position, pointed out that 'its provisions or some of them were substantially identical with those of a former Act, which had been declared by the High Court to be unconstitutional'.[22] Hyde then declined to sign the Bill and a meeting of the Council of State was called to determine whether the Bill should be referred to the Supreme Court. McDunphy privately noted his approval of this decision and wrote that the President was 'bound to regard the Bill as one of those contemplated by Article 26 of the Constitution which provides for reference of Bills to the Supreme Court on the question of their constitutionality.'[23] In advance of the Council of State meeting, Fine Gael was still maintaining that, given the security situation, it would be better if the Bill was signed immediately by the President. Richard Mulcahy and James Dillon were among six members of the Oireachtas appointed by Hyde to the Council of State on the evening that the President had declined to sign the Bill. In a statement to the Press Association, they said that they would advise the President at the meeting that they were 'as determined as the Government that the only authority must be the elected Government and we will give full support to any measure which might end the activities of any section trying to abrogate to itself the powers of the Government'.[24]

The first meeting of the Council of State took place in Áras an Uachtaráin on 8 January 1940 for the sole purpose of offering advice to the President as to whether he should refer the Offences Against the State Amendment Bill 1940 to the Supreme Court. Hyde was conscious that there were diverging political views between the Government and Fine Gael members of the Council of State as to whether he should refer the Bill (as well as the opinion of William Norton, whose Labour Party had voted against the legislation). He was also clearly determined that the Council of State would not turn into a verbal brawl where each of the partisans rehashed their political opinions. As the procedural memo that McDunphy retained shows, Hyde seized control of the meeting from the outset. McDunphy recorded:

> At the first meeting of the Council of State on 8 January 1940, the President in the course of his opening statement laid down three rules or principles to be observed in the conducting of the meeting, viz:
>
> a) The proceedings should be strictly private.
> b) Political references should be avoided.
> c) Legal arguments should be equally avoided.[25]

Extracts from the President's opening statement, kept by McDunphy on a procedural file, show that Hyde said:

> I think you will agree with me also that reference to political considerations should be carefully avoided. We are not concerned here with whether the Bill is a desirable one or not, or with what consequences may or may not result in the event of its becoming law. The only matter which is before the meeting is whether or not I should refer the Bill to the Supreme Court . . . I think you will agree with me also that anything in the nature of legal arguments would be equally out of place. It is not the purpose of the meeting to express any opinion on the constitutionality of the Bill. This is a matter entirely for the Supreme Court, in the event of my deciding to refer the Bill to the Supreme Court.[26]

McDunphy subsequently noted, 'the result was that members of the council confined themselves merely to simple expressions of opinion for or against reference of the Bill to the Supreme Court, and that there was practically no discussion'.[27]

Hyde had succeeded in keeping the first Council of State meeting free from party-political posturing, which in itself was an important precedent, but he had done so by stifling almost all discussion. This was something that would be relaxed in future meetings of the Council of State, but it seems, irrespective of any discussion at the first meeting, Hyde had his mind already set on referring the Offences Against the State Amendment Bill 1940 to the Supreme Court. The Council of State meeting had lasted for only an hour and the President did not mull long over matters. As McDunphy later recorded, 'following the first meeting of the Council of State, on 8 January, 1940, the President personally informed the members of his decision before they left the Áras'.[28] Given the legal uncertainties, as well as the tense political climate, Hyde's decision to let the Supreme Court adjudicate on the matter was a wise one. On 14 February 1940, the Supreme Court upheld the constitutionality of the Offences Against the State Amendment Bill 1940.[29] The legal minefield that this Bill had posed, vindicating the President's decision to let the Supreme Court decide, was evident from the Chief Justice indicating at the commencement of his judgement that the court had actually divided on the constitutionality of the Bill.[30]

The President's decision to refer the Bill, combined with the Supreme Court's subsequent positive decision, gave legal certainty to important security measures to tackle the IRA and was met with some relief in Government.[31] Hyde's decision did cause some disquiet in the Labour Party. At the party's national conference, in April 1940, the Dublin North West branch tabled a motion that the party leader, William Norton, should withdraw from the Council of State 'which exists for the purpose of endorsing the Fianna Fáil restrictions of liberty, which the Labour Party have publicly opposed'.[32] This motion was stoutly opposed by the chairman of the Labour Party, Michael Keyes, a Limerick TD, who maintained that the functions of the Council of State were 'advisory' and that 'members of the Oireachtas should pull their weight in the instruments of the state'.[33] Norton also vigorously rejected the motion, arguing that he should continue to serve on the Council of State 'to preserve the principle of labour representation' on public bodies.[34] The motion was roundly defeated.

The main Opposition party made no immediate criticism of the President's decision to refer the Bill, although what Hogan describes as

Cosgrave's 'rather curmudgeonly attitude to the entire procedure' – as displayed at the UCD Law Society at the end of February 1940 – hinted at some Fine Gael frustration with the President.[35] Cosgrave, who had absented himself from the Council of State meeting, summed up his criticism by stating that 'we have reached a stage in the making of laws when on one occasion recently the proceedings were suspended and the question 'how's that, Umpire' was fired by the President from the Council of State gun at the Supreme Court. The consideration of that question was costly in terms of time and money. By a majority the Supreme Court gave its decision – a rare tribute to the ambiguity of the Constitution or the Bill or both.'[36]

If Cosgrave's comments contained a mild criticism of the President's action in exercising his constitutional powers, this was not the only occasion on which Hyde would be subjected to the verbal frustrations of the Opposition. In 1944, Fine Gael and Labour were livid when the President granted an election to de Valera in debatable circumstances and, while the brunt of their ire focused on the Taoiseach, implicit criticism was made of Hyde's decision-making capacities. These circumstances saw the presidency drawn into a contentious political row that was unsurpassed until the events surrounding the resignation of Cearbhall Ó Dálaigh in 1976.

The row grew out of the Government's unexpected defeat on the second stage of the Transport Bill 1944 late on the evening of 9 May 1944. After the Government's defeat, de Valera immediately convened a meeting of the cabinet to discuss his options before proceeding to the Áras to seek a general election. The possibility of an election had emerged at a highly favourable juncture for Fianna Fáil. In the previous general election, in June 1943, Fianna Fáil had lost the absolute majority that it had held since 1938. De Valera was left with the difficulty of a minority Government, yet Fianna Fáil's public standing began again to increase steadily in the early months of 1944.

De Valera's strong handling of the American Note episode in February/March 1944, in which the US Government unsuccessfully sought to pressurise de Valera to close down the German and Japanese legations in Dublin, coupled with his firm assertion of Ireland's right to remain neutral, enhanced the Taoiseach's appeal.[37] At the same time, Fianna Fáil's political rivals were experiencing unprecedented organisational difficulties. In early 1944, a vicious split had occurred within the Labour Party and the *Irish Press* exploited this to the full, carrying damaging headlines such as 'Story of the Red Coup in the Party' and 'Communist Victory over Irish Labour Party'.[38] Fine Gael was also at a low ebb. W. T. Cosgrave had resigned as leader in January 1944 and the party's weakness was highlighted by the fact that his successor, Richard Mulcahy, was at that time not a member of the Dáil.[39] De Valera's authorised biographers suggest that, though de Valera had not been planning an election, when the opportunity presented itself he could not resist the temptation to seek an overall majority. Longford and O'Neill recorded that 'he had been reluctant to take the initiative of going to the country again so soon to resolve the difficulty. The defeat of his Government, however, gave him good reason for resigning, even though he might well have won a vote of confidence on the following day.'[40]

President Hyde very nearly caused de Valera's electoral calculations to backfire. Indeed, if it were not for the decisive intervention of Michael McDunphy, who counselled the President against his initial instinct to refuse the Taoiseach an election, de Valera's later career trajectory might have been very different.

The Government's defeat in the Dáil was, like elsewhere, shock news in the Áras. McDunphy was at his home in Clontarf when he got a phone call shortly after 9 p.m. from the Taoiseach's Assistant Private Secretary informing him of the Government's defeat.[41] McDunphy was told to arrange an appointment with the President for the Taoiseach 'to discuss' the question of a general election and McDunphy was told that the Taoiseach thought that he 'as Secretary to the President should also come to the Áras'.[42] With his own car unavailable, McDunphy had to cycle to the Áras and, though he arrived somewhat behind schedule, he still managed to paint a vivid picture of a very tense and slightly incongruous scene. McDunphy recorded:

> Having reached the Áras I found that the Taoiseach was already there with the President in his bedroom, the latter, a man of eighty-four years, having been practically bedridden for some years. I went to my office and waited there for a few minutes until the President sent for me. I found him lying in

> bed looking somewhat expectant. The Taoiseach, who seemed to be very thoughtful, was seated at the bedside but rose on my entrance. After the President and he had spoken a few words of greeting to me, the Taoiseach explained to me that in view of the constitutional position which had arisen out of the defeat of his Government, he had suggested to the President, and the President had agreed, that discussion of the matter by them should be postponed until I as the President's adviser should be present.[43]

De Valera then proceeded to explain the matter to Hyde 'at length'.[44] The Taoiseach pointed out that his Government had been defeated on a matter that he regarded as 'a major one' and he considered that in those circumstances he, as Taoiseach, had 'ceased to retain the confidence of Dáil Éireann within the meaning of Article 13.2.1 of the Constitution'.[45] McDunphy noted:

> He [the Taoiseach] therefore proposed to advise the President to proclaim a General Election. He realised that the President was entitled under that Article as amended for the period of the war emergency (General Election Emergency Provisions Act, 1943, No. 11 of 1943) to refuse to accept that advice. The Taoiseach explained that he was not at that moment formally advising the President, but was merely asking him if he would act on that advice if so given.[46]

It became clear to McDunphy that the President had major qualms. With de Valera's immediate political future resting in the balance, the career civil servant politely moved to eject the Taoiseach from the room. It was to be McDunphy's first decisive intervention of the evening. He noted:

> The President looked at me, and then at the Taoiseach, and again back to me. Realising that the situation was a delicate one, I suggested to the Taoiseach that in view of the fact that the President after consultation with me might possibly decide to refuse to act on the advice of the Taoiseach, a decision which

> naturally could not be very acceptable to the latter, it might perhaps be difficult for the President to discuss the matter freely with me, his Secretary, in the presence of the Taoiseach. I said that in my view it would be important as a constitutional precedent and as a matter of historical record that, in making his decision, the President should be free from any embarrassment or influence which might subsequently be argued were the Taoiseach present during the discussion. The President and the Taoiseach both concurred, and the President having expressed a wish to that effect, the Taoiseach withdrew.[47]

At this point, it seems Hyde's view was clear-cut. McDunphy recorded that 'when the Taoiseach had left the room the President turned to me and said immediately "I must refuse; the country does not want a General Election."'[48]

According to McDunphy's memo, which is the only account of the conversation that transpired between the President and his Secretary, McDunphy then made his second and most significant intervention of the evening. He wrote:

> I suggested that the matter was not quite so simple. If he refused, the Taoiseach would be forced by Article 13.2.2 of the Constitution, as amended by the Act of 1943, to resign with his Government, and the Dáil would then have the onus of nominating a new Taoiseach. There was however, no single party or combination of parties, which could secure such a nomination, and there was consequently no practicable alternative to the existing Government. We discussed the matter at length, and finally the President agreed that the wisest thing to do from the point of view of the country's interest would be to act on the Taoiseach's advice.[49]

The President's decision to grant de Valera a general election 'shortly before midnight' on 9 May 1944 caused fury among the ranks of the Government's political critics.[50] The following morning's *Irish Independent* led the charge. In an editorial entitled 'A Reckless Decision', the newspaper did not spare the President in its criticism. The editorial stated that 'the President has, apparently, exercised his discretion in favour of Mr de Valera. In our opinion it is an improper use of the discretion, and the action of the President calls for the censure of the people'.[51] Although the Opposition parties were not so explicit in their attacks, they too made it known that they were not happy with the President's decision.

Given the provisions of the General Elections (Emergency Provisions) Act 1943 (which ensured that there would be no hiatus in Oireachtas sittings for the duration of the war), the Dáil met the morning after de Valera's visit to the Áras, notwithstanding the calling of an election. In the ensuing debate, the Opposition accused the Taoiseach of taking advantage of the President's ill health to secure an election. Prior to this, all parties had been circumspect about publicly referring to the President's precarious health; however, the Opposition's annoyance over what they viewed as an unwanted election seemed to suggest that all bets were off. Despite the best attempts of the Ceann Comhairle to protect Hyde's sensitivities, the Opposition, while expressing sympathy with the President's condition, suggested that the Taoiseach had taken advantage of a person who was not physically up to the job. While the Opposition's tactic – which was in some ways inevitable with an election now in the offing – was to suggest that the Taoiseach had acted dishonourably and irresponsibly, no effort was made to spare Hyde collateral damage.

Dr T. F. O'Higgins, leader of Fine Gael in the Dáil, who believed that in the circumstances a national government should have been formed, denounced 'plunging this country into an unnecessary general election at, perhaps, or definitely, the most dangerous and critical weeks that the people of this country were ever asked to live through'.[52] In direct criticism of the Government and implicit criticism of the President, O'Higgins said: 'After astute manoeuvring, politically corrupt practices and un-national activity, guided by political exigencies rather than consideration for the safety and security of the country, opportunists decided to take advantage of the failing health of a great figure in order to cheat Parliament of the right of fulfilling its destiny'. When the Ceann Comhairle interrupted to state that 'there must be no criticism, direct or indirect, of any action of the President'. O'Higgins continued:

> My remarks are in sympathy with the President. I am expressing the views of all decent men, inside and outside the Parliament. We sympathise with him in his affliction, and we sympathise with him in the predicament he was placed in last night, roused out of bed – a man in his state of health – in order that a political junta would cheat Parliament of its rights. There is – and well the Taoiseach knows it – enough material inside this House at the present moment, with or without the cooperation of any elements in the Government Party, to give to this nation a Government that would carry on its business more efficiently than did the last Government for the remaining period of this emergency.[53]

The Labour leader, William Norton, continued the theme that Hyde had been too weak to face the Taoiseach down:

> High treason was committed in the Park last night. We find the Taoiseach arriving in the darkness of the night in the house of an aged man whom everyone knows to be in anything but a perfect state of health. One can imagine the scene – the Taoiseach full of venom against a democratic Parliament which had unseated his Government. One is left to imagine the tone in which the demand for a dissolution was presented to the aged man in the Park last night. Like Deputy O'Higgins I want to express sympathy with the President in the advantage which was taken of him last night and of the nocturnal intrusion of an annoyed and outraged Taoiseach.[54]

The most venomous speech came from James Dillon, who excoriated 'de Valera for storming up to the Phoenix Park in the middle of the night', and went on to portray the President in an unflattering light:

> Surely that is undesirable. In any circumstances for the Taoiseach to go and root the President, who is eighty-four years of age, out of his bed in order to ask for a general election would be disagreeable, but it is more so bearing in mind the

> circumstances in which this particular thing was done . . . Well it is a 'quare' picture of the gentleman in a motor-car, blazing through the night up to the Viceregal Lodge to get poor President Hyde out of his bed to sign the dissolution: the Olympian calm, the Olympian patience, the Institute of Higher Studies and the President in his night-shirt, tottering down the stairs to sign the dissolution.[55]

Dillon's comments attracted the hostility of the Ceann Comhairle, who told the independent TD, 'the Chair deprecates any reference to the President. The Deputy's reference is objectionable.'[56] McDunphy later noted that 'the President's sister, Mrs Kane, who lives at the Áras, has been very hurt by Mr Dillon's comments'.[57] McDunphy was of the view that the President 'should consider carefully in the circumstances whether he should again receive Mr Dillon', but this appears to have been advice that Hyde chose to ignore.[58]

In his own contribution to the debate, de Valera sought to defend both himself and the President. The Taoiseach argued that the advice he gave the President was proper and that Hyde had made a sensible decision. De Valera said:

> I have no apology whatever to make for the advice which I gave. The advice could have been rejected. It is set out in the Constitution that a Taoiseach who, apparently, has lost the confidence of the House can ask for a dissolution or, in these particular circumstances, if he wants the alternative, he can ask for a general election. It is clearly set out that the President, at his own discretion completely, can refuse it if he wishes. I asked for it. I put myself in the position of the President and asked myself what I would do if I had been appealed to in circumstances of that sort. So far as I am concerned in any case, I would do exactly what the President has done, for this reason, that there is in this House, as everybody knows, no other Party which could form a Government and no other combination of Parties that would be able to carry on the Government for any length of time against the united opposition of this Party.[59]

Though de Valera was adamant that he had behaved appropriately towards the President, this did not end the matter. The question of whether de Valera had manipulated the President became an undercurrent of the election campaign. From the outset, *the Irish Press* saw this as a bogus argument that sprang from the Opposition's anger at an election taking place at a favourable time for Fianna Fáil. In defending de Valera against the initial charges made in the Dáil relating to the Taoiseach's late-night visit to Hyde, the *Irish Press* wrote: 'The volume of the protests made against the holding of a general election indicated the measure of the uneasiness felt by the speakers regarding their parties' fate in the coming contest. The nature of virulent attacks on the Taoiseach and the tone of references made to the President during the debate evoked unfavourable comment from observers.'[60]

The suggestion that de Valera had in some way manipulated the President was one that Fine Gael was clearly using on the doorsteps because, on the campaign trail, de Valera felt compelled to return to this matter on a number of occasions. In Portlaoise, on 17 May 1944, de Valera said 'there had been suggestions that he had acted improperly in asking the President to declare or order an election'.[61] The Taoiseach maintained that he had acted within his 'constitutional rights' and that the President 'need not have accepted' his 'advice'.[62] In declaring that both he and Hyde had acted wisely, de Valera claimed that they had established a new and important precedent. The Taoiseach said, 'my asking for the election and the President granting it will stand out in Irish constitutional history as a classic example of a Taoiseach who had not the confidence of the Dáil getting an election'.[63]

In Limerick, on 27 May, de Valera made a scathing response to newspaper criticism of the manner in which he sought a dissolution. The Taoiseach insisted that he had always shown 'respect and deference' to the President's office and he vehemently rejected as a 'falsehood' the suggestion that he had acted towards the President 'in an unbecoming manner'.[64] De Valera blamed such suggestions on newspapers that 'since 1914 . . . had worked in a direction quite opposite to that which was desired by the vast majority of the Irish people'.[65]

Fianna Fáil won a massive seventy-six seats, fourteen more than the combined Opposition.[66] Though there were numerous factors that contributed to the election result, de Valera sought to use it as a vindication of the course of action he and Hyde had taken on the night of the Government's defeat in the Dáil. In the course of a victory statement issued to the press, de Valera maintained: 'The result of the elections proves incidentally that the advice which, as Taoiseach, I gave the President to direct that an election should be held was democratically sound, and that the President's decision to accept my advice was also the right one.'[67]

This view was not one subsequently shared by Michael McDunphy, the individual who had done so much to persuade President Hyde to accept de Valera's advice. In a reflective memorandum drawn up in 1949 after John A. Costello's Government had lost a vote in the Dáil, McDunphy noted:

> While the President, the Taoiseach and myself were of opinion at the time of the defeat of the Government on a single issue on 9 May 1944 that the Taoiseach had thereby ceased to retain the support of the majority in Dáil Éireann within the meaning of Article 13.2 of the Constitution, I am not so satisfied now that we were right. I believe that if the Taoiseach, following his defeat in Dáil Éireann on that occasion, had gone back the next day and asked for a vote of confidence, he would in all probability have got it. Such a possibility raises a very serious doubt as to the value of a single defeat as evidence of loss of confidence.[68]

McDunphy's second thoughts reflect an ambiguity at the heart of the Constitution. As Kelly points out, in regard to the important discretion accorded to the President by Article 13.2.2, 'a serious uncertainty seems to lurk in the sub-section . . . namely: what is the test of the Taoiseach's having "ceased to retain the support of a majority?"'[69] This lack of definition means it is arguable as to when a Taoiseach has actually lost the support of the Dáil. The question is posed by Robert Elgie: 'Is it simply when the government has lost a vote of confidence, or when it has been defeated over a single item of legislation, or when a party announces that it is leaving the governing coalition, or even when an independent TD withdraws his or her support?'[70] De Valera and Hyde's action in 1944 brings a little clarity to this conundrum.

As de Valera suggested in his campaign remarks in Portlaoise, a precedent was established by the circumstances in which Hyde granted him this election. McDunphy's memo makes clear that both the Taoiseach and Hyde had concurred that this was a situation in which the President had the right to refuse an election. A Government defeat on a motion of confidence is obviously clear-cut, but the 1944 precedent suggests a defeat on another kind of motion can also be seen as presumptive evidence that the Government has lost the confidence of the Dáil.[71] Arising from this interpretation, Charles Haughey, Brian Lenihan and Sylvester Barrett sought to make it known to President Hillery that Fianna Fáil was willing to form a Government should the President have refused Garret FitzGerald a dissolution, following the Government's defeat on John Bruton's budget in January 1982.[72] In another scenario with roots in the 1944 precedent, President Robinson made it known that she would not have granted Albert Reynolds an election following the breakdown of the Fianna Fáil/Labour coalition in 1994.[73] Elgie has argued that Article 13.2.2 is 'controversial because at times of extreme political tension it draws the President into the party political process whether or not the article is actually invoked. Either to grant or to refuse a dissolution might lay the President open to charges of favouring one political party over another'.[74]

This certainly accords with the situation in which Hyde was placed in 1944. Though the Opposition parties did not directly accuse the President of favouring Fianna Fáil, they did make it known that they were unhappy with the President's decision, even going so far as to suggest that Hyde had been manipulated or was not physically capable of making the correct decision. Yet it is hard to argue with the ultimate logic of his decision. Hyde eventually chose, with some strong prompting from McDunphy, to grant de Valera an election because he believed no stable alternative could be formed from the existing Dáil. Though Fine Gael and Labour had been advocating a national government throughout the war, in 1944, Fianna Fáil would not have supported this arrangement and, given that Fianna Fáil had lost the crucial Dáil vote only because of the illness of three of their TDs (including the temporary hospitalisation of the Tánaiste for an operation), the parliamentary arithmetic made it highly unlikely that any other administration could have been formed or would have lasted for any length of time without recourse to an election.[75]

McDunphy's memo also underlines that much of the Opposition's attack on de Valera for manipulating the President was unfounded and that the Taoiseach did not unduly lean on Hyde but, in fact, showed a sense of probity in having McDunphy witness the conversation. The Opposition's implicit criticisms of the President for not refusing de Valera a general election are, perhaps, understandable given their long political wait to unseat the Taoiseach, but, in the circumstances of the time, Hyde would have generated far more controversy and instability had he effectively forced de Valera's resignation as Taoiseach by declining his appeal to go to the people. However, had the Opposition been aware that it was McDunphy – and not de Valera – who had convinced the President that an election was a necessity, bringing about a total U-turn on Hyde's original position, it is hard to believe that their confidence in Hyde's political decision-making capacities would have been enhanced.

End of Term

Despite Hyde's poor health, McDunphy was eager for the President to serve a second term. In December 1943, McDunphy had sought the advice of the Attorney-General, Kevin Dixon, on the appropriate nomination procedure for a President seeking a second term.[76] On 1 October 1944, McDunphy raised this issue with Hyde, but did not get much insight into the President's intentions. McDunphy noted: 'I have explained the position to the President, Dr Douglas Hyde, and he will give his decision as regards himself in due time.'[77] Upon Seán T. O'Kelly's death in 1966, de Valera explained that Douglas Hyde had been 'too ill to continue for a second term'.[78] There is no record as to whether Hyde and de Valera actually formally discussed the prospect of Hyde letting his name go forward for a further term, but, even as only a courtesy, it is likely that the Taoiseach would have privately sounded out Hyde's view as he entered into the last year of his term. Certainly, within Fianna Fáil, there seems to have been a prevailing opinion that Hyde would not seek a second term. In August 1944, a letter sent by Gerry Boland and Senator William Quirke, the

Secretaries of the Fianna Fáil National Executive, to units of the party organisation mentioned the possibility of a presidential election in the summer of 1945 and accordingly requested that each cumann be brought 'to the highest possible pitch of efficiency'.[79] Hyde would turn eighty-five prior to his first term expiring in 1945 and, given his poor physical condition, it does not seem credible that he would have seriously considered another seven-year stint in the Áras. In any case, over seven months prior to his office falling vacant, Hyde's mind had turned to an exit strategy. In a terse memo dated 23 November 1944, McDunphy wrote: 'The President informed me today that he did not intend to nominate himself for a second term.'[80] On 22 December, President Hyde formally conveyed this decision to the Taoiseach. In explaining this decision, the President wrote to de Valera: '*Tá mé in aois go ro mór agus bad cóir fear níos óige a beit in áit-se.* [I am too old now and it would be better to have a younger man in my place].'[81]

Hyde's letter to de Valera was accompanied by a covering letter from McDunphy to Moynihan, which underlined that the President would be guided by the Taoiseach on how and when his retirement should be announced. McDunphy wrote: 'The President wishes the Taoiseach to understand that the information contained in that letter is not confidential, and that the Taoiseach is free to use it in any way and at any time he may consider desirable.'[82] De Valera's initial response was to sit on this information for over a fortnight. Hyde's decision not to seek a second term was not publicly disclosed until 5 January, following a cabinet discussion that decided the 'most appropriate manner' to break this news was 'a statement to the Press by the Secretary to the President'.[83] The delay in making this announcement may be explained by the Christmas break, but it also gave Fianna Fáil advance warning on the President's definitive decision. Though Hyde had been originally put forward for the presidency by both Fianna Fáil and Fine Gael, he decided to inform solely the Taoiseach – rather than all the party leaders – of his choice not to seek a second term. This set a dubious precedent, which McDunphy tried to explain away by stating that the President's idea was that 'the communication of this decision to the Dáil and to the general public might perhaps come from the Taoiseach rather than from himself, although he had no strong views on the matter . . . Since then, however, the Taoiseach has given the matter a good deal of consideration and his view now is that the publication of the decision would more appropriately come from the President himself.'[84]

This back-and-forth delay provided time for Fianna Fáil to clear the decks by deciding who would be their preferred candidate to succeed Hyde. It is hardly coincidental that on 6 January 1945, the day after a statement issued from the Áras said that Hyde would not run again, the *Irish Independent* wrote that Seán T. O'Kelly was being 'freely mentioned' as the Fianna Fáil candidate.[85] Two days later, *The Irish Times* also hinted at an orchestrated press briefing, when the paper noted it was 'the opinion in well-informed circles that Fianna Fáil will nominate Mr Seán T. O'Kelly'.[86] The speed with which O'Kelly's name was circulated as a favoured candidate may well have been credited to an efficient Fianna Fáil press operation, but had the Opposition been aware that de Valera had known the detail of Hyde's announcement a fortnight in advance and had ultimately decided on when this information was publicly disclosed – then certainly their suspicions would have been roused. It would also be fair to say that they may well have felt that Hyde, in allowing this to happen, had not dealt them a straight hand in the succession stakes.

Though this precedent was problematic, it was observed, though sensibly adapted, by President Mary Robinson. Robinson was the first Irish President since Hyde to have almost completed a full first term and definitively decided not to seek a second. Robinson made her intention to retire public in early 1997, seven months before her term of office was due to expire[87] (though Robinson would subsequently choose to resign two months before completing this full term to take up an appointment in the United Nations). Like Hyde, Robinson also decided to inform the Taoiseach of the day, John Bruton, of her decision not to seek a second term in advance of communicating this information to the other party leaders in the Oireachtas. However, Robinson, unlike Hyde, could not be accused of giving the governing party any real advantage as, though precedent was observed and the Taoiseach was told first, this happened only on the day in which the news was released from the Áras.[88] In this respect, Robinson showed more political acumen than Hyde, albeit in a different era, in which the presidency had more leeway to alter precedents and to act independently of Government.

On the day prior to Hyde's presidential term expiring, de Valera wrote to him expressing his appreciation for Hyde's service to the country:

> I regard it as a signal honour to be privileged to serve as Head of Government with you as head of state. The period in which we have worked together has been one of great anxiety and difficulty but your kindness and understanding made the task much lighter than it otherwise would have been. In you were symbolised for us the efforts and ideals that inspired our generation. It was fitting indeed that the first person to hold the office of President, which symbolises the realisation of those ideals, should have been yourself. It is my wish for the nation that the highest post will always be filled with as much honour and dignity as it has been by you.[89]

At the same time, de Valera made a short, private, handwritten assessment of the first President, which was not unkind: 'Had his health permitted he would have established many precedents which would make the path of his successor easy. For some years, his health did not enable him to move about and meet the people on a number of occasions when it would have been appropriate to do so.'[90] In regard to Hyde's official duties, de Valera remarked that he 'performed . . . with such a grace that it made dealing with him a pleasure'.[91] In conclusion, de Valera noted that 'we all regret that he has found it necessary to retire. Were his health equal to all the tasks there would not now be any question of an election of a successor. All would have asked him to continue.'[92]

9

Forgotten Patriot

Shortly after it was announced in January 1945 that Douglas Hyde intended to retire, Michael McDunphy contacted Éamon de Valera with concerns that the move back to his native Roscommon would prove too much for Hyde. Douglas Hyde's wife had died on the last day of 1938, less than six months after Hyde had taken office, and Áras an Uachtaráin had provided him with a support infrastructure, including round-the-clock nursing care, that would not be available to him if he returned to live alone in rural Frenchpark. Over the course of seven years working together, the professional relationship between the punctilious senior civil servant and the elderly President had developed into a warm and affectionate friendship. McDunphy was genuinely upset at the prospect of Hyde being put into a position where he had to fend for himself. His entreaties to de Valera were met with a receptive ear.

In February 1945, after consultation with McDunphy, the Taoiseach made a proposal to Hyde that Little Lodge, a house near to Áras an Uachtaráin in the Phoenix Park, which had in previous times been the official residence of the Private Secretary to the Lord Lieutenant of Ireland, would be let to him.[1] Hyde had hoped to return to Roscommon on the expiration of his term, but reluctantly agreed, given his physical infirmities, that this would no longer be practical. Accordingly, the Taoiseach issued instructions that 'the House in the Park, known as the Private Secretary's House, should be put in order by the Board of Works, as far as exterior and structural work are concerned'.[2] Until August 1944, the house had been used by the Plans and Operations Section of the Irish Army and this meant that considerable renovation and refurbishment had to be undertaken. The enthusiasm of de Valera and McDunphy for this project was a source of some frustration to the Commissioner of the Board of Public Works, Joseph Connolly. He wrote to Moynihan complaining that over £1,000 was spent 'rehabilitating and furnishing' the house and he added that 'we are in the difficult position of having to take our instructions from McDunphy and we are not in a position to challenge or question any of his directions'.[3] Connolly did manage to have the retiring President make a once-off payment of £118 for linoleum, carpets and blinds; however, Hyde's annual rent on the property was a very modest sum of 'about £120 per annum'.[4]

Hyde's final home had an unusual history. It was the first childhood home that Winston Churchill could remember. In 1876, Churchill's grandfather, the Duke of Marlborough, was appointed as Viceroy to Ireland and he appointed his son, Randolph Churchill, father of Winston, as his Private Secretary. As a result, the future British Prime Minister lived in Little Lodge, as the house was then known, between the ages of two and six. In his memoirs, Churchill recalled that he had his first engagement with formal learning in this house and that 'it was at the Little Lodge I was first menaced with education. The approach of a sinister figure described as "the Governess" was announced.'[5] Churchill's brother, John, was also born in the house in 1880, just prior to the family returning to England.[6] At Hyde's insistence, the name of the house was changed to Little Ratra in memory of Hyde's own private home in Roscommon, which was also called Ratra and had been gifted to him by the Gaelic League in 1906.[7]

Although Hyde's term did not officially terminate until midnight on 24 June 1945, he quietly moved into Little Ratra on 20 June and, from this point, he completely disappeared from public sight. His failing health prevented him from attending his successor's inauguration. Hyde was joined in Little Ratra by his sister and his nurse, Kathleen Fitzsimons, who had been by his side since his stroke in 1940. McDunphy, de Valera and Éamonn de Buitléar, Hyde's first aide-de-camp and the father of the renowned Irish naturalist and film-maker, were regular visitors, but Hyde's life during these final years was distressful. Entirely bedridden, he was plagued with uncomfortable skin ailments that often made sleep difficult.[8]

Douglas Hyde died at 10.15 p.m. on 12 July 1949 after 'a prolonged illness'.[9] He was eighty-nine years old. The following day in a statement to Dáil Éireann, the Taoiseach, John A. Costello, said that 'with the death of Dr Douglas Hyde there has passed from the Irish scene one whose name will occupy a permanent and unique place in the records of Irish history. Dr Hyde's life was a very long, very full and very varied one. No Irishman of our time, or indeed of any time, played a greater part in shaping the history of his own age and few men have ever carried so many distinctions with so much modesty.'[10]

Hyde's death gave rise to numerous tributes and large crowds of citizens took to the streets to pay tribute to the first President of Ireland, as Hyde's funeral cortège, accompanied by a military guard of honour, travelled from St Patrick's Cathedral to Portahard, Frenchpark, in Hyde's native Roscommon. The funeral service was not without controversy. Though the Government had accorded Hyde a state funeral, almost the entire cabinet chose not to attend the service in St Patrick's Cathedral. The poet Austin Clarke satirised this non-attendance in 'Burial of an Irish President':

> At the last bench
> Two Catholics, the French
> Ambassador and I, knelt down.
> The vergers waited. Outside:
> The hush of Dublin town,
> Professors of cap and gown,
> Costello, his Cabinet
> In Government cars, hiding
> Around the corner, ready
> Tall hat in hand, dreading
> Our Father in English. Better
> Not hear that 'which' for 'who'
> And risk eternal doom.[11]

Maurice Dockrell, a Protestant Fine Gael TD for Dublin South Central, represented the Taoiseach at the service; however, Costello and almost his entire cabinet skulked outside the church. The Minister for Health, Noël Browne, who would later vehemently clash with the Catholic hierarchy, did attend Hyde's funeral service.[12] Hyde's successor, President O'Kelly, and the then leader of the Opposition, Éamon de Valera, were also absent from the St Patrick's Cathedral funeral, though the latter was represented by Erskine Childers, a Fianna Fáil TD and member of the Church of Ireland, who had performed a similar duty for de Valera eleven years previously at the Protestant religious ceremony prior to Hyde's inauguration.[13] There was a similar lack of official representation at Hyde's burial in Portahard, though *The Irish Times* pointedly noted that in this instance, at least, both President O'Kelly and de Valera stayed in the graveyard 'right to the end of the service'.[14]

The absence of major state dignitaries from Hyde's funeral service was not because of any political or personal animus – the late President was held in high regard by many of those who stayed away from his funeral – but because the Catholic Church's doctrine, at this time, made participation in Protestant ceremonies a reserved sin that only a bishop could absolve.

Bert Smyllie, under his pseudonym of 'Nichevo', wrote a column bluntly pointing the finger at Catholic regulations for the 'sparsely occupied pews' in St Patrick's Cathedral, which gave rise to angry debate in the paper's letters page.[15] One letter writer to *The Irish Times* regretted that 'the President, the Taoiseach or Mr de Valera did not see their way to give a lead by flouting a decree, which treats them as schoolchildren' and another correspondent expressed 'a sense of bewilderment and frustration from beholding the spectacle of the members of the Government of our newborn sovereign and independent Republic waiting outside of the ancient Irish Cathedral Church of St Patrick, in the capital of the Republic, in obedience to a decree emanating from foreign sources'.[16]

The lingering sectarian divide in Irish society highlighted by Hyde's funeral stood in stark contrast to the hopes of a new spirit of religious toleration that had accompanied his inauguration. *The Irish Times* in May 1938 had congratulated the political parties for 'their choice of a Protestant to be the head of the state, they have shown an example of broad minded tolerance which will not be lost upon our own people and upon the world at large'.[17]

Hyde's religion as President mattered because it allowed the parties, and in particular Fianna Fáil, to stress the ecumenical character of the Irish state both for its own sake and as a means to tackle partition. Williams has observed that 'Hyde's background represented an attempt to signify and emphasise the non-sectarianism of the state.'[18] That there was an immediate need to emphasise the non-sectarian nature of the Irish state at this juncture has been highlighted by Lee. He notes that 'insofar as one can judge from the constituency returns, it seems that the overwhelming majority of Protestants voted heavily against the Constitution'.[19]

Though de Valera had consulted with and secured the approval of Dr Gregg, Church of Ireland Archbishop of Dublin, Rev. Massey, head of the Methodist Church in Ireland, and Dr Irwin, Moderator Designate of the Presbyterian Church of Ireland, the public debate that followed on the merits of the draft Constitution in 1937 caused some unease in the Protestant community.[20] In Fianna Fáil's eagerness to seek popular support for the Constitution, a number of ministers seemed to equate Irishness with Catholicism. Seán T. O'Kelly claimed the Constitution was 'worthy of a Catholic country and worthy to be voted for by every right-minded Catholic Irishman'.[21] In the Dáil debate, Seán MacEntee had spoken about the need to ratify 'the Constitution of a Catholic state'.[22] In the plebiscite campaign, while acknowledging that some people had expressed concerns of 'Rome Rule', he dismissed this notion before going on to boast that Fianna Fáil had 'the moral courage almost unique in the world today to adopt as part of the Constitution the fundamental teachings of the Holy Father in regard to the Family'.[23] Bowman's research notes that the 'Constitution's debt to the social teaching of the papal encyclicals was widely commented upon' at the time of the Constitution being debated.[24] At the same time, Article 44 of Bunreacht na hÉireann recognised the 'special position' of the Roman Catholic Church. As Deputy Frank MacDermott predicted in the Dáil debate on the draft Constitution, this clause had the potential to 'create misunderstandings' among the Protestant community.[25]

The strong emphasis placed on Catholicism in the Constitution caused many southern Protestants to feel the passing of Bunreacht na hÉireann amounted to a further decline in their status. This point was recognised within Fianna Fáil by Gerry Boland, who had staged a vociferous cabinet revolt in response to an earlier incarnation of Article 44. He had remonstrated angrily:

> If this clause gets through as now worded, then it would be equivalent to the expulsion from our history of great Irishmen like Tone, Emmet, Russell, McCracken and even Parnell, Childers and many more. None of these men would live in Ireland under a sectarian Constitution, and I would not live under it either. I would take my wife and children and put myself out of it. It seems to me that it is bowing down before all of those who were against the Republicans all the time, and still are.[26]

In the aftermath of the passing of the Constitution, there was a definite political need to make a gesture to Irish Protestants to assure them that there would be no religious discrimination. For de Valera, there was also a need to keep on board Boland and 'other senior Fianna Fáil men' who had genuine fears that the religious clauses in the Constitution might be 'sectarian, anti-republican and a hindrance to prospects for national reunification'.[27] A means to do this was to put a Protestant in the role that Seán MacEntee had described as the 'apex' of the Irish people's 'political organisation' in the Constitution.[28] Fianna Fáil was conscious that a Protestant in the highest office in the state would visibly demonstrate that there was no political bigotry in the state, while at the same time serving to undermine the arguments of the proponents of partition. It may also be significant that Boland was one of the two Fianna Fáil plenipotentiaries that negotiated with Fine Gael on who the first President would be.

News of Hyde's selection was well received by southern Protestants. In 1988, Dr Donald Caird, Church of Ireland Archbishop of Dublin, recalled: 'As a schoolboy in Dublin in 1938, I remember the mild surprise and sense of gratification expressed by my teachers, parents and generally the older members of the community, at the news that Dr Douglas Hyde had been unanimously elected as first President of Ireland under the new 1937 Constitution.'[29]

For the political parties, but especially Fianna Fáil, the selection of Hyde was a further attempt at reconciling all shades of Protestant opinion with both republicanism and the Irish state. In Ó Tuathaigh's words, Hyde's selection was popular because it underpinned 'what Tone had advocated and what many generations of Irish nationalists had hoped and striven for, namely, a symbol of an inclusive form of Irishness'.[30]

John MacVeigh, Secretary of the American legation in Dublin, described Hyde's nomination as a 'fine gesture of goodwill towards the minority religious group' in the state, but de Valera undoubtedly hoped that it would also be interpreted as a gesture of goodwill to the majority religion in the North.[31] The subject of partition was never far from de Valera's mind. As MacEntee later commented on de Valera's political motivation, 'there recurs, like the clanging of a bell, one theme: Partition, Partition, Partition! Every argument came back to it. Every decision was affected by it.'[32] This was certainly the case with Hyde's nomination. Fianna Fáil's agreement on Hyde's candidacy must also be examined in the context of the Anglo-Irish negotiations in 1938, which were drawing to a conclusion after over three months of stop-start talks. The parties agreed on Hyde's nomination on 21 April 1938. The following day, it was announced that the negotiations had been completed and the ceremonial signing of the Anglo-Irish Agreement subsequently took place on 25 April.[33]

This agreement saw de Valera isolate partition as the one remaining source of grievance between Britain and Ireland. Privately, in the course of the talks, Chamberlain had told de Valera that he would be glad to see partition removed, provided only Northern Ireland would consent.[34] Chamberlain had been conciliatory in the talks, but was insistent that the disagreement lay between the two administrations on the island of Ireland. Chamberlain had also told de Valera that there was a need for a shift in British public opinion and, according to MacEntee, who was part of the Irish delegation, Chamberlain had encouraged Irish involvement 'in the evangelising of the great British public'.[35]

Against this immediate backdrop, for Fianna Fáil, agreement on a Protestant President made perfect political sense. De Valera would have been acutely aware that a non-Catholic head of state gave him a trump card in the propaganda stakes to deploy against those who portrayed the Irish state in terms of 'Rome Rule'. What de Valera did not know was that the intervention of the Second World War would give him little opportunity to play this card. Though de Valera established the Anti-Partition League in every major Irish centre in Britain, by the time the major distraction of the war had finished so too had Hyde's presidency.

A further significant reason for the readiness of Fianna Fáil and Fine Gael to agree on Hyde was the boost his presidency would give to the revival of the Irish language. The former Cumann na nGaedheal minister and co-founder with Hyde of the Gaelic League, Eoin MacNeill, acclaimed the choice of Hyde as 'a victory for Irish popular culture'.[36] Leading figures in both of the main parties had come into politics via the language movement. For the Taoiseach, the language question would remain of utmost political importance. A number of months after Hyde's inauguration, de Valera told the Seanad that the Irish language was more important to him than the issue of partition because 'as long as the language remains you have a distinguishing characteristic of nationality which would enable the nation to persist'.[37] Hyde's presidency was a means for the Fianna Fáil Government to underline its enduring political commitment to the Gaelic revival.

Hyde's journey to Áras an Uachtaráin was facilitated by the evolution of views on the role of a head of state in early twentieth-century Ireland. By exploring the offices that preceded that of the President of Ireland, as well as nationalist Ireland's reaction to them, this book underlines the fact that the ultimate *raison d'être* of the office of President was most definitely political. It grew out of the fundamental debate on sovereignty that dominated Irish politics up until the enactment of Bunreacht na hÉireann.

The office of President of Ireland has its roots in de Valera's unwillingness to reconcile himself to the Governor-Generalship as the British Crown's representative in Ireland, which was a key component of the 1921 Anglo-Irish Treaty. During the Treaty debates, de Valera made it clear that he genuinely believed that the King having a role as head of state in Ireland would be used as a pretext for British political interference in Irish affairs. He said: 'It is not King George as a monarch they choose, it is Lloyd George, because it is not the personal monarch they are choosing, it is the British power and authority as sovereign authority in this country.'[38]

The office of President emerged out of a gradualist and, at times, torturous political campaign, which had at its core de Valera's determination to assert the fullest measure of Irish sovereignty. By 1936, he had made good on his privately stated intention to Moss Twomey, the IRA Chief of Staff, to make a '*sean na scuab*' (i.e., a stuffed dummy) of the Governor-General.[39] At the end of that year, the office was consigned to history as part of the fallout from the abdication crisis in London. By this stage, de Valera had already begun formulating his thoughts as to what a form a new Irish head of state should take.

Gallagher has correctly pointed out that 'it was not enough that there should be a head of state provided for under an Irish constitution; it was important that it be made quite unambiguous that this head of state was chosen by the Irish people themselves'.[40] For de Valera, with his fundamental political focus on showcasing Ireland's enhanced sovereignty, a key aspect of the new presidency was that it affirmed the Irish people's right to elect their own head of state. Despite the Opposition's increasingly hysterical fears that a president with a superior national mandate to the head of government would result in a dictatorship, de Valera refused to budge from his conviction that an Irish head of state should be directly elected by universal suffrage.

In relation to the nature of the office, it is hard to dispute de Valera's assertion that the political purpose of the President was to 'guard the people's rights and mainly to guard the Constitution'.[41] Though in modern times political scientists have taken issue with de Valera's assertion that the President was given six 'substantial powers', dismissing these powers as 'a distinct anticlimax', in the context of the 1930s, these powers were politically appropriate and provided a significant democratic reserve to guard against an aspiring dictator.[42]

The Opposition's allegations of dictatorship in the debate on the draft Constitution were largely based on unfounded fears that extra-constitutional powers might be conferred upon the new President. This was undoubtedly influenced by the slide away from democracy already well under way on the continent. It was also indicative of their political mistrust of de Valera.

The challenge to European democracy clearly also had a marked impact on how de Valera politically conceptualised the President's role. In this regard, de Valera was keen to emphasise in the Dáil debate that the new office's powers, in relation to the dissolution of the Dáíl, convening a meeting of the Oireachtas and requesting the Supreme Court to validate the constitutionality of legislation, were of real significance because they provided important democratic safeguards.

Gallagher has suggested that if instead of compromising on Hyde 'all the main parties had nominated heavyweight political candidates and the President had been elected on a partisan platform, the subsequent development of the office might conceivably have been quite different'.[43] It was to prevent such an eventuality coming to pass that de Valera acquiesced to a non-contest. In the debate on the draft Constitution, de Valera had set out an important distinction. While maintaining that the new presidency was a political office, he also set his face against it taking on a party-political hue. He maintained that it would be the President's responsibility to be 'interested in the broad politics as far as the state as a whole is concerned, but he should not be involved in what you might call party politics or in matters where there are differences of party view'.[44] Hyde neatly fitted this bill.

Historians and commentators have largely ignored Hyde's presidency, justifying this oversight on the erroneous basis that nothing significant happened. The dismissal of the presidency as nothing more than a 'retirement home' in relation to the period from 1938 to 1945 is, though misguided, perhaps understandable given the fact that Hyde was seventy-eight years old on assuming office. However, it is a mistake to assume that because of the advanced age of the incumbent, the office of President by corollary was inactive. In Hyde's seven-year term, the office of President was extraordinarily busy. Much of the legwork in this regard was initiated and undertaken by a highly productive and efficient if, at times, zealous, civil servant, Michael McDunphy. As the first Secretary to the office of President, McDunphy was scrupulous about lines of authority and, while Hyde gave him wide latitude, it is clear from the voluminous files from the office of the President that Hyde remained the key decision maker.

Both Hyde and McDunphy took on a huge workload in establishing the office of President in its formative years. At a political level, this involved standing up to a number of powerful interests in Irish society who seemed unwilling to recognise the constitutional prerogative of 'precedence over all other persons in the state' that was bestowed upon the new President.[45]

Hyde's presidency was undoubtedly constrained by his deteriorating health as well as wartime restrictions, which in any case would have curtailed his ability to travel to engagements around the country. However, critics, who attribute inertness to the first President, need to be careful of not engaging in a backwards reading of history. The visibility of modern Presidents is explained, at least in part, by a 24/7 news era and faster news cycles. It is unfair and unhistorical to impose these modern media standards on Presidents who served when the political pace was much more sedate and at a time when even Taoisigh or ministers regularly went home for lunch or finished for the evening at 5.30 p.m.[46]

While hardly scientific, it is worth pondering the fact that an *Irish Times* archives search for the period in which Douglas Hyde was President shows that he was mentioned more often in that newspaper than Seán Lemass, who was considered possibly the most dynamic minister in Government.[47] Rumours of Hyde's anonymity, it seems, are much exaggerated. Certainly, for those who measure inertia or activity in terms of column inches, President Hyde's comparative strong coverage should give cause for reflection, especially given the fact that ministers had the regular platform of speeches to the Dáil, which were then a staple of newspaper coverage.

Similarly, the unfair comparison that extols modern Presidents for expanding the role of their office, while implicitly criticising early Presidents, such as Hyde, for taking a more restrained approach, again lacks historical context. This criticism completely misses the point that a more expansionist role for the presidency could not have come about without the diligent and often unglamorous work of early Presidents in establishing initial credibility and respect for the office. Specifically, in this regard, Keogh has praised the work 'collectively' done by successive Presidents of Ireland from 1938, arguing that this has 'helped to change a negative public perception of the office which was there when the draft Constitution was first discussed in the Dáil in 1937. Cynical views have often been expressed about the presidency having been a "retirement home" for long-serving politicians. That was never the case.'[48] Much of this work, which, as Keogh validly argues has made the presidency 'an integral part of the constitutional life of the state', has been highly political.[49] Gerard Hogan's contention that the 'ceremonial role of the President is by far the most important one in practice' does not tally with de Valera's view in creating the office nor with how the office evolved in Hyde's formative early presidency.[50]

It is popular, but not historically correct, to assert that the presidencies of Mary Robinson and Mary McAleese were in some way groundbreaking for the emphasis they placed on non-partisan political themes, such as, in Robinson's case, the Irish diaspora and humanitarian issues and, in McAleese's case, the Irish peace process.[51] In fact, from the office's inception, Hyde made a number of political themes synonymous with his tenure in the Áras. President Hyde was to the forefront on the key political issues of his day on which there was a broad national consensus, such as protecting Ireland's neutrality, healing Civil War bitterness and restoring the Irish language.

Between 1938 and 1945, Hyde diligently engaged with the political system and reacted to political events while exercising his powers and performing his duties. In Douglas Hyde's time as President, the office and the incumbent, far from being seen as removed from or above politics, were on a number of occasions the focus of severe attack by political forces unhappy with the manner in which the President had exercised his constitutional powers. In particular, his decision in 1944 to grant a dissolution of the Dáil to de Valera in debatable circumstances saw the presidency become immersed in heated political debate that was not matched until the events surrounding the resignation of Cearbhall Ó Dálaigh more than three decades later.

Despite his failing health and his consequent lack of visibility, President Hyde remained one of the most talked about figures in Irish life and, indeed, the subject of numerous rumours. Hyde's stroke gave rise to gossip that 'spread throughout the civil service and the Dáil to the effect that the President had become senile'.[52] However, the professional manner in which Hyde dealt with his constitutional obligations, as well as the fact that while in office, after his stroke, he published three volumes of poetry for private circulation – *The Children of Lir* (1941), *Songs of Columcille* (1942) and *Dánta Éagsamhla agus*

Béarla Curtha Ortha (1943) – underline that Hyde's sharp intellect remained very much intact. Furthermore, the ever scrupulous McDunphy, aware of the rumours, composed an explicit memo for the historical record maintaining that the President was not senile.[53]

Rumours that Hyde was a ladies' man had surfaced throughout his long public career, but these gained widespread currency during his presidency. Brian O'Nolan, a civil servant in the Department of Local Government who used the pen name Myles na gCopaleen, composed a vulgar limerick about the President:

> There once was a man called an t-Uachtaráin
> who lived in Áras an Uachtaráin,
> He was fond of his nookie,
> he had a go at the cookie,
> And there is the couch that he f-uchtaráin.[54]

Despite the fact that the octogenarian Hyde was confined to a wheelchair and was unlikely to have had the physical capacity to engage in sexual intercourse with anyone, this irreverent verse was 'very popular at the time'.[55]

Stories of Hyde's womanising have persisted down through the years. In 1991, the respected journalist and author Proinsias Mac Aonghusa, who was also the serving President of the Gaelic League, claimed that Hyde had entered into a relationship in the Áras with one of the nurses who had been assigned to care for the widowed President after his stroke. Mac Aonghusa's story, which first appeared in the Irish-language newspaper *Anois*, created a minor media sensation and was based on accounts given by personal friends of Hyde and an unidentified army officer who was working at Áras an Uachtaráin at the time.[56]

The essence of the story was that Hyde's family had 'objected strongly' when the President told them he intended to remarry with a young nurse; however, Hyde ignored these protests, causing his family to confront the Taoiseach.[57] On hearing of Hyde's plans, de Valera, allegedly, 'headed straight to Áras an Uachtaráin' and 'he ordered Dr Hyde not to marry, and the President acquiesced'.[58] An anonymous source for Mac Aonghusa's original story subsequently told the *Irish Press* that de Valera's motive 'in advising against the marriage' was 'to maintain the dignity' of the presidential office.[59] The Taoiseach was apparently 'worried about the impact on public opinion of a marriage between an elderly holder of high office and a much younger woman'.[60]

Irrespective of whether Hyde ever really did wish to remarry or whether the Taoiseach ever did have to advise the President not to enter into nuptials, there is no doubt that de Valera was deeply concerned with maintaining the dignity of the presidency. A significant level of political priority was attached by Government to ensuring that the new office of President was perceived with sufficient respect. De Valera's decision to appoint Michael McDunphy, a respected career civil servant, as Secretary to the office of President was a wise political choice. It helped to ameliorate Opposition concerns about the nature of the office and it gave administrative responsibility to a capable individual who would become a fervent defender of the dignity and independence of the President's office.

In a newly emerging postcolonial society, it is understandable, especially given the confusions of the External Relations Act, that there was a resolute determination to ensure that the President would not be overshadowed by representatives of the old order. The office of President's refusal to allow the Punchestown Race Committee or anyone else to treat Hyde with less precedence than either the British Representative or his spouse was an important political marker that both underpinned the President's status and asserted Irish sovereignty. Similarly, the office of President's insistence that *The Irish Times* accord Hyde precedence in their social column was indicative of a zero-tolerance approach to any suggestion that the President's rank was in some way inferior to other heads of state and, in particular, the British sovereign.

In the presidency's earliest days, the office's precedence was also challenged when Hyde refused to submit to the GAA's policy of sporting apartheid. The GAA's action in expelling the President of Ireland for attending a soccer match was a despicable attempt to elevate the narrow politics of the ban above Hyde's objective of a pluralist presidency. The GAA's action caused fury across the body politic. Hyde's dignified response was important in building public support and respect for his office, but, de Valera's principled dressing-down of the GAA's two leading officials was also of real political significance. The

Taoiseach's willingness to vent his wrath on the country's most popular sporting organisation underlined the high political priority Government attached to upholding the President's precedence and to the development of a truly national office.

Hyde's presidency was benign, paternalistic and pursued a healing agenda. Although some influential figures in Irish public life stubbornly refused to respond to the President's quiet diplomacy, Hyde's effort to foster political reconciliation was important national work. He enjoyed some success in easing Civil War tensions and in using the Áras as a space to bring former foes together as part of a strategy to make Irish politics less fractious. Hyde also used his presidency to reach out to those who felt politically alienated from the new Irish state. Though his efforts met with little gratitude from Ulster unionists or militant republicans, this does not take away from his noble intentions. Hyde's work underlined the bridge-building potential of an inclusive presidency, and this theme has been significantly developed by later Presidents, particularly so in the case of Mary McAleese.

Hyde also established a number of important constitutional precedents against a backdrop of fraught political events. In 1940, in the aftermath of the IRA's raid on the Magazine Fort, Hyde became the first President to refer a piece of legislation to the Supreme Court. The Offences Against the State Amendment Bill had become a contentious political football, with the Government and Opposition taking diametrically opposed views on whether it was desirable that this Bill be referred to the Supreme Court. Hyde showed political dexterity in ensuring that his office was not sucked into the dispute and in keeping his office independent. The President's appointments to the Council of State, made almost immediately prior to its first meeting, were representative of all shades of opinion in the Oireachtas. By subsequently taking a rigid procedural approach in chairing the first Council of State meeting, Hyde ensured that the meeting did not degenerate into a party-political squabble. This helped establish the Council of State as a forum where Presidents receive a broad range of opinions and impartial advice.

The second occasion that Hyde referred legislation to the Supreme Court was also of political note. Despite his lifelong advocacy of the Irish language, Hyde wisely chose to refer a Bill that provided for compulsory Irish in schooling to the Supreme Court when it became clear that this legislation could impinge on the constitutional rights of minorities, especially members of the Protestant community. Hyde's decision underlined that a President's primary duty is to defend the Constitution and that this factor must outweigh any personal opinions they may have on whether or not legislation may be politically desirable.

As President, Hyde performed an important role in putting a human face on the national policy of neutrality. He was scrupulously impartial in his dealing with the diplomatic representatives of the belligerent nations as part of the state's effort to portray an even-handed approach in its relations with the Axis and Allied powers. It should, however, be noted that Hyde's personal lack of empathy for the plight of Professor Pokorny does his reputation little favours. Nonetheless, the office of President played a key role in the state's diplomatic intelligence-gathering operation, and this sensitive political work was taken seriously by de Valera, who was regularly briefed on McDunphy's conversations about the wartime situation with foreign visitors to the Áras. McDunphy was also accorded a considerable degree of political trust by the Government and President Hyde in being allowed to strongly enunciate what Irish policy was in his conversations with foreign representatives, and this facet of his work, in particular, negates any impression that the Áras existed in splendid isolation from the dominant political concerns of the day.

Douglas Hyde's contribution to Ireland was immense. As a cultural campaigner, he did more than any other individual to save the Irish language from national extinction. His persuasiveness and his perseverance were central to reviving a language that, in his own words, had been thrown away 'like dirty water out of a house'.[61] The Gaelic League was one of the most profoundly influential grass-roots organisations in Irish history, but at the very root of its success was Hyde's own personal dynamism. W. B. Yeats, though he viewed Douglas Hyde with condescension, grudgingly admitted that Hyde 'was to create a great popular movement, far more important in its practical results than any movement I could have made'.[62] In his poem 'The Man and the Echo', written in 1938, Yeats rather vaingloriously asked, 'Did that play of mine send out / Certain men the English shot?'[63] However, in reality, it was Hyde and the Gaelic League that provided the intellectual and emotional foundation for the majority of those who led the political and military campaigns for Irish separatism in the period prior to 1916 up until the coming into being of the Irish Free State. Hyde had fought a fruitless battle to keep the cultural nationalism he had pioneered free from the political nationalism it had spawned, but ultimately he recognised and took pride in the central role the Gaelic League had played in bringing about Irish independence. In an essay printed in the *Manchester Guardian* in 1923, Hyde wrote: 'the movement which has resulted in the establishment of our Government is the descendant of the Gaelic League, and the Gaelic League goes back to Gaelic Ireland, to ancient Ireland for its inspiration. The Gaelic League grew up and became the spiritual father of Sinn Féin, and Sinn Féin's progeny were the Volunteers, who forced the English to make the Treaty. The Dáil is the child of the Volunteers, and thus it descends directly from the Gaelic League, whose traditions it inherits.'[64]

If Hyde was both the cultural saviour of the Irish language and the spiritual father of the Irish revolution, this was not his only national service. His personality and his patriotism were integral to how the office of President quickly established itself as a relevant, political and popular institution. Hyde's popularity was a big factor in this regard.

On his eighty-second birthday, in 1942, Hyde told a gathering of his intimate friends that his 'supreme wish' was that he 'might live to complete his period of office'.[65] In an interview with *The Irish Times* that day, he said 'my greatest pleasure is to serve my country'.[66] The manner in which Hyde went about this service was appreciated by the public. Hyde's style was low-key; he was uncomfortable with any ostentatious displays and his whole disposition exuded decency. Ireland's first two Governor-Generals had left themselves open to charges of delusions of grandeur, either through donning an air of self-importance or through some extravagant entertainment expenses.

Hyde, however, had a healthy contempt for excessive formality and was determined not to be seen to lose touch with 'the ordinary people' that he viewed as his greatest allies in his quest to preserve the Irish language.[67] At Hyde's insistence, 'the cost of entertaining' was 'borne out of the President's pocket'.[68] He was deeply sensitive to the poverty that was still rampant in Irish society and he was keen to show his solidarity with the less well-off. When the Second World War made heating fuel a scarce commodity, Hyde swiftly donated the contents of the coal cellars in Áras an Uachtaráin to the poor of Dublin. This gesture was extraordinarily well received. Even forty-five years after the event, the impact it had on people living in straitened circumstances was acknowledged by the then Taoiseach Charles Haughey, who as a teenager growing up in Donnycarney had experienced the austerities arising from the Second World War.[69]

Similarly, Hyde was very engaged in the effort to tackle the real food shortages that Irish society experienced during the Second World War and, in particular, to keep the population nourished. Detailed files in the National Archives in Dublin highlight the President's keen interest in the growing of crops in the grounds of the Áras during the war.[70] To the chagrin of some of the Board of Works' gardeners, Hyde instructed that the spectacular flower and plant displays in the old Viceregal Gardens be cleared in order to feed Dublin's poor. In January 1942, *The Irish Times* reported that 'most of the arable land' in the Áras an Uachtaráin estate was 'under tillage' and that the gardens had been mostly 'ploughed for wheat this year, making twenty-five acres altogether under cultivation'.[71] The same newspaper report, highlighting Hyde's gentle nature, also referred to the fact that the President had 'made an animal sanctuary of the grounds' of Áras an Uachtaráin and that 'he will not permit any living thing to be killed within its boundaries'.[72]

Hyde's generosity had been publicly evident in September 1940 when he made a gift from his own personal resources of six motor ambulances to the Irish Red Cross.[73] His kindness and his geniality also combined with a genuine bravery, which contributed to the affection that the Irish people had for him. Hyde valiantly soldiered on in office, despite serious ill health, because he recognised that political stability was crucial in the wartime situation. Unlike President Roosevelt, whose administration made his disability 'virtually a state secret' and were prepared to use forceful censorship to prevent photos of the US President in his wheelchair appearing in public, Hyde had no personal qualms about being photographed in his wheelchair and he said that he hoped it would offer encouragement to other people contending with similar disabilities.[74]

Historians have rightly given enormous credit to the British royal family's courageous refusal to leave London during the Second World War and the positive effect that this had on public morale. Though almost entirely forgotten, Hyde's bravery in declining all entreaties to vacate the Áras should be viewed in a similar light. While not contending that Ireland came even remotely close to experiencing the same extent of the horrors of the German Blitzkrieg as the United Kingdom, German bombs fell on locations in the Irish state in August and December 1940 and in January, May, June and July 1941.[75] Like Buckingham Palace, Áras an Uachtaráin had no proper air-raid shelter facilities when the sustained period of German bombing began. However, in the British King's primary residence, a bomb shelter was rapidly constructed, affording maximum protection.[76] The safety precautions surrounding President Hyde were far more precarious.

At the outbreak of the war, an outdoor coal cellar in the grounds of Áras an Uachtaráin had been converted into a temporary, if amateur, air-raid shelter by reinforcing it with 200 sandbags.[77] At the end of July 1940, after a lengthy correspondence between McDunphy and the Board of Works, work began on a dedicated air-raid shelter on the Áras's grounds. However, this project was rendered redundant even before construction commenced. In this period, Hyde was largely bed-ridden and McDunphy noted that 'owing to the state of [the President's] health the use of the outdoor air-raid shelter is not regarded as either practicable or wise'.[78] When German bombs fell on Dublin in late December 1940 and on successive days in January 1941, Hyde declined entreaties from McDunphy to vacate the Áras unless an indoor shelter was provided.

The risk to the President was brought crashing home on the night of 31 May 1941 when the Luftwaffe dropped four high-explosive bombs across north Dublin. The most severe carnage occurred in North Strand, where twenty-eight people lost their lives and hundreds of homes were damaged or destroyed. One of the bombs came within a whisker of killing Douglas Hyde. McDunphy recorded: 'A bomb dropped beside the Dog Pond in the Phoenix Park, which is only about half a mile in direct line from the Áras, [it] smashed a number of windows in the Áras itself. One of the windows of the President's bedroom in which he was at the time sleeping was broken and a portion of the mantelpiece was dislodged.'[79]

In 1997, an aviation researcher, Leo Sheridan, claimed to have unearthed archival evidence in a Munich army base that proved that the May 1941 Luftwaffe bombings of Dublin were designed 'to teach the [Southern] Irish a lesson' after de Valera had, in the previous month, sent fire brigades across the border to fight bomb blazes in Belfast. Sheridan claimed, 'it was also intended to bomb Áras an Uachtaráin – and President Douglas Hyde being the main target . . . Dr Hyde, being a Protestant, was perceived by German intelligence to have sympathies with Northern unionists.'[80] Though Sheridan's claims initially made news headlines, they remain largely unsubstantiated and now are viewed with scepticism.

More credence is given to an appeal for forgiveness broadcast on RTÉ radio in 1999 by an anonymous elderly German, resident in Canada, who claimed to have been one of the Luftwaffe pathfinder pilots on the night of the Dublin bombings. According to this source, the intended target of the mission was Belfast, and Dublin had been inadvertently bombed through 'military error'.[81]

Irrespective of whether the Nazis had deliberately intended to bomb Dublin or not, it is hard not to imagine that the course of Irish history would have been radically different if the Luftwaffe bomb had landed a short distance further north in the Phoenix Park and caused the death of President Hyde. In this scenario, it would have been considerably more difficult for de Valera to keep Ireland out of the war.

Hyde was shaken by the German bombing, but he still declined to leave the Áras out of concern that this would generate panic amongst the public. De Valera immediately gave sanction for the construction of a new, indoor bomb shelter, bringing to an end further Board of Works foot-dragging on the issue. McDunphy noted that 'the Taoiseach, who visited the President some hours after the explosion, expressed the view that a blast-proof shelter should be provided within the Áras itself, to which the President could be removed should occasion occur'.[82] Work on the indoor shelter in Áras an Uachtaráin was completed in December 1941, but Hyde never had occasion to use it. From June 1941, the Luftwaffe's military focus was increasingly on the Soviet Union, and Dublin escaped further bombings. Nevertheless, Hyde showed immense personal fortitude and solid political judgement in not evacuating the Áras in order to convey a sense of normalcy to the public.

Though President Hyde was not always publicly visible, he was still able to exert influence and leadership, and he was often at the fulcrum of political events. His presidency laid solid foundations upon which the credibility of the office was established. Far from being irrelevant, the Irish presidency during Hyde's tenure built up a strong reservoir of public goodwill.

While never partisan, Douglas Hyde's presidency was undoubtedly political. Hyde's work in building credibility and support for his office was political; his skill in protecting the independence of his office was political, and his wise judgement in the exercise of his constitutional responsibilities was political. The engagement of President Hyde with the personalities and issues that dominated Irish politics in mid-twentieth-century Ireland was also decidedly political.

Hyde's presidency has been dismissed as a 'sleepy presidency' and one that did not politically matter. But, in fact, an understanding of Douglas Hyde's career and the foundation of the office of President is central to a deeper understanding of the dynamic of Irish politics in this period. Even today, Hyde's wider achievements remain central to the life of our nation. He preserved for us our vibrant culture and, through his benign presidency, he progressed stability and constitutional order. He deserves more from history than to be a forgotten patriot.

Endnotes

Introduction

1 Thomas Carlyle, *History of Friedrich II of Prussia* (London, 1858), p. 125.

2 Douglas Hyde, 'The Necessity for De-Anglicising Ireland' (Dublin, 1892).

3 *Ibid.*

4 National Gallery of Ireland, NGI31.

5 *United Press International*, 18 February 2013.

6 Barbara J. Mitnick (ed.), *George Washington: American Symbol* (New York, 1999).

7 *The Irish Times*, 21 May 1973.

8 Janet E. Dunleavy & Gareth W. Dunleavy, *Douglas Hyde: A Maker of Modern Ireland* (California, 1991).

9 Risteárd Ó Glaisne, *Dúbhglas de h-Íde: Náisiúnach Neamphspleách* (Dublin, 1993).

10 Cormac Moore, *The GAA v Douglas Hyde* (Cork, 2012).

11Joseph McKenna, *The Irish-American Dynamite Campaign: A History 1881–1896* (North Carolina, 2012), p. 179.

12 Pádraic Pearse, *Collected Works of Padraic H. Pearse: Political Writings and Speeches* (Dublin, 1924), p. 84.

13 Garret Fitzgerald, *Ireland in the World: Further Reflections* (Dublin, 2005), p. 115.

14 *The Irish Times*, 16 December 1972.

15 Dermot Keogh, 'Office of the Presidency has served the State well' *The Irish Times*, 20 October 1997.

16 *'Uachtaráin,'* TG4 Documentary Series, April–May 2007; Kevin Kenna, *The Lives and Times of the Presidents of Ireland* (Dublin, 2010).

1. 25 June 1938

1 Robert Rozett & Shmuel Spector (eds), *Encyclopedia of the Holocaust* (New York, 2000), p. 325.

2 *Ottawa Citizen*, 24 June 1938.

3 Molefi Kete Asante, *The African People: A Global History* (New York, 2012), p. 133.

4 *Irish Independent*, 27 June 1938.

5 *The Irish Times*, 27 June 1938.

6 Donald Cameron Watt, *How War Came* (London, 1989), p. 26.

7 *Daily Illini*, 25 June 1938.

8 *Evening Times*, 23 April 1938.

9 *News Review*, 30 June 1938.

10 *Ibid.*

11 *News Review*, 30 June 1938.

12 *The New York Times Magazine*, 29 May 1938.

13 *Ibid.*

14 *Irish Independent*, 29 July 1938.

15 T. Ryle Dwyer, 'JFK in Ireland: The early visits of a future US president', *Irish Examiner*, 23 July 2015.

16 *Ibid.*

17 *The Irish Times*, 9 July 1938.

18 *Ibid.*

19 *Ibid.*

20 NAI DFA 147/43, Irish Legation in Washington Memo, 11 May 1938.

21 *Irish Press*, 21 July 1938.

22 Alan J. Ward, *The Irish Constitutional Tradition: Responsible Government and Modern Ireland 1782–1992* (Dublin, 1994), p. 234.

23 *Ibid.* p. 234.

24 *Manchester Guardian*, 30 December 1937.

25 John M. Kelly, *The Irish Constitution*: 2nd Edition (Dublin, 1984), p. 723.

26 *Hansard, House of Commons Debate*, vol. 335 col. 1071–1854, 5 May 1938.

27 *Ibid*, vol. 335 col. 1071–1854, 5 May 1938.

28 NAI 1/PRES P235.

29 *The Times*, 27 June 1938; *The Daily Telegraph*, 27 June 1938; *British Pathé*, www.youtube.com/watch?v=nx0Ml2nJhis

30 *The Observer*, 24 April 1938, 26 June 1938; *News Chronicle*, 24 June 1938, 27 June 1938; *Daily Express*, 23 April 1938, 25 June 1938, 27 June 1938.

31 *News Chronicle*, 25 June 1938.

32 *Ibid.*, 24 June 1938.

33 *Daily Express*, 25 June 1938.

34 *Ibid.*

35 *Manchester Evening News*, 22 April 1938, 25 June 1938; *Yorkshire Observer*, 27 April 1938; *Nottingham Journal*, 27 June 1938; *Birkenhead News*, 2 July 1938.

36 *Edinburgh Evening News*, 26 April 1938.

37 *Ibid.*

38 *Irish News*, 25 June 1938.

39 *Irish Press*, 4 July 1938.

40 *Northern Whig*, 13 July 1938.

41 *Ibid.*

42 *Irish Press*, 4 July 1938.

43 *Belfast Telegraph*, 12 July 1938.

44 *Ibid.*

45 *Northern Whig*, 27 June 1938.

46 *Ibid.*, 13 July 1938.

47 *Irish Press*, 4 July 1938.

48 Michael Lennon, 'Douglas Hyde', in the *Bell*, 1951, vol. 16, no. 6, pp. 46–54 & vol. 17, no.1, pp. 41–52. Royal Irish Academy, *Documents on Irish Foreign Policy: 1937–1939*, vol. 5, pp. 308–11, Joseph P. Walshe to Éamon de Valera, 2 June 1938.

49 NAI, PRES 1/P479, memo by Michael McDunphy, 3 November 1938.

50 *The Irish Times*, 22 April 1938; *The New York Times Magazine*, 29 May 1938.

51 *Belfast News Letter*, 27 June 1938.

52 *Daily Express*, 25 June 1938.

53 *The New York Times Magazine*, 29 May 1938.

54 Statement by President Hyde, 27 June 1938, quoted in Dunleavy & Dunleavy, *op. cit.*, p. 391.

55 Ulick O'Connor, *Celtic Dawn: A Portrait of the Irish Literary Renaissance* (Dublin, 1984), p. 379.

56 Basil Peterson, 'Aiding the President', *The Irish Times*, 1 July 1980.

57 *Ibid.*

58 Dunleavy & Dunleavy, *op. cit.*, p. 383; Peterson, 'Aiding the President', *op. cit.*

59 Peterson, 'Aiding the President', *op. cit.*

60 *Ibid.*

61 *Ibid.*

62 *Ibid*; *Saturday Herald*, 25 June 1938.

63 Peterson, 'Aiding the President', *op. cit.*

64 Dunleavy & Dunleavy, *op. cit.*, p. 391.

65 *Saturday Herald*, 25 June 1938.

66 *Ibid.*

67 Peterson, 'Aiding the President', *op. cit.*; *Saturday Herald*, 25 June 1938; Dunleavy & Dunleavy, *op. cit.*, pp. 384–5.

68 *Weekly Cork Weekly Examiner*, 2 July 1938.

69 *Ibid.*

70 Peterson, 'Aiding the President', *op. cit.*; *Weekly Cork Weekly Examiner*, 2 July 1938.

71 *Saturday Herald*, 25 June 1938.

72 *Ibid.*

73 *Derry Journal*, 26 June 1938.

74 *Northern Whig*, 27 June 1938.

75 *Belfast News Letter*, 27 June 1938.

76 *Evening Mail*, 25 June 1938.

77 *Ibid.*

78 *Ibid.*

79 *Derry Journal*, 26 June 1938.

80 *Evening Mail*, 25 June 1938.

81 *Ibid.*

82 *Evening Herald*, 16–28 May 1938.

83 Peterson, 'Aiding the President', *op. cit.*

84 *Belfast News Letter*, 27 June 1938.

85 Peterson, 'Aiding the President', *op. cit.*

86 Lawrence William White, 'Timothy Sullivan' in James McGuire & James Quinn (eds), *Dictionary of Irish Biography*, vol. 9, (Cambridge, 2009), pp. 161–2; *The Irish Times*, 25 June 1938.

87 *Birkenhead News*, 2 July 1938; *Irish Press*, 27 June 1938.

88 *Derry Journal*, 26 June 1938.

89 *The Irish Times*, 22 May 1963 and 14 August 1981.

90 *Irish Independent*, 24 June 1938.

91 *Saturday Herald*, 25 June 1938.

92 Peterson, 'Aiding the President', *op. cit.*

93 *The Irish Times*, 25 June 1938.

94 *Ibid.*

95 *Saturday Herald*, 25 June 1938.

96 Peterson, 'Aiding the President', *op. cit.*; *The Irish Times*, 25 June 1938.

97 *The Irish Times*, 25 June 1938.

98 *Ibid.*; *The Irish Times*, 2 July 1938.

99 Dunleavy & Dunleavy, *op. cit.*, p. 254.

100 *The Irish Times*, 27 April 1938.

101 *Cork Weekly Examiner*, 5 May 1938.

102 *Saturday Herald*, 25 June 1938.

103 *Ibid.*

104 *Ibid.*

105 *The Irish Times*, 27 June 1938.

106 Ashley Jackson, *Buildings of Empire* (Oxford, 2013), p. 20.

107 Denis McCarthy & David Benton, *Dublin Castle at the Heart of Irish History* (Dublin, 1997), p. 62.

108 Jackson, *op. cit.*, p. 33.

109 *Ibid.*

110 Basil Peterson, 'All the President's Men,' *The Irish Times*, 2 July 1980.

111 *The Irish Times*, 27 June 1938.

112 *Irish Press*, 24 June 1938.

113 *Bunreacht na hÉireann*, Article 12.8.

114 *Saturday Herald*, 25 June 1938.

115 *The Irish Times*, 27 June 1938

116 *Saturday Herald*, 25 June 1938.

117 *Belfast News Letter*, 27 June 1938; *The Daily Telegraph*, 27 June 1938.

118 *Irish Independent*, 27 June 1938.

119 *Saturday Herald*, 25 June 1938.

120 *Northern Whig*, 27 June 1938; *Belfast News Letter*, 27 June 1938; *Irish Daily Telegraph*, 27 June 1938; *Evening Mail*, 25 June 1938.

121 *Saturday Herald*, 25 June 1938; *The Irish Times*, 27 June 1938;

122 *Saturday Herald*, 25 June 1938; *The Irish Times*, 27 June 1938.

123 *Saturday Herald*, 25 June 1938.

124 *Ibid.*; *Evening Mail*, 25 June 1938.

125 *The Irish Times*, 27 June 1938.

126 Seán T. Ó Ceallaigh, *Seán T.* (Dublin, 1963), p. 31; Patrick Maume, 'Seán T. O'Kelly' in McGuire & Quinn (eds), *op. cit.*, vol. 7, pp. 615–19.

127 *Saturday Herald*, 25 June 1938.

128 *Evening Mail*, 25 June 1938.

129 *The Irish Times*, 2 July 1938.

130 *Belfast News Letter*, 27 June 1938.

131 O'Connor, *op. cit.*, p. 377.

132 *Saturday Herald*, 25 June 1938.

133 *Belfast News Letter*, 27 June 1938; *Cork Weekly Examiner*, 2 July 1938; *The Irish Times*, 27 June 1938.

134 *Cork Weekly Examiner*, 2 July 1938.

135 *Evening Mail*, 25 June 1938.

136 Dermot Keogh & Andrew McCarthy, *The Making of the Irish Constitution 1937* (Cork, 2007), p. 206.

137 *Saturday Herald*, 25 June 1938.

138 *Ibid.*

139 *Cork Weekly Examiner*, 2 July 1938.

140 Maurice Moynihan (ed.), *Speeches and Statements by Éamon de Valera 1917–73* (Dublin, 1980), p. 354.

141 *Ibid.*

142 *Ibid.*

143 *Ibid.*

144 *Ibid.*; *The Irish Times*, 27 June 1938.

145 NAI, PRES 1/P324, memo by Michael McDunphy entitled 'Entry on office of President', 11 June 1938.

146 *Saturday Herald*, 25 June 1938.

147 *Ibid.*

148 *Belfast News Letter*, 27 June 1938.

149 *Cork Weekly Examiner*, 2 July 1938; Peterson, 'All the President's Men', *op. cit.*

150 Keogh & McCarthy, *op. cit.*, p. 206.

151 *Cork Weekly Examiner*, 2 July 1938.

152 *The Irish Times*, 25 June 1938.

153 *Cork Weekly Examiner*, 2 July 1938; *Irish Daily Telegraph*, 27 June 1938.

154 *Derry Journal*, 26 June 1938.

155 *Saturday Herald*, 25 June 1938.

156 *Cork Weekly Examiner*, 2 July 1938.

157 *Saturday Herald*, 25 June 1938.

158 *Ibid.*

159 *Cork Weekly Examiner*, 2 July 1938.

160 *Derry Journal*, 26 June 1938.

161 *Ibid.*

162 *Saturday Herald*, 25 June 1938.

163 *The Irish Times*, 27 June 1938.

164 *Saturday Herald*, 25 June 1938.

165 *Evening Mail*, 25 June 1938.

166 *Derry Journal*, 26 June 1938.

167 *The Irish Times*, 27 June 1938.

168 Dunleavy & Dunleavy, *op. cit.*, pp. 315–21.

169 White, 'Timothy Sullivan' in McGuire & Quinn (eds), *op. cit.*, vol. 9, pp. 161–2; Brendan Ó Caothair, 'Patrick Lynch' in McGuire & Quinn (eds), *op. cit.*, vol. 5, pp. 647–8.

170 *The Irish Jurist*, vol. 31 (1996), p. 219.

171 Diarmaid Ferriter & Lawrence William White, 'Frank Fahy' in McGuire & Quinn (eds), *op. cit.*, vol. 3, p. 691; Maume, 'Seán T. O'Kelly' in McGuire & Quinn (eds), *op. cit.*, vol. 7, p. 616.

172 *Saturday Herald*, 25 June 1938.

173 *The Irish Times*, 24 June 1938.

174 Peterson, 'All the President's Men', *op. cit.*

2. The Political Origins of the Presidency

1 Tim Pat Coogan, *De Valera: Long Fellow, Long Shadow* (London, 1993), p. 29.

2 Arthur Mitchell & Padraig Ó Snodaigh, *Irish Political Documents 1916–49* (Dublin, 1985), pp. 18–19.

3 F. S. L. Lyons, *Ireland Since the Famine* (London, 1973), pp. 370–71.

4 Tom Garvin, *The Evolution of Irish Nationalist Politics* (Dublin, 1981), p. 105.

5 Moynihan (ed.), *op. cit.*, p. 7.

6 *Ibid.*, p. 8.

7 *Dáil Éireann*, vol. T, no. 4, cols 185–6, 16 December 1921.

8 Lord Longford & Thomas P. O'Neill, *Éamon de Valera* (London, 1970), p. 175.

9 *Ibid.*, pp. 172–73.

10 J. Bowyer-Bell, *The Secret Army: The IRA 1916–79* (Dublin, 1979), p. 17.

11 Malcolm Pearce & Geoffrey Stewart, *British Political History 1867–2001: Power and Decline* (London, 2002), p. 585.

12 Longford & O'Neill, *op. cit.*, p. 146; Brendan Sexton, *Ireland and the Crown 1922–1936: The Governor-Generalship of the Irish Free State* (Dublin, 1989), p. 25.

13 John Coakley, 'The Prehistory of the Irish Presidency,' *Irish Political Studies*, vol. 27, no. 4 (2012), p. 546.

14 *Ibid.*

15 Sexton, *op. cit.,* p. 99; NAI, S1909.

16 *Dáil Éireann,* vol. T, no. 6, cols 26–8, 19 December 1921.

17 *Dáil Éireann,* vol. 1, no. 16, cols 1082–3, 3 October 1922.

18 Ward, *op. cit.*, p. 171; Frank Callanan, *T. M. Healy* (Cork, 1996), p. 599; Sexton, *op. cit.,* p. 177.

19 John L. McCracken, *Representative Government in Ireland: A Study of Dáil Éireann 1919–48* (Oxford, 1958), p. 157.

20 Terence de Vere White, *Kevin O'Higgins* (Dublin, 1966), p. 142.

21 Mary Bromage, *De Valera and the March of a Nation* (London, 1967), p. 84; NLI, William O'Brien Papers, MS 8556 (31).

22 *The Irish Times*, 6 December 1922.

23 Sexton, *op. cit.,* p. 102.

24 *Ibid.*

25 *Ibid.,* p. 103.

26 *The Irish Times*, 17 November 1926.

27 *Dáil Éireann*, vol. 17, no. 1, cols 28–9, 16 November 1926.

28 *The Irish Times*, 1 June 1927; *The Irish Times,* 4 June 1927.

29 *The Irish Times*, 9 January 1928; Sexton, *op. cit.,* p. 105; *Daily Express*, 2 February 1928.

30 NAI, PRES 1/P327.

31 Jim Maher, *The Oath is Dead and Gone* (Dublin, 2011), pp. 243–4.

32 Sexton, *op. cit.,* p. 122.

33 *The Irish Times*, 2 June 1927.

34 Sexton, *op. cit.,* p. 107.

35 *Dáil Éireann*, vol. 30, no. 16, cols 2067–8, 28 June 1929.

36 M. J. McManus, *Éamon de Valera: A Biography* (Dublin, 1947), p. 313.

37 Kevin Casey, 'Áras an Uachtaráin: The Story of a House,' article in the author's possession, p.18; Michael Kennedy, 'James McNeill' in McGuire & Quinn (eds), *op. cit.,* vol. 6, pp. 155–8; Terence de Vere White, 'Social Life in Ireland 1927–37,' in Francis MacManus (ed.), *The Years of the Great Test, 1926–39* (Cork, 1967), p. 23.

38 Bromage, *op. cit.*, p. 125.

39 NAI, S8536/A, costings on file.

40 *Dáil Éireann*, vol. 30, no. 16, cols 2067–8, 28 June 1929.

41 *The Irish Times*, 24 June 1937; *Dáil Éireann*, vol. 72, no. 8, cols 897–904, 14 July 1938.

42 *Dáil Éireann*, vol. 72, no. 8, cols 897–904, 14 July 1938.

43 *Dáil Éireann*, vol. 72, no. 8, cols 903–907, 14 July 1938.

44 *Dáil Éireann*, vol. 72, no. 8, cols 899–900, 14 July 1938.

45 *The Irish Times*, 28 October 1931.

46 *The Irish Times*, 10 March 1932.

47 T. Ryle Dwyer, *De Valera: The Man and the Myths* (Dublin, 1991), p. 163.

48 Sexton, *op. cit.,* p. 126; Seán Farragher, *Dev and His Alma Mater: Éamon de Valera's Lifelong Association with Blackrock College 1898–1975* (Dublin, 1984), pp. 164–5.

49 *The Irish Times*, 12 July 1932.

50 Longford & O'Neill, *op. cit.,* p. 284.

51 John N. Young, *Erskine H. Childers: President of Ireland* (Buckinghamshire, 1985), p. 184.

52 *Dáil Éireann*, vol. 67, no. 10, cols 1279–1280, 28 May 1937.

53 UCDA, Hugh Kennedy Papers, P4/1259.

54 Sexton, *op. cit.*, p. 140.

55 UCDA, Hugh Kennedy Papers, P4/1259, memo from Kennedy to de Valera, 6 October 1932.

56 Patrick Murray, *Oracles of God: The Roman Catholic Church and Irish Politics 1922–37* (Dublin, 2010), p. 264.

57 *Dáil Éireann*, vol. 48, no. 19, cols 2753–2755, 14 July 1933.

58 Sexton, *op. cit.*, p. 153.

59 *The Irish Times*, 1 July 1937.

60 *Ibid.*

61 Morley Ayearst, *The Republic of Ireland: Its Government and Politics* (New York, 1970), p. 117.

62 McCracken, *op. cit.*, p. 158.

63 Deirdre McMahon, *Republicans and Imperialists: Anglo-Irish Relations in the 1930s* (New Haven, 1984), p. 128.

64 *Dáil Éireann*, vol. 56, no. 15, cols 1853–1854, 28 May 1935.

65 Keogh & McCarthy, *op. cit.*, p. 297.

66 Sexton, *op. cit.*, p. 161.

67 Longford & O'Neill, *op. cit.*, p. 292.

68 D. George Boyce, *The Irish Question & British Politics 1868–1986* (London, 1988), p. 82.

69 John Bowman, *De Valera and the Ulster Question 1917–1973* (Oxford, 1989), p. 146.

70 Longford & O'Neill, *op. cit.*, p. 292.

71 *Dáil Éireann*, vol. 64, no. 9, cols 1276–1283, 11 December 1936.

72 *Dáil Éireann*, vol. 64, no. 10, cols 1385–1389, 12 December 1936.

73 Keogh & McCarthy, *op. cit.*, p. 91.

74 Owen Dudley Edwards, *Éamon de Valera* (Cardiff, 1987), p. 118.

75 Ward, *op. cit.*, p. 230.

3. The Custodian of the People's Constitutional Liberties

1 Kelly, *op. cit.*, p. 57.

2 Jim Duffy, 'The Presidency of Ireland: An Inherently Unsatisfactory Office' (MA Politics Thesis, UCD, 1991), p. 37.

3 Keogh, 'Office of the Presidency has served the State well' *op. cit.*

4 *Dáil Éireann*, vol. 67, no. 1, cols 154–155, 11 May 1937.

5 *Dáil Éireann*, vol. 67–8, no. 1–8, 11 May 1937–14 June 1937.

6 *Dáil Éireann*, vol. 68, no. 4, cols 359–360, 14 May 1937.

7 Seán Faughnan, 'De Valera's Constitution: The Drafting of the Irish Constitution of 1937' (MA History Thesis, UCD, 1988), p. 119.

8 David Gwynn Morgan, *Constitutional Law of Ireland: The Law of the Executive, Legislature and Judicature,* (Dublin, 1990), p. 52.

9 UCDA, Éamon de Valera Papers, P150/2370, draft heads of constitution, 17 May 1935.

10 *Dáil Éireann*, vol. 67, no. 1, cols 40–41, 11 May 1937.

11 *Dáil Éireann*, vol. 67, no. 8, cols 1035–1036, 25 May 1937.

12 *Dáil Éireann*, vol. 67, no. 8, cols 1015–1016, 25 May 1937.

13 *Dáil Éireann*, vol. 67, no. 1, cols 131–133, 11 May 1937.

14 *Dáil Éireann*, vol. 67, no. 2, cols 303–304, 12 May 1937.

15 *Ibid.*

16 *Dáil Éireann*, vol. 67, no. 3, cols 381–382, 13 May 1937.

17 *Dáil Éireann*, vol. 67, no. 2, cols 266–277, 12 May 1937; *Dáil Éireann*, vol. 67, no. 8, cols 1006–1010, 25 May 1937.

18 *Dáil Éireann*, vol. 67, no. 2, cols 226–227, 12 May 1937.

19 *Dáil Éireann*, vol. 67, no. 3, cols 341–342, 13 May 1937.

20 *Dáil Éireann*, vol. 67, no. 3, cols 423–424, 13 May 1937.

21 *Dáil Éireann*, vol. 68, no. 4, cols 423–424, 14 June 1937.

22 *Dáil Éireann*, vol. 67, no. 3, cols 438–439, 13 May 1937.

23 *Irish Independent*, 5 May 1937.

24 *The Irish Times*, 21 June 1937.

25 *Irish Press*, 30 August 1975.

26 Dáil Éireann, vol. 67, no. 3, cols 356–357, 13 May 1937.

27 Dáil Éireann, vol. 67, no. 8, cols 1042–1044, 25 May 1937.

28 Mark O'Brien, *De Valera, Fianna Fáil and the Irish Press: The Truth in the News* (Dublin, 2001), pp. 154–5. In September 1976, President Ó Dálaigh referred the Emergency Powers Bill to the Supreme Court for a decision on its constitutionality. The purpose of this Bill was to give additional power to the security forces to combat the IRA. In mid October, the Supreme Court ruled that the Bill was constitutional. Shortly afterwards, on 18 October, the Minister for Defence, Paddy Donegan, described the President as 'a thundering disgrace' when he addressed troops at Columb Barracks, Mullingar. Donegan subsequently apologised for this comment and Taoiseach Liam Cosgrave declined to sack the Minister. When a Dáil motion of no confidence in Donegan was defeated, Ó Dálaigh resigned, in his own words, 'to protect the dignity and independence of the presidency as an institution'. See J. J. Lee, *Ireland 1912–85: Politics and Society* (Cambridge, 1989), p. 482

29 UCDA, Éamon de Valera Papers, P150/2370, draft heads of constitution, 17 May 1935.

30 NAI, S9715, draft constitution, May 1937.

31 *Dáil Éireann*, vol. 67, no. 8, cols 1073–1074, 25 May 1937.

32 *Ibid.*

33 *Dáil Éireann*, vol. 67, no. 9, cols 1085–1086, 26 May 1937.

34 *Dáil Éireann*, vol. 67, no. 8, cols 1077–1078, 25 May 1937.

35 *Dáil Éireann*, vol. 67, no. 9, cols 1086–1088, 26 May 1937.

36 *Dáil Éireann*, vol. 67, no. 9, cols 1096–1097, 26 May 1937.

37 *Dáil Éireann*, vol. 67, no. 9, cols 1086–1088, 26 May 1937.

38 John Walsh, *Patrick Hillery: The Official Biography* (Dublin, 2008), p. 486.

39 Interview with Bertie Ahern, Drumcondra, Dublin (6 March 2012).

40 *Dáil Éireann*, vol. 67, no. 1, cols 42–43, 11 May 1937.
41 *Dáil Éireann*, vol. 67, no. 1, cols 51–52, 11 May 1937.
42 *Dáil Éireann*, vol. 67, no. 2, cols 233–235, 12 May 1937.
43 *Dáil Éireann*, vol. 67, no. 8, cols 1032–1033, 25 May 1937.
44 *Dáil Éireann*, vol. 67, no. 3, cols 382–383, 13 May 1937.
45 *Dáil Éireann*, vol. 67, no. 3, cols 343–344, 13 May 1937.
46 *Dáil Éireann*, vol. 67, no. 1, cols 46–47, 11 May 1937.
47 Ward, *op. cit.*, p. 287.
48 *Dáil Éireann*, vol. 67, no. 1, cols 52–53, 11 May 1937.
49 Kelly, *op. cit.*, pp. 67–8.
50 *Dáil Éireann*, vol. 67, no. 8, cols 1054–1055, 25 May 1937.
51 *Dáil Éireann*, vol. 67, no. 10, cols 1295–1296, 28 May 1937.
52 UCDA, Éamon de Valera Papers, P150/2416, memo from James Douglas to de Valera, 21 May 1937.
53 *Dáil Éireann*, vol. 67, no. 8, cols 1042–1043, 25 May 1937.
54 *Dáil Éireann*, vol. 67, no. 8, cols 1042–1043, 25 May 1937.
55 Keogh & McCarthy, *op. cit.*, p. 175.
56 *The Irish Times*, 28 June 1937.
57 *The Irish Times*, 26 June 1937.
58 R. A. H. Robinson, *Contemporary Portugal* (London, 1979), p. 45.
59 Robin Okey, *Eastern Europe 1740–1985: Feudalism to Communism* (London, 1991), p. 121.
60 *Dáil Éireann*, vol. 67, no. 8, cols 1054–1056, 25 May 1937.
61 *Dáil Éireann*, vol. 67, no. 10, cols 1271–1272, 28 May 1937.
62 *Dáil Éireann*, vol. 67, no. 2, cols 275–276, 12 May 1937.
63 *Dáil Éireann*, vol. 67, no. 10, cols 1247–1248, 28 May 1937.
64 *Dáil Éireann*, vol. 67, no. 1, cols 141–142, 11 May 1937.
65 *Dáil Éireann*, vol. 67, no. 9, cols 1224–1226, 26 May 1937.
66 *Dáil Éireann*, vol. 67, no. 10, cols 1252–1253, 28 May 1937.
67 *Dáil Éireann*, vol. 67, no. 3, cols 326–327, 13 May 1937.
68 Michael Forde, *Constitutional Law of Ireland* (Cork, 1987), p. 100.
69 Gerard Hogan, *The Origins of the Irish Constitution 1928–41* (Dublin, 2012), p. 152, p. 527.
70 Hogan, *op. cit.*, p. 152.
71 Kelly, *op. cit.*, p. 68.
72 *Dáil Éireann*, vol. 67, no. 10, cols 1295–1296, 28 May 1937.
73 *Dáil Éireann*, vol. 67, no. 2, cols 260–262, 12 May 1937.
74 *Irish Independent*, 5 May 1937.
75 *Dáil Éireann*, vol. 67, no. 10, cols 1274–1275, 28 May 1937.
76 Arthur Jacobson, *Weimar: A Jurisprudence of Crisis* (California, 2002), p. 114; John Traynor, *Mastering Modern German History* (Hampshire, 2008), p. 166.
77 *Dáil Éireann*, vol. 67, no. 1, cols 39–41, 11 May 1937.
78 Stephen J. Lee, *The Weimar Republic* (London, 1998), p. 16.

79 UCDA, Éamon de Valera Papers, P150/2373, draft constitution, 14 October 1936.

80 *Bunreacht na hÉireann,* Article 28.5.2.

81 *Dáil Éireann*, vol. 68, no. 4, cols 423–424, 14 June 1937.

82 Lee, *The Weimar Republic, op. cit.*, p. 19.

83 Jim Duffy, 'Overseas Studies: Ireland' in *Report of the Republican Advisory Committee – An Australian Republic, vol.2 The Options – The Appendices*, p. 136.

84 *Dáil Éireann*, vol. 748, no. 4, cols 771–797, 2 December 2011.

85 *Dáil Éireann*, vol. 67, no. 9, cols 1104–1105, 26 May 1937.

86 *Dáil Éireann*, vol. 67, no. 9, cols 1109–1110, 26 May 1937.

87 *Dáil Éireann*, vol. 67, no. 9, cols 1097–1098, 26 May 1937.

88 *Dáil Éireann*, vol. 67, no. 2, cols 194–105, 12 May 1937.

89 *Dáil Éireann*, vol. 67, no. 1, cols 38–40, 11 May 1937

90 *Dáil Éireann*, vol. 67, no. 3, cols 354–355, 13 May 1937.

91 Thomas P. O'Neill, 'The Legacy of the Constitution' *Irish Press,* 14 October 1982.

92 *Ibid.*

93 *Dáil Éireann*, vol. 67, no. 1, cols 51–52, 11 May 1937.

94 *Dáil Éireann*, vol. 67, no. 1, cols 38–39, 11 May 1937.

95 *Dáil Éireann*, vol. 67, no. 1, cols 59–60, 11 May 1937.

96 *The Irish Times*, 10 May 1937.

97 *Dáil Éireann*, vol. 67, no. 2, cols 300–301, 12 May 1937.

98 *Dáil Éireann*, vol. 67, no. 9, cols 1230–1231, 26 May 1937.

99 *Dáil Éireann*, vol. 67, no. 3, cols 411–412, 13 May 1937.

100 *Dáil Éireann*, vol. 67, no. 3, cols 437–438, 13 May 1937.

101 *Dáil Éireann*, vol. 67, no. 3, cols 430–431, 13 May 1937.

102 NAI, PRES 1/P52, file entitled 'Council of State: composition and personnel 1937–1977'; NAI, PRES 1/P96, file entitled 'Appointments by President Douglas Hyde.'

103 NAI, 2005/3/105, file entitled 'Appointments by President Seán T. Ó Ceallaigh'; NAI, PRES 1/P52.

104 *Dáil Éireann*, vol. 67, no. 1, cols 46–47, 11 May 1937.

105 Michael McDunphy, *The President of Ireland: His Powers, Function and Duties* (Dublin, 1945), p. 47.

106 *Dáil Éireann*, vol. 67, no. 1, cols 45–46, 11 May 1937.

107 *Dáil Éireann*, vol. 67, no. 2, cols 266–277, 12 May 1937; *Dáil Éireann*, vol. 67, no. 9, cols 1204–1208, 26 May 1937.

108 *Dáil Éireann*, vol. 67, no. 9, cols 1206–1207, 26 May 1937.

109 *Dáil Éireann*, vol. 67, no. 9, cols 1212–1214, 26 May 1937.

110 McDunphy, *op. cit.,* p. 52.

111 *Dáil Éireann*, vol. 67, no. 9, cols 1208–1209, 26 May 1937.

112 Michael Gallagher, 'The President, the People and the Constitution' in Brian Farrell, *De Valera's Constitution and Ours* (Dublin, 1988), pp. 85–6.

113 Ward, *op. cit.*, p. 288.

114 *Dáil Éireann*, vol. 67, no. 9, cols 1206–1208, 26 May 1937.

115 *Dáil Éireann*, vol. 67, no. 9, cols 1210–1212, 26 May 1937.

116 *Bunreacht na hÉireann,* Article 13.7.1, Article 13.7.2.

117 *Dáil Éireann*, vol. 67, no. 10, cols 1277–1278, 28 May 1937.

118 *Dáil Éireann*, vol. 67, no. 10, cols 1278–1279, 28 May 1937.

119 *Ibid.*

120 *Ibid.*

121 *Dáil Éireann*, vol. 67, no. 10, cols 1271–1272, 28 May 1937.

122 Gallagher, 'The President, the People and the Constitution' *op. cit.*, pp. 79–80.

123 *Dáil Éireann*, vol. 67, no. 2, cols 198–199, 12 May 1937.

124 *Dáil Éireann*, vol. 67, no. 3, cols 434–435, 13 May 1937.

125 Ayearst, *op. cit.,* p. 201.

126 *Dáil Éireann*, vol. 67, no. 1, cols 49–50, 11 May 1937.

127 *Dáil Éireann*, vol. 67, no. 3, cols 430–431, 13 May 1937.

128 *Dáil Éireann*, vol. 67, no. 1, cols 50–51, 11 May 1937.

129 *Dáil Éireann*, vol. 67, no. 1, cols 49–51, 11 May 1937.

130 *Dáil Éireann*, vol. 67, no. 3, cols 435–437, 13 May 1937.

131 *Dáil Éireann*, vol. 67, no. 1, cols 50–51, 11 May 1937.

132 *Dáil Éireann*, vol. 67, no. 1, cols 46–47, 11 May 1937.

133 *Dáil Éireann*, vol. 67, no. 3, cols 438–439, 13 May 1937.

134 *Dáil Éireann*, vol. 68, no. 4, cols 349–350, 14 June 1937.

135 *The Irish Times*, 24 June 1937, 30 June 1937.

136 *Dáil Éireann*, vol. 68, no. 4, cols 419–420, 14 June 1937.

137 *Dáil Éireann*, vol. 67, no. 2, cols 218–229, 12 May 1937.

138 *Dáil Éireann*, vol. 67, no. 1, cols 40–41, 11 May 1937.

139 Duffy, 'The Presidency of Ireland' *op. cit.*, p. 42.

140 James Casey, *Constitutional Law in Ireland* (London, 1992), p. 14.

141 Ward, *op. cit.* p. 284.

142 *Bunreacht na hÉireann,* Article 13.1.1, Article 33.2.

143 *Dáil Éireann*, vol. 67, no. 1, cols 41–43, 11 May 1937.

4. The Successor of Our Rightful Princes

1 *Sunday Independent*, 26 June 1938; *Irish Press*, 27 June 1938; *The Irish Times,* 27 June 1938; *Irish Independent,* 27 June 1938.

2 Moynihan (ed.), *op. cit.*, pp. 353–4.

3 *Dáil Éireann*, vol. 67, no. 9, cols 1113–1114, 26 May 1937.

4 Seán Donnelly, *Elections 2002* (Dublin, 2002), p. 416.

5 *Dáil Éireann*, vol. 67, no. 2, cols 302–303, 12 May 1937.

6 McMahon, *op. cit.*, p. 215, p. 318.

7 NAI, PRES 1/P2196.

8 NAI, PRES 1/P2196.

9 McMahon, *op. cit.,* p. 215.

10 Michael Kennedy, 'Seán Lester' in McGuire & Quinn (eds), *op. cit*, vol. 5, pp. 469–70.

11 Kennedy, 'Seán Lester' in McGuire & Quinn (eds), *op. cit.*, vol. 5, pp. 469–70.

12 Douglas Gageby, *The Last Secretary General: Seán Lester and the League of Nations* (Dublin, 1999), p. 158.

13 Lindie Lunney, 'Robert Mitchell Henry' in McGuire & Quinn (eds), *op. cit.*, vol. 4, pp. 633–4.

14 Nicholas Allen, 'Bernard Duffy' in McGuire & Quinn (eds), *op. cit.*, vol. 3, p. 504.

15 NAI, S10431A.

16 NAI, S10431A.

17 *The Irish Times*, 13 Janaury 1938.

18 *Ibid.*

19 Dunleavy & Dunleavy, *op. cit.*, pp. 370–1.

20 Michelle Gibbs, *Generations of Pride: A Centennial History of Cudahy, Wisconsin* (Wisconsin, 2006), p. 12.

21 McMahon, *op. cit.*, p. 215.

22 *Liverpool Daily Post*, 23 April 1938; NAI, PRES 1/P2196.

23 NAI, PRES 1/P2196.

24 *Ibid*; *The Irish Times*, 7 October 2011.

25 NAI, PRES 1/P2196.

26 *Evening Herald*, 24 January 1942.

27 Janet E. Dunleavy, 'The Myths of Douglas Hyde's Boyhood' in Brendan Ó Conaire (ed.), *Comhdháil an Chraoibhín 1988 – Conference Proceedings* (Roscommon, 1993), pp. 68–9.

28 Dunleavy & Dunleavy, *op. cit.*, pp. 377–8.

29 *Ibid.*

30 Diarmuid Coffey, *Douglas Hyde: An Craoibhín Aoibhinn* (Dublin, 1917); Diarmuid Coffey, *Douglas Hyde: President of Ireland* (Dublin, 1938).

31 Coffey, *Douglas Hyde: President of Ireland*, p. 8.

32 *The Irish Times*, 27 May 1937

33 *Ibid.*

34 *The Irish Times,* 6 August 1937.

35 *The Irish Times,* 13 October 1937.

36 *The Irish Times,* 3 January 1938.

37 *The Irish Times*, 8 January 1938.

38 *Ibid.*

39 UCDA, Fianna Fáil Papers, P176/442.

40 *Irish Press*, 10 January 1938.

41 *Ibid.*

42 Tony Gray, *The Irish Answer: An Anatomy of Modern Ireland* (London, 1966), p. 207.

43 McMahon, *op. cit.*, p. 228.

44 *Ibid.*, p. 227.

45 *Ibid.*

46 *Irish Press*, 9 April 1938.

47 *The Irish Times*, 22 April 1938.

48 *Daily Express,* 22 April 1938; *The Irish Times,* 29 October 1949.

49 *Daily Express,* 22 April 1938.

50 Marie Coleman, 'Conor Maguire' in McGuire & Quinn (eds), *op. cit.,* vol. 6, pp. 265–6.

51 *Daily Express,* 22 April 1938.

52 Liam Cosgrave in correspondence with the author, 8 May 2012.

53 *Ibid.*; Patrick Long, 'Richard Francis Hayes' in McGuire & Quinn (eds), *op. cit.,* vol. 4, p. 543.

54 Pauric Dempsey, 'Cahir Davitt' in McGuire & Quinn (eds), *op. cit.,* vol. 3, p. 87.

55 Donal McCartney, 'Denis Coffey' in McGuire & Quinn (eds), *op. cit.,* vol. 2, p. 625; Tony White, *Investing in People: Higher Education in Ireland from 1960 to 2000* (Dublin, 2001), p. 23.

56 *The Irish Times,* 22 April 1938.

57 *Catholic Herald,* 29 April 1938.

58 Stephen Collins, *The Cosgrave Legacy* (Dublin, 1996), p. 59; Liam Cosgrave in correspondence with the author, 8 May 2012.

59 NAI, S9783A.

60 *Daily Express,* 23 April 1938.

61 *The Irish Times,* 22 April 1938; *Irish Press,* 22 April 1938; *Daily Express,* 23 April 1938.

62 *Irish Press,* 22 April 1938.

63 *Ibid.*

64 *Daily Express,* 23 April 1938.

65 NAI, S9783A.

66 *Ibid.*

67 *The Irish Times,* 23 April 1938.

68 NAI, S9783A.

69 *Ibid.*

70 *Irish Press,* 23 April 1938.

71 *Ibid.*

72 *The Irish Times,* 22 April 1938.

73 *Irish Independent,* 22 April 1938.

74 *Irish Press,* 23 April 1938.

75 *The Irish Times,* 6 December 1937.

76 NAI, PRES 1/P1475.

77 Anne Dolan, 'Alfred Byrne' in McGuire & Quinn (eds), *op. cit.,* vol. 2, p. 202.

78 *Ibid.*

79 *The Times,* 23 April 1938.

80 *Irish Press,* 20 April 1938.

81 *Irish Press,* 2 April 1938.

82 *The Irish Times,* 22 April 1938.

83 *Ibid.*

84 *Sunday Independent,* 17 April 1938.

85 *Ibid.*

86 *Irish Press,* 21 April 1938.

87 *The Irish Times*, 23 April 1938.

88 *Catholic Herald*, 29 April 1938.

89 *The Irish Times*, 22 April 1938; *Irish Independent*, 22 April 1938; *Irish Press*, 22 April 1938.

90 *The Irish Times*, 22 April 1938.

91 *Catholic Herald*, 29 April 1938.

92 *Ibid.*

93 UCDA, Fianna Fáil Papers, P176/444.

94 *The Irish Times*, 5 May 1938; *Irish Independent*, 5 May 1938; *Irish Press*, 5 May 1938.

95 *The Irish Times*, 5 May 1938.

96 *Irish Press*, 5 May 1938.

97 *Ibid.*

98 *Ibid.*; *Sunday Independent*, 26 May 1938; Peterson, 'All the President's Men' *op. cit.*

99 *Dublin Opinion*, May 1938.

100 *The New York Times Magazine*, 29 May 1938.

101 McManus, *op. cit.*, p. 217; *The Irish Times*, 5 May 1938; NLI, Seán T. O'Kelly Papers, MS 27,721 (T. D. Williams, Typescript Thomas Davis Lecture – 'The Presidency in historical perspective); Donald Caird, 'Douglas Hyde: Observed from a Distance' in Ó Conaire (ed.), *op. cit.*, p. 48.

102 Lyons, *op. cit.*, p. 227.

103 Colm Ó Lochlainn, 'The Literary Achievements of Douglas Hyde: President of Ireland,' in *The British Annual of Literature* (London, 1938), p. 63; Moynihan (ed.), *op. cit.*, p. 354.

104 Caird, 'Douglas Hyde: Observed from a Distance' in Ó Conaire (ed.), *op. cit.*, p. 49.

105 Paul Bew (ed.), *The Memoir of David Gray: A Yankee in De Valera's Ireland* (Dublin, 2012), pp. 77–80.; Gearóid Ó Tuathaigh, 'Douglas Hyde and Irish Nationalism' in Ó Conaire (ed.), *op. cit.*, p. 25.

5. The Foundations of Presidential Precedence

1 O'Brien, *op. cit.*, p. 36.

2 Paul Rouse, 'Seamus Hughes' in McGuire & Quinn, *op. cit.*, vol. 4, pp. 832–3; Thomas J. Morrissey, *A Man Called Hughes: The Life and Times of Seamus Hughes 1881–1943* (Dublin, 1991), p. 216.

3 Morrissey, *op. cit.*, p. 216.

4 Norman Vance, 'Douglas Hyde' in H. C. G. Matthew & Brian Harrison, *Oxford Dictionary of National Biography* (Oxford, 2004), vol. 29, p. 117.

5 Patrick Maume, 'Douglas Hyde' in McGuire & Quinn (eds), *op. cit.*, vol. 4, p. 883.

6 Domhnall Ó Cuill, 'Douglas Hyde: An Craoibhin Aoibhinn 1860–1949,' in the *Capuchin Annual 1961*, p. 365; *The New York Times Magazine*, 29 May 1938.

7 Maume, 'Douglas Hyde' in McGuire & Quinn (eds), *op. cit.*, vol. 4, p. 883; *The Times* (Literary Supplement), 17 September 1938.

8 Hyde, *op. cit.*

9 *Ibid.*

10 Patsy McGarry, 'The Gaelic Dream of Douglas Hyde' *Magill Magazine*, July 1988, p. 37.

11 Cormac Moore, *The GAA v Douglas Hyde: The Removal of Ireland's First President as GAA Patron* (Cork, 2012), p. 27; Patricia Bourden, *The Emergence of Modern Ireland 1850–1966* (Dublin, 1986), p. 66.

12 Moore, *The GAA v Douglas Hyde*, p. 29.

13 McGarry, *op. cit.*, p. 37; Bourden, *op. cit.*, p. 66.

14 Gareth W. Dunleavy, *Douglas Hyde*, (New Jersey, 1974), p. 11; McGarry, *op. cit.*, p. 37.

15 Gareth W. Dunleavy, *op. cit.*, p. 49.

16 *Irish Press*, 23 April 1938.

17 McGarry, *op. cit.*, p. 37.

18 *The Irish Times*, 22 April 1938; *The Irish Times*, 25 April 2007.

19 Brendan Walsh, *The Pedagogy of Protest: The Educational Thought and Work of Patrick H. Pearse* (Berne, 2007), p. 187.

20 Gareth W. Dunleavy, *op. cit.*, pp. 50–51.

21 Kenna, *op. cit.*, p. 22.

22 Gareth W. Dunleavy, *op. cit.*, p. 51.

23 *Irish Press*, 21 May 1938; *The Spectator*, 5 May 1938.

24 Gareth W. Dunleavy, *op. cit.*, p. 11.

25 *Yorkshire Observer*, 27 April 1938.

26 Gareth W. Dunleavy, *op. cit.*, p. 51.

27 Dunleavy & Dunleavy, *op. cit.*, p. 354.

28 Moore, *The GAA v Douglas Hyde*, p. 59.

29 *Irish Press*, 22 April 1938.

30 *Irish Independent*, 22 April 1938.

31 *Daily Express*, 28 April 1938.

32 Dunleavy & Dunleavy, *op. cit.*, p. 369.

33 Jim Duffy, 'Poorly Conceived, Badly Funded, Needing Reform' *The Irish Times*, 24 December 1990.

34 UCDA, Éamon de Valera Papers, P150/2686, Fianna Fáil election circular, 18 May 1945.

35 Keogh, 'Office of the Presidency has served the State well' *op. cit.*

36 NAI, PRES 1/P1396; NAI, PRES 1/P862.

37 NAI, PRES 1/P862, memo by McDunphy entitled 'Disrespectful press references to President', 12 April 1939.

38 Hugh Oram, *The Newspaper Book: A History of Newspapers in Ireland, 1649–1983* (Dublin, 1983), p. 198.

39 *Evening Mail*, 18 October 1939.

40 NAI, PRES 1/P1396, memo by McDunphy entitled 'Offensive References to President' 23 October 1939.

41 NAI, S3204; NAI, S10199; NAI, S2979; NAI, S5610.

42 NAI, PRES 1/P2901, memo by McDunphy, 31 October 1938.

43 NAI, PRES 1/P350, undated memo by McDunphy entitled 'Notes: Secretary to the President', c. 1939.

44 NAI, PRES 1/P350, undated memo by McDunphy entitled 'Notes: Secretary to the President', c. 1939.

45 NAI, S10332B, civil service personnel file of Michael McDunphy.

46 Keogh & McCarthy, *op. cit.*, p. 65.

47 *The Irish Times*, 6 November 1937.

48 NAI, S10332B, civil service personnel file of Michael McDunphy; NAI, S1288.

49 Marie Coleman, 'Michael McDunphy' in McGuire & Quinn (eds), *op. cit.*, vol. 5, 985.

50 NAI, S10332B, civil service personnel file of Michael McDunphy.

51 NAI, S1288.

52 Faughnan, *op. cit.*, p. 224.

53 NAI, PRES 1/P1473, memo by McDunphy entitled 'Secretary to the President: Relations with the Taoiseach – Political Matters: Taoiseach's authorisation', 19 January 1940; NAI, PRES 1/P1473, memo by McDunphy entitled 'Secretary to the President: Personal Coversations with Taoiseach – Official Matters: Taoiseach's further authorisation', 19 April 1940; NAI, S10332B; NAI, S9798A.

54 NAI, PRES 99/2/30, letter from McDunphy to Mairtin Ó Flathartaigh, Secretary to the President, 22 February 1968 & letter from Michael McDunphy to Joseph Holloway, Secretary of 'the Constitution Amendment Committee', 24 February 1967; NAI, S9798A; Hogan, *op. cit.*, p. 700.

55 NAI, S14553, memo by McDunphy entitled 'Department of State Bill 1949: Comment by the Secretary to the President', 20 July 1949.

56 NAI, S10199, letter from McDunphy to Moynihan, 21 November 1939.

57 NAI, S9798A, letter from Moynihan to McDunphy, 15 December 1939.

58 NAI, S9798A, letter from Moynihan to McDunphy, 23 December 1939.

59 NAI, S10484, memo by Maurice Moynihan, 10 January 1940.

60 NAI, PRES 1/P1473, memo by McDunphy entitled 'Secretary to the President: Personal Coversations with Taoiseach – Official Matters: Taoiseach's further authorisation', 19 April 1940.

61 NAI, 2005/3/121, memo by McDunphy entitled 'Conversation with Secretary to the Government', 10 January 1940.

62 NAI, 2005/3/121, memo by McDunphy entitled 'Comment on Mr. Moynihan's note of 23 Dec 1939', 30 December 1939.

63 Morgan, *op. cit.*, pp. 50–1.

64 NAI, S9777

65 *Ibid.*

66 *Ibid.*

67 NAI, DFA/P345.

68 *Ibid.*

69 *Ibid.*

70 NAI, PRES 1/P2223, memo by McDunphy entitled 'The President: Position vis-à-vis the King – Decision of the High Court 23.4.42', 26 April 1942.

71 NAI, P2223.

72 Risteárd Ó Glaisne, *op. cit.*, pp. 599–600.

73 John Horgan, 'Douglas Hyde – An Irishman's Diary', *The Irish Times*, 21 February 1998.

74 NAI, PRES 98/1/09, memo by McDunphy entitled 'British National Anthem', 11 June 1938.

75 *Ibid.*

76 NAI, PRES 1/P2257, memo by McDunphy to de Valera, October 1939.

77 NAI, PRES 1/P2257.

78 NAI, PRES 1/P2257, memo by McDunphy, April 1940.

79 *Ibid.*

80 *Ibid.*

81 *Ibid.*

82 *Ibid.*

83 *Ibid.*

84 *Ibid.*

85 NAI, PRES 1/P2257, memo by McDunphy, June 1942.

86 NAI, PRES 1/P2257.

87 NAI, PRES/1/P1076, memo by McDunphy entitled 'Paintings and Other Pictures', 1 December, 1938.

88 NAI, PRES/1/P1076, memo by McDunphy entitled 'Inspection by Director of Natl. Gallery', 5 December, 1938.

89 NAI, PRES/1/P1076, letter from Michael McDunphy to Maurice Moynihan, April 1939.

90 *Ibid.*

91 NAI, PRES/1/P1076, memo by McDunphy entitled 'Replacement of Pictures: Desirability of Early Replacements', 3 February 1942.

92 *Ibid.*

93 NAI, PRES/1/P1076, memo by McDunphy entitled 'Removal of portraits from walls of Áras', 16 September 1942.

94 Kathleen Clarke, *Revolutionary Woman: An Autobiography* (Dublin, 1991), p. 220; *Sunday Business Post*, 8 January 1995.

95 NAI, PRES/1/P1076, memo by McDunphy entitled 'Removal of portraits from walls of Áras', 16 September 1942; NAI, PRES 1/P2278; NAI, PRES 1/P4339.

96 NAI, 98/1/9, memo by McDunphy entitled 'Wedding of Miss Molly O'Connor, Lucan', 22 January 1942.

97 *Ibid.*

98 NAI, P98/1/17.

99 *Ibid.*

100 *Ibid.*

101 *Ibid.*

102 NAI, S9777.

103 *Ibid.*

104 NAI, PRES 1/P685, letter from McDunphy to Moynihan, 24 September 1938.

105 NAI, PRES 1/P685, letter from McDunphy to Moynihan, 17 October 1938.

106 NAI, PRES 1/P685, memo by McDunphy, 28 October 1938.

107 NAI, S9777, memo by Moynihan, 27 October 1938.

108 *The Irish Times,* 1 November 1938; *The Irish Times,* 7 November 1938.

109 NAI, PRES 1/P685, letter from McDunphy to Moynihan, 26 March 1939.

110 NAI, S9777, memo by Moynihan, 25 July 1939.

111 NAI, PRES 1/P685, letter from McDunphy to Moynihan, September 1939.

112 *Ibid.*

113 *Ibid.*

114 NAI, PRES 1/P685, letter from Moynihan to McDunphy, 8 December 1939.

115 NAI, PRES 1/P685, letter from McDunphy to Moynihan, 19 December 1939.

116 NAI, PRES 1/P685, letter from McDunphy to de Valera, February 1940.

117 *Ibid.*

118 NAI, PRES 1/P685, memo by McDunphy entitled '*The Irish Times:* Attitude vis-à-vis the King, Conference with Minister 6.8.40', 7 August 1940.

119 *Ibid.*

120 Donal Ó Drisceoil, *Censorship in Ireland 1939–45* (Cork, 1996), pp. 160–69.

121 NAI, PRES 1/ P685, memo by McDunphy, March 1942.

122 Ó Drisceoil, *op. cit.*, p. 161.

123 *Dáil Éireann*, vol. 69, no. 10, cols 1534–1536, 25 April 1944.

124 *Dáil Éireann*, vol. 69, no. 10, cols 1535–1537, 25 April 1944.

125 *Dáil Éireann*, vol. 69, no. 10, cols 1537–1544, 25 April 1944.

126 *The Irish Times*, 27 April 1944.

127 *Ibid.*

128 NAI, PRES 1/P685, memo by McDunphy entitled '*The Irish Times:* Attitude towards the President – Debate in the Dáil on censorship', 28 April 1944.

129 *Ibid.*

130 *The Irish Times*, 28 April 1944.

131 *Ibid.*

132 Dunleavy & Dunleavy, *op. cit.*, pp. 402–3.

133 Cormac Moore, 'An Astounding Moment of Aberration: The Removal of Dr Douglas Hyde as Patron of the GAA' (MA History Thesis, UCD, 2010), p. 8.

134 NAI, PRES 1/P1131; *Irish Press*, 5 December 1938; *The Irish Times,* 19 December 1938.

135 NAI, PRES 1/P1131; *The Irish Times*, 14 November 1938.

136 Moore, 'An Astounding Moment of Aberration', p. 4.

137 *Ibid.*, p. 17.

138 *Ibid.*, p. 16.

139 *Irish Press*, 20 December 1938.

140 *The Irish Times*, 19 December 1938.

141 Moore, *The GAA v Douglas Hyde*, pp. 107–8.

142 NAI, PRES 1/P1131.

143 *Ibid*; Dunleavy & Dunleavy, *op cit.*, p. 403.

144 *Irish Independent*, 17 January 1939.

145 NAI, PRES 1/P1170.

146 NAI, PRES 1/P1131, memo by McDunphy, 30 December 1938.

147 *Ibid.*

148 *Dáil Éireann*, vol. 74, no. 12, cols 1562–1563, 7 March 1939.

149 Dunleavy & Dunleavy, *op. cit.*, p. 403.

150 *Ibid.*

151 *Irish Independent*, 17 January 1939; *Irish Press*, 17 January 1939.

152 Dick Walsh, *The Party: Inside Fianna Fáil* (Dublin, 1986), p. 39.

153 *The Irish Times*, 30 September 1943.

154 Brian Murphy, 'Ard Fheiseanna Gone By', *Cuisle Magazine*, Spring 2012.

155 NAI, PRES 1/P2577, letter from Seamus Gardiner & Padraig Ó Caomh to Seán T. O'Kelly, August 1945.

156 NAI, PRES 1/P1131, memo by McDunphy, August 1945.

157 NAI, S13715, note on file, 10 August 1945.

158 NAI, PRES 1/P2577, minute by Padraig Ó Cinnéide of meeting of de Valera with Gardiner and Ó Caomh, 10 August 1945.

159 *Ibid.*

160 *Ibid.*

161 *Ibid.*

162 *Ibid.*

163 *Ibid.*

164 *Ibid.*

165 Moore, 'An Astounding Moment of Aberration', p. 38.

6. A Healing and a Gaelic Presidency

1 *The New York Times*, 29 May 1938.

2 *Irish Press,* 23 April 1938.

3 *The Irish Times,* 22 April 1938.

4 Robert Briscoe, *For the Life of Me* (Boston, 1959), p. 254.

5 *The Irish Times*, 22 April 1938.

6 *Irish Independent,* 23 April 1938; *Irish Independent,* 5 May 1938.

7 *The Irish Times*, 5 May 1938.

8 Donnacha Ó Beacháin, *Destiny of the Soldiers: Fianna Fáil, Irish Republicanism and the IRA, 1926–1973* (Dublin, 2010), p. 58.

9 NAI, PRES 1/P350, undated memo by McDunphy entitled 'Notes: Secretary to the President', c. 1939.

10 NAI, PRES 1/P444, memo by McDunphy of meeting of President Hyde with W. T. Cosgrave and Richard Mulcahy, 24 June 1938.

11 *Ibid.*

12 *Ibid.*

13 NAI, PRES 1/P444.

14 NAI, PRES 1/P1210, memo by McDunphy entitled 'Wm. T. Cosgrave: Invitations to Presidential Functions', 27 April 1939.

15 *Irish Independent*, 28 April 1939.

16 NAI, PRES 1/P1210, memo by McDunphy entitled 'Wm. T. Cosgrave: Invitations to Presidential Functions', 27 April 1939.

17 NAI, PRES 1/P829, letter from Cosgrave to McDunphy, 20 April 1939.

18 NAI, PRES 1/P1210, memo by McDunphy entitled 'Wm. T. Cosgrave: Personal File – Membership of Council of State', 27 July 1945.

19 NAI, PRES 1/P1348, memo by McDunphy entitled 'Appointment as Member of the Council of State', 1 February 1940.

20 *Ibid.*

21 Ronan Fanning, 'Richard Mulcahy' in McGuire & Quinn (eds), *op. cit.*, vol. 6, p. 751; NAI, PRES 1/P1348; NAI, PRES 1/P96; NAI, S9808.

22 NAI, PRES, 1/P96, memo by McDunphy entitled 'Appointment by first President (Dr. Hyde)', 6 January 1940.

23 NAI, PRES, 1/P96, memo by McDunphy entitled 'Appointment of members by First President', 25 May 1938.

24 NAI, PRES, 1/P96, memo by McDunphy entitled 'Appointment by first President (Dr. Hyde)', 9 January 1940.

25 Interview with Bertie Ahern, Drumcondra, Dublin (1 May 2012).

26 NAI, PRES 1/P447.

27 NAI, PRES 1/P1018; *News Chronicle*, 13 December 1938.

28 NAI, PRES 1/P1018, memo by McDunphy, January 1940.

29 NAI, PRES 1/P447; *The Irish Times*, 19 June 1939.

30 NAI, PRES 1/P447; *Irish Independent*, 19 June 1939.

31 Áine Lawlor, 'Mary McAleese: A Hard Act to Follow', *Irish Independent*, 21 October 2011.

32 Uinseann MacEoin, *The IRA in the Twilight Years 1923–48* (Dublin, 1997), p. 399.

33 *The Irish Times*, 5 May 1938.

34 *The Irish Times*, 14 November 1938.

35 *Ibid.*

36 Dunleavy & Dunleavy, *op. cit.*, p. 398.

37 NAI, PRES 1/P499, letter from Maud Gonne MacBride to Hyde, 8 June 1939.

38 Maume, 'Douglas Hyde' in McGuire & Quinn (eds), *op. cit.*, vol. 4, p. 883.

39 Dunleavy & Dunleavy, *op. cit.*, p. 417.

40 Dunleavy & Dunleavy, *op. cit.*, p. 417, p. 447; Anne Dolan, 'Joseph Clarke' in McGuire & Quinn (eds), *op. cit.*, vol. 2, p. 554.

41 Dunleavy & Dunleavy, *op. cit.*, pp. 417–8.

42 Lorna Siggins, *Mary Robinson: The Woman Who Took Power in the Park* (Edinburgh, 1997), pp. 166–9.

43 Michael Kennedy, *Division and Consensus: The Politics of Cross Border Relations in Ireland 1925–1969* (Dublin, 2000), p. 72.

44 *Ibid.*

45 Donald Harman Akenson, *Conor: A Biography of Conor Cruise O'Brien vol. 1 – Narrative* (Montreal, 1994), p. 402.

46 NAI, PRES 1/P1727.

47 *Ibid.*

48 NAI, S10332B.

49 NAI, S10332B; Gerry McElroy, 'James Andrews' in McGuire & Quinn (eds), *op. cit.*, vol. 1, p.118.

50 NAI, S10332B.

51 *Ibid.*

52 *Ibid.*

53 Pauric Dempsey, 'Anthony Brutus Babington' in McGuire & Quinn (eds), *op. cit.*, vol. 1, p. 209.

54 NAI, S10332B.

55 *Ibid.*

56 *Ibid.*

57 Deirdre McMahon, 'John Charles McQuaid' in McGuire & Quinn (eds), *op. cit.*, vol. 6, p. 178.

58 DDA, McQuaid Papers, xviii/1/1/1, letter from McDunphy to Fr Glennon, 3 July 1942.

59 DDA, McQuaid Papers, xviii/1/1/2, letter from Fr Glennon to McDunphy, 21 July 1942.

60 *Ibid.*

61 Robin Tobin, *The Minority Voice: Hubert Butler and Southern Irish Protestantism 1900–1991* (Oxford, 2012), p. 185.

62 *Irish Independent*, 23 April 1938.

63 NAI, S9783A, letter from de Valera to Hyde, 23 April 1938.

64 Dunleavy & Dunleavy, *op. cit.*, p. 381.

65 Fergus Finlay, *Mary Robinson, A President with a Purpose* (Dublin, 1990), pp. 62–3.

66 *The New York Times Magazine*, 29 May 1938.

67 Casey, 'Áras an Uachtaráin,' *op. cit.*, p. 21; Office of Public Works, *Áras an Uachtaráin: A History of the President's House* (Dublin, 2013), p. 18.

68 Michael McDunphy Papers, letter from McDunphy to de Valera, 21 January 1969.

69 *Dáil Éireann*, vol. 71, no. 12, col. 1630–2, 24 May 1938.

70 NAI, PRES 1/P61, memo by McDunphy entitled 'Suggested Re-Conditioning of the Former Viceregal Lodge', 16 December 1940.

71 NAI, PRES 1/P382, letter from McDunphy to Moynihan, 23 December 1938.

72 NAI, PRES 1/P382, letter from McDunphy to Moynihan, 28 November 1939.

73 Terence Brown, *Ireland – A Social and Cultural History 1922–79* (London, 1981), pp. 53–4; Ronan Fanning, *Independent Ireland* (Dublin, 1983), p. 82.

74 Fanning, *op. cit.*, p. 134.

75 *Ibid.*

76 Diarmaid Ferriter, *The Transformation of Ireland 1900–2000* (London, 2005), p. 429.

77 Tim Pat Coogan, *Ireland Since the Rising* (London, 1966), p. 196.

78 *The Irish Times*, 11 October 1954.

79 *The Irish Times*, 28 March 1939; NAI, PRES 1/P37; *Irish Press*, 1 September 1939.

80 *The Irish Times*, 28 March 1939; NAI, PRES 1/P37; *Irish Press*, 1 September 1939.

81 *Irish Press*, 1 September 1939.

82 Dunleavy & Dunleavy, *op. cit.*, p.427.

83 *The Irish Times*, 25 October 1943.

84 NAI, PRES 1/P3041, School Attendance Bill 1942.

85 *Dáil Éireann*, vol. 88, no. 12, cols 1558–1559, 28 October 1942; *Bunreacht na hÉireann,* Article 42.

86 *Seanad Éireann*, vol. 27, no. 12, cols 1111–1112, 1137–1138, 3 February 1943.

87 *The Irish Times,* 22 January 1943; *Seanad Éireann*, vol. 27, no. 12, cols 1082–1095, 3 February 1943; J. Anthony Gaughan (ed.), *Memoirs of Senator James G. Douglas 1887–1954: Concerned Citizen* (Dublin, 1998), pp. 39–40.

88 Paul Rouse, 'Liam Ó Buachalla' in McGuire & Quinn, *op. cit.*, vol. 7, pp. 108–9; *Seanad Éireann*, vol. 27, no. 9, cols 819–820, 21 January 1943; *Seanad Éireann*, vol. 27, no. 12, cols 1136–1137, 3 February 1943.

89 NAI, PRES 1/P3041.

90 *Seanad Éireann*, vol. 27, no. 12, cols 1107–1108, 3 February 1943; *The Irish Times*, 4 February 1943.

91 NAI, PRES 1/P3041, letter from eight Oireachtas members to Douglas Hyde, 15 February 1943.

92 *Ibid.*

93 UCDA, John A. Costello Papers, P190/329(7); David McCullagh, *The Reluctant Taoiseach: A Biography of John A. Costello* (Dublin, 2010), p. 143, p. 260.

94 NAI, PRES 1/P3041, letter from eight Oireachtas members to Douglas Hyde, 15 February 1943.

95 *Ibid.*

96 *Irish Independent,* 23 February 1943.

97 NAI, PRES 1/P3041.

98 NAI, PRES 1/P3041, memo by McDunphy entitled 'Document read at meeting, 25 February 1943', 26 February 1943.

99 NAI, PRES 1/P3041, memo by McDunphy entitled 'Procedure at Meeting: Relaxation of restrictions', 1 March 1943.

100 *Irish Independent,* 26 February 1943.

101 NAI, PRES 1/P3041.

102 *Irish Press,* 26 March 1943.

103 Irish Reports, *Supreme Court 1943* (Dublin, 1943), p. 346.

104 *Irish Press,* 16 April 1943.

105 Morgan, *op. cit.,* p. 221.

106 *Round Table: A Quarterly Review of the Politics of the British Commonwealth*, vol. 35 (September 1945), no. 307, pp. 312–3.

107 *The Irish Times,* 14 June 1945.

7. The Politics of Neutrality

1 NAI, PRES 1/P521, memo by Michael McDunphy, entitled 'Sudden Illness', 13 April 1940.

2 *Ibid.*

3 *Ibid.*

4 *Ibid.*

5 NAI, PRES 1/P521, press statement from office of President, 13 April 1940.

6 *Sunday Independent*, 14 April 1940; *Irish Independent*, 15 April 1940; *Irish Press*, 15 April 1940.

7 Dunleavy & Dunleavy, *op. cit.*, pp. 422–3.

8 Robert Fisk, *In Time of War* (London, 1985), pp. 350–1; Dermot Keogh, *Twentieth Century Ireland: Nation and State* (Dublin, 1994), p. 113.

9 Keogh, *Twentieth Century Ireland, op. cit.,* p. 113.

10 NAI, PRES 1/P521, memo by McDunphy, 16 April 1940.

11 NAI, PRES 1/P521, letter from McDunphy to Moynihan, 22 April 1940.

12 NAI, PRES 1/P521, medical report of Dr. William Boxwell, 22 April 1940.

13 NAI, PRES 1/P1691.

14 *Ibid.*

15 NAI, PRES 1/P1722.

16 Leon Ó Broin, *Just Like Yesterday*, p. 131.

17 NAI, PRES 1/P730; NAI, PRES 1/P1692.

18 NAI, S9787.

19 NAI, PRES 1/P521, press statement from office of President, 15 May 1940; *Irish Independent,* 16 May 1940.

20 *Irish Independent,* 27 May 1940.

21 NAI, PRES 1/P2335, memo by McDunphy, June 1945.

22 Bew (ed.), *op. cit.*, pp. 77–80.

23 NAI, PRES 1/P521, memo by McDunphy, 27 June, 1940; NAI, PRES 1/P1753.

24 NAI, S12156, PRES 1/P1753.

25 NAI, S13549, memo by Moynihan, February 1942; NAI, PRES 1/P521, memo by McDunphy, 9 July 1949.

26 NAI, S13549.

27 NAI, PRES 1/P1769.

28 *Ibid*; *Sunday Press*, 2 June 1940.

29 *The Irish Times*, 19 March 1943

30 *Irish Independent,* 26 June 1945.

31 *Dáil Éireann*, vol. 97, no. 16, cols 1273–1274, 27 June 1945.

32 Dwyer, *op. cit.,* p. 163.

33 *Irish Independent*, 24 November 1938.

34 *Ibid*; NAI, PRES 1/P1067.

35 Patrick Brogan, *Eastern Europe 1939–1989: The Fifty Years War* (London, 1990), pp. 213–4.

36 NAI, PRES 1/P1067, memo by McDunphy, November 1938.

37 Dunleavy & Dunleavy, *op. cit.*, p. 408.

38 *Ibid.*, p. 409.

39 NAI, PRES 1/P1378.

40 NAI, PRES 1/P1820, memo by Michael McDunphy, October 1939.

41 *Ibid.*

42 NAI, PRES 1/P1820; *The Daily Telegraph*, 28 October 1939.

43 NAI, PRES 1/P1820, memo by Michael McDunphy, October 1939.

44 *Ibid.*

45 NAI, S10332B, civil service personnel file of Michael McDunphy.

46 NAI, S10332B, 'Ireland and World War II, 1939–1945, Conversations with Mr Michael McDunphy', Explanatory Note, 20 August 1954.

47 *Ibid.*

48 NAI, S10332B, 'Ireland and World War II, 1939–1945, Conversations with Mr Michael McDunphy', 'European War 1941: Conversation with Mr Vinton Chapin, Secretary to the American legation', 22 March 1941.

49 NAI, S10332B, 'Ireland and World War II, 1939–1945, Conversations with Mr Michael McDunphy', 'Discussion with Mr Antrobus, Secretary to Sir John Maffey', 11 July 1940.

50 *Ibid.*

51 *Ibid.*

52 *Ibid.*

53 *Ibid.*

54 *Ibid.*

55 *Ibid.*

56 Fisk, *op. cit.*, pp. 350–1; Keogh, *Twentieth Century Ireland, op. cit.*, p. 160.

57 Fisk, *op. cit.*, pp. 350–1; Keogh, *Twentieth Century Ireland, op. cit.*, p. 248.

58 NAI, S10332B.

59 NAI, S10332B, 'Ireland and World War II, 1939–1945, Conversations with Mr Michael McDunphy', 'Conversation with Capt. Lauriston Arnott', 24 August 1940.

60 *Ibid.*

61 *Ibid.*

62 *Ibid.*

63 *Ibid.*

64 *The Irish Times,* 26 March 1975.

65 *Ibid.*

66 *Ibid.*

67 *Ibid.*

68 *Ibid.*

69 *Ibid.*

70 NAI, S10332B, 'Ireland and World War II, 1939–1945, Conversations with Mr Michael McDunphy', 20 August 1954.

71 Michael McDunphy Papers, note entitled 'Experience and Qualifications of Michael McDunphy', undated.

72 *Irish Independent,* 8 October 1934; *Irish Independent,* 2 May 1935; *Irish Independent,* 7 February 1936; *Irish Independent*, 21 May 1937.

73 *The Irish Times,* 20 December 1937; Gerry Mullins, *Dublin Nazi No.1: The Life of Adolf Mahr* (Dublin, 2007), pp. 64–6.

74 NAI, PRES 1/P519.

75 Dermot Keogh, *Jews in Twentieth Century Ireland: Refugees, Anti-Semitism and the Holocaust* (Cork, 1998), p. 103.

76 Aideen Breen, 'Julius Pokorny' in McGuire & Quinn (eds), *op. cit.,* vol. 8, p. 197.

77 Pól Ó Dochartaigh, 'Professor Pokorny of Vienna: Austrian Catholic, German Nationalist, Celtic Professor and Jew', *History Ireland,* Issue 1, vol. 8, Spring 2000.

78 Breen, *op. cit.*, p. 197.

79 Ó Dochartaigh, 'Professor Pokorny of Vienna', *op. cit.*; Breen, *op. cit.*, p. 198.

80 Pól Ó Dochartaigh, *Julius Pokorny 1887–1970: Germans, Celts and Nationalism* (Dublin, 2004), p. 15.

81 Ó Dochartaigh, 'Professor Pokorny of Vienna', *op. cit.*

82 NLI, Letters to Douglas Hyde, letter from Pokorny to Hyde 5 May 1933, MS 17, 996.

83 *Ibid.*

84 Keogh, *Jews in Twentieth Century Ireland, op. cit.*, p. 103.

85 *Ibid.*

86 *Ibid.*; Breen, *op. cit.*, p. 197.

87 Gisela Holfter, Siobhan O'Connor and Birte Schulz, 'Resources Relating to German Speaking Refugees in Ireland, 1933–1945 – Some Initial Thoughts and Results', in Andrea Hamill and Anthony Greenville (ed.), *Refugee Archives: Theory and Practice* (Amsterdam, 2007), p. 43.

88 Keogh, *Jews in Twentieth Century Ireland*, p. 127.

89 Ó Dochartaigh, *Julius Pokorny 1887–1970, op. cit.*, p. 113.

90 *Ibid.*, p. 117.

91 *Ibid.*

92 NAI, 2002/7/4.

93 NAI, 2002/7/4, letter from Pokorny to Hyde, 24 June 1938.

94 *Ibid.*

95 NAI, 2002/7/4, letter from Hyde to John Glyn Davies, 16 September 1938.

96 NAI, 2002/7/4, letter from John Glyn Davies to Hyde, 11 September 1938.

97 NAI, 2002/7/4, letter from Hyde to John Glyn Davies, 16 September 1938.

98 NAI, 2002/7/4, memo by Julius Pokorny, 21 September 1938.

99 NAI, 2002/7/4, memo by McDunphy, 21 September 1938.

100 NAI PRES 1/P350, undated memo by McDunphy.

101 Eoghan Ó Raghallaigh & Lesa Ní Mhunghaile, 'Liam Gógan' in McGuire & Quinn (eds), *op. cit.*, vol. 4, pp. 122–3.

102 NAI, 2002/7/4, Liam Gógan to Michael McDunphy, 1 April 1939.

103 *Ibid.*

104 *Ibid.*

105 NAI, 2002/7/4.

106 NAI, 2002/7/4, memo by Michael McDunphy, 4 April 1939.

107 *Ibid.*

108 NAI, 2002/7/4, memo by McDunphy, 4 April 1939.

109 NAI, 2002/7/4, letter from McDunphy to Liam Gógan, 12 April 1939.

110 NAI, 2002/7/4, memo by McDunphy, 20 April 1939.

111 Ó Dochartaigh, *Julius Pokorny 1887–1970, op. cit.*, p. 120.

112 *Ibid.*, p. 123.

113 NAI, 2002/7/4, letter from Frederick Boland to McDunphy, 2 August 1940.

114 *Ibid.*

115 Ó Dochartaigh, *Julius Pokorny 1887–1970, op. cit.*, p. 122.

116 Ó Dochartaigh, 'Professor Pokorny of Vienna,' *op. cit.*; Ó Dochartaigh, *Julius Pokorny 1887–1970, op. cit.*, p. 124.

117 NAI, DFA 438/146, letter from McDunphy to Frederick Boland, 7 August 1940.

118 Ó Dochartaigh, *Julius Pokorny 1887–1970, op. cit.*, p. 122.

119 *Ibid.*, p. 124.

120 *Ibid.*, p. 125.

121 *Ibid.*, p. 17.

122 NAI, 2002/7/4, letter from Liam Gógan to McDunphy, 21 September 1943.

123 NAI, 2002/7/4.

124 NAI, 2002/7/4, telegram from Julius Pokorny to Hyde, 16 January 1944.

125 NAI, 2002/7/4.

126 Ó Dochartaigh, *Julius Pokorny 1887–1970, op. cit.*, p. 17.

127 NAI, 2002/7/4, memo by McDunphy, 15 February 1944.

128 NAI, 2002/7/4, report of the Irish Ambassador to Switzerland, April 1970.

129 Breen, *op. cit.*, p. 198.

130 NAI, 2002/7/4, report of the Irish Ambassador to Switzerland, April 1970.

131 Aengus Nolan, *Joseph Walshe: Irish Foreign Policy 1922–46* (Cork, 2008), p. 122.

132 Nolan, *op. cit.*, p. 122.

133 NAI, PRES 1/P519.

134 *Ibid.*

135 NAI, PRES 1/P519, letter from Eduard Hempel to Hyde, 17 February 1941.

136 John P. Duggan, *Neutral Ireland and the Third Reich* (Dublin 1985), p. 31.

137 John P. Duggan, *Herr Hempel at the German legation 1937–45* (Dublin, 2003), p. 76.

138 Fisk, *op. cit.*, p. 372.

139 Duggan, *Herr Hempel at the German Legation, op. cit.* p. 77.

140 *Ibid.*, p. 76.

141 *Ibid*, p. 74.

142 Michael Kennedy, 'William Warnock' in McGuire & Quinn (eds), *op. cit.*, vol. 9, p. 803.

143 Duggan, *Herr Hempel at the German Legation, op. cit.*, p. 77.

144 *Ibid.*, p. 77.

145 Michael McInerney, 'The Seán MacEntee Story', *The Irish Times*, 25 June 1974.

146 NAI, PRES 1/P519.

147 Longford & O'Neill, *op. cit.*, p. 411.

148 *The Irish Times*, 3 May 1945; *Irish Press*, 3 May 1945; *Irish Independent*, 3 May 1945.

149 *Irish Independent*, 31 December 2005; *The Guardian*, 31 December 2005; *Los Angeles Times*, 31 December 2005; *Sarasota Herald Tribune*, 31 December 2005.

150 *Irish Independent*, 31 December 2005; NAI, 2005/163/5, 'Deaths of Heads of State', book of protocol records from Áras an Uachtaráin 1938–1957.

151 *Ibid.*

152 *Ibid.*

153 *The Irish Times*, 4 May 1945.

154 *Irish Press*, 4 May 1945; *Irish Independent*, 4 May 1945.

155 *The Irish Times,* 31 December 2011.

156 Dermot Keogh, 'Éamon de Valera and Hitler: An Analysis of International Reaction to the Visit to the German Minister, May 1945', *Irish Studies in International Affairs*, vol. 3, no. 1 (1989), p. 73.

157 Dermot Keogh, *Ireland and Europe 1919–48* (Dublin, 1988), p. 191.

158 Keogh, 'Éamon de Valera and Hitler,' *op. cit.*, pp. 83–4.

159 NAI, PRES 1/P519, memo by McDunphy, 9 May 1945.

160 NAI, PRES 1/P519, press statement issued by Government Information Bureau, 8 May 1945; *Irish Independent*, 9 May 1945.

161 NAI, PRES 1/P519, memo by McDunphy, 9 May 1945.

162 *Ibid.*

163 *Ibid.*

164 NAI, PRES 1/P47, memo by McDunphy entitled 'Consuls; Reception by the President', 5 July 1945.

165 *Ibid.*

166 NAI, PRES 1/P1597, letter from Nils Jaenson to McDunphy, 9 July 1945.

167 NAI, PRES 1/P1597, memo by McDunphy, 25 July 1945.

168 *Dáil Éireann*, vol. 97, no. 25, cols 2754–2756, 19 July 1945.

169 Coogan, *De Valera, op. cit.*, p. 543.

170 NAI, PRES 1/P521, memo by McDunphy, 18 April 1940.

171 Dunleavy & Dunleavy, *op. cit.*, p. 422.

172 *Ibid.*

173 NAI, S10332B, 'Ireland and World War II, 1939–1945, Conversations with Mr Michael McDunphy', 'European War 1941: Conversation with Mr Vinton Chapin, Secretary to the American legation', 22 March 1941.

174 *Ibid.*

175 NAI, S10332B, 'Ireland and World War II, 1939–1945, Conversations with Mr Michael McDunphy', memo by McDunphy of conversation with David Gray, 5 May 1941.

176 *Ibid.*

177 Nolan, *op. cit.*, p. 294.

178 Coogan, *De Valera, op. cit.*, p. 628.

179 *Ibid*; Dunleavy & Dunleavy, *op. cit.*, p. 423.

180 Keogh, 'Éamon de Valera and Hitler', *op. cit.*, pp. 84–5.

181 Nolan, *op. cit.*, p. 294.

182 *Ibid.*

183 NAI, DFA P98, letter from David Gray to Jospeh Walshe, 22 June 1945.

184 Bew (ed.), *op. cit.*, p. 80

185 Dunleavy & Dunleavy, *op. cit.*, p. 422.

186 NAI, DFA P98.

187 *Ibid.*

188 Coogan, *De Valera, op. cit.*, p. 543.

189 Keogh, 'Éamon de Valera and Hitler', *op. cit.*, p. 85.

190 NAI, PRES 1/P2510, memo by Michael McDunphy, 4 July 1945.

191 *Ibid.*

192 *Ibid.*

193 Nolan, *op. cit.*, p. 294.

194 Keogh, *Twentieth Century Ireland, op. cit.*, p. 162.

195 NAI, PRES 1/P2594, memo by McDunphy, 25 September 1945.

196 Keogh, *Twentieth Century Ireland, op. cit.*, p. 162.

197 *Ibid.*

198 Ronan Fanning, 'The Anglo-American Alliance and the Irish Application for Membership of the United Nations', *Irish Studies in International Affairs*, vol. 2, no. 2 (1986), p. 45.

8. Playing the Game or Blowing the Whistle

1 Michael McDunphy Papers, letter from McDunphy to de Valera, 21 January 1969.

2 *Ibid.*

3 NAI, S9791.

4 *Dáil Éireann*, vol. 67, no. 1, cols 50–51, 11 May 1937.

5 *Report of the Committee to review the Offences Against the State Acts 1939–1998 and Related Matters,* p. 53.

6 Ronan Fanning, 'The Rule of Order: Éamon de Valera and the IRA', in John A. Murphy & John P. O'Carroll (eds), *De Valera and His Times* (Cork, 1983), p. 168.

7 *Report of the Committee to review the Offences Against the State Acts 1939–1998 and Related Matters,* p. 56; Hogan, *op. cit.*, p. 24.

8 Hogan, *op. cit.*, p. 24; Tim Pat Coogan, *The IRA* (London, 1986), p. 178.

9 *Dáil Éireann*, vol. 74, no. 10, cols 1296–1297, 2 March 1939.

10 *Dáil Éireann*, vol. 74, no. 10, cols 1408–1410, 2 March 1939.

11 Fanning, 'The Rule of Order', in Murphy & O'Carroll (eds), *op. cit.*, p. 168; Tim Pat Coogan, *Ireland in the Twentieth Century* (London, 2003), p. 329.

12 Coogan, *The IRA*, *op. cit.*, p. 178.

13 Hogan, *op. cit.*, p. 24.

14 *Dáil Éireann*, vol. 78, no. 10, cols 1323–1324, 3 January 1940.

15 *Dáil Éireann*, vol. 78, no. 11, cols 1527–1528, 4 January 1940.

16 *Dáil Éireann*, vol. 78, no. 11, cols 1528–1529, 4 January 1940.

17 *Dáil Éireann*, vol. 78, no. 10, cols 1352–1353, 3 January 1940.

18 *Dáil Éireann*, vol. 78, no. 10, cols 1355–1356, 3 January 1940.

19 *Dáil Éireann*, vol. 78, no. 10, cols 1345–1346, 3 January 1940.

20 *The Irish Times,* 5 January 1940.

21 *The Irish Times,* 4 January 1940.

22 NAI, PRES 1/P1451, memo by McDunphy, 6 January 1940.

23 *Ibid.*

24 *Irish Press,* 8 January 1940; *The Daily Telegraph*, 9 January 1940.

25 NAI, PRES 1/P2, memo by McDunphy, January 1940.

26 *Ibid.*

27 NAI, PRES 1/P3041, memo by McDunphy entitled 'Procedure at Meeting: Relaxation of restrictions,' 1 March 1943.

28 NAI, PRES 1/P3041, memo by McDunphy entitled 'Notification of President's decision to members of Council', 1 March 1943.

29 Hogan, *op. cit.*, p. 689.

30 *Ibid.*, p. 694.

31 *Ibid.*, p. 689.

32 *Irish Press*, 18 April 1940.

33 *Ibid.*

34 *Ibid.*

35 Hogan, *op. cit.*, p. 689.

36 *Ibid.*, p. 689.

37 Alvin Jackson, *Ireland 1798–1998: War, Peace and Beyond* (Sussex, 2010), p. 300.

38 Noel Whelan, *Fianna Fáil: A Biography of the Party* (Dublin, 2011), p. 73.

39 Michael Gallagher, *Political Parties in the Republic of Ireland* (Manchester, 1985), p. 47.

40 Longford & O'Neill, *op. cit.*, p. 409.

41 NAI, PRES 1/P2385, memo by McDunphy entitled 'General Election: May, 1944,' 20 May 1944.

42 *Ibid.*

43 *Ibid.*

44 *Ibid.*

45 *Ibid.*

46 *Ibid.*

47 *Ibid.*

48 *Ibid.*

49 *Ibid.*

50 *Ibid.*

51 *Irish Independent*, 10 May 1944.

52 *Dáil Éireann*, vol. 93, no. 15, cols 2469–2470, 10 May 1944.

53 *Dáil Éireann*, vol. 93, no. 15, cols 2469–2471, 10 May 1944.

54 *Dáil Éireann*, vol. 93, no. 15, cols 2474–2475, 10 May 1944.

55 *Dáil Éireann*, vol. 93, no. 15, cols 2482–2484, 10 May 1944.

56 *Dáil Éireann*, vol. 93, no. 15, cols 2483–2484, 10 May 1944.

57 NAI, PRES 1/P1531, memo by Michael McDunphy entitled 'General Election, May 1944: Objectionable reference to President', 25 May 1944.

58 *Ibid.*

59 *Dáil Éireann*, vol. 93, no. 15, cols 2498–2499, 10 May 1944.

60 *Irish Press*, 11 May 1944.

61 *The Irish Times*, 18 May 1944.

62 *Ibid.*

63 *Ibid.*

64 *Sunday Independent*, 28 May 1944.

65 *Ibid.*

66 Anthony Jordan, *Éamon de Valera 1882–1975 – Irish: Catholic: Visionary* (Dublin, 2010), p. 246.

67 *Irish Press*, 2 June 1944.

68 Michael McDunphy Papers, memo entitled 'Loss of Support of Majority in Dáil Éireann', 1949.

69 Kelly, *op. cit.*, p. 62.

70 Robert Elgie, 'Political leadership: the President and the Taoiseach' in John Coakley & Michael Gallagher (eds), *Politics in the Republic of Ireland* (London, 1999), p. 235.

71 Ward, *op. cit.*, p. 290.

72 UCDA, Patrick Hillery Papers, P205/145, Áras an Uachtaráin telephone log, 27 January 1982; Elgie, 'Political leadership: the President and the Taoiseach' in Coakley & Gallagher (eds), *op. cit.*, p. 235.

73 Elgie, 'Political leadership: the President and the Taoiseach' in Coakley & Gallagher (eds), *op. cit.*, p. 235.

74 *Ibid.*

75 *Irish Independent*, 10 May 1944.

76 NAI, PRES 1/P2464.

77 *Ibid.*

78 *The Irish Times*, 24 November 1966.

79 *The Irish Times*, 27 August 1944.

80 NAI, PRES 1/P2464.

81 *Ibid.*

82 NAI, S9783A.

83 *Ibid.*

84 NAI, PRES 1/P2464, memo by McDunphy, 8 January 1945.

85 *Irish Independent*, 6 January 1945.

86 *The Irish Times*, 8 January 1945.

87 *Irish Independent*, 13 March 1997.

88 Siggins, *op. cit.*, p. 217.

89 NAI, S9783A, letter from de Valera to Hyde (English translation), 23 June 1945.

90 UCDA, Éamon de Valera Papers, P150/3157.

91 *Ibid.*

92 *Ibid.*

9. Forgotten Patriot

1 NAI, PRES 1/P2473.

2 NAI, PRES 1/P2473, memo by Michael McDunphy entitled 'Conversation with Secretary to the Government', 8 February 1945.

3 Padraic O'Farrell, *Down Ratra Road: Fifty Years of Civil Defence in Ireland* (Dublin, 2000), p. 83.

4 NAI, PRES 1/P2473, memo by Michael McDunphy entitled 'Conversation with Secretary to the Government', 8 February 1945; O'Farrell, *op. cit.*, p. 83.

5 Winston Churchill, *A Roving Commission: My Early Life* (New York, 1930), p. 3.

6 O'Farrell, *op. cit.*, p. 79.

7 NAI, PRES 1/P2473, memo by McDunphy entitled 'Transfer of Dr Hyde from Áras', 20 June 1945; McGarry, *op. cit.*, p. 38.

8 O'Farrell, *op. cit.*, p. 84.

9 *The Irish Times*, 13 July 1949.

10 *Dáil Éireann*, vol. 117, no. 6, cols 737–738, 13 July 1949.

11 Quoted in Ian D'Alton, 'A Protestant Paper for a Protestant People: *The Irish Times* and the southern Irish minority', *Irish Communications Review*, vol. 12 (2010), p. 70.

12 Tobin, *op. cit.*, p. 151.

13 McGarry, *op. cit.*, p. 38.

14 *Ibid.*

15 *The Irish Times*, 16 July 1949.

16 *The Irish Times*, 17–19 July 1949.

17 *The Irish Times*, 5 May 1938.

18 NLI, Seán T. O'Kelly Papers, MS 27,721 (T. D. Williams, 'Typescript Thomas Davis Lecture – The Presidency in historical perspective').

19 J. J. Lee, *Ireland 1912–85: Politics and Society* (Cambridge, 1989), pp. 210–11.

20 UCDA, Éamon de Valera Papers, P150/2419.

21 *Irish Press*, 24 June 1937.

22 *Dáil Éireann*, vol. 67, no. 1, cols 155–156, 11 May 1937.

23 *Irish Press*, 18 June 1937.

24 Bowman, *op. cit.*, p. 154.

25 *Dáil Éireann*, vol. 67, no. 1, cols 1890–1891, 4 June 1937.

26 Michael McInerney, 'The Gerry Boland Story', *The Irish Times,* 11 October 1968.

27 McInerney, 'The Gerry Boland Story,' *op. cit.*; Lawrence William White, 'Gerald Boland' in McGuire & Quinn (eds), *op. cit.,* vol. 1, p. 634.

28 *Dáil Éireann*, vol. 67, no. 2, cols 204–205, 12 May 1937.

29 Caird, 'Douglas Hyde: Observed from a Distance' in Ó Conaire (ed.), *op. cit.,* p. 48.

30 Ó Tuathaigh, *op. cit.*, p. 25.

31 Dunleavy & Dunleavy, *op. cit.*, p. 369.

32 UCDA, Seán MacEntee Papers, P67/480.

33 McMahon, *op. cit.,* p. 280.

34 Bromage, *op. cit.*, p. 137; Longford & O'Neill, *op. cit.,* p. 320.

35 Bowman, *op. cit.*, p. 191; McInerney, 'The Seán MacEntee Story', *op. cit.*

36 O'Lochlainn, *op. cit.*, p. 64; NAI PRES 1/P1943.

37 *Seanad Éireann*, vol. 22, no. 11, cols 988–990, 7 February 1939.

38 *Dáil Éireann*, vol. T, no. 6, cols 26–27, 19 December 1921.

39 Coogan, *Ireland Since the Rising*, *op. cit.*, p. 263.

40 Gallagher, 'Republic of Ireland' in Robert Elgie (ed.), *Semi Presidentialism in Europe* (Oxford, 1999), p. 106.

41 *Dáil Éireann*, vol. 67, no. 1, cols 51–52, 11 May 1937.

42 Gallagher, 'Republic of Ireland' in Elgie (ed.), *op. cit.*, p. 107.

43 *Ibid*, p. 106.

44 *Dáil Éireann*, vol. 67, no. 1, cols 59–60, 11 May 1937.

45 *Bunreacht na hÉireann,* Article 12.1.

46 Brian Farrell, *Seán Lemass* (Dublin, 1983), p. 111; Ronan Fanning, 'Jack Lynch' in McGuire & Quinn (eds), *op. cit.*, vol. 5, p. 639.

47 623 articles relating to 'Douglas Hyde' versus 505 relating to 'Seán Lemass' for the period 25/6/38–24/6/45. Search undertaken 26 February 2011.

48 Keogh, 'Office of the Presidency has served the State well', *op. cit.*

49 *Ibid.*

50 Gerard Hogan, 'Ceremonial role by far most important for the President', *The Irish Times*, 21 October 1997.

51 Brian Murphy, 'Presidential Themes', *CU Focus*, Winter 2011.

52 Duffy, 'Overseas Studies: Ireland', *op. cit.*, p. 136.

53 Donnchadh Ó Corráin, 'Douglas Hyde: Multitext Project in Irish History,' http://multitext.ucc.ie/d/Douglas_Hyde3344120424 [Accessed 28 July 2015]; Duffy, 'Overseas Studies: Ireland', *op. cit.*, p. 136.

54 Lisa Hannigan, 'Hyde's Path to the Park', *Daily Mail*, 12 January 2007.

55 *Ibid.*

56 Pronsias Mac Aonghusa, '*Chuir de Valera cosc ar de h-Íde athphósadh*', *Anois*, 20–21 July 1991; 'Dev stopped Hyde seeking new love with Áras nurse', *Sunday Press*, 21 July 1991.

57 'Dev stopped Hyde seeking new love with Áras nurse', *Sunday Press*, 21 July 1991.

58 *Ibid.*

59 'Hyde marriage was prevented for dignity of office', *Irish Press*, 22 July 1991.

60 *Ibid.*

61 Century Ireland website, comments made by Douglas Hyde, 17 March 1915, www.rte.ie/centuryireland/articles/hyde-says-irish-language-thrown-away-like-dirty-water-out-of-a-house.

62 William O'Donnell & Nicholas Archibald (eds), *The Collected Works of W. B. Yeats vol. III: Autobiographies* (New York, 1999), p. 182.

63 Augustine Martin (ed.), *W. B. Yeats: Collected Poems* (London, 1990), p. 361.

64 Gareth W. Dunleavy, *op. cit.*, p. 30.

65 *The Irish Times*, 17 January 1942.

66 *Ibid.*

67 Dominic Daly, *The Young Douglas Hyde: The Dawn of the Irish Revolution and Renaissance 1874–1893* (Dublin, 1974), p. 33.

68 NAI PRES 1/P1353, letter from McDunphy to Moynihan, 16 August 1939.

69 O'Connor, *op. cit.*, p. 379; Charles Haughey, 'Douglas Hyde: An Appreciation' in Ó Conaire (ed.), *op. cit.*, p. 66.

70 NAI PRES 1/P2112–3.

71 *The Irish Times*, 17 January 1942.

72 *Ibid.*

73 *Red Cross World*, vol. 22–23 (1941), p. 74–5; *The Irish Times*, 5 October 1940.

74 *The Guardian*, 'Rare footage shows Franklin D Roosevelt using wheelchair', 10 July 2013; Hugh Gallagher, *FDR's Splendid Deception: The Moving Story of Roosevelt's Massive Disability and the Intense Efforts to Conceal it from the Public* (Florida, 1999), p. 94.

75 *The Irish Times*, August 1940–August 1941.

76 Egbert Kieser, *Hitler on the Doorstep: Operation Sea Lion: The German Plan to Invade Britain, 1940* (Annapolis, 1997), p. 55.

77 NAI PRES 1/P1753.

78 NAI PRES 1/P1753, memo by McDunphy entitled 'Necessity for Indoor Shelter', 4 June 1941.

79 *Ibid.*

80 'Nazi bombing of Dublin was not accidental', *The Irish Times*, 19 June 1997.

81 Robert Fisk, 'Why the Nazis bombed Dublin', *Independent*, 24 January 1999.

82 NAI PRES 1/P1753, memo by McDunphy entitled 'Necessity for Indoor Shelter', 4 June 1941.

Sources and Bibliography

Primary Sources

Archives

Dublin Diocesan Archives (DDA)
John Charles McQuaid Papers

National Archives of Ireland (NAI)
Cabinet Minutes
Dáil Éireann Archives
Department of External Affairs
Department of Finance
Department of Foreign Affairs
Department of the Taoiseach
Government Information Services
Office of the Attorney-General
Office of the President of the Executive Council
Office of the Secretary to the President

National Library of Ireland (NLI)
Douglas Hyde Letters
Sean T. O'Kelly Papers
William O'Brien Papers

Papers in Private Possession
Michael McDunphy Papers

University College Dublin Archives (UCDA)
Eamon de Valera Papers

Fianna Fáil Archives
Hugh Kennedy Papers
John A. Costello Papers
Patrick Hillery Papers

Newspapers, periodicals & magazines

Belfast News Letter; Belfast Telegraph; Bell, The; Birkenhead News; Catholic Herald; Cork Examiner; Daily Express; Daily Illini; Daily Telegraph; Derry Journal; Dublin Opinion; Edinburgh Evening News; Evening Herald; Evening Mail; Evening Times; Guardian, The; Independent, The; Irish Independent; Irish Jurist; Irish News; Irish Press; Irish Times, The; Liverpool Daily Post; Los Angeles Times; Magill Magazine; Manchester Evening News; Manchester Guardian; News Chronicle; News Review; New York Times; New York Times Magazine; Northern Whig; Nottingham Journal; Observer, The; Ottawa Citizen; Red Cross World; Round Table; Saturday Herald; Sarasota Herald Tribune; Spectator, The; Sunday Business Post; Sunday Independent; Sunday Press; Sunday Tribune; Times, The (London); United Press International; Yorkshire Observer.

Official Publications

Dáil Éireann Debates
Hansard, House of Commons Debate
Irish Reports (Supreme Court)
Report of the Committee to review the Offences Against the State Acts 1939–1998 and Related Matters
Seanad Éireann Debates

Constitutions

Dáil Constitution, 1919 (Constitution of the First Irish Republic 1919–22)
Irish Free State Constitution, 1922
Bunreacht na hÉireann (Constitution of Ireland, 1937)
Constitution of the First German Republic (Weimar Constitution), 1919

Correspondence and Interviews

Bertie Ahern
Liam Cosgrave
Desmond McDunphy
Risteárd Mulcahy

Secondary Sources

Books

Akenson, Donald Harman. *Conor: A Biography of Conor Cruise O'Brien Vol. 1 – Narrative*, Montreal, 1994.

Asante, Molefi Kete. *The African People: A Global History*, New York, 2012.

Ayearst, Morley. *The Republic of Ireland: Its Government and Politics*, New York, 1970.

Bell, J. Bowyer. *The Secret Army: The IRA 1916–79*, Dublin, 1979.

Bew, Paul (ed.) *The Memoir of David Gray: A Yankee in De Valera's Ireland*, Dublin, 2012.

Bourden, Patricia. *The Emergence of Modern Ireland 1850–1966*, Dublin, 1986.

Bowman, John. *De Valera and the Ulster Question 1917–1973*, Oxford, 1989.

Boyce, D. George. *The Irish Question & British Politics 1868–1986*, London, 1988.

Briscoe, Robert. *For the Life of Me*, Boston, 1959.

Brogan, Patrick. *Eastern Europe 1939–1989: The Fifty Year War*, London, 1990.

Bromage, Mary. *De Valera and the March of a Nation*, London, 1967.

Brown, Terence. *Ireland – A Social and Cultural History 1922–79*, London, 1981.

Callanan, Frank. *T. M. Healy*, Cork, 1996.

Carlyle, Thomas. *History of Friedrich II of Prussia*, London, 1858.

Casey, James. *Constitutional Law in Ireland*, London, 1992.

Chubb, Basil. *The Constitution and Constitutional Change in Ireland*, Dublin, 1978.

Churchill, Winston. *A Roving Commission: My Early Life*, New York, 1930.

Clarke, Kathleen. *Revolutionary Woman: An Autobiography*, Dublin, 1991.

Coakley, John & Gallagher, Michael (eds.) *Politics in the Republic of Ireland*, London, 1999.

Coffey, Diarmuid. *Douglas Hyde: An Craoibhín Aoibhinn*, Dublin, 1917.

– *Douglas Hyde: President of Ireland*, Dublin, 1938.

Collins, Stephen. *The Cosgrave Legacy*, Dublin, 1996.

Coogan, Tim Pat. *De Valera: Long Fellow, Long Shadow*, London, 1993.

– *The IRA*, London, 1986.

– *Ireland in the Twentieth Century*, London, 2003.

– *Ireland Since the Rising*, London, 1966.

Daly, Dominic. *The Young Douglas Hyde: The Dawn of the Irish Revolution and Renaissance 1874–1893*, Dublin, 1974.

De Vere White, Terence. *Kevin O'Higgins*, Dublin, 1966.

Donnelly, Sean. *Elections 2002*, Dublin, 2002.

Duggan, John P. *Herr Hempel at the German Legation 1937–45*, Dublin, 2003.

– *Neutral Ireland and the Third Reich*, Dublin, 1985.

Dunleavy, Gareth W. *Douglas Hyde*, New Jersey, 1974.

Dunleavy, Janet E. & Dunleavy, Gareth W. *Douglas Hyde: A Maker of Modern Ireland*, California, 1991.

Dwyer, T. Ryle. *De Valera: The Man and the Myths*, Dublin, 1991.

Edwards, Owen Dudley. *Eamon de Valera*, Cardiff, 1987.
Elgie, Robert (ed.) *Semi Presidentialism in Europe*, Oxford, 1999.
Fanning, Ronan. *Independent Ireland*, Dublin, 1983.
Farragher, Sean. *Dev and His Alma Mater: Eamon de Valera's Lifelong Association with Blackrock College 1898–1975*, Dublin, 1984.
Farrell, Brian. *Chairman or Chief: The Role of the Taoiseach in Irish Government*, Dublin, 1971.
– (ed.) *De Valera's Constitution and Ours*, Dublin, 1988.
– *Sean Lemass*, Dublin, 1983.
Ferriter, Diarmaid. *The Transformation of Ireland 1900–2000*, London, 2005.
Finlay, Fergus, *Mary Robinson: A President with a Purpose*, Dublin, 1990.
Fisk, Robert. *In Time of War*, London, 1985.
Fitzgerald, Garret. *Ireland in the World: Further Reflections*, Dublin, 2005.
Forde, Michael. *Constitutional Law of Ireland*, Cork, 1987.
Gageby, Douglas. *The Last Secretary General: Sean Lester and the League of Nations*, Dublin, 1999.
Gallagher, Hugh. *FDR's Splendid Deception: The moving story of Roosevelt's massive Disability and the intense efforts to conceal it from the public*, Florida, 1999.
Gallagher, Michael. *Political Parties in the Republic of Ireland*, Manchester, 1985.
Garvin, Tom. *The Evolution of Irish Nationalist Politics*, Dublin, 1981.
Gaughan, J. Anthony (ed.) *Memoirs of Senator James G. Douglas 1887–1954: Concerned Citizen*, Dublin, 1998.
Gibbs, Michelle. *Generations of Pride: A Centennial History of Cudahy, Wisconsin*, Wisconsin, 2006.
Gray, Tony. *The Irish Answer: An Anatomy of Modern Ireland*, London, 1966.
Hogan, Gerard. *The Origins of the Irish Constitution 1928–41*, Dublin, 2012.
Jackson, Alvin. *Ireland 1798–1998: War, Peace and Beyond*, Sussex, 2010.
Jackson, Ashley. *Buildings of Empire*, Oxford, 2013.
Jacobson, Arthur & Schlink, Bernhard (eds.) *Weimar: A Jurisprudence of Crisis*, California, 2002.
Jordan, Anthony. *Eamon de Valera 1882–1975 – Irish: Catholic: Visionary*, Dublin, 2010.
Kelly, John M. *The Irish Constitution* (2nd Edition), Dublin, 1984.
Kenna, Kevin. *The Lives and Times of the Presidents of Ireland*, Dublin, 2010.
Kennedy, Michael. *Division and Consensus: The Politics of Cross-Border Relations in Ireland, 1925–1969*, Dublin, 2000.
Keogh, Dermot. *Ireland and Europe 1919–48*, Dublin, 1988.
– *Ireland and the Vatican: The Politics and Diplomacy of Church-State Relations 1922–1960*, Cork, 1995.
– *Jews in Twentieth-Century Ireland: Refugees, Anti-Semitism and the Holocaust*, Cork, 1998.
– & McCarthy, Andrew. *The Making of the Irish Constitution 1937*, Cork, 2007.
– *Twentieth Century Ireland: Nation and State*, Dublin, 1994.

Kieser, Egbert. *Hitler on the Doorstep: Operation Sea Lion – the German Plan to Invade Britain, 1940, Annapolis, 1997.*

Lee, Joseph. *Ireland 1912–1985: Politics and Society*, Cambridge 1989.

Lee, Stephen J. *The Weimar Republic*, London, 1998.

Longford, Lord & O'Neill, Thomas P. *Eamon de Valera*, London, 1970.

Lyons, F. S. L. *Ireland Since the Famine*, London, 1973.

McCarthy, Denis & Benton, David. *Dublin Castle at the Heart of Irish History*, Dublin, 1997.

McCracken, John L. *Representative Government in Ireland: a study of Dáil Éireann 1919–48*, Oxford, 1958.

McCullagh, David. *The Reluctant Taoiseach: A Biography of John A. Costello*, Dublin, 2010.

McDunphy, Michael. *The President of Ireland: His Powers, Function and Duties*, Dublin, 1945.

MacEoin, Uinseann. *The IRA in the Twilight Years 1923–48*, Dublin, 1997.

McGuire, James & Quinn, James (eds.) *Dictionary of Irish Biography: From the earliest times to the year 2002*, Cambridge, 2009.

McKenna, Joseph. *The Irish-American Dynamite Campaign: A History 1881–1896*, North Carolina, 2012.

McMahon, Deirdre. *Republicans and Imperialists: Anglo-Irish Relations in the 1930s*, New Haven, 1984.

MacManus, Francis (ed.) *The Years of the Great Test 1926–39*, Cork, 1967.

McManus, M. J. *Eamon de Valera: A Biography*, Dublin, 1947.

Maher, Jim. *The Oath is Dead and Gone*, Dublin, 2011.

Martin, Augustine (ed.) *W. B. Yeats: Collected Poems*, London, 1990.

Mitchell, Arthur & Ó Snodaigh, Padraig. *Irish Political Documents 1916–49*, Dublin, 1985.

Mitnick, Barbara J. (ed.) *George Washington: American Symbol*, New York, 1999.

Moore, Cormac. *The GAA v Douglas Hyde: The Removal of Ireland's First President as GAA Patron*, Cork, 2012.

Morgan, David Gwynn. *Constitutional Law of Ireland: The Law of the Executive, Legislature and Judicature,* Dublin, 1990.

Morrissey, Thomas J. *A Man Called Hughes: The Life and Times of Seamus Hughes 1881–1943*, Dublin, 1991.

Moynihan, Maurice (ed.) *Speeches and Statements by Eamon de Valera 1917–1973*, Dublin, 1980.

Mullins, Gerry. *Dublin Nazi No.1: The Life of Adolf Mahr*, Dublin, 2007.

Murphy, John A. & O'Carroll, John P. (eds.) *De Valera and His Times*, Cork, 1983.

Murray, Patrick. *Oracles of God: The Roman Catholic Church and Irish Politics 1922–37*, Dublin, 2010.

Nolan, Aengus. *Joseph Walshe: Irish Foreign Policy 1922–46*, Cork, 2008.

Ó Beacháin, Donnacha. *Destiny of the Soldiers: Fianna Fáil, Irish Republicanism and the IRA, 1926–1973,* Dublin, 2010.

O'Brien, Mark. *De Valera, Fianna Fáil and the Irish Press: The Truth in the News,* Dublin, 2001.

Ó Broin, Leon. *Just Like Yesterday: An Autobiography*, Dublin, 1986.

Ó Ceallaigh, Sean T. *Sean T.*, Dublin, 1963.

Ó Conaire, Brendan (ed.) *Comhdháil an Chraoibhín 1988 – Conference Proceedings*, Roscommon, 1993.

O'Connor, Ulick. *Celtic Dawn: A Portrait of the Irish Literary Renaissance*, Dublin, 1984.

Ó Dochartaigh, Pól. *Julius Pokorny 1887–1970: Germans, Celts and Nationalism,* Dublin, 2004.

O'Donnell, William & Archibald, Nicholas (eds.) *The Collected Works of W. B. Yeats vol. 3: Autobiographies,* New York, 1999.

Ó Drisceoil, Donal. *Censorship in Ireland 1939–45*, Cork, 1996.

O'Farrell, Padraic. *Down Ratra Road: Fifty Years of Civil Defence in Ireland,* Dublin, 2000.

Ó Glaisne, Risteárd. *Dúbhglas de h-Íde: Náisiúnach Neamphspleách*, Dublin, 1993.

Office of Public Works. *Áras an Uachtaráin: A History of the President's House,* Dublin, 2013.

Okey, Robin. *Eastern Europe 1740–1985: Feudalism to Communism,* London, 1991.

Oram, Hugh. *The Newspaper Book: A History of Newspapers in Ireland, 1649–1983*, Dublin, 1983.

Pearce, Malcolm & Stewart, Geoffrey. *British Political History 1867–2001: Power and Decline*, London, 2002.

Pearse, Padraic. *Collected Works of Padraic H. Pearse: Political Writings and Speeches*, Dublin, 1924.

Robinson, R. A. H. *Contemporary Portugal*, London, 1979.

Royal Irish Academy, *Documents on Irish Foreign Policy: 1937–1939*, vol. 5, Dublin, 2006.

Rozett, Robert & Spector, Shmuel (eds.) *Encyclopedia of the Holocaust*, New York, 2000.

Sexton, Brendan. *Ireland and the Crown 1922–1936: the Governor-Generalship of the Irish Free State*, Dublin, 1989.

Siggins, Lorna. *Mary Robinson: The Woman Who Took Power in the Park*, Edinburgh, 1997.

Tobin, Robert. *Hubert Butler and Southern Irish Protestantism 1900–1991*, Oxford, 2012.

Traynor, John. *Mastering Modern German History*, Hampshire, 2008.

Walsh, Brendan. *The Pedagogy of Protest: The Educational Thought and Work of Patrick H. Pearse*, Berne, 2007.

Walsh, Dick. *The Party: Inside Fianna Fáil*, Dublin, 1986.

Walsh, John. *Patrick Hillery: The Official Biography*, Dublin, 2008.
Ward, Alan J. *The Irish Constitutional Tradition: Responsible Government and Modern Ireland 1782–1992*, Dublin, 1994.
Watt, Donald Cameron. *How War Came*, London, 1989.
Whelan, Noel. *Fianna Fáil: A Biography of the Party*, Dublin, 2011.

Index